# REST AND BE THANKFUL

## AUTOBIOGRAPHY OF A BELFAST MISSIONARY

**Daniel Cummings C.Ss.R.**

**COLOURPOINT**

Each of us dances to our own individual music, and those who do not hear the music to which I am dancing will be unable to make sense of my movements and gestures.
(Thoughts from a Spanish Mystic)

There are three things my soul delights in, and which are delightful to God and to men: concord between brothers, friendship between neighbours, and a wife and husband who live happily together.
(Ecclesiasticus 25:1–2)

Vita enim mortuorum in memoria vivorum est posita.
(The life of the dead is retained in the memory of the living.)
(Cicero)

Published 2015 by Colourpoint Books
an imprint of Colourpoint Creative Ltd
Colourpoint House, Jubilee Business Park
21 Jubilee Road, Newtownards, BT23 4YH
Tel: 028 9182 6339
Fax: 028 9182 1900
E-mail: sales@colourpoint.co.uk
Web: www.colourpoint.co.uk

First Edition
First Impression

Text © Daniel Cummings
Illustrations © Rosemary Doherty

A catalogue record for this book is available from the British Library.

Designed by April Sky Design, Newtownards
Tel: 028 9182 7195
Web: www.aprilsky.co.uk

Printed by W&G Baird Ltd, Antrim

ISBN 978-1-78073-074-5

*Published with support from the*
*Ulster Local History Trust*

# Contents

# Acknowledgments

FIRST AND FOREMOST I would like to acknowledge the Local Ulster History Trust. From the outset, when the book was a large hand-written volume, they have been most generous with their grant, invaluable advice, encouragement and trust in the project. I would like to thank Malcolm Johnston and Colourpoint Books for fulfilling my dream of having the book in print.

Thanks to my cousins for their family photographs: Martin Holland (Holland photographs), Fr Dan Cummings (James Cummings photographs) and Colette and Nora McEvoy (Magennis photographs).

I must also acknowledge my family who have shown considerable patience and tolerance in support of my commitment to the project. And, of course, I am in awe of my uncle, the author, who with sterling effort during his busy working life was able to produce such a volume in response to my simple suggestion as a child, that he should "write his life story".

*Rosemary Doherty*
*(née Rooney)*

# Foreword

IT MADE THE young girl cry and retch. The grainy, jolting image on the black and white television could not dull the horror recorded: emaciated bodies with pleading eyes, death piled high, unimagined barbaric atrocities. She knew someone who had been in this grim war and decided to investigate.

Her uncle, Fr Dan who had never spoken to her of the horrors he witnessed, was not surprised at her reaction to the graphic TV programme.

"Were you really in the war? You must have been through some times. I wouldn't have believed those things actually happened, without that original footage."

When he confirmed that he had been there as an army chaplain, and was part of the forces who liberated Belsen concentration camp, she immediately demanded:

"Well, you just must write it all down. You've had such a varied and interesting life that you should write your life story."

Many years later, a letter arrived to the girl from her uncle. The task was complete. Dan Cummings had written his story.

It was on 30 November 1970, in my twentieth year, during my teacher training while I boarded at Ewanrigg Road, Maryport in Cumberland, that I received the following letter from my uncle:

Personal and Secret

Erdington Abbey<br>Birmingham 23

Dear Rosemary,

I asked Mammy for your address! Now I write to you in what looks awfully like "Eariwig" St. So Miss R. (in Eariwig Street), accept my good wishes for your health and prosperity.

Many months – many, many months – ago, you gave me some counsel – advice, a suggestion, an idea, a proposal – about something. It concerns myself! You probably forget all you said, but I never forgot it. And now I write to ask you to promise me complete secrecy over what I will reveal to you. Here comes the crunch! The shock! Wait for it!

You said to me one day in 410: "Fr Dan, you should write an account of your experiences!" (I think you said "your life".)

Well, I thought over your suggestion, and finally I decided that if I set down my story in clear, simple, straightforward language, others might be interested, and what I have learnt as a child, boy, student, priest and missionary might help them. (I'm now forty years a priest, forty-five years a C.Ss.R.)

The first draft is completed – believe it or not, it runs to approx. 120,000 words. I have some work yet to do with it. But if anything happens to me – if death (in blunt language) takes me soon, remember what I say: I am giving this typescript to you – so, come and claim it here! It lies in a green cardboard folder on my table for you, here in my room in Erdington Abbey. (This is awfully dramatic, isn't it?)

Again – this is all very dramatic, isn't it? Why do I say all this? Because I was very, very ill last winter and another bout of similarly dimensional flu might easily prove too much for me! Hence this dramatic message.

What concerns me at the moment is this: that you keep what I have told you as a serious secret, the revelation of which would perhaps put me in a very embarrassing position.

You agree? Please write and reassure me in writing on this point.

You are young: you will outlive me by ever so many years. It is my hope that in the years to come, when I have passed on, you might find a use for the so varied and strange picture of my life I have put in words.

You wonder how I got time (in all my work here) to write so much. I made time; I sacrificed other things. I have never been at a cinema since I came here to Birmingham; I gave up attendance at football matches. But the most valuable time of all was secured in the bright, clear mornings of spring and summer – for then I used to rise at 4.45 or 5.00 am and work at my story steadily until 10.00 or 10.30 am. It has taken me about three years.

Write, dear, and tell me you understand; I will then write again. At the moment and indeed for the present I don't want you to do anything about – I just want you to know about it.

God bless you!
Love, Fr Dan


My uncle died seven years later. This is his book. I selected the title *Rest and Be Thankful*, and I hope it is to his liking.

*Rosemary Doherty*
*(née Rooney)*

# Family Tree

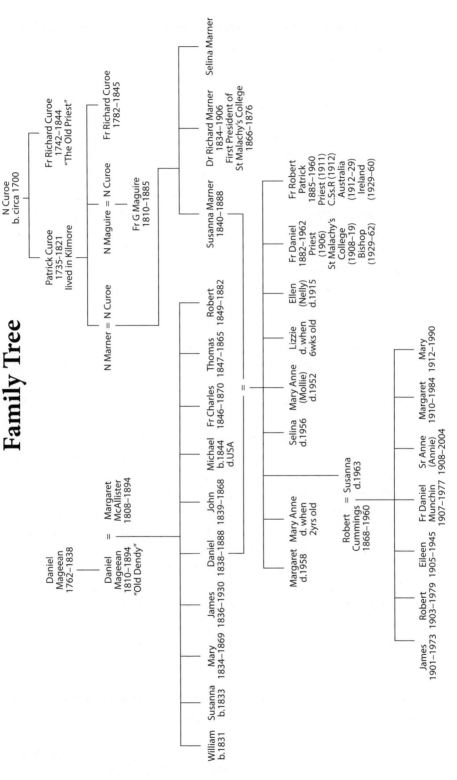

# Introduction

TODAY IS A glorious, heart-warming day in early spring. Seated in a quiet corner of the Abbey garden, I begin this story of my life.

I start my narrative in very pleasant surroundings. In the sky above me, fleecy white clouds drift slowly and silently along. High to the west, a jet-airliner speeds swiftly on its way, its vapour trail becoming a white woollen line across the blue sky. A light breeze gently sways the bare, drooping branches of the willow tree in the central lawn. The sun throws a trembling pattern of light and shade on the grass beneath. The hawthorns near the dark elm colonnade are dappled with soft green leaves now unfolded from the buds of spring. The bright sunlight plays among the quivering leaves and heightens their colour. Already the low rose bushes near the middle wall display their small copper-red leaves, harbingers of the rich red roses of the coming summer.

In this lovely sunlight the clusters of fresh new daffodils, the line of red and yellow wallflowers, and the mauve aubrietia border, add their glory to the breathtaking beauty of an enchanting spring day. The birds also sing their part in the universal song of joy. From the shadowed depths of the still, sombre holly bushes arises an unbroken melody, as thrush vies with blackbird in welcoming the spring. Even the humble sparrows make merry and keep chirping away at their best. Now I pause – I see a sparrow who has temporarily halted his efforts at song: he darts across the lawn, twisting and turning, in eager pursuit of a large black fly.

Today the pallid rays of the winter sun are replaced by rays that bear some heat. The red sandstone of the Abbey sacristy wall, near which I am seated, is quite warm to the touch. It is near the end of April: "Winter is now past … The flowers have appeared in our land" (Song of Solomon 2: 11–12). Tossed by the breeze a brown leaf dances along the grey pathway and flutters among the rose bushes. For an instant I think it is a bird – but no! It is only a leaf, only a withered brown leaf: a leaf once fresh and green, and now old and withered. The autumn that killed it is gone; so also is the winter that buried it in the snow. And now the spring has come again, to robe the trees in new green leaves – which in turn shall fade and die.

While I thus consider how the leaves and the seasons come and go from year to year, my thoughts turn to the years of my life. They too come and go:

but they are not altogether dead – they live on in my memory. Sometimes in the quiet of the evening I go into our library here in the Abbey and wander from one bookshelf to another. Picking out a volume which has caught my attention, I stand in the silent room and read. The past years of my life are like so many books – now written and closed. I will pause before the shelf on which they stand; I will open these volumes and tell you what I find therein recorded. As in your own life, so in mine – there will surely be a lot to regret and much to be grateful for.

Regret is important: so also is gratitude. The traveller from Glasgow to Inveraray comes at last to a high point on the road above Glen Croe. It is a spot known far and wide as, "Rest and be Thankful". In obedience to this silent command the traveller, as he rests there, looks back on the winding road he has travelled. A long section of his journey is done: let him rest and be thankful!

The greater part of my life's journey is done. So now I rest for a while and look back with gratitude at the years I have lived. Cahir Healy once said: "Autobiographies are too often boasts of one's own self or one's family." Heaven forbid this here! What I am offering in these pages is the story of an ordinary priest belonging to a very ordinary family. We have nothing to exult over – except perhaps our Faith in God. I will stop speaking in this strain, however, because self-deprecation can be an oblique and subtle form of self-praise.

The world, life in Ulster, in Belfast, life in the priesthood and in the religious Order to which I belong – all have changed. The ways I knew, the laws and customs I followed, have all disappeared. The old order has changed, yielding place to the new. I will endeavour to record in these pages the life I knew, and the people's customs and manners of the years gone by. I will show you how we lived.

Take my slender story as you find it! There may be elements in it which will interest and even encourage you! I sincerely hope so, for that is my chief reason for writing it.

# CHAPTER ONE
# My Father and His People

I BEGIN WITH the unimportant fact that my name is Scots in origin. It has different forms, viz, Comings, Cummins, Cummings, Cumming, Cumings, Cumine. There is also the phonetically similar name, Comyn, or Comyns. In a modern book, *Dictionary of Surnames*, I read that forms of the name ending in '–ng' are mostly Scots, and that the form 'Cummings' means 'son of Cumming'. Perhaps my forebears belonged to the Scots clan Cummings – an ancient clan which is still found in Western Scotland. Mason's *Survey of Ireland* (1816) gives the name 'Cummins' among the inhabitants of Glenavy and Tullyrusk. (See **Appendix 1**.)

So at my father's request, in Baptism I was given the name Munchin. Admirable saint though Munchin of Limerick no doubt was, his odd name thus thrust on me at Baptism, brought me a succession of miseries through the ridicule and merciless teasing of my school companions. My first name, Daniel, was no doubt conferred on me because it was my maternal grandfather's name and perhaps also because my uncle was then Father Daniel Mageean – he it was who baptised me. Knowing his meticulous care in such matters, I have no doubt about the validity of my Baptism, but he did err in recording the date of my birth as 3 January 1907: the actual date being 2 January. When, as a priest, I gave a mission in Holy Rosary Church, Belfast, I looked up the entry of my Baptism and found that mistake.

I realise that all this is very unimportant to the reader, but it leads me up to one fact which has been of immense importance in my own life, namely, that I was born in a Protestant district in Belfast – Agincourt Avenue, off the Ormeau Road. I say this has been a fact of immense importance in my life, because the Protestant environment of my early days has meant much to me. To a great extent it moulded my existence. A lot of what I hope to say in these pages has resulted from my early surroundings. The neighbourhood and the people of Agincourt Avenue have had a lasting influence on my life.

For example, I am always conscious that I am an Ulsterman and a Belfast man. One day a few years ago I met the Reverend Ian Paisley in Lombard Street in the city. He stopped and stared at me.

"Good Heavens!" he exclaimed, "Are you back here again?"

"Listen, my dear sir!" I instantly replied. "This is where I belong! But you – you were born in County Derry, or near Ballymena, and the sooner you go back there, the better!"

At this retort he burst out laughing – but he had no answer for me.

As a city Belfast has many defects. Its rapid industrial development was perhaps too rapid. It does not possess a fine collection of buildings, such as is found in Dublin. Neither has it Dublin's central situation. Yet, given my choice, I would rather live in Belfast than in Dublin. This is the old preference for one's homeland, sung of in song and told in story. Belfast speaks to me as no other city or town does. There the streets and the houses fill my mind with memories. There most of my life-long friends live. There I would willingly – nay, gladly – spend my days, and there I hope to die.

In a Belfast church I first met God. In a Belfast graveyard the remains of my parents, my sister Eileen, my relatives, my teachers (to whom I owe so much) and my friends, lie at rest. Belfast has done so much for me. I would like – and have tried – to do something for my city in return.

Belfast, busy, grimy, red-bricked, cradled in the hills, at the head of the Lough's blue waters – if I forget thee, may my right hand forget its cunning!

## My Grandfather Cummings

And now I must go on to say something more about my forebears. My paternal grandfather, James Cummings, was a County Antrim man. (In a report entitled, "Statements to a Secret Committee, Ireland 1797", we are told that: "A spy named Donaldson went to Donaghadee to meet Henry Joy McCracken, McCabe, Neilson and Cummings, but these failed to turn up.") My grandfather hailed from the district around Dundrod and the Bohill, some six or seven miles from Belfast. He married Catherine McClarnon, a girl from the district. She died in childbirth sometime between 1870 and 1872. From the marriage there were two children: my father and the baby who died at birth.

My grandfather was a carpenter. He worked in various places in and around Belfast. At one period he worked in Holywood. In those days work started at a very early hour. The hours were long; the wages small. There were no Trade Unions – employers dictated everything: wages, working hours, your retention or dismissal. If you did not accept their terms, they sent you away – they would let you go without any hesitation, knowing they could easily find others to do your job.

In order to have breakfast and have time to walk from his home in

McMillans Place, Falls Road, to the job five or six miles away in Holywood, my grandfather had to rise before dawn. Nowadays, after such a trek, carpenters would not face a twelve-hour day of work. They certainly would not do it for fifteen shillings a week – as my grandfather had to. In his day you had no option: you did what he did, or you starved.

He was sturdily built, wore a beard and was always neat and tidy. He was rather quick-tempered, liked a drink, and frequently backed his fancy in a horse race.

He had a hard life. His wife died an early death, leaving him with a young boy – my father – to be brought up. Friends and neighbours helped to rear the lad while my grandfather himself kept working at his trade. He was skilled, intelligent and industrious. At times he took on carpentry jobs for which he needed men. He was a Master Carpenter and knew the men to employ. With reliable men he never feared taking on important jobs.

He worked to the end of his life. He died when he was about seventy years of age. His sufferings at the end were excruciating. Father always held the view, rightly or wrongly, that the doctor had failed to diagnose his father's ailment – common appendicitis and peritonitis, which perhaps could have been remedied, had the doctor recognised it in time. Mother used to tell me that my poor grandfather's cries of pain, as he lay a-dying, were heartrending. He died about 1906 and was buried among his relatives and friends in the old graveyard at Tullyrusk, in the district where he was born.

## My Father

My father, named Robert, was born in 1868 at 10 McMillans Place, off Durham Street. This place no longer exists: it has been demolished quite recently to make way for one of those modern blocks of flats which, while providing the people there with proper amenities, make the area resemble a human warren. My father did not live to see this change.

His maternal grandmother was Molly McClarnon. She was then a woman of about sixty years of age. She could easily recall events of the early part of the nineteenth century. In those sad years Ireland was experiencing epidemics, agrarian problems and military repression. Many of these events were most clear in her memory. She was a contemporary of Daniel O'Connell, Father Mathew, Michael Davitt, John Mitchell, O'Donovan Rossa, and the Fenian Movement. She remembered contemporary accounts of Napoleon's campaign in the snows of Russia and his final defeat at Waterloo. Among her neighbours were Irish soldiers who had served under Wellington in that famous battle.

Before coming into Belfast, she had lived with her daughter Catherine in the countryside around Dundrod. In my grandmother's young days the Catholic religion was outlawed in Ireland. There were no permissions to have Catholic churches. It is quite likely that she attended Mass at the Mass Rock on Collin Hill. In 1829 she saw the passing of the Catholic Relief Bill: it emancipated Catholics from serfdom and allowed them freedom to practice their religion.

Her daughter, Catherine, my father's mother, died in childbirth around 1870. The baby also perished. My father, born in 1868 was still a very young child. Unfortunately his grandmother who was helping to rear him also died a few years later. He was not without friends, however: two neighbours – sisters – who kept a small general store near his home looked after him. As he grew older he was able in some measure to repay them, by helping to serve customers in their shop. These two ladies were named Cregan: my father always spoke of them with great gratitude.

Father was an apt pupil at school. The curriculum in those days was not too extensive; but what was prescribed was done intensely. The chief emphasis was on reading, writing and arithmetic. In our later school years, when we children had picked up a smattering of these subjects and thought we could match our ability with his, he soon proved we were mistaken. His penmanship, even when he was an old man in his eighties, was copperplate. His spelling was amazingly accurate. He knew the precise meaning of words from his knowledge of their Latin and Greek roots.

We used to test him! We would open a dictionary and try him with all sorts of strange, awkward words – he had to spell them for us and tell us their meaning! My memory may be at fault – for I'm quite sure the dictionary holds words which will baffle experts – but I have no recollection of father ever failing his test.

His best subject, however, was mathematics. He always preferred to work at arithmetic, algebra and geometry. We children made good use of his preferences: how often we turned to him when we were in difficulties with our homework!

When he was only sixteen years of age, my father was appointed a Monitor in Raglan Street School. He also taught in a number of other schools in the Falls Road area. In 1899 he was admitted as a Queen's Scholar to the Teachers' Training College, Drumcondra, Dublin. This scholarship had been devised in the middle years of the nineteenth century to facilitate pupil teachers like Father in gaining teaching practice and training.

On completing his training, he taught for a while in 'The Rock' school, Hannahstown. After his marriage to my mother, he went to teach at Cary, near Fair Head. When he married my mother, Father's weekly wage was £1 per week. All during his teaching career, his wage – it was dignified by the term 'salary' – was wretched. How did people live in those days? In the mid-1890s farm labourers earned about 10 shillings a week, and a bricklayer's labourer in Belfast earned 18 shillings. As late as 1910, men and women working in the Belfast linen industry earned, on an average, about twelve shillings and sixpence per week. Those were the "good old days"!

In our days Cary is not counted as important. In bygone centuries, however, it was perhaps the most important place in North Antrim. In the Abbey's library today I came on a copy of *The British Isles* taken from Mercator's *Atlas,* or *Meditations of a Cosmographer on the Creation of the World and on the Form of Created Matter,* dated 1595. In this ancient production the only town or place named and marked on the North Antrim coast is 'Cary'.

When going to teach there, Mother and he set up their home in Ballycastle, a few miles away. Close by, on the same shore road, Marconi took over one of the cottages and there tried out his experiments – sending messages by wireless telegraphy across the six miles of sea to Rathlin Island.

Father's next appointment was as Principal Teacher in St Colman's School, Eliza Street, Belfast. He taught in this school for about thirty years, until his retirement.

On coming to Belfast my parents went to live at 77 Agincourt Avenue, Ormeau Road. While we lived there Mother was a friend to all the neighbours. Everybody knew her and everybody liked her. Father, on the other hand, never mixed with the neighbours. He was friendly towards them all, but never entered into any kind of close, personal friendship with them. He kept on associating with his old friends, who lived around the Catholic areas of the city. Some were his fellow teachers in other city schools, but most of them were members of the various Catholic Clubs in the city parishes. In those days, all these Clubs had billiard teams. Father was popular with the members, for he was deemed a good billiard player.

He had learned the finer points of the game in St Peter's Club, Divis Street. As a boy he had tried to teach himself. When alone, in charge of the shop belonging to the two Cregan sisters, he spent his free moments trying to play billiards. The shop counter was his billiard table. On its smooth surface, with a stick or cane as cue, and marbles as billiard balls, he practised the different strokes.

It is easy to recall parallel enthusiasms in the acquiring of skill in craftsmanship, games, and the higher arts. In literature we have the example of Robert Louis Stevenson: in the early days of his literary apprenticeship, he used to carry a notebook around with him. In it he noted down short descriptions of things he saw or heard – endeavouring all the while to find the apposite and precise words he needed. In his room at home, he tells us, he sedulously copied extracts from the great essayists. He tried to write as they did. Day after day he kept up his efforts to learn what he called "the trade of words".

And to take an example from the high art of music, we have Handel. As a child, instead of peacefully sleeping in his cot at night, he would creep silently up the stairs to play the spinet he had secretly smuggled into the attic of his home. Alone there with that humble instrument, he began to elicit the astonishing powers which gave to the world such tuneful melodies.

So it was with my Father on the level of a much humbler skill. A time came when, if he started to play a game of billiards in St Peter's Club, the word went quickly round the neighbourhood, and the Club soon filled up with spectators. Often, in a game of 'one hundred up', he began and finished the game without his opponent getting one shot. He was frequently invited to play an exhibition game at the opening of a new billiard hall. Many of the teams on which he played won championships. At home we once had a collection of gold medals he had won. I need not say what happened to them when money was in short supply in our home!

He would not however encourage me to take up the game. He used to say, "Proficiency at billiards is the sign of a misspent youth!" I disagree with the absoluteness of this statement. Youth needs an interest, a hobby, a pastime. In winter, or on cold, wet days when outdoor games are not feasible, a game of billiards in a good social club is surely to be recommended.

Scripture tells us wisely: "Whatever influence gets the better of a man becomes his master." (2 Peter 2:19). In the Revised Version, the Greek of this text is translated thus: "For whatever overcomes a man, to that he is enslaved." I like this succinct version; but Monsignor Knox's version, which I adopted, is plainer English. A game, a hobby, or a pastime may, but need not, rule a man's life. Like everything else in life, if used or played in moderation a game is beneficial and usually necessary.

One other relevant point deserves mention: in my father's early days – that is to say, a hundred years ago or more – the working class people of Belfast had a very limited number of forms of recreation. Wages were low – twelve to fifteen shillings per week in many, many cases – and what was earned was needed for rent, food, clothing and other essentials. There were no motorcars, radio sets, TV sets, cinemas, skating rinks or buses. Only the well-to-do could enjoy golf, holidays and travel. The ordinary, working-class families had no money to spare. Games of football or billiards were the main pastimes for men and boys. Times have changed radically – but that was the situation in those days. So I think Father's dictum, which I quoted above, needs careful qualification.

Although he mixed a lot among men of all classes, Father never adopted their solecisms or slangy modes of speech. This was due, not to any snobbishness on his part, but rather to his teacher's outlook as well as his practice in the school classes. He was constantly correcting the boys in these matters, and out of school he practised what he preached in the classroom.

He never used profane language. I cannot recall him ever using the name of God or Jesus Christ in ordinary conversation. To express his annoyance or amazement or pleasure, he had an odd expression he sometimes used – ie, "James Street!" Where he got this odd exclamation, I cannot guess. It was the most vehement expression I ever heard him using. Never in his life was he known to tell a blue story or use an improper expression. Awareness of this came forcibly to my mind as we stood around his grave on the day we buried him. On that sad occasion Canon McSparron, one of his lifelong friends, came over to me and in expressing his sympathy, said: "Your Father was a good man! He was a very pure man!" It has always seemed to me that being pure in heart, he was pure also in speech.

My Father had a very accurate ear for music. He also enjoyed it and sang well. He often played our piano and sang the songs of the "good old days". He clearly had a talent for music which circumstances, alas, had not permitted him to develop. In later years when radio was introduced, he would stop whatever he was engaged in to listen with obvious pleasure to some song or piece of music that was being broadcast.

All his life long he was a splendid walker. As I have said already, he grew up in a Belfast which had neither trams nor buses as we have had them. For him there was no other way of getting about, except by walking. On Sundays in the fine weather, after attending Mass in St Peter's Church, Divis Street, his father and he would walk the eight or nine miles to Dundrod to visit their relatives and friends. At the close of the day they walked back to the city. This meant that on their "day of rest", they walked about eighteen miles. Such a Sunday programme would be given little consideration nowadays by all those millions held in bondage by their motorcars.

The advent of the electric tramcar system in Belfast did not affect Father's life very much. Had the Belfast City Tramways depended for support on people like him, they had long since gone into bankruptcy! All his life long, he liked to walk. I often reflect that his love of walking was the secret of his longevity and his perennial good health.

A medical expert said the other day that in his opinion, the secret of good health and all-round fitness is to walk briskly two miles at least every day, and to take six really deep breaths morning and night. I think my Father would have agreed with him.

Father had a good sense of humour. His stories about the old days in Belfast were always interesting and often very amusing. He had a story of a man, a well-known character on the Falls Road, who lived by his wits and who resorted to all kinds of tricks to get money. One day this artful dodger caught a rat, put it in a sack, and went into a pawnbroker's shop. He told the pawnbroker what was in the sack.

"Give me what you like, for sack and all!" he said to the pawnbroker.

"Take it out of my shop at once!" exclaimed the pawnbroker.

"Alright! If you don't feel like giving me something, you can have the whole lot, sack and all, for nothing!" said the trickster.

The pawnbroker, aghast at the thought of having a rat loose in his shop, gave him half a crown and told him to take sack and rat to hell out of his shop. In parting with his money, the pawnbroker knew he was choosing the lesser of two evils.

Another event which Father used to recall for us concerned a very different matter. In those bygone days, when something of unusual interest or importance occurred, the *Belfast Telegraph* issued a 'Special Edition' giving the news. Nowadays, a 'newsflash' on TV or radio speedily informs the world – but these communication media did not exist then: the 'Special Edition' was relied upon to spread the news. One Sunday while Father as a boy was attending Mass in St Peter's Church, he heard the newsboys shouting, "Special Edition!" as they ran past the church. Out in the street after Mass, he would learn the news of the Phoenix Park murders, which had taken place on the previous afternoon, 6 May 1882.

## St Colman's

The school where Father taught was in the Markets' area of Belfast. Most of the pupils were from homes that were poor or close to the borderline of poverty. When the Bishop was coming to the parish to confer Confirmation, the Parish Council of St Vincent de Paul bought clothes for the poorer boys who were in need of them. It fell to Father to keep these new clothes in a school press or cupboard and to fit them on the boys who needed them. This involved much extra work for him, but it was worthwhile to see all his boys respectably dressed as they stood at the altar rails to be confirmed by the Bishop.

In those days Confirmation was usually given on a Sunday. It often happened that a poor boy, to whom new clothes had been given during the previous week, appeared in school the next morning, Monday, clad in his old tattered rags. On being asked what had become of his new clothes, the lad would explain that his mother had pawned the lot – the new boots, the new stockings, the new corduroy pants, and the new shirt and blue jersey. Nothing could be done about it – the boy was to be pitied and made to understand that he was not to be blamed.

It was very difficult to maintain high standards in such a school. The attendance of the boys was irregular. Most of them had only one horizon – their fourteenth birthday, after which they could leave school behind and go out into the big, wide world to earn a few shillings at some humble job. Yet in spite of the difficulties, St Colman's was a school where the boys were thoroughly grounded in writing, spelling and arithmetic. Some of the boys were very brainy. Unfortunately their parents lacked either the means or interest needed to give them a higher education. What a boon it then would have been, if a grant from some fund or trust had been available to help such boys to go to college and university! Some system of repayment on their graduation could easily have been devised.

The school was in the parish of St Malachy. Our home in Agincourt Avenue was in Holy Rosary parish, but normally we attended our religious duties in St Malachy's Church. A fine, noble church it is! Those qualified to judge say it is the finest late-Georgian building in Belfast. It was built in 1844. As I write, its red brick is now dingy, but the general external appearance of the building is still impressive. In contrast to the sooty exterior, the interior is bright and cheerful. If ever you visit the church, you must observe the ceiling: it is fan-vaulted in imitation of Henry VIII's chapel in Westminster Abbey. One worker says: "Its plasterwork is a creamy colour, rather lace-like and frothy." This luscious description, however, may not fit your ideas of the ceiling. Let it not put you off! St Malachy's Church is well worth a visit.

On Sundays then, all our family went to Mass in St Malachy's. The ten o'clock Mass was the Children's Mass. My two older brothers were usually altar-servers at the early Masses. As a rule I went with my sisters to the Children's Mass. The organist, Mr Murphy, played the hymns that were specially composed for this Mass. All the children joined in the singing. My memory is that, as children, we liked this Mass and never found it wearisome.

To be in time for this Children's Mass at ten o'clock, my sisters – Eileen, Annie, Margaret and Mary – and I had to leave our home in Agincourt Avenue at about 9.35 am or 9.40 am. As we neared the church, we used to hear the great deep-toned bell booming out its call to all the children to come to their Mass. The low, sonorous, vibrating tones of the bell became for us as children almost the living voice of the Church assembling to worship God.

Alas, some years ago the great bell and its tower were removed, because, it is said, the tolling of the bell interfered with the proper maturing of the whiskey in Dunville's distillery nearby! That is the story – I wonder, is it correct?

At the Children's Mass, all the parish schools were present in their section of the church, each under the supervision of a teacher. My father was always present with his boys at this Mass. In the afternoons he came back to the church for the Children's Catechism, or Sunday School, at three o'clock. All the teachers were expected to be present at this Sunday School. The Catechism instruction lasted about twenty minutes, after which the Parish Priest, Fr Daniel McCashin, came to the sanctuary and gave us a short talk on some saint or doctrine or religious practice. This talk lasted about ten minutes; we then had Benediction.

Saturday was the only free day Father had. His Sundays were busy days. Often he acted as a church collector at other Masses. Often on Sunday nights he was Master of Ceremonies at the parish whist drives. I do not recall that he ever complained about his Sunday commitments. He may have done so – but I cannot recall him doing so.

I have mentioned the parish whist drives: this leads me to say a word about Father's love of a game of cards. He had a good sense for the game. He was always an amiable and understanding partner: the post-mortems following a game were merely gentle interludes.

Chess was a game of which he was also very fond. On one occasion, when we were children, he had a slight accident which confined him to the house for a few weeks. During that enforced rest period, he bought a set of chess and patiently taught every one of us the game. For me this knowledge of chess has been a valuable acquisition. I have frequently, with much interest and pleasure, re-played the games of the great masters of chess. And when I was in charge of altar boys in St Joseph's, Dundalk, I taught the game to all of them. I regret to say that some of them quickly became experts at beating me at my own game! Each Christmas I organised among them a senior and junior Knock-out Competition, with valuable prizes for the winners – usually a very acceptable box of sweets.

## Later Years

Father retired from teaching about 1929. At that time my family was living on the Springfield Road. On his retirement he began to attend Mass and receive Holy Communion daily. For many years Mother and he attended our church at Clonard. I often saw them there at my Mass and gave them Holy Communion. As they grew older, however, they found the journey to St Paul's Church easier, and from 1950 onwards they walked to St Paul's each morning.

The years passed by; both of them grew older and feebler. In the street en route to Mass, one would have to support the other against falling. When Mother stumbled, Father held her up and when he faltered, she steadied him. At times we used to laugh over this – we used to tell them their guardian angels were being forced to work overtime! Particularly on winter mornings, when frost or icy patches lay on the pavement, their progress to the church was necessarily slow. On such mornings they shrewdly took care to walk close to the iron railings that ran along the front of our terrace of houses. There was sound reason in their strategy: when both stumbled simultaneously, Father, who was nearer the railings, would seize hold of them.

One cold morning, Mother fainted at the Communion rails. On another morning Father fell on the granite steps leading up to the main door of the church. News of these incidents quickly spread through our neighbourhood. People stopped me in the street and in a friendly way advised me to persuade them both not to continue going to Mass on icy mornings. Earnest neighbours insisted that my parents were not really able to go out to Mass daily. They even said my parents would surely die on the street if they kept up what they were doing. I did not follow the advice of these well-intentioned friends. I decided that, if my parents did die on the street or on the steps of the church, then that was the way they wanted it to be. I also felt certain they would sweep aside all my objections to their practice and calmly go on as before – death or no death, they would go to Mass and Holy Communion every morning. And that was their way, every morning for the last thirty years of their lives.

A day came however when Father was so ill he was not able to go to Mass. He accepted that situation. It was not the only cross he had to bear. In the last three years of his life he was totally blind. I was sitting beside his bed the night his blindness fell on him. Towards morning he wakened up and began fumbling for his watch, which he kept under his pillow. Having found it, he peered closely at it again and again.

"Put on the light, please!" he said to me.

"Father, the light is already on!"

He then started to feel for the glass face of his watch, and finding it, he kept peering at it – holding it more and more closely to his eyes. Finally he put it back under the pillow and said quietly, "I cannot see a thing!" He was now blind, and he knew it.

From that moment onwards his eyes were closed to the sights of this world. But never again did he refer to his blindness. Never did he murmur or complain. One could not but admire his courageous acceptance of what must be one of the most severe trials in human life – blindness.

Since that night when I sat and watched beside his bed, I have often thought about his fortitude when he realised his sight was gone. I can explain it only by assuming he had received, at that moment when he needed it, a special helping grace from God. In his last twenty or twenty-five years of life, he daily spent a long time in prayer: and this was the way God answered his prayers when he most needed His help.

In his extreme old age, Father went as a patient to the Bon Secours Nursing Home in Belfast. Gradually he became weaker and weaker. At last, one day when Mother was visiting him, he said to her:

"Mother, I am afraid I am going to die!"

(In the context this phrase, "I am afraid", does not really refer to fear. As Father used it, it means what we say, for example, in the expression "I am afraid the shop will be closed!")

Having observed a distinct change in his condition, Mother answered him quite simply and candidly: "Yes, I think you are!"

"Well," Father went on, "I have had a long life and a happy one!"

"I am very glad to hear you saying that," replied Mother.

He died peacefully next morning. The day was 22 August 1960: the Feast of the Immaculate Heart of Mary. He was ninety-two years of age.

Like every one of us he had his faults and failings. None of us are free of these – as St James says, "In many things we all offend!" I do think that those who knew my Father well would agree that his good points outweighed his defects. I, his son, cannot do otherwise but dwell on his good qualities.

Father won a victory over two habits he had in early life. At the time of his marriage, he had a drink problem. Mother insisted he must stop all drinking!

He did so at once. All his life long he never touched a drink. When he was over eighty years of age, my brothers used to treat him to an occasional glass of ale. I do not think he was keen on this – but he pleasantly accepted it for their sake: he knew it pleased them.

He was also rather a heavy smoker. One day he came home from the school, had his meal, lit up his pipe and sat down by the fire to enjoy a read of the daily paper. Suddenly he decided "to quit the smoking" – that was his mode of expressing it! He put his pipe aside, and for the rest of his life never smoked again.

When I reflect on these two victories over drink and tobacco, I can see that he had a very strong will. His strength of will was what enabled him to be an early riser – never did he stay in bed in the morning.

Now, when he has left this world, I see more clearly his grand qualities of will, and mind, and heart.

# CHAPTER TWO
# My Mother and Her People

MY MOTHER'S MAIDEN name was Susanna Mageean. She was born around 1874 or 1875 in the townland of Lisowen, which lies a few miles beyond Saintfield on the Crossgar Road in County Down.

In the period 1800–50, on which I will focus mainly in this chapter about my mother's family, County Down was of course less thickly populated than it is now. The towns and villages were then much smaller. Roads were generally in bad condition, with very rough, broken surfaces – in winter they were sometimes impassable. Traffic on the roads was negligible, except on market days in local towns, which meant more farmers would be driving their horses and carts along the roads. Usually however one would perhaps meet just a few horsemen now and then, or a coach on trunk roads, or again a herdsman guiding a flock of sheep or a herd of cattle to new pastures.

The farms of families of planter stock were generally prosperous – "large farms and slated, two-storeyed houses" is one description of them of the time. The native Irish families, whose forebears had been earlier dispossessed of their lands and driven to the hills and more remote parts of the county, had a poorer way of farming and living.

Thanks to the infamous Penal Laws in the first two or three decades of the century, many of these native men of Down were 'marksmen'. This name has nothing to do with marksmanship: it was the name given to those who, being illiterate and unable to write their name, could put only their 'mark' to any document which required signing.

Early in the nineteenth century, Irish was the everyday language of many people in the county. As the years passed by, English became more widely used. The story of the Gaelic language in County Down is a sad one.

In the middle of the sixteenth century, Gaelic was spoken throughout Down, except in the area around Strangford and Ardglass, where there were colonies of English and Scots planters. The continued arrival of these planters increased the use of English year by year. By the seventeenth century, English was mostly spoken in the widespread planter areas. Wherever the native Irish population remained, Gaelic was the everyday language. This was generally so up until the middle of the nineteenth century.

As late as 1880, a resident in the Mourne country wrote in a letter:

"There are a good many Irish-speaking people in the neighbourhood of Hilltown. Nearly all of them can speak English: when, however, they frequent fairs in the upper parts of County Armagh – for instance at Newtownhamilton or Crossmaglen – they meet numbers of people who speak English very imperfectly: with these people, the Down men converse altogether in Irish."

My great-grandfather on my mother's side, Dendy Mageean (1810–94) probably knew a good lot of Gaelic. Quite possibly he was bilingual. My maternal grandfather, Daniel Mageean (1838–88) knew a little Irish. He had, however, many Irish words in his vocabulary. My mother spoke no Irish, but, like her father, she had many words from Irish or Scots Gaelic in her vocabulary. (See **Appendix 2**.)

The Mageeans, cousins of mine, are still to be found in the district of Lisowen, a few miles beyond Saintfield. They must be one of the oldest Catholic families in Down. Some ancient records to hand inform us that two Mageean brothers fought on the Continent in the armies of Spain or of Queen Anne (1702–14), and returned to County Down in the latter half of the eighteenth century. One of these settled in the Loughinisland area; the other at Carryduff, near Belfast.

In Kilmore graveyard, outside Crossgar, there is the grave of a Daniel Mageean, who was born in 1676 and died in 1748. This man had a grandson, also named Daniel Mageean, who was born in 1762 and died in 1838. He lived at Creevyloughgare, near Saintfield. He was my mother's great-grandfather and it is certain that he lived through troubled times. When he was born, England was at war with Spain; when he was ten years old, the American War of Independence broke out; when he was about twenty-seven, the French Revolution began. This was followed by the wars of Napoleon.

All these events however were remote from Daniel Mageean's life. Yet there was one war which was not remote – the Irish Rebellion of 1798. The United Irishmen fought battles with British troops at Saintfield and Ballynahinch, with a skirmish with the British yeomanry taking place around Daniel Mageean's homestead at Creevyloughgare. It is very probable, if not quite certain, that he took part in these battles as a United Irishman. My cousins, the Mageeans of Ballygowan House, treasured a sword and a pike used by their forebears at the battles of Ballynahinch or Saintfield.

In the Public Record Office, Belfast, I found the Deed of Sale or Rent of a farm of nine acres at Ballydian, near Ballygowan, to Daniel Mageean in 1804. The rent to be paid was eleven guineas per annum. In those days, that was a lot of money to pay for the use of a mere nine acres of land. What interested me most however in the faded yellow document was the startling fact that Daniel Mageean, a respectable Catholic farmer in County Down in 1804, could not write his own name – he was illiterate! On the old document you can see the cross he made in substitution for his name – and beside it the words (written in the Protestant solicitor's bold, dashing handwriting) "Daniel Mageean – his mark".

This brought home to me most vividly the fact that in my great-great-grandfather's days, the harsh, unjust Penal Laws (the forerunners of the Special Powers Act in Northern Ireland) made it practically impossible for a Catholic to acquire an education in his own country. It is one thing to read the Penal Laws in a history book; it is another to see them working out in a man's ordinary way of life. Under the Penal Laws, Irish Catholics could not have schools at home or attend schools abroad. The historian, Canon D'Alton says of these laws:

> "Passed by Protestants possessing confiscated Catholic lands, the Penal Code's object was to impoverish, to debase, to degrade, to leave the despoiled Catholics incapable of rebellion and ignorant of their wrongs…"

## "Old Dendy"

The name "Daniel" had always been a popular one in the Mageean family. The Daniel Mageean, of whom I have just now spoken, had a son also named Daniel. He was born at Creevyloughgare, Saintfield in 1810. When grown to manhood he was familiarly known throughout the countryside as "Dendy Mageean" – this no doubt being a friendly, euphonious form of Daniel. In County Antrim, a Daniel is called "Dinty"; in County Down he is "Dendy".

Dendy was an intelligent person, and, unlike his father, he was educated. His education and industry made him well-respected among the people of the area. Since he was a District Councillor, his help and advice were sought by the country folk from a wide area. To his several sons I rather think he must have been something of a taskmaster – he worked hard himself, and saw to it that they did likewise. By his industry and thrift, later on in life, he was able to provide each of his sons with a fair-sized farm.

For men like Dendy, life in the middle of the nineteenth century was one long struggle. Each day brought its quota of arduous tasks which could not be shirked or postponed. In those distant years farming was not the machine-worked business of today. There were no tractors, no potato or seed planters, no harvesters – none of the ruthlessly efficient mechanisms to help the modern farmer.

Often, while on the up-to-date farms of my County Down cousins and friends, I have mentally brought "Old Dendy" back to earth, to survey some of the present-day farming machinery at work. I pictured him by my side; I watched his reactions! At first speechless, Dendy would recover his breath and perhaps exclaim, "Farming is not what it was in my day – now machines, not men, do the work."

Like other farmers in Down, Dendy had his horse-drawn plough, his harrow, scythes, forks and spades. He also had a pony trap and an old, heavy country cart. The only horsepower available to Dendy was horse-power: he knew no other. Farm work was slow, wearisome drudgery. And to crown it all, prices for crops, cattle and farm produce were low and uncertain.

On many Fridays throughout the year Dendy had to rise before dawn to go to the Belfast market. As the morning light filled the sky, Dendy was on his way. His horse, pulling the heavy, cumbersome country cart, plodded slowly along the rough stone road. Today, if you travel that same road from Saintfield to Belfast by car, you can easily do the journey in less than twenty minutes. It would have taken Dendy and his horse and cart the best part of three hours.

It was on one of these market journeys to Belfast, accompanied by his young grandson, Charles Mageean, that Dendy pointed with his whip to a house at Carryduff and said, "Charles, there is the house where my grandfather was born!"

That brings one a long way back in time, for Dendy's grandfather was born over two hundred years ago. Ever since hearing this item of information, I have never passed through Carryduff without thinking of the ancient home of the Mageeans, and wondering about its exact location and whether any signs of it still remain.

To return to Dendy: if the market was a good one and prices were right, he would often pause on his way home at Black's Public House, Ballynafeigh. There he suitably refreshed himself before continuing his homeward journey. On such occasions it was his practice to renew his energy slowly by sleeping soundly in the lumbering, creaking cart as it travelled. He always arrived home safely: his old horse knew every yard of the road. Traffic in those days presented no hazard. Nowadays the sleeping Dendy would be fined or even imprisoned for his dangerous driving!

It is interesting to go back across the years and see the world as Dendy saw it. How different it was from our world of today! None of the following 'necessities' existed in his lifetime – radio, television, phone, typewriter, motorcar, plane, cinema, buses, dance-halls and showbands. Dendy had none of these. He had no electric light. His home at Creevyloughgare was lighted by a few candles or a paraffin lamp. On special occasions, when he needed more light, he would light a rush candle – this was a kind of homemade torch or taper. To have a supply of these in the home, Dendy gathered the rushes in due season from marshy land. They were then peeled, dried, and drawn through melted fat or castor oil. A handful of these bound together and fixed into a crude iron holder greatly increased the light in a room. They were normally brought out only on festive occasions. Such occasions did not occur every week or fortnight, for the people could not afford frequent festivity.

Life in those days in County Down was a dour struggle – but it was not the hurried struggle of the modern rat-race: it was a long, slow process. Men worked steadily, no doubt, but at a leisurely pace.

For example, two men with scythes would come on a fine morning to cut a field of corn or hay. With fair accuracy they knew how long it would take them to finish a job. They started work at a regular, even pace, keeping it up throughout the day, stopping once in a while to sharpen their scythes or to quench their thirst from the can of buttermilk or cold tea brought down from the house by one of the children. There was a break for lunch about noon. Afterwards the men rested for half-an-hour or so for a smoke and a chat there in the field. Resuming their task, they worked away steadily, without slacking, yet without feverish haste.

Theirs was a craft which they had truly mastered. They had learned all the tricks of their trade: a dry blade, which would be rubbed carefully before you whet it; your whetstone would be laid on your coat on the ground so that during the work it remained quite dry. You would listen to the sound of the blade as you whet it – first there would be a harsh, changing note, next, a single musical note, and finally, as it became quite keen, it would hum and sing contentedly. At the work, you were not to force the scythe, but to let it swing easily and sweetly like a pendulum rather than the blade of a knife that is cutting. You would get into your most comfortable posture or stance, keeping as erect as the design of the scythe permitted, and swing the blade rhythmically in time and nicely away from you. You would follow up each stroke, always first moving the left foot forward. These are the hints born of experience: the men made use of them all. Although they lightened the job, they did not make it a light one. The men had still to work hard.

Unless the rain came, they would work at an unhurried pace right through the day. They were not on 'piece work', where haste meant more money; nor were they 'going slow' and prolonging the work unduly in order to get overtime money. They had a job to do: they would do it at the right pace and in the right time. They would do an honest day's work, and would be accordingly weary at sundown.

As the sun was setting, the men would go home to their first real meal of the day. Their usual food came from the products and produce of the farm. So far as I know, meat was not a frequent dish in the old days: it appeared only on the Sunday dinner table and also perhaps once during the week.

At the end of the harvest each year, there would of course be a celebration and a get-together of workers and neighbours. A special supply of 'good things' was prepared for the occasion. One quaint custom still survives in County Down: the last handful of oats is brought home and fixed up on the kitchen wall. This small sheaf is called "the Churn" – I cannot explain this word's origin or meaning – but all must have a drink for the Churn! This was a rigorous tradition, which is still followed. (See **Appendix 3**.)

Such was the life and the work of men like Dendy Mageean in the nineteenth century. By the sweat of their brow, they laboured on their land and with gladness gathered its fruits.

Dendy lived in constant anxiety about his occupation of his farm. He depended on his landlord for his very livelihood. This landlord allowed him no vested interest or right in his holding. He could charge Dendy any rent he pleased. He could raise the rent because of any improvements his tenant made; whenever it suited him, he could evict Dendy – even though he was faithful in paying the rents. And Dendy could do nothing about it – every power was against him: landlord, land-agent, police, military, law-courts. Were he to give up farming, he could hope to earn five pence a day as a labourer. His poor wife would then have the task of raising the family on the princely sum of half-a-crown per week.

In his early life as a farmer, Dendy had one really good field which he had rented from the landlord, Colonel Crawford. It was called the Hill Field. One day Crawford came up to where Dendy was working in the fields and said to him, "Mageean! I am going to take over the Hill Field! In compensation, I'll give you six shillings an acre for it!"

"Colonel, you cannot do that!" replied Dendy in alarm. "The Hill Field is my livelihood!"

"Well, whether you like it or not, I am going to take it over!" said the Colonel, as he turned away. Dendy was so upset and so indignant he felt like murder. On his next encounter with the Colonel, his manner clearly revealed his inner feelings. Crawford sensed the danger he was in and shouted to some of his workmen. These quickly gathered round him. Dendy was outnumbered and could do nothing. In due course the Hill Field was taken away from him. His compensation was six shillings per acre.

This was but one of Dendy's many trials: he had countless others. His family suffered from ill-health. Tuberculosis, then a killer disease, seemed to run in the family. A number of the Mageeans died in early life. Dendy saw them carried to their graves, one by one.

He must have been a remarkable man. He worked hard all through his life, and by his intelligence and industry, was able to improve his status. He was one peasant who profited immediately from the Catholic Emancipation Act of 1829, which gave such relief to Irish Catholics. In the humble cottage at Creevy, outside Saintfield, he reared a family of ten children, educating them and settling his sons in fair-sized farms. He tended to be headstrong and domineering – while he lived, he ruled. His sons feared and respected him: none of them ever thought of defying him.

Dendy lived to the grand old age of eighty-four, dying in 1894. He is buried in the family grave in Kilmore graveyard, near Crossgar. As you enter the graveyard, you will see his grave, twenty or thirty yards to the left.

As I have said a moment ago, Dendy Mageean's family were not all as long-lived as he was. As the headstone over his grave in Kilmore shows, five of his children died in early life. At the back of my mind is a memory of my mother telling me that they all died of tuberculosis. I have no written evidence to confirm this, but there is other oral testimony confirmed by my cousin, Fr Quinn. The early deaths of William, Susanna, Mary, Fr Charles and John seem to suggest that they all fell victims to this disease.

William was born in 1831. He was the father of the Ballygowan Mageeans. This family (Mary Agnes, Thomas, Robert and Charles) worked hard. While Robert and Charles worked the farm, Thomas endured about forty or fifty years as a bookkeeper and clerk in a whiskey firm in Belfast. Every day for a lifetime, he travelled by the same trains, at the same times, to the same desk, to deal with the same entries and transactions – a life like something you would read in Dickens.

Mary Agnes attended to the running of the house and the dairy side of the work. In her old age she used to tell me about her early life and her long hours of work in her uncle's public house in Saintfield. However, she always used to wind up her harrowing account of her toil there with the comforting reflection that the work was not so difficult after all, because the takings were so good. At the end of the day, the till made the toil worthwhile.

The family lived first on their farm at Carsonstown, near Ballygowan. The house there has always had the reputation for being haunted. Recently, in Birmingham, I met the young married couple who have now made their home in it. They never referred to the ghost – neither did I! Obviously they knew nothing of the house's history, so I let them go away without breathing a word to them about the ghost who shares their abode.

The Mageeans of Ballygowan were industrious and made money. In the early days of the twentieth century, they acquired that extensive and valuable holding – as the auctioneers would have put it – of some one hundred acres of excellent land, with a splendid Georgian residence approached by a tree-bordered avenue, and conveniently situated at Ballygowan, close to the main Ballygowan–Belfast road.

This property belonged to Mary Agnes. On her death, she left practically all her assets to charities in the Down and Connor diocese. It was indeed a generously charitable will – one that will, down the years, assist thousands of really deserving people.

I must now say a word about some of Dendy's other children. After Dendy's death, his son James occupied the family homestead and farm at Creevyloughgare near Saintfield. James lived a long life, dying in 1930 at the age of 94. He remained hale and hearty to the end. On Sundays, dressed in style, flower in buttonhole, he would walk the two miles into Saintfield to attend Mass – knowing, and known by, every man, woman and child along the road, in the chapel, and outside the chapel.

James' sons were Daniel, Robert, John and Thomas. Daniel and Robert were skilled at ploughing and won several championships. For many years they were judges of the ploughing contests at agricultural shows in County Down.

On that farm at Creevy is a Mass rock, wonderfully hidden. (My cousin, Peter Mageean, has searched the Mageean land at Creevyloughgare, but cannot rediscover the Mass rock now: perhaps it is in a field beside the Mageean farm and not in the farm itself.) One day many years ago, Daniel brought me to see it. He led the way through several fields to a clump of bushes. Behind these lay a concealed dell, near the bottom of which was a smooth, flat table of rock. On this rock-table, Mass was offered in the Penal Times. More bushes were growing along the slopes of the dell. There was also an open grass space in front of the rock. Fifty or sixty people could easily have gathered there for Mass. Daniel said truthfully that no one passing along the nearby lane or crossing the adjoining fields would discover this dell. He was justly proud of having such a relic from the Penal Days on his land. He had learned all about this Mass rock from his father and grandfather. The family tradition was strongly Catholic: the Mass rock was a precious possession none of them could forget.

John, the second youngest of Dendy's sons, was born in 1839. He became the owner of the farm at Leggygowan. His son John inherited it from him. The present Daniel Mageean of Darragh Cross is his grandson. One of the younger of Dendy's sons, Charles, became a priest. He was born at Creevy in 1846. As a boy he must have known of the Mass rock on his father's land. Probably he often visited it – perhaps it was in that hallowed spot that his thoughts first turned to the priesthood.

The normal age for ordination at the time was twenty-four: Charles was ordained at the age of twenty-three. Why? I am sure it was because of his ill-health. Within the year following his ordination, he died. He lies buried in front of the altar in Crossgar Church. A tablet in the sidewall commemorates him. It reads:

> "To the memory of the Reverend Charles Mageean, CC Dunean (1846–70) who departed this life at the early age of twenty-four years, after having been eleven months in the sacred ministry. R.I.P. Erected by his father, Daniel Mageean, Leggygowan."

I believe Fr Charles was a very sick man – if not actually a dying man – when he was ordained. The Bishop ordained him so that he would die a priest. Fr Charles had the same disease as so many of his brothers and sisters: tuberculosis. Effective remedies nowadays make minimal the dangers of the disease: in Charles' time, it was a death-sentence.

## Daniel Mageean of Lisowen

Among all Dendy's sons my main concern in these pages is with Daniel, who worked a farm at Lisowen outside Saintfield. He was the father of Dr Mageean (Bishop of Down and Connor, 1929–62), Fr Robert Mageean

C.Ss.R., and their sisters – my own mother being one of these. So this Daniel Mageean is my grandfather.

He was born in 1838. He received an education well above what was then normal in the countryside. He became a bank official, holding an appointment in one of the local banks in Downpatrick. His health was very poor: he suffered from the same disease as the others in his family – tuberculosis. Since it was clear to Dendy that the indoor work of a bank official would not improve his son's health, he made Daniel abandon his banking career and take up farming. With this in mind, Dendy bought him the farm at Lisowen, a mile or more from Saintfield.

About 1869 or 1870 Daniel Mageean married Susanna Marner from Drumnaconnor near Crossgar. They lived and reared their family at Lisowen. Both of them died there in 1888.

As will later become clear in my narrative, this family went through some hard times at Lisowen. The land was of poor quality. There was always plenty to worry about – bad crops, low prices at the markets, the death of a cow or a horse. All these were serious blows to a family, who were barely able to pay their way with the farm's normal revenue. No doubt Dendy helped his son financially when possible. He often visited Lisowen and advised Daniel about the farm's problems and activities – crop rotation, drainage, the keeping of stock and prices.

Daniel's wife, Susanna Marner, was a most devout Catholic. In her life she offered her children an inspiring example of a lively faith in God. Her large family of nine children meant that she was never idle. Her work in looking after them and in dealing with the work around the farmhouse left her little leisure. Each day she persevered at her work and her prayers. Even when going through the field to the well for water, she would recite her Rosary – in a day of continual work, this was one of her few opportunities to say some prayers.

Was it the constant hard work and worry that hastened the death of these two parents? They both died within six weeks of each other, in the year 1888. When Daniel saw death beckoning to him, one sorrow flooded through him: his orphaned children! To kind neighbours and friends who came to visit him, he would say sadly, "What will happen to my poor children when I am gone from them?"

Later I will take up the story of what did happen to these orphaned children. First, however, I would like to speak now about the Marner side of my mother's family.

## Susanna Marner's Family: Dr Marner

My grandmother, Susanna Mageean, née Marner, of whom I have been speaking, had a brother who was a priest, Dr Richard Marner. His was an interesting life, and I must say a word about it here. He was born in the townland of Kilmore, near Crossgar, in 1834. Having finished his preparatory studies in St Malachy's College, Belfast, he went to Maynooth College in 1850. He must have had more than average ability, for at the end of his theological studies he was assigned to a higher line of study in the Dunboyne Establishment attached to the College. On 4 April 1857 he was ordained a priest in Clarendon Street Church, Dublin. Two years later, having been awarded his Doctorate in Theology in Maynooth, he was appointed Professor of Classics and Mathematics at St Malachy's College.

In 1866 Dr Marner became the first President of the College. While in this position, he widened the course of studies available there. He himself taught classes in Logic and Natural Philosophy for those students who intended to study for the priesthood: this meant they could start their theological studies at once on entering Maynooth. (Under the old system, they normally would have had to spend a period in Maynooth studying these subjects first.)

His health became impaired, unfortunately. What was the cause of this? I had thought it was perhaps due to overwork; however my cousin, Fr Quinn has reminded me of something else that may have caused it. In mid-Down, even to this day, the people speak of "Marner's Ghost". The story behind this expression is as follows: a person living in County Down at the time was possessed by an evil spirit. Dr Marner was delegated by the Bishop of the Diocese to exorcise this person, using the formal, solemn ritual of the Church's prayers for exorcism. He faithfully carried out the duty imposed on him, with the result that the evil spirit was driven out from the person in question. That was all very well, but the strain of the work involved told on Dr Marner's health. His bishop granted him a long leave of absence, in the hope that a lengthy sea journey and a tour abroad might help him to forget his experience in the exorcism. He toured the Mediterranean and the countries of the Near East, hoping he would regain his health. Although the trip improved his health, he was never the same man again.

I have often heard that a priest who performs an exorcism pays a toll in one way or another. Dr Marner is a case in point.

On his return to his diocese, he was appointed Parish Priest – first in Ardglass, and then in Kilkeel. He remained in Kilkeel until his death in 1906.

What kind of person was he? My mother told me he was of short stature, very dapper, precise in manner and speech, and possessed of a very firm mind of his own. I say he was dapper, as he had a very fixed idea that a priest should be always smartly dressed. I have been told Dr Marner could rightly claim a highly original 'first' among the priests of Down and Connor diocese – he was the first priest in the diocese to put a crease in his trousers! I am sure this action did not shake the diocese to its foundations, but it was a clear departure from the custom then existing among fellow priests. In those days it was thought more becoming for a priest to appear poorly dressed. He however set a style in the diocese: he felt he should be just as well-dressed as the Church of Ireland or Presbyterian Ministers living down the street.

And so he was always immaculately dressed, complete with top hat and walking stick, as he proceeded with dignity through the little streets of Kilkeel. Invariably, he was excessively polite to anyone whose person or function did not please him. It is said, for example, that the local sergeant of police constantly received an overdose of politeness from the parish priest, Dr Marner!

A scholarly person, Dr Marner was of a very studious type of mind, and was very widely read. On his death he bequeathed his large collection of books to St Malachy's College. When I was a boy at the college, these books reposed on shelves in the upstairs room known as the Library. There, in the quietness, they have steadily accumulated dust – I doubt if anyone has ever opened them.

When Dr Mageean and Fr Robert Mageean were students at Maynooth, they spent their holidays with their uncle, Dr Marner, in Kilkeel. One of the daily chores required of them was to read aloud to him from the newspaper the entire news, from first page to last. Robert noticed that his brother, Dan, when reading his share of the paper, blithely skipped whole passages here and there. Robert was astonished at this audacity, for he himself never omitted a word from his reading task. When he challenged Dan about this, his long-headed brother told him bluntly he should make more use of his discretion!

I have said above that Dr Marner was of low build. The altars erected by him in the churches of Ardglass and Kilkeel testify to this; for his height determined theirs, and they are rather low. In his churches he erected many memorial tablets for his relatives. He seemed to have a mania for this. When the word went round among his relatives and friends that another tablet had appeared, they threw up their hands in dismay. The thing had become a painful joke! From what I have written, one can deduce that Dr Marner was not the informal type, given to back-slapping, noisy laughter and idle frivolities. I see him as a very correct person, a thoroughly good priest, but one who was rather unapproachable for ordinary folk. I see him too as a tough disciplinarian, one who was strict with himself and equally strict with others. That was his character. I am not at all disparaging him. He was a sterling priest: his name and memory have always been held in the highest regard, not only by his own kith and kin, but also by the priests of his diocese.

Dr Marner had his own share of serious problems to face. On his shoulders fell the whole burden of looking after the Mageean children when their parents died. He was parish priest of Kilkeel at the time. He had to make frequent visits to Saintfield to see how the children were getting along and to attend to the family's affairs. Today a car could easily do the journey in an hour. It was a different matter in his day. He had to do the forty odd miles from Kilkeel to Saintfield either on horseback or in his pony trap: especially in bad weather, this would mean a good deal of trouble and weariness for him.

All credit to him for what he did for the Mageean children. He saw to the education of the younger ones, sending the two boys, Daniel and Robert, as boarders to St Malachy's College. He watched carefully over their studies. One year it happened that Daniel failed an examination. Dr Marner spoke seriously to the boy about this lapse – apparently with good effect, for Daniel never failed another examination. Dr Marner could not be expected to replace completely for the Mageean children the parents they had lost – but he certainly did his best, at least for the younger ones. He is buried in a cemetery adjoining Massforth Church, Kilkeel. (See **Appendix 4**.)

### "The Old Priest"

Dr Marner's granduncle was the Reverend Richard Curoe. In nineteenth-century Ulster he was known as "The Old Priest". His was a most remarkable life too, which I would like to write here. My link with him is that he was my great-great-granduncle.

He was born in 1742 in the townland of Ballynagarrick in Kilclief parish, Strangford. I cannot explain how, having made up his mind to become a priest, he went on to pursue his studies. He must have learned the elements at some 'hedge school', and been taught by one of those peripatetic geniuses who earned a subsistence of a kind by teaching in such 'schools'. Where, however, did young Richard Curoe go to do his studies for the priesthood? By the Penal Laws then in force a Catholic lad could not be educated. In Ulster, as elsewhere throughout the country, there was no formal seminary for clerical students. So Richard Curoe had to travel here and there to meet his teachers. His studies were interrupted: at times he had to set them aside, then take them up again when opportunity offered. All this helps to explain why Fr Curoe was ordained before he had completed his studies. He was ordained somewhere in County Down in 1773 by his bishop, the Most Reverend Dr McCartan. After his ordination, Fr Curoe went to Paris and there finished his studies at the College of the Lombards.

At that time the streets of Paris had not yet witnessed the bloody scenes of the French Revolution. The aristocrats with all their wealth, their chateaux, their gilded carriages, their imperious ways, and their luxurious mode of living, still ruled the country. Louis XIV and his dazzling queen, Marie Antoinette, continued to hold royal court and preside at lavish entertainments: they and their entourage seemed blind as a serpent's slough to the sinister signs of sorrowful days ahead.

This was the Paris Fr Curoe saw, this the city in which he lived and studied. He walked about its streets, passing men and women who some years later would howl for the blood of priests and bishops. He was gone from those streets and those broad open squares and places when that blood began to flow.

On his return to Ireland, he was appointed Curate in the parish of Bright, County Down. In 1778, on the feast of St Patrick he became Parish Priest of Ballykinlar. It was while he was in the parish that 'the fun' began.

When Dr Hugh McMullin became Bishop of Down and Connor, he decided that Ballykinlar parish was too extensive. He blandly informed Fr Curoe of his intention to take away the northern section of it (which once upon a time had been the ancient parish of Drumcaw – probably the Bishop based his decision on this fact), and annex it to the Loughinisland parish. He little knew his man!

Fr Curoe objected. He claimed that this section was canonically part of his parish and that the Bishop had no power to deprive him of it. A clerical storm on a grand scale followed! The Bishop stood his ground; so also did the Parish Priest. Fr Curoe continued as usual to look after the northern section of his parish, saying Mass each Sunday in Drumaroad. Finally, the Bishop forbade Fr Curoe to say Mass there – all that area, he said, must henceforth be considered part of Loughinisland parish.

This was by no means the end of the affair. Fr Curoe decided to take action. Through the Primate in Armagh, Most Reverend Dr Blake, he appealed to the Pope.

It must have taken months and months to get this case settled. There was no postal system as we have it nowadays. Letters to Rome, if very important, were usually brought personally by students returning to one of the Roman Colleges, or by some bishop or priest going to Rome on business. If other means had to be used, communication with the Holy Father was slow, expensive and hazardous. Considering all this, one wonders how this dispute was ever settled. But settled it was – and in favour of Fr Curoe. The Pope decided that Drumcaw (the area in question) was indeed part of the parish to which Fr Curoe had been canonically inducted as Parish Priest, and therefore the Bishop was prohibited from disturbing him in "the enjoyment [sic] of his lawful rights".

In due course, at a Conference of all his clergy, the Bishop publicly promulgated the term of the papal rescript. He was a humble man to do this – or perhaps he had no option: perhaps Rome had said he must promulgate the decree in his diocese. In a public matter, such as this had become, Rome usually insists on its judgement being made public.

And so Fr Curoe was vindicated in his just claim. And now see what happened! Having proved his point and won his case, he requested his Lordship the Bishop to transfer him to Kilmore parish (ie Crossgar), so that when Ballykinlar parish became vacant he could make in it the change he desired. This would go to show that he withstood the Bishop solely on a point of principle, and not for any personal reason relating to Drumcaw.

So it all ended amicably: in 1780 the Bishop transferred Fr Curoe to Kilmore parish and was thus able to incorporate the Drumcaw area into Loughinisland parish.

In his new parish of Kilmore, Fr Curoe soon settled down. He lived and worked in it for sixty-four years. Surely this is a record in the diocese of Down and Connor, if not in the whole of Ireland!

May I here quote a passage about him taken from O'Laverty's *History of the Diocese of Down and Connor*:

"After ministering to his flock for upwards of 64 years, Fr Curoe died at his residence in Lisnamore on 31 July 1844, and was interred in the chapel yard of Kilclief. (There is still a plaque to his memory in Kilclief church erected by Dr Marner.) "The Old Priest", as he was called, had arrived at the patriarchal age of 102. He was the last priest in Down and Connor of those who had to worship God with the canopy of heaven for a covering, and rude stone in an open field for an altar whereon to celebrate the sacred mysteries."

(Note – I have not seen this plaque anywhere in the new church which replaces the old one at Kilclief.) O'Laverty continues:

"Previous to the erection of the chapels at Inch, Kilmore and Killyleagh, Mass was celebrated in secluded places, one of which was a few yards distant from the Rocks chapel, where the rock altar still remains. The high cliff, where the watchmen stood to sound the alarm on the approach of the priest-hunters is still pointed out."

Fr Curoe doubtless offered Mass frequently in these secluded places. O'Laverty gives us further information about other Mass rocks:

"Another Mass rock was in a field belonging to John Burns in Castle Quarter, in the townland of Annacloy: the rock, however, was quarried away for the erection of the county jail. Another 'station' was in a field in the townland of Cluntagh. Mass was also offered during the times of persecution on a rock in John Quinn's glen in the townland of Cluntaghaglar, and, in the same townland, the altar of sods, on which the great sacrifice of the New Law was offered up, is still religiously preserved on James Killen's farm."

These details serve to give us a picture of the parish in which Fr Curoe laboured as a priest. What a pity he did not write his memoirs! Alas, the record of his life and experiences died with him. He would perhaps have written in Irish; for Irish was surely his first language. In his early life it was the common everyday language of the people of County Down.

He was a kindly, zealous priest, as is shown by a document now in the parish archives of Kilmore. A Catholic tradesman wrote this in a letter to the Parish Priest in Crossgar in 1875:

"I lived in Killyleagh in 1824–25. I was told there was no chapel there and the nearest was in Crossgar. Me and my wife had to go to Crossgar every Sunday to Mass. I was not long going there when I got acquainted with the PP, a Rev. Fr Curoe, an elderly gentleman, who took compassion on my wife to have to walk every Sunday. Fr Curoe asked me, if he sent a priest to Killyleagh, where he could say Mass. I said he could celebrate Mass in the house I lived in, as I had the house to myself. This was in 1825. Fr Curoe sent a priest, a Father

McMullan, and a boy with the vestments. The first Sunday he came we had but six of a congregation; the next time we had more; and the third time there was more than the house could contain. The Rev Fr Curoe told me there was not a Mass celebrated in Killyleagh for upwards of 300 years before it was celebrated in my house."
(Martin Lyons, Clonmona Cottage, Birr, King's County, 8 December 1875)

One other interesting point about Fr Curoe is this: being one of the few Catholic priests in that central area of County Down (so close to Saintfield and Ballynahinch, where battles were fought), he surely attended to the spiritual needs of the many Catholic men who, as United Irishmen, fought at these places during the 1798 Rebellion. He would have heard their confessions in the fields, said Mass for them when possible, anointed their dying, and buried those who had fallen in battle. In his article, "Killyleagh and Killinchy in 1798" (*Irish News,* 1945), Colin J Robb says:

"Father Curoe became Parish Priest of Kilmore in Jan. 1780, and was Pastor during that epoch. History is silent about his experiences during those days. The following pass was issued to him: 'The bearer Mr Richard Curoe of Lisnamore, priest of Kilmore, has permit to pass upon his lawful business at all hours between sundown and sunrise, and to carry letters not under seal. Given at Finnebrogue under my hand this 15th day of May 1798. John Waring Maxwell.' The old Mass House at Kilmore, which was built by the priest, was fired by a troop of the 22nd Light Dragoon Guards on 15 June 1798, according to the Duty Book of that Regiment."

The battles of Saintfield and Ballynahinch took place some days previously, so the Mass House was probably burned in the follow-up operations.

It is quite possible also that Fr Curoe met Thomas Russell, "the Man from God Knows Where", who stopped at The Buck's Head in Loughinisland on his journey to rouse the North men to join in the Rebellion.

Fr Curoe must have had an iron constitution. He was out in all kinds of weather. His journeys often took him through difficult country. To avoid imprisonment or fines, he had to keep away from the roads and highways when carrying out his priestly duties. With his Catholic people he endured much for the Faith. To his – and their – loyalty to the Faith we owe our Faith under God today.

In his *Memoirs of the Whig Party*, the Protestant writer, Lord Holland, shows us something of what this priest and his people had to suffer for their Faith:

> "The fact is incontrovertible that the people of Ireland were driven to resistance by the free quarters and excesses of the soldiery, which were such as are not permitted in an enemy's country. Dr Dickson, the Protestant Lord Bishop of Down, assured me he had seen families, returning peacefully from Mass, assailed without provocation by drunken troops and yeomanry, and their wives and daughters exposed to every species of indignity, brutality and outrage, from which neither his remonstrance, nor those of other Protestant gentlemen could rescue them."

Such was the life of Fr Richard Curoe, such were the times and circumstances in which he, with his local people, remained true to the Catholic Faith.

Before passing on in my narrative to other matters, may I here subjoin a brief word about Fr Curoe's nephew, who was also named Richard Curoe. This second Richard Curoe was born in the townland of Cluntagh, near Killyleagh in 1782. As a boy he witnessed the turmoil and unrest in 1798 in County Down. The year after the Rebellion, when he was just seventeen years of age, he entered Maynooth College as a student. In 1808 he was ordained a priest in Belfast. So far as I can ascertain, his was the first ordination to take place in that city.

His bishop, Most Rev Dr McMullin, appointed him Assistant Priest to the Rev Hugh O'Donnell, to help him "in the arduous duties of the Belfast Mission". At that time Fr O'Donnell was the only priest in Belfast. He offered Mass in a shed near Castle Street. The Catholics in the city did not number more than a couple of hundred. At the most a couple of dozen might have received Holy Communion at the Sunday Mass. (Compare that with the situation to-day! During the year 1967, St Mary's Church alone in the city of Belfast had a daily average of about 400 taking Communion, with a total figure for the year of 150,000.)

Why then did Dr McMullin speak of, "the arduous duties of the Belfast Mission"? Because it was work that was underground, work proscribed, work carried out in spite of constant repression and danger, work that demanded much zeal and courage from the priests engaged in it. The Catholic Church in

Belfast was then a Church of the Catacombs – a Church not legally permitted to emerge from the darkness into the light of day, until in 1829 the Catholic Emancipation Act was passed.

So ends all I have to say here about the Curoe family. The history of the family is in some ways unique in the Diocese of Down and Connor. There are two main reasons for this: firstly, because many of their family and their descendants became priests – up to 1970, there were sixteen in all; and secondly, because the Curoe priests are the link in the diocese between the Church of the harsh, cruel Penal Days and the Church of the years since Emancipation.

## The Mageean Children: Dr Mageean

I will now take up the story of the orphaned children of Daniel and Susanna Mageean of Lisowen, Saintfield. Margaret, the eldest girl, was about 15 years of age when her parents died. For a while she looked after the home and the other children. When the home was later broken up, she went to a college in Liverpool. Not long after her return to Ireland, she married.

Selina went into business in Belfast. She too married after a few years. Mollie became a teacher. Nelly acted as housekeeper to Dr Marner. Both these girls – Mollie and Nelly – were married in their twenties.

Daniel and Robert stayed at Creevy, attending the local primary school until they were old enough to enter St Malachy's College as boarders. Daniel was ordained a priest in Maynooth in 1906. He taught in St Malachy's College from 1908 until 1919. He then went as Dean to St Patrick's College, Maynooth. In 1929 he was consecrated Bishop of Down and Connor. He died in 1962.

Daniel's career, his efforts to influence Ulster's affairs, his long years as Bishop in the most difficult diocese in Ireland – all deserve more than a passing mention here. I shall begin with his student days. As a student in Maynooth, he favoured the study of philosophy – so he once told me when I was studying philosophy. To it perhaps he owed that accuracy of mind and that impatience with vagueness, which characterised him in his dealings with others.

The Spartan routine in the Maynooth of his time formed in him a habit of early rising and a general adherence to a daily programme of work. His were laborious days. I feel sure he would have achieved success in his higher Dunboyne studies, had he not been called out to fill a need in his diocese. In St Malachy's College he taught English and History. I now wonder how he fared in his first months there. He had a slight stammer in his speech, which he fairly well concealed by speaking slowly and with very great deliberation. The College boys must not have noticed his difficulty, for it would have prompted a nickname – his nickname in fact was "Wee Dan". All down the years his efforts to hide his defect must have cost him a great deal. He had always a burning love for Ireland, its people, its history, and its language. In this regard I want to mention a few points.

While teaching in the College, he asked Fr Toal to give him some lessons in Gaelic. So, on an evening after his very fatiguing day in his classes, he got out his Irish books and went through them with Fr Toal until a late hour. He once admitted to me that at the end of such a day he felt worn out.

Fr Seamus Clenaghan and he spent part of their holidays in the Gaelic-speaking district of Donegal. There they attended Irish classes at Cloughaneely Irish College. This cost some money. Only through making sacrifices could Daniel afford this Irish course. His income in St Malachy's College was small. He once said to one of his priests:

"I remember beginning my three month summer vacation with £13 in my pocket and cycling down the College avenue on a BSA bicycle on which I had paid the first instalment!"

That green bicycle – which I well remember – was useful and used. With my cousin Patrick McGouran (later Canon and PP in the Sacred Heart Parish), he cycled out to Templepatrick to visit the grave of Sir Samuel Ferguson, the Ulster poet. On its wheels he made journeys through the city and into neighbouring counties. He used it also on his frequent visits to the ancient monastic ruins on Mahee Island – a spot he dearly loved.

During one vacation, Rev Dr Hendley and he cycled to Omeath Irish College. En route they stopped to consult a Dromore priest about the roads before them. This priest advised them, chatted with them, and discovered they were Down and Connor priests. He looked at them sharply and asked,

"Who are the two men – Hendley and Mageean – who have volunteered to go as Chaplains to the army?"

There was a silence on the roadside, until the cyclists muttered some neutral remarks to cover the situation. Here is the explanation: World War 1 was being waged, and Bishop McRory of Down and Connor had a few weeks earlier asked his priests for volunteers to become Army Chaplains. Dr Hendley and Fr Mageean had volunteered but had not disclosed the fact to each other. The Bishop, however, needed them in the College – hence their volunteering was in vain.

Instead, Fr Mageean was appointed Chaplain to the Catholic prisoners in Crumlin Road Gaol – work he could carry on while teaching in the College. There he attended to the spiritual needs of IRA prisoners – among them Éamon de Valera.

In 1919, Fr Mageean was appointed Junior Dean in Maynooth College. Students under him agreed he was very strict but just. He was also deemed ubiquitous! If you judiciously paused in your studies or prudently broke a rule, the Dean always happened to see it. Also he could knock your door and be standing in the middle of your room at one and the same instant. Anyone whose name did not appear on the List for Major or Minor Orders could go to the Dean and find out why. The Dean would bring him into his room and there, man-to-man, explain the causes of the failure. He never relished 'Orders List' day. But it had to be! And his decisions thereon were utterly conscientious: fear or favour had no part in them.

In 1929 he was appointed Bishop of his native diocese, Down and Connor. On his Consecration Day he spoke to the assembled priests of the Diocese. His theme was simple and direct, viz, "I am a Down and Connor priest!" He meant – and they all knew it – that there would henceforth be one Diocese of Down and Connor, with no divisions or distinctions. I never heard anyone accusing him of having gone back on this principle.

Since I am not here writing his life, what I say about him as Bishop will be put with great brevity. I will begin with his faults. Firstly, I know he was rather autocratic – and I think I know why: he dreaded anyone having undue influence on him or even trying to sway him. He sought advice, asked opinions, and listened to others – but he made up his own mind, for he was not going to be a puppet on another man's string.

He was on occasion very long-winded. He often wiped out the value of his speech or address by going on and on and on – until his listeners became wearily impatient and longed for him to have done. His Lenten Pastorals, I felt, were far too long and at times dull.

He was said to be odd and eccentric. In what way, I wonder? I never could pinpoint instances of this. At times he could be very blunt and rather sullen with us his closer relatives. He could quickly give one of us the cold shoulder. I suppose he had his moods, as we all have.

As Bishop, he always distinguished what he knew as Dan Mageean from what he knew officially as Bishop of the Diocese. This seemed to be an obsession with him. It developed in him almost a dual personality. As Dan Mageean, he frequently got to know 'things', but he would not act until he knew them officially. When anyone – priest or layman – called to see him on business, he was 'The Bishop' – courteous, but reserved and serious. But once the matter in hand had been settled, he changed manner at once, and, producing a bottle of excellent sherry for his visitor, he became, especially with the priest caller, the light-hearted, friendly, generous Dan Mageean of old.

The Apostolic Nuncio, Monsignor Paschal Robinson, once said to me, "That Bishop up there in Belfast is a very hard worker." The Diocese was a busy one. He kept his correspondence up-to-date, answering all letters promptly. Diocesan affairs never got out of hand – he attended to them immediately.

He had grave anxieties, such as the Catholic Schools Question, the 1935 Riots, the IRA troubles. In his heart he longed for a United Ireland. He distrusted the Unionist Government in Northern Ireland. Had that Government then hearkened to his repeated demands for fair play for Catholics, Northern Ireland would not have sunk into it the present day shambles (ie, from 1969 onwards). Had Catholics then got just dealing on housing, jobs, promotion and social life, English and Scots soldiers would not be needed to bolster up Stormont's efforts to maintain peace and its security. Bigotry, like pride, often defeats its own purposes – this is an instance of it. The House of Ulster is tumbling down – and for this dénouement the Unionists can but blame their own sweet selves.

Dr Mageean loathed doing or saying anything against those who struggled for an Ireland Gaelic and free. When Fr Mangan asked him in 1936 about some Catholic men who wondered if they should retain their guns, he said,

"Tell them to keep their guns for their own self-defence and the protection of their homes!"

When I started the correspondence course for Non-Catholics at Clonard in Belfast, which I will talk about later in this book, he urged me to proceed very quietly with the work:

"What you are doing will annoy many Protestants. We don't want another pogrom!" He knew the North and its Orange hatred and bigotry. Rome itself knew of his difficulties. Pope Pius XI once asked him: "How are the Orangeisti?"

And yet he loved the North. It was his homeland. He loved its people. He was proud of their strong, lively Faith. How proud he was too of Saul and of Slemish! How keenly interested he was in the growth and expansion of St MacNissi's College. "I hope," he said one day to Fr Agnew, "that it will mean many vocations for the Diocese!" In his mind the Diocese was the one thing that mattered! It was his life.

He was most at ease in a gathering of his priests. With them he thoroughly enjoyed a good hard game of poker. The priests had no qualms whatever about relieving him of his funds when a suitable opportunity came their way. They could not go too far, however, for he usually imposed a five-shilling bet limit on all playing. For their part, his priests were at ease in his company. Their experience at the Christmas dinners he gave for their benefit had shown them what a friendly, generous host he was.

My one lifelong impression of him is that he was very dedicated to his work in the vineyard of God. First and foremost, he was a spiritual man. Rising at 6.00 am, he made his morning meditation before his Mass at seven. Each day he made his visit to the Blessed Sacrament, said his Breviary and at night, with his household staff, recited the Rosary in his private Oratory. His mornings were given to letters and interviews; his afternoons to visiting the sick in St John's Nursing Home or the Mater Hospital (less frequently in the latter, because he discovered his visits meant an extra strain on nurses and staff). Any of his priests who were sick were visited, not once only but often.

Every Friday at about 4.00 pm, he rang the bell at Clonard Monastery for Confession. He made his annual retreat with his priests in St Malachy's College. At a very late hour one night, during the retreat, one of the College priests had to go to the Chapel (perhaps because of a sick call) – he was to find the Bishop kneeling alone in the darkness before the Blessed Sacrament.

In his last months of life he suffered agonies from coronary thrombosis. I asked him was the pain very bad, to which he replied,

"It is as if someone plunged a screwdriver into your heart and twisted it around." When the end was drawing near, he sent for all who had attended him and thanked them earnestly. He died as he lived, calmly and quietly yielding up his soul to God. I helped to place his dead body in the coffin. He is buried as he wished, among his priests of the Down and Connor Diocese in Milltown Cemetery. In life he was happy to be one of them; in death's long sleep he will still like to be in their company. (See **Appendix 5**.)

What about his will? He left about £6000 – every penny of which went to Diocesan needs! His relatives – even my own mother, his only surviving sister – received nothing of it.

## Fr Robert Mageean C.Ss.R.

Robert was the youngest of all the Mageean children. In 1911, like his brother, he became a priest. In the following year he took his vows as a Redemptorist. He spent seventeen years on the Australian Mission. Part of this period he spent teaching classics in the Redemptorist Juniorate there. A sound classical scholar, he was a successful teacher, with some of his pupils achieving first place in the State examinations in Classics. Returning to Ireland, he preached many missions and retreats throughout the country until his saintly death in 1960.

In his latter days, Fr Robert had a heart condition. He knew he could die at any moment, but he was quite ready to go whenever God called him. Finally one night he wakened from sleep, feeling ill. He got up and went to Fr Patrick Whelan, who lived in the room beside his. Fr Whelan got him back to bed, gave him the last Sacraments, prayed by his bedside, and saw him breathe his last. Within an hour from the time he had wakened, he was dead.

Fr Robert's reputation among Redemptorists was very high. They looked on him as being a man of God – abstemious, prayerful, observant of his Rules and Vows, and quite unusually charitable and obliging. They knew he was sincerely zealous for the salvation of souls and completely dedicated to God.

"I would willingly take his chances! I would willingly change places with him!" said one of the Brothers to me, as we stood near the dead body of Fr Robert. Of him too, we can say, "He died as he lived!" His chief interests in life were God, prayer, work for souls, and his own Redemptorist brethren.

## My Mother: Susanna Mageean

Susanna was my mother. When her parents died, she was about thirteen years of age. She helped her sister, Margaret, with the work of rearing the children. She lived a long life. She survived all the others, dying at the age of 86.

I wish to speak here of her life in some detail. I owe it to her memory. My debt to her is incalculably great. Heaven alone knows all she did for me.

Like the other Mageean children, she was born in Lisowen, near Saintfield, and spent her childhood there. She attended the local school at Doran's Rock. Although this was not a Catholic school, many Catholic children attended it. At that time the teacher was Master Adams. (In County Down, then as now, the country schoolteacher was always given this title of "Master".) Master Adams thought Susanna Mageean a bright child. She was quite lively in mind and manner. She was never unduly troublesome. He felt she would go far.

Susanna was very devoted to her father. In the evenings after school, she would go across the fields to find him and help him where possible in his work. As she grew up, she was able to help him quite a lot. In this she was a contradiction of the accepted belief of those times – that girls were of little or no use in the working of a farm. Mother once told me that as a child she knew that boys, but not girls, were wanted in farming families. Boys were assets – they could work the farm; they could make a good match in marriage – perhaps marrying into a wealthy family. Girls were regarded more or less as a nuisance: "second-class" citizens, they would be called in modern parlance.

Until our own days, even in the Church, have women not been treated and regarded as second-class citizens? This goes a long way back. In his book, *Daily Life in Palestine at the Time of Christ*, Daniel-Rops writes (pg 102) that when a child was born in a Jewish family, neighbours flocked in to congratulate the parents:

> "The congratulations were particularly warm in the case of a son; if it were a daughter they were less enthusiastic – with so little enthusiasm indeed that sometimes they were more like expressions of sympathy. Daughters were no addition to the family fortunes, since as soon as they were married, they belonged to other families."

"Girls are but an illusory treasure," observes the Talmud, and then adds, "Besides, they have to be watched continually." This was the Jewish traditional outlook. I seem to see it also in the words of the Psalmist in Psalm 127: "Sons are a bounty from Yahweh, he rewards with descendants: like the arrows in a hero's hand are the sons you father when young. Happy the man who has filled his quiver with arrows of this sort."

Even in the Gospels, you can notice this poor regard for women. Read Matthew 15: 37–8: "Four thousand men shared in this meal, to say nothing of women and children." Why say nothing about them? Was it because they did not matter? Apparently it was not thought worthwhile to go to the trouble of even making a rough guess about the number of women present. The Evangelist is merely echoing the outlook of his times – nowadays, we would ask why the women were not counted.

St Paul would not let women speak at the early Christian gatherings. He directed that they were not to wear braided hair, gold, jewellery or expensive clothes, stating, "Woman is the reflection of man's glory!" (1 Corinthians 11:7) A friend told me that her grandmother, a very devout Anglican, had said she could not endure being in the same room with the Apostle Paul! I can understand her feelings. Saints have felt much the same about the Church's attitude to women.

In the early editions of the autobiography of the Little Flower, St Thérèse of Lisieux, the following passage was omitted, lest it shock readers and diminish their esteem for the saintly writer:

"I still cannot understand why it is so easy to get excommunicated in Italy! All the time, people seemed to be saying: "No! You must not go here! You must not go there! You will be excommunicated!" There is no respect for us poor wretched women anywhere. *[I would add "in the Church and its laws!"]* And yet you will find the love of God much commoner among women than among men, and the women at the Crucifixion showed much more courage than the Apostles, exposing themselves to insult, and wiping Our Lord's face. I suppose He lets us share the neglect He Himself chose for His lot on earth. In Heaven, where the last will be first, we shall know more about what God thinks."

Theologians followed suit in their general attitude towards women. You can see their want of consideration for women in such matters as the duties of women in the married state. Our own St Alphonsus says that a married woman may not go out of the house without her husband's permission: "Quapropter domi libenter se contineat, nec sine viri permissu exeat." (Damen Vol 1, No 552) (I have not been able to find these words in Gaudé's edition – I am wondering where Fr Aertnys, whose text Fr Damen edited, found them.)

Monsignor Knox points out that if you consult the Index of Suarez's *Theology*, you will find that under the word 'woman', the Index bluntly says: "See Scandal"! That is in harmony with the unflattering note sounded about women down through the centuries in the Church.

The puzzle of it all is that the Church elevated and honoured Our Lady so highly, while this "women are second-class citizens" theme was maintained in Catholic laws and writings. Things have improved since Vatican Council II. Nearly fifty women now work in the Roman Curia. Two women saints have been declared Doctors of the Church – St Theresa of Avila and St Catherine of Sienna. Religious women are now being consulted about matters affecting their life in religion. Most of us think it is about time all this was done.

That digression, as you can guess, is on a point about which I have had strong ideas for many a year – but now I will leave it alone and continue with the story of my mother's life.

As she worked with her father in the fields and helped him out of some difficulty, he always applauded her and cried out: "Bully, Susanna! Bully, Susanna!" This word "bully" in common similar use throughout Ulster is surely the Gaelic word "baile", found in such phrased as "Bail O Dhia ort!", "Baile ar Sean!", meaning "blessing" on a person. The everyday Ulster use of the word means: "Good for you! Good man! Fine!" When Susanna's father wanted some tobacco from the village, she would go for it. She led the mare out along the lane to that part of the bank she could climb, so as to get sufficient height for scrambling on to the mare's back. This planned operation having been successfully carried out, a slightly breathless but happy little girl went trotting off to Saintfield village some miles away.

Susanna was courageous; she feared nothing. No person living or dead could frighten her. As mothers sometimes will, Susanna's mother used to threaten her with 'the bogeyman'. In the Catholic homesteads of Down in those days 'the bogeyman' was Lord Castlereagh – a most feared and hated landlord, a horrible man in the people's eyes. So what was said to Susanna was this: "If you are not a good child, I'll give you to Castlereagh!" Yet I doubt if even that execrable name frightened Susanna!

When Old Dendy, her grandfather was alive, he was a constant visitor to Lisowen where his son Daniel lived. Dendy was feared by all – except Susanna! If she spotted him coming up the lane, she would instantly run back to the house to warn all of his approach. If her father was smoking, he instantly emptied his pipe into the fire. Out of respect, he would never smoke in his father's presence.

Dendy knew, of course, that Susanna had heralded his approach. He thought her too bold. In his opinion her father had spoiled her. At any rate there were times when Dendy deemed it necessary to chastise Susanna himself. With this punitive intention written in his eyes, he would walk towards her. When she saw him coming on the warpath, she quickly took evasive action. One line of retreat near at hand for her was the gable wall of the house – in it she had made footholds by which she could climb to the roof of the loft. With speed she ascended the wall and remained on high, out of Dendy's reach, and quite unrepentant. She was safe and she knew it: Dendy could never use the footholds in the wall, and would certainly not make any attempt.

If Dendy ever cunningly barred this escape route, she had another one available – the tall pear tree in front of the house. Susanna could get up that tree with almost the speed of a squirrel. Perhaps Dendy was right in thinking that her father spoiled her. In the circumstances one can understand and make allowance for her father's indulgent attitude towards her. In his poor state of health, he needed someone to assist him in the work of the farm. Susanna was the only one to provide this help. He depended a lot on her: perhaps she did get too much of her own way.

Her father's health became so poor that he was forced to take her away from school to work on the farm. Susanna was then about twelve or thirteen years of age. She had reached the Fourth Book at school. Her formal education at the humble school at Doran's Rock was thus abruptly ended. Master Adams, on hearing what had happened, was quite upset. He walked out to Lisowen to have a chat with her father. He begged him to let the girl come back to school: she was intelligent; she was doing well at her books; it would be a tragedy to take her away from school.

This was a most distressing interview for Daniel Mageean: one cannot but feel sorry for him in his dilemma. He agreed with Master Adams that she was intelligent. He agreed it was a great pity to take her away from her books. However, he had to look at the problem from the other side. His poor state of health made it impossible for him to run the farm without Susanna. He hated to take her from school. He loved her; he would do anything possible for her; but now he needed her help. He could not spare her: he was no longer able to work the farm alone. The family's livelihood depended on this child. He would have to stick to his decision. He was sorry about it, but he could do nothing else!

Master Adam's journey to Lisowen that evening had been in vain. He walked home in pensive mood, sad over the whole business, and rather disappointed.

Mother never again put her foot inside the school at Doran's Rock. Her school days were finished. She now faced life at twelve or thirteen years of age – possessed of only a Fourth Book education! The hard decision reluctantly made by her father, affected her whole future life. All her days she was to be painfully aware of her educational deficiencies. She remained forever conscious of the gaps in her knowledge.

When writing letters, her penmanship was neat and clear; but she was sometimes hesitant about points of spelling and grammar. In conversation she was at times cautious and slightly reticent, particularly before strangers. She read a lot, she asked us questions, and she relied on us. She tried to improve her knowledge. Almost every week for years, I used to bring her some books from the Carnegie Library, Donegall Road. She loved reading. In the evening, when the day's work was done, she would sit down contentedly to read a book. In the course of her reading, she would ask us the meaning of some word she had come upon. She kept learning and improving all the time. We all helped her – Father and the rest of us. And the more she learned, the more keenly she felt the loss of an educational opportunity in her childhood.

On one point she excelled over us: she had a curious vocabulary of words quite strange to us. When we would challenge her over these, she would confidently bid us search the dictionary. This we did promptly, only to find to our chagrin that she was right! Such a word existed: there it was, in black and white, in the family dictionary. Thus for our own selves we often discovered a new word and its meaning. Sometimes the dictionary informed us that the word was derived from the Gaelic; sometimes we were told it was indeed a genuine word, but one which had become archaic.

"The wind is coming from a good airt!" she announced to us one day. That was one word I learned from her – a good word derived from the Gaelic "ard", meaning a height or point of the compass. "I don't care a "thraneen" what you do!" Gaelic again, meaning "a little reed". "Watch that trinket!" she would say to my sister, Margaret and me, as we three walked through the fields. She was referring to a little trench or runnel that lay in our path. When we challenged her on this one, she maintained she was right. I'm sure she learned this word from her father when working in the fields with him. Although the dictionaries do not give the meaning she put on the word, it may be a very old word, a diminutive from "trinkette", bearing a French or Norman influence on the Latin word *truncare* (sometimes spelt *trincare*), meaning to cut or channel. (In French, *une tranchée* is a trench; *une tranchette*, a small trench.)

This kind of gentle 'conversational' challenge went on all through our lives with Mother. I wish I had noted down her many quaint words and turns of phrase. (See **Appendix 2**.)

I must get on with my story! On leaving school, Susanna worked with her father on the farm. Within a year or so, however, Daniel Mageean's health became completely undermined. He took to his bed, never to rise again. In the year 1888, he died. His wife and he would die in the same year, within six weeks of each other.

Neighbours now rallied around the orphaned Mageean family and worked the farm for them. Susanna helped her older sister, Margaret, in running the home and attending to the other five smaller children.

What a sad home it was! Both parents dead, and a large family of young children to be reared and educated! The two girls, Margaret and Susanna, did their best. During the day they were too busy to mourn their loss; but at night, when the five younger children were abed, the two girls sat in the silent cottage and wept for their parents. They often opened the doors of the kitchen where they sat – and then earnestly begged God, if only once, to allow their father or mother to walk through the room.

For several months, life in Lisowen went on in this way. But it was an impossible situation and could not last. Finally Dr Marner, uncle of the children, decided, in his capacity as executor of their parents' will, to dispose of the farm, and with the proceeds to educate the children.

This was done. Susanna went to stay with her aunt, Selina Marner, who was married to a man named John Davey and lived in Saintfield.

This was not what Dr Marner had planned, however. His arrangement was that Susanna should go to a certain convent of nuns and become a lay-sister. She would be able to do domestic work there. The question of whether the girl had a vocation for the life of a nun did not seem to arise! The line of thought seems to have been: "She can do that kind of work – let her go and do it!" Despite the many years that have elapsed since my Mother told me of this, I am still astonished and rather shocked at this utterly impersonal and heartless solution to an orphaned girl's problem. That a man of Dr Marner's education and background should even consider it, much less proffer it himself, surpasses my understanding!

When the lay-sister suggestion was made to Susanna, she gave a very prompt answer: "If I am to be a maid-of-all work, I can be that in the world, without going into a convent!" So Susanna lived with her aunt in Saintfield. She helped her with the work of the house. John Davey had a shop or a public house in the village. Susanna helped in it also. She was well worth her keep.

Her Aunt Selina somehow reminds me of David Copperfield's aunt, Betsy Trotwood – like Betsy, Selina was an old-timer, a tireless worker, and as hardy as a snipe. One day, feeling out of sorts, Susanna said to her, "Aunt, I think I have got indigestion!"

"You have got what?" exclaimed the aunt, wrinkling her forehead and half-closing her eyes.

"Indigestion!" replied Susanna.

"Gracious goodness, child, what is that? I never heard of it before!" said her aunt.

Selina was kind to the young girl however: she gave her a home when she stood badly in need of one. She guided her through some of the most difficult years of a girl's life. She advised her. She taught her all she knew about domestic work. Hence my mother Susanna was a very competent cook, rather an expert with the knitting and sewing needles, and a capable manager of a home. These were the accomplishments for which she was often praised by her friends. I feel that a good share of the credit should go to her Aunt Selina, who taught her so much of it.

Selina seems to have been kind to everyone – even to "the wee people" – the fairies. At night she used to put some bread and milk in a bowl on the windowsill for them, "if they feel like it"! A kindly, thoughtful soul!

And yet it never occurred to this good woman to give Susanna any wages or pocket money. And around the house and in the shop, she was surely entitled in justice to some wage. But she never received a penny! In the end the girl helped herself on one occasion to one half-crown. It was a small sum, undoubtedly due to her – indeed, many times over. But how she worried over this 'theft' in later years. She had acted quite correctly in what she had done – but she did not see it that way. Her conscience troubled her. I put her mind at rest when, years later, she sorrowfully recalled the story of the purloined half-crown.

My mother lived in Saintfield with her aunt for three or four years. She then went to Belfast and stayed with her sister, Margaret, who was now married. In the city Susanna obtained work as a shop-assistant. Her wages were five shillings per week. On this wage she had to provide herself with food, clothes and lodging.

What about the money obtained from the sale of her father's farm: did she get any part of it? She got about £60. In Belfast she gave it to her brother-in-law to keep for her. Later on when she asked him for it, he told her he regarded it as his money – it was payment he had a right to receive from her for her keep. And that was that! She left the house and went into the city to look for a new place to stay. She was just eighteen years of age; she was alone and almost destitute. She now had to live on five shillings per week.

She took a room in Broughton Street in the city, paying half a crown per week for it. With the remaining half-crown, she had to supply all her other needs. I have often wondered, with great sadness of heart, how she survived.

At one point she lived in lodgings in some house near the Shankill Road. The landlady wanted her, on one occasion, to allow another girl to share the bedroom with her. When the landlady's own sons heard of this proposal, they said they would not allow it. They protested against the idea, saying,

"This new girl is not a good type, we think, and Miss Mageean will keep her own room. This new girl is not fit company for Miss Mageean!"

All this brings home to me vividly the very difficult circumstances in which my mother found herself in those days. Of course as she gained experience in business, she was able to get other jobs which carried better wages. In some of the houses where she lodged, she would give a hand with the housework. When people discovered her skills in laundering, sewing, knitting and baking bread, they made use of her. I am sure the families she helped would in return readily provide her with a meal. This would have saved her from having to buy food.

Such was Mother's life until she married my father about the year 1900. All during her married life she worked hard, rearing a big family on little money, and teaching us all – chiefly by her example – to live a good Christian life.

The strongest influence in my life has been my mother. I think of her smile, her kindness and generosity. I think back to her unlimited spirit of forgiveness and her astonishing ability to overlook completely our repeated offences and temperamental displays.

We ought to have realised how much it cost her to spend her days amid the red-bricks of the city. She longed for the country life of her childhood. How often from the Tuesday markets she carried home a flowering plant for the window-box of our living room. If when I visited her, I did not comment on the new plant, she would draw my attention to it, pointing out its loveliness and expressing the hope that I liked it. In our backyard she kept several large boxes filled with earth in which she grew shrubs and flowers. In late spring and early summer she would transform our small front garden in Agincourt Avenue into a glowing mass of red, orange, and pale lemon nasturtiums. These were her substitute for the green fields and bright flowers of the Lisowen of her childhood.

When we moved house – from Agincourt Avenue to Springfield Road – she was appalled by the very high wall at the back of our new dwelling. The high curtain of red bricks lessened considerably her view of the open blue sky she loved so much.

Her interest in flowers did not deflect her from her work in the home. Undoubtedly her housekeeping skill brought us safely through the trying, impoverished years of the First World War. She knitted socks, cardigans and pullovers; she made dresses and suits; she prepared meals – such as they were, in wartime – all at minimal expense. An expert at price values, she spent money wisely. By doing all our laundry work herself, she saved a lot of money. On washing day, after a hard morning's work, she would hang two long lines of clothes and linens out to dry.

My mother's outings were simple and inexpensive – a visit to the theatre to hear Eugene Stratton singing "The Lily of Laguna" and the other popular songs of Leslie Stuart; or perhaps a night at the play, *East Lynne* (her eyes filled with tears at the sad death of Little Willie); or possibly a visit to one of her sisters living in the city.

In pain and suffering, she was admirable. Cancer attacked her throat. Operation followed operation – altogether, she underwent eight operations. Professor Negas in King's College Hospital, London, removed the infected parts. Since Father at the time was too feeble to accompany her there, I said I would stay in our monastery at Clapham and visit her each day. But to this, Father said, "No! If she is dying in London, you may go. Not otherwise!" The utter heartlessness of that reply stunned me! My sister Mary had to leave her family of eight young children to go with Mother in my stead. Mary said later that the hospital staff marvelled at Mother's patient endurance of excruciating pain. The operation was successful, and Mother lived for many more years. She died in February 1963. It snowed heavily on the day we buried her. I thought it a sign of the innocence and goodness of her life. May Almighty God grant her eternal rest!

# CHAPTER THREE
# My Childhood

MY PARENTS, AS I have already said, were married about the year 1900. Shortly after their marriage, Father was appointed teacher in the small country school at Cary, near Fair Head in County Antrim. Mother and he went to live in a cottage on the sea road running along the bay at Ballycastle.

Father's next appointment was that of Principal Teacher in St Colman's School, Eliza Street, Belfast. Therefore Mother and he moved house from Ballycastle to 77 Agincourt Avenue, in the Ormeau Road district of Belfast. Except for a baby girl who died in infancy and my eldest brother, James, who was born in Ballycastle, all the children of our family were born in that red-bricked terrace house in Agincourt Avenue, viz, Robert, Eileen, Annie, Margaret, Mary and myself.

This district in which we were born was a network of red-brick streets. I can easily recall their names: Carmel Street, Palestine Street, Jerusalem Street, Damascus Street, and so on. With such biblical names to the fore, the area was popularly known as the "Holy Land". There I lived for the first thirteen years of my life – years which left on me a profound, indelible impression.

In Agincourt Avenue our neighbours were either Presbyterians, or members of the Church of Ireland, or Methodists. They were all working-class people. Many of the men were plasterers, riveters, or carpenters in the shipyards. Their work was strenuous; their days long. As a child I remember lying in bed in the early morning and listening to the distant, low-sounding horn of the shipyards at six o'clock, calling the workers to their jobs.

In a way, is it not ludicrous to call those days "the good old days"? The truth is, that compared with our modern standards of living and working, they were "the bad old days". Only some elements in those far-off days were good. Life then was certainly more leisurely – there was less rush, less tension. The roads were safe: the newspapers gave no columns over to lists of those dead or injured in traffic accidents. Diseases indigenous to foreign lands – smallpox, cholera, influenza of certain types – could not quickly spread throughout the world, as they can today via air passengers. The era of the gangster, the super-criminal, the dope addict, the hippie, the beatnik, the motor-cycle mobs had not yet begun. All this, however, is but one side of the story: another side must be considered also. Even allowing for the changing value of money, people in those days had to work harder and longer for less money. In the Belfast flax-spinning mills, for example, young girls worked barefoot on very wet floors from 6.00 am til 6.00 pm for ten or twelve shillings per week. The shipyard men also worked a twelve-hour day for about twenty or twenty-four shillings per week. Bricklayers, carpenters and painters earned about eighteen shillings per week. When my parents married, my Father's weekly wage as a teacher was one pound! A working boy's average wage was three or four shillings. To earn that paltry sum, boys in the bakery trade worked from 5.00 am to 9.00 pm, with Sunday work as well. You could be sacked any day. There were no unions to safeguard and advance the interests of the workers.

It would remind you of the circus games in ancient Rome. A gladiator vanquished in combat in the arena depended for his life on the whim of the Emperor: if he gave a thumbs-down signal, the victor would promptly put the vanquished opponent to death. Likewise in "the good old days", the employee's livelihood depended on the whim of the employer: the latter could, at will, keep him in work or sack him.

The overall standard of living for the working classes, and for many of the professional classes was extremely low. In those days, ever so many houses were small. They offered little privacy, and usually there was no bathroom. Meals were unvaried: many lived on porridge, bread and butter, and tea. Only in some homes was meat eaten once or twice a week.

The arrival of a new baby meant more debt: money would be needed for doctors, nurses and for clothes for mother and child. Many young boys and girls ran about the streets barefoot in all weathers: there was no money to buy boots or shoes. Clothing was so often shabby and threadbare. Garments which would now quickly be thrown aside were carefully brushed, sponged and pressed, to make them respectable. When a man bought a new suit, he took special care of it: outside the home, he wore it with caution; in the home, he would take off the jacket and go about in his shirt-sleeves – all this "to save his new suit".

In Belfast the women of the working class ignored the dictates of fashion: they had no choice! When out shopping, visiting friends, or going to work, they wore black or grey shawls draped over their heads.

In those "good old days" there were no school meals for children; no bottles of milk to build up their strength and their resistance to ailments. If you look at photographs – group photographs – of school children taken in those "good old days", you can see how thin, puny and hungry-looking they were. Indeed, the working classes – and many of the professional classes – of those days merely existed rather than lived.

Disease met no resistance in the people: it mowed them down. Tuberculosis was a death sentence; so also, appendicitis; so also, pneumonia and a score of other illnesses which nowadays are speedily remedied. To call in a doctor or to go to his surgery meant money had to be paid. A visit to a doctor was an event, a highly important event, occurring only when something obviously serious was wrong.

Few families among the working classes were entirely free from debt. Were it not for the numerous pawnshops, where family treasures or worthwhile articles could procure a loan, hundreds of families would have often gone hungry.

As in the army in those days, so in ordinary life: the well-to-do, like the officers, rode on horseback; the working people, like the common soldiers, marched the long road, mile by mile, mile by mile.

When my mother heard anyone referring to the "good old days", she would merely shake her head. She knew the truth: she had lived through those days. She used to tell me, for example, that with her sister Margaret, she would walk from Saintfield to Ballynahinch to sell a few pieces of embroidery or sprigged muslin, over which they had toiled for weeks at home in Lisowen. The journey there and back totalled roughly twelve miles – a twelve-mile walk crowning the work's own drudgery! All this to earn two or three shillings! Those were the "good old days".

In spite of all, the people had their hours of fun and laughter too. Within their limited resources, they occasionally had "the gay hour". They wrung the last drop of enjoyment from a day's excursion to the sea, a visit to the nearby park, a local football game, a meal with friends. Simple pleasures were enjoyed all the more, because they so often came after long stretches of undiluted, hard, monotonous work. Neighbour helped neighbour in life's daily struggle: they shared their joys as well as their sorrows.

My family got along very well with all our neighbours. These were nearly all Protestants, yet we, a Catholic family, had no serious clashes or conflicts with any of them. Mother was very popular with all the womenfolk. They liked her friendliness and light-heartedness. She was kind to them in many ways. In one respect, they found her help invaluable: they discovered that she was really gifted in nursing sick children. How often a neighbour would come knocking at our door, asking her to see a child who was ill. My mother was almost a specialist in curing ringworm, for example. She had learned a particular form of treatment which was always successful. No doubt in rearing her own large family, she had learned a number of useful remedies for sick children. She was always ready to set aside her own housework to go to the help of a neighbour. She was a friend to everyone.

Of course, in our district she had no monopoly on these grand qualities. The women there, especially the mothers of families, despite their own problems and worries, were very kind-hearted and always ready to do a neighbour a good turn. When an emergency arose in any particular home, all the neighbours – men and women – helped in any way possible.

Our neighbours had few inhibitions when they met with each other: they talked candidly about home and domestic affairs. They would come to the garden gate at the front of their homes and chat amiably and unconcernedly across the street with one another. It was like an open-air parliament or debating society. The topics of conversation varied according to their moods and tensions. Never was there a dearth of subjects! For example, they might have talked about their 'menu' for that day's dinner, the price of different foodstuffs, a sick member of the family, some accident or mishap in the district, some startling item in the newspaper. The Crippen murder case kept them going for long enough. And then when Crippen and Ethel Le Neve were captured, there had to be a special session of discussion – although I am bound to say that this was more a group meeting than the usual, across-the-street exchange. (I have always thought that women, especially married women, were more interested in that murder case than historians have realised.)

There was in those days a candour and openness among the people which, I fear, has disappeared. Modern ways and means, such as the telephone, apartment blocks or towers, planes, television, radio, have in one sense brought people closer and in another sense forced them further apart. Nowadays I can telephone a neighbour, yet never meet him. I can live in an apartment building under the same roof as a hundred families, yet never get to know one of them. I can share a seat on a plane with a German or an Indian, yet remain a complete stranger to him. In motorcars the neighbours in a street may come and go, yet never meet face-to-face on the pavement. Sixty years ago in our district, everybody knew everybody else: neighbours visited neighbours, met one another in the street, and joined in frequent neighbourly gatherings.

Such was the district, such were the people where I was born. The most vivid memories of my life are of those streets in "the Holy Land" and of those good people.

All this leads me now to speak of some of my earliest memories. I have a vague recollection that I became aware of my own self and the world about me while I was still very, very young. As an infant I cried one day in the brown wickerwork cradle in which I reposed. To quieten me, Mother told one of my older brothers to rock the cradle – at that moment for the first time I was conscious of my own existence and of the world around me.

I have been informed by reliable sources that I started to go to school at the age of three. I have no memory of this. I often wonder, did I benefit in any way by going to school so young? One thing I do know: I was not forced to take up school life. I escaped my mother's vigilance one fine day, and made my way to the school in Eliza Street. Thus through no superlative element in my make-up, I was spared the awful misery of children who are highly sensitive and feel intensely the separation from the warmth of home life in exchange for the rough, rude climate of the average school.

At an early age I learned to read. This was largely due to a long section of hoarding outside the Northern Ireland cricket grounds on the Ormeau Road. This long hoarding was covered with advertising posters: Pears Soap, Oxo, Raleigh bicycles, Andrews' Liver Salts, current films in local picture houses, current shows in the music halls, and so on. I was just as eager as my brothers to read these posters as we walked to school. With my brothers' help, I was gradually able to decipher more and more. In this way I learned many 'big' words long before I learned them in my class at school. It was thanks to these brotherly tutorials on the way to school that I was fairly able as a child to read books in advance of what I read in my classroom.

The reading books used by my older brothers at school were always available to me. These I read avidly. I found that words I understood led me to the meaning of new words: I proceeded, as the philosophers would say, from the known to the unknown. The Donegall Road Branch of the Carnegie Library provided us boys with plenty of adventure books. I used to read so much that my brothers – no doubt with the connivance of my parents – hid the library books from me. For a long time I searched the house for the hidden treasures, but without success. Then one day I decided to search again in the top back attic. My efforts were fruitless, it seemed: I remember I was about to admit defeat. I stood dejectedly in the centre of the room, surveying my surroundings – and then it happened! I gazed wearily at the four walls, the floor – and then my eyes wandered to the ceiling! There, at the end of the long roof where the beam entered the wall, on a narrow, cunningly contrived shelf, reposed the library books. I quietly exulted in my discovery. With what I deemed to be equal cunning, I kept my discovery to myself – but henceforth I read every library book that came into the house. My parents and brothers were happy, and so was I!

One particular book which I often read in my childhood was Schuster's *Bible History*. It was well illustrated, with line drawings of all the outstanding personages and events of the Old and New Testaments. I pored over this book: the pictures became alive for me. Even now, after sixty years, I have but to close my eyes and these pictures come vividly before me. This book was one which helped to give me a lively faith in God. No doubt it contributed to the forming of my vocation.

Perhaps this is the place for me to say that under God, I owe my vocation to the Priesthood to the good influences of the Catholic home in which I was reared. In our home there was an enduring reverence for God. We were taught to pray, to go to Mass, to receive the Sacraments, and to be grateful to God for our faith. We were never permitted to use God's name in ordinary conversation.

During the dreadful years of World War I, a neighbour of ours was called to the Colours and fought in Flanders in the 36th Ulster Division. On one occasion while home on leave, he came to visit us. He frightened us children at first, because he had donned a goatskin jacket, wore a German helmet, and carried his Lee-Enfield rifle with bayonet affixed to it. Whoever opened the door to him was badly shaken at seeing this frightening figure, with rifle and bayonet at the ready. Indeed all of us got a severe shock – but when we recognised our friend, we soon recovered.

He put his armament aside, sat down, and told us stories about his life as a soldier in the trenches in Flanders. For us children, it was an intoxicating pleasure to listen to his adventures. Fascinated, we gathered around him as he spoke of his experiences in the Line near Arras, Ypres, and other sections of the Western Front. In the course of his stories, he let fall some common profane expressions. Before leaving our home that night, however, he apologised to our parents for using these expressions in front of us children. He knew our home: he knew that we as children had never heard any profane language there – and he therefore apologised. We had heard all these expressions while out playing in the streets or in the park – but we never heard them in our home.

As was the common practice in Catholic families in those distant days, we recited the Family Rosary every night. When assembling us for this devotion,

Mother used a weird expression with a nautical ring about it: "All hands on their knees! All hands on their knees!" Since the floor of our living room was tiled with cold bare tiles, there was an instant rush for cushions, papers, or something else to kneel on.

Father led the prayers, with Mother and the older children in turn reciting a Mystery. There were no protests, and there was no demurring: we accepted and said the Family Rosary. Not only did we have the Rosary, there were other prayers added – "trimmings" as they are called – which were often lengthy enough. Early on Sundays we were all up and about, to be in good time for Mass. We were never late. There was Mass every Sunday, and Confession once a month. Mother would remind each one of us, saying, "This is your Saturday for Confession – off you go!"

We went to Holy Rosary Church for Confession. Sometimes the priests were late coming for the Confessions. I remember often kneeling in the dark church at a confessional, longing for the priest to come. Confession itself was not the worry – it was getting to Confession that was my concern. Maybe only two priests would come to the church and, to my dismay, go to the other confessionals. I would be left kneeling outside an empty one. I would then be puzzled to know what to do. Should I go and join the queue at one of the occupied confessionals – or should I stay where I was? I often elected to stay, kneeling in the dark corner of the church, hoping and hoping "our" priest would come along. People came into the church long after my arrival and were being "heard" and able to go away, while I still knelt on! In the end I had often to rise from my knees and join the queue at one of the other confessionals.

I had never anything really serious to tell the priest. Sometimes I thought some of my small sins were serious. Usually my confession did not delay the priest. I would soon emerge from the confessional, say my small penance of prayers, and run all the way home, as light-hearted as a lark.

The point I am trying to make here is that our parents helped us and watched over us: by word and example they showed us the way to God. Among ourselves we priests readily admit that our vocations were fostered and nourished in our Catholic homes. The piety of the mother of the home influences the children mightily. It was so in our home: Mother would often attend Sunday evening devotions, and usually some of us accompanied her. My memory now is still most vivid about her fervour at prayer. She seemed to pray with her whole heart and soul. The force of her example has always been compelling to me in my efforts to pray.

Mother made certain we all attended Sunday School – at 3.00 pm in St Malachy's Church. All the schoolchildren of the parish were present at these gatherings. Their teachers, my Father included, would come to take their own classes for about twenty minutes of Catechism. Then the parish priest, Father Daniel McCashin, would come out to the Sanctuary and give us a talk on some doctrine of the Catholic Faith. He then imparted Benediction of the Most Blessed Sacrament.

In the autumn we attended the October Devotions at 9.30 am Mass each morning. Father McCashin recited the special prayers at the Mass. Since those dim, misty mornings long ago, I have never said the October prayer without thinking of the earnest and solemn tones of Fr McCashin's voice as he recited them for us schoolchildren at those morning Masses.

In our eyes, priests were very important people. We talked about them, repeated things they had said, imitated their mannerisms, and revered them sincerely. A priest's visit to our home was a major event. He was received with profound respect. While our parents chatted with him, we children were quiet as mice – listening, watching, but speaking only when spoken to. When answering a question put to us by the priest, we always gave him his proper title: "Yes, Father", "No, Father". When I started as a pupil at St Malachy's College, I was much surprised to hear the boys addressing the priest professors as "Sir". None of the priests took umbrage at this: they knew, as one of them in later years explained to me, that the boys were unconsciously following the practice they had learned in their primary schools.

Although our home was very Catholic in tone and outlook, it was not always calm and peaceful. Our parents had their differences, their hours of annoyance, their conflicting viewpoints. There were indeed times of great tension. Few homes are free from such troubles.

On our side, we children argued, cried, shouted, quarrelled, played up and gave heaps of trouble. On this score our home was no better and no worse than any other home. Like other homes, we had our happy times too. No matter what her troubles were, Mother could always see the humour of a situation. She had a hearty laugh – a merry, infectious laugh which knocked us all into good humour. Her quaint expressions, her memory for funny incidents, her ability to tell a story well, her sense of the ridiculous – all these helped to cheer us up in the gloomy hours we inevitably sometimes had.

I recall the fun we had when she read aloud for us Cathal O'Byrne's stories about "Mrs Twigglety" in our local paper, *Ireland's Saturday Night*. She put on the real Belfast accent when reading these humorous sketches; she spoke them to us rather than simply reading them. There were frequent pauses, because we all burst out laughing at the sayings and doings of Margit Bella, wee Hugh Robert, the childers' father and wee Mrs McCrum. (I wish someone would assemble all these stories of Cathal and publish them in book form!)

## The Outbreak of World War I

I come now to deal with the year 1914. I was then seven years old. In the August of that year, war broke out in Europe. Nurse Spence was in our home that morning: she had come to attend Mother, who was unwell. I remember her opening the morning paper and showing us all the banner headlines: "Britain Declares War on Germany".

Some friends advised Mother to lay up a store of food, because sooner or later there would be a shortage and prices would soar. So, among other commodities, Mother stored a ten-stone bag of flour and a quantity of sugar. Optimistically she thought the war would not last very long – it would be over by Christmas! Everybody was saying England's might would soon crush Germany. Mother was quite confident that these stores of food she had bought would last as long as the war lasted. The months until Christmas were now, she thought, secure. But Christmas 1914 came and went, so also the Christmases of 1915, 1916 and 1917 – and still the war raged. We had to wait until Christmas 1918 for our first Christmas of peace. By that time, our squirrelled reserves of flour, sugar, tea, etc, had long since been consumed. In the intervening years my family, like so many millions of others, suffered from prolonged shortages of almost every article of food.

Bread became darker in hue; butter was precious – a half pound made a splendid reward or gift; sugar was very scarce; meat, eggs, fish and poultry reached prices ordinary folk could not afford.

To this day journalists agree that the biggest news any paper could print would be the *Parousia Christou* – "The Second Coming of Christ". In the first few weeks of the First World War, the daily press gave us "Second Coming" headlines about war events, viz, "Germans Advance through Belgium"; "Belgium Army Resisting Strongly"; "Germans Capture Belgian Forts"; "Brussels Falls". And so it went on, until the Battle of the Marne halted the German advance to Paris. The stalemate of trench warfare in Flanders and Northern France followed. From then onwards, we occasionally read the headline, which later was so strikingly adopted by Erich Maria Remarque for his war book's title, *All Quiet on the Western Front*. On their side the Germans used the same phrase in their newspapers: "Im Westen, Nichts

Neues". So for his book Remarque used a title which would be known by all of Europe, and indeed the world.

In Ulster, in the pre-war period 1911–13, the Protestants had formed two military groups to resist Home Rule: the Ulster Volunteers and the Young Citizen Volunteers. As a small boy I used to watch out for the local Company of the Ulster Volunteers as they did their drills in the streets. They wore no distinctive uniform, but each man had a bandolier and carried a rifle. I remember how urgently their Commanding Officer addressed them. One remark he made puzzled me: "We must not forget our own brave soldier comrades, now fighting the Germans in Flanders. They are up against it! They are holding on by the skin of their teeth!" This last sentence baffled me – I could not understand anyone talking about teeth having skin. I looked at the Volunteers to see how they took it – but they neither frowned nor looked at one another enquiringly: at still attention they listened impassively to the officer's fervent harangue.

Lord Carson and the Ulster Unionists decided to form an army Division amongst the ranks of the Ulster Volunteers and the Young Citizen Volunteers. Recruiting started on a wide scale. Military bands played in public places, while recruiting sergeants moved through the crowds. From various platforms prominent ladies and elderly gentlemen made earnest appeals for men to come forward and join the Colours. Recruiting posters were pasted up everywhere: Lord Kitchener's stern eyes glared from innumerable walls and hoardings, as he pointed directly to you and shouted: "Your Country Needs You!" Soon a good number of the men in our district appeared in the streets – smiling and a little self-conscious – in their new uniforms.

Thus the famous 36th Ulster Division was brought into being. It was trained at Clandeboye, Ballykinlar, and other camps throughout Ulster. Several months passed by. One fine day news went around that the Division was soon to leave for some final training at the army camp at Aldershot, before going to the Western Front.

Before leaving Ulster, the entire Division marched through Belfast. I was about eight or nine years of age at the time. On the side path of the Lisburn Road, I stood and watched the Division marching past. I was speechless with wonder at the sight of it all: the endless, ordered ranks of tramp-tramp-tramping soldiers, the row upon row of sloped rifles with fixed bayonets glinting in the sun – shining like pins on a pin-sheet. And not marching soldiers only, for here came also the strong teams of horses pulling the guns and the sturdy supply wagons.

The officers were mounted on gleaming chargers behind them, then, section by section, came the regimental Colours – and with it all, the tramp, tramp, tramp of the marching men and the stirring, heady music of the military bands.

I thought the Division unconquerable, invincible – these words were not then in my vocabulary, but I certainly had the ideas they convey. I must have been standing for the best part of two hours on the footpath watching this gorgeous, fascinating cavalcade. My feet and legs were sore. I came home aching and weary, but my heart was filled with pity for the poor German soldiers who would have to face such a mighty Division.

How little I then knew about German machine guns! How little I knew about trench warfare and the murderous fire of those guns across no man's land.

In due course the Division sailed for France and Western Front. On 1 July 1916, they launched their first great attack against the Germans on the Somme. According to the plan of operations, this prolonged heavy bombardment would erase the German trenches! True enough, this heavy shelling flattened and crushed their trenches – but it did not crush or wipe out the Germans' resistance.

During the bombardment the German soldiers stayed safe below ground level in their deep, strongly constructed dug-outs. They sat there, listening to the *Trommelfeuer* – the 'drum fire' of the British guns. Tight-lipped and silent, they awaited the lifting of the shelling – their cue that the Tommies were about to attack. The moment the shells ceased falling, the German soldiers rushed up the steps of their dug-outs, hauling light and heavy machine guns and boxes of ammunition. Planting these deadly weapons on the smashed parapets of their trenches, they met with withering fire the men of Ulster advancing towards them across the open spaces of no man's land. It was merciless slaughter! The rapid, hammering fire of these machine guns cut Ulster's soldiers down, as a scythe cuts through corn or grass. "We felt they were mad," a German soldier said later. "They went down in their hundreds! You did not have to aim. You just fired into them!"

Despite it all, one Brigade led by the Inniskillings achieved remarkable success. At a good, steady pace they advanced through the tumbled and broken barbed-wire defences of the Germans. Keeping well up behind their own creeping barrage, they crossed the front fire trench between the Ancre river and Thiepval. They continued on for a mile and captured the maze of German trenches called the Schwaben Redoubt. Their reserve Brigade overran the Germans' second line. But the soldiers of Ulster had advanced too quickly – they had now no adequate support. Besides, they had lost their Battalion Commanders, and communication with Divisional and Brigade Headquarters had broken down. Hence they could not consolidate their gains. At night, when their ammunition was exhausted, they withdrew.

In that battle the Ulster Division's casualties were appalling. According to the official history, about five thousand men were killed, wounded or missing. The Division was never the same again.

The aftermath in Ulster, and particularly in Belfast, was extremely sad. Ever so many Ulster homes had dear ones in the ranks of that proud Division. In the few days immediately after the attack, word of the disaster came filtering through to the people: that things had not gone well in the battle and that the 36th Division, particularly, had suffered heavy losses. How grievous then was the anxiety of thousands of families as they awaited further news!

They had not long to wait: the news came too soon. Those who had a close relation killed, wounded or missing, received the news by telegram from the War Office in London.

I have now no clear recollection of those particular days, but Mother told me that people were shocked and horrified. In our own district the neighbours gathered in small groups in the streets, trying bravely to reassure and comfort one another. And as they did so, they watched the streets all the while for the arrival of another Post Office Telegram messenger.

When one of these dark-blue uniformed boys came riding his bicycle up the street, everyone stopped talking: they waited to see what home he would approach. When he knocked at a particular door, the neighbours knew at once who the casualty was. But was he wounded, or missing, or killed?

And so it went on in the streets, every day for a week or more. In the columns of the local newspapers the lists of casualties grew longer and longer. The tragic losses of the Division were grieved by the district, the city of Belfast, and indeed the entire province of Ulster. No wonder such names as the Somme, Thiepval, Bapaume are laden with sorrow in many Ulster homes – for by that slow, reedy, meandering river of the Somme and in the chalk fields of Thiepval and Bapaume, thousands of Ulster lads fell on that first day of July 1916.

During the following week hospital trains brought many of the wounded to army hospitals in Northern Ireland. I used to watch these men being carried on stretchers from the ambulances into one of the hospitals near home. Many of their faces were ashen grey. All of them were labelled like luggage! This amazed me – grown men, labelled? I finally decided they must be so badly wounded that they could not answer questions about themselves, their wounds, or treatment received: the labels would tell doctors and nurses all they wanted to know.

The war continued. The daily life of the people became more difficult. Air-raids by German Zeppelins were expected in Belfast. To guard against this threat, parts of the street lamps were darkened. Those bright, friendly lights, where we boys had gathered of a night to laugh and chat and play our games, became dim and muted. And the food situation worsened month by month: bread was a mixture of flour and rye: margarine, which for us had long since replaced butter, was often unobtainable. Some families had kind friends in the country to help them; we had none. Eggs and bacon were scarcer than ever, and when available, too expensive for ordinary folk like us.

My parents' difficulties multiplied. In those war years a teacher's salary, even a principal teacher's salary, was meagre. Father was in charge of a seven-teacher school with over three hundred pupils, yet his salary was only about ten or twelve pounds per month. This miserable sum was paid to him every three months. During those grim years, the prices of many necessities doubled or trebled. How Mother fed and clothed us all is still to me incomprehensible. For her, it was a heart-searing existence. Of course, there were millions like her – millions of mothers, millions of families in these islands – enduring the same privations.

During this period (1917–18), something happened which Mother had always abhorred: we fell into debt. It was not her fault, for she never wasted a penny. Rising prices and a low income were the partial causes of our misfortune. The war went on and on and on. She did her best to make ends meet, but it was impossible – we owed money which we could not pay. This was a sore blow!

And now when, through no fault of my mother's, things had gone against us, our Catholic grocer refused us further credit. For the previous twenty years we had faithfully paid his bills! Now he cast us off. With very deep gratitude, I recall the Protestant grocer who came to our aid in that crisis. He is long since dead, but I can still see him in his dimly-lighted shop, wearing his long white apron as he shuffled about the place, serving his customers, - now peering over his spectacles at your basket to see what groceries you had bought, now going to his ledger to inscribe with a scratchy pen all he had given you.

Mother spent nothing on herself. She had no money for new clothes. When going to Mass in the autumn or winter, no one bothered very much about the wearing of new clothes: the mornings were darkish, sometimes wet or foggy, and no new styles were expected. Sooner or later however, old clothes had to be discarded. Mother postponed their discarding as long as possible.

On the clear, bright Sunday mornings of spring and summer, to avoid embarrassment in meeting her friends on Sundays, Mother used to go to an early Mass, in a church other than the one we usually attended. I usually accompanied her. Sometimes we went through Botanic Gardens to St Brigid's Church in Derryvolgie Avenue; more frequently we went to St Mary's in the centre of the city.

On fine mornings it was pleasant to walk along the silent, empty streets. We usually met no one, except a policeman on his morning beat, or a workman coming back from his night shift in a factory. I felt we owned the whole place. We sometimes kept our eyes alert for any money lying on the pavement. I cannot recall that we ever found any. All this was for us a kind of game – we were like children seeking nice shells on the sands.

Our route to St Mary's Church lay along Botanic Avenue and Great Victoria Street. At the end of Great Victoria Street I knew I would hear the pigeons cooing in the high towers of the Municipal Technical College. I knew I would also pass the statue known commonly as "The Black Man".

I would like to interrupt my narrative for a moment to say a word about this statue and the person it represents. As a small boy, gazing at it frequently on my way to Mass, I knew nothing of its history or meaning. As the years passed by, I came to know that it represented the Reverend Henry Cooke, who has been called "the Father of the Present Partition of Ireland". The Reverend Doctor's statue is green – why then is it called "The Black Man"? The explanation is simple: in 1855 the citizens of Belfast erected a bronze statue of the Earl of Belfast in College Square. For some unknown reason, it was painted black – was it perhaps because the loyal Orange citizens saw it turning into a disloyal green hue in the open air? Hence it soon became known as "The Black Man".

I used to wonder how the unity and comradeship of Irish Catholics and Protestants, once displayed in the ranks of the United Irishmen, came to be broken up and dissolved. Doubtless the atrocities committed by Catholic rebels on Protestants in Wexford during the 1798 Rebellion horrified and antagonised Ulster Protestants. It would seem then that the Wexford massacres in some measure initiated the split; that they marked, for Irish Catholics and Protestants, the parting of the ways.

Historians, however, tell us that this Reverend Henry Cooke made the separation of the two groups complete and final. He it was who steered the Ulster Presbyterians away from their nationalist or republican ideals and moulded them into the earnest Unionists they are today. In 1832, at a huge gathering of Protestants at Hillsborough, County Down, he announced "The Banns of Marriage" between the Presbyterians and the other Protestant churches in Ulster. This man, through his dourness, bigotry, and raucous and explosive speeches, did more than anyone else to keep Irishmen apart. The irony of it all is this – Catholics made it possible for him to do this, not merely by the drunken follies of some of them in Wexford, but also by educating him! How many local and bitter Protestants know that their "Black Man" was educated at a hedge school in Penal Times in his native County Derry by the local hedge-school master, Frank Glass, who was a Catholic?

Nowadays the Northern Ireland Protestants are urging the principle that all Ulster schools should be inter-denominational. In 1826 the Catholic Bishops of Ireland were willing, because of the circumstances of those harsh days, to accept this principle, but insisted that Catholic children at such schools should receive separate instruction in their own Catholic Faith. In 1837 Henry Cooke, giving evidence before a Commission on behalf of the Presbyterian Synod of Ulster, was asked:

"Would you object to separate religious instruction of Roman Catholic children in such schools?" To this, Cooke replied,

"To the separate religious instruction in Roman Catholic doctrine, I object *in toto*, for that makes me a party to its inculcation!" Oh, delicate conscience!

Quite clearly, this man abhorred the Catholic Church and its teaching. The rights of a Catholic conscience meant nothing to him. This basic principle of the Lutheran and Calvinistic Reformation – the right of conscience – which Cooke theoretically upheld, was set aside when he came to deal with Catholic people.

I knew none of this when, as a child, I walked past "The Black Man" on my way to Mass with Mother. And, having said it, I will now leave this digression and get back to the story of Mother's difficulties in the days of the First World War…

As I have already said, we survived as a family because of the kindness of the Protestant grocer who accepted us as customers when our Catholic grocer had discarded us. We survived because of that dry, wizened, kindly little man who daily lived the same routine of serving customers, keeping accounts, interviewing commercial travellers, weighing goods, changing money. Through it all, he trusted Mother: he judged that she was honest and would sooner or later pay all she owed. Because of her courage and thrift, we owed him nothing when we left that district of the city in 1920. This man's name was Davidson. His shop was in University Street.

We still owed money to the Catholic grocer in 1920, but it was all paid eventually. It took Mother some years to do this; she never forgot the debt. I remember well as a boy walking across the city to the shop and paying this Catholic grocer his last farthing.

We also owed money to our bread server. He was a Protestant and hailed from Mother's own native district in County Down. He was always very kind to us children. He did not press for the money we owed him. When Mother had finally saved up the amount due to him, she did not know where to find him. He had by then given up his job and was living in retirement somewhere in the city. But where? I phoned the bakery where he used to work. The office girl was able to give me his new address. I went to his house with the money. It was a wonderful experience to meet him again, after all the intervening years, and in Mother's name, to pay him and thank him.

This has brought me too far ahead in my story. I must go back some years. In 1916 the Irish Rebellion broke out in Dublin, on Easter Monday. One of its leaders afterwards declared, "We went out to waken up the country!" They succeeded, although they roused their country not by victory, but by their own defeat and death. The citizens of Dublin jeered at the Republican prisoners marching along the city streets under British guards. Much of the country felt very bitter towards these Irishmen, who had attempted a hopeless struggle against the might of England. All the Dublin people saw, as a result of the Republican effort, was their city in ruins.

The execution of the ten or eleven leaders of the Rebellion however completely changed all public opinion in Ireland: those who had jeered, now cheered; those who had mocked, now applauded. From England's viewpoint these executions were a blunder; from Ireland's viewpoint they were a tragedy, which brought success to the cause for which the rebels had died.

In that same week of the Rebellion, I remember accompanying Mother on one of her shopping expeditions in Belfast city. In Chapel Lane she stopped to chat with a friend. While we stood there, a newsboy came running along the street and calling out, "Special! Special Edition!" The special news was that Stephen's Green – up till that day in rebel hands – had been captured by the British.

Although those days and events in Dublin meant so much to Ireland, they somehow did not enter our lives in Belfast in the same way, or affect us as deeply as the dreadful losses of the 36th Ulster Division on the Somme in that same year.

Despite the fact that I was an army chaplain in the Second World War, the war of 1914–18 made a more profound impression on my mind. Somehow in those dark days of the First World War, we were all more involved, more concerned. Perhaps this was due to our outlook as children, for we lived the war in our thoughts and imaginations. So much around us constantly reminded us of the war: the shaded street lamps, the almost black bread, the shortage of butter and sugar, the many people in uniform on the streets. Add to these the daily newspapers with their headlines exultant over some trifling victory. At times the very battlefield came closer to us when news arrived that some neighbour of ours had been killed in action. Then we sat round the fire at night and talked about him – we wondered how he had met his death, if he suffered much, if he was killed instantly. The daily news concerned the war, and all else in our young lives touched on the war in some way.

A friend of my brothers used to lend us a weekly magazine entitled *The War Illustrated*. This magazine gave page after page of photographs of the war – many of them taken on the battlefield or in the trenches. I pored over these magazines: every time I opened a copy, I was plunged right away into the war. I was no longer a small boy in Belfast, instead I was far away in Flanders: I was doing lonely sentry duty in a trench, or I was sweeping no man's land with a Lewis machine gun, or silently awaiting the officer's signal to crawl out on a raid to bring back prisoners from the German lines. A boy's imagination…

No wonder I found it easy to accept on three occasions the Queen's University ex-Service Graduates' invitation to propose the toast of "Our Fallen Comrades". I had my vivid memories of the First World War, as well as my experiences in the Second World War, to call on. In a real sense, I had experienced both.

## A Childhood Scene

The river Lagan flowed near our home. Its own channel was not much broader than a city street, but being tidal as far as Stranmillis, the river spread out to reach the higher banks on both sides. At low tide these lateral stretches, now uncovered, were unsightly, evil-smelling mud flats. All this has since been changed for the better: through the damming of the river lower down, these mud flats are now hidden in the water. What a different scene is now presented to my eyes whenever I pause on the Ormeau Bridge to look around me!

Along the then high banks on the northern side of the Lagan we played as children. When the tide was in, we used to play 'ducks and drakes', skimming flat stones along the calm, shining levels of the river. We diligently searched for flat stones; we learned to bend our bodies sideways, so as to make the stone alight flatly on the water – only in this way could we expect to make the stone skip, skip, skip along. The boy who secured the most 'skips' with a stone was the winner. As is usual with boys, ours was an earnest competition, not just an exhibition.

At low tide we used to throw stones across the river channel. Because of the wide stretches of mud, we were a good distance from the channel, so that it was a feat for a small boy to succeed in flinging a stone across the water.

One day, I remember, our puny efforts were altogether out-classed by a boy who used a sling. Never having seen a sling in operation, I was amazed at its powers. The humming speed of the stone; the mighty distance it travelled; the surprising accuracy of the slinger – these were all beyond our feeble powers.

That incident came back to me very vividly many years later. One night I was reading the Bible. I was studying the Old Testament. I had reached Chapter 17 of the First Book of Samuel, and I read the following passage:

> "David took his staff in his hand, picked five smooth stones from the river bed, put them in his shepherd's bag, in his pouch and, with his sling in his hand, he went to meet the Philistine… No sooner had the Philistine started forward to confront David, than David left the line of battle and ran to meet the Philistine. Putting his hand in his bag, he took out a stone and slung it and struck the Philistine on the forehead; the stone penetrated his forehead and he fell on his face to the ground. Thus David triumphed over the Philistine with a sling and a stone, and struck the Philistine down and killed him."

For this passage I did not need any help from a scripture commentary. I knew quite well what had happened and how it happened – I had seen it at the Lagan.

At high tide many barges used the river. It was a fine sight, to see two of the three-man crew on the tug lowering the funnel – with perfect timing – to allow their boat passage under the Ormeau Bridge.

Sometimes we used to see a single barge poled up the river by two men – one on either side. Simultaneously they plunged the long pole down to the stony bed of the river; they then leaned on it, facing the stern, and slowly and laboriously pushed the boat forward with their feet. Starting at the prow, they thus stepped the length of the barge away from them. Having reached the stern, they lifted the pole out of the water, walked back to the prow, dug the pole down again into the river-bed and repeated the process.

As I write this there comes to mind a dreary, depressing picture of the poor boatmen on the Volga, ropes over their shoulders, pulling a heavily-laden boat. Both the Lagan and the Volga had their weary workers, but if I remember rightly, the bargees on the Lagan sang no songs. Yet the Volga men sang! How did they do it?

Despite its mud, despite the seemingly long intervals between the desired high tides, in our world as children the Lagan was a precious asset. Another of our assets was the nearby public park – the Botanic Gardens. What a crowd of memories the name brings to my mind! The maze of walks around the beds of strange, exotic plants – we called them the "puzzle walks" – was one of our playgrounds: there we could hide when playing hide-and-go-seek; there we could pick bamboo canes and blackberries; there we had competitions to see who had discovered the "nicest" flower or plant.

Near the puzzle walks was the pond where the snow-white swans paddled slowly and lazily along, dipping their heads and strange elongated necks deep down into the water in quest of food. It was a thrilling sight for us youngsters to be at the pond when the swans took off in flight. What sudden, powerful flurry and flapping of those great wings! What strong beating of the air! What a foaming, turbulent track in the waters as they gathered speed and rose into the air.

Their departure was always temporary. They came back, sooner or later: our pond was their home – and it is with animals as it is with us humans – they tend to return to the homeland. Moreover, on the pond's only island they built their shapeless nests. There they reared broods of cygnets and proudly showed them to visitors. When these exhibitions were in progress, the cygnets became the star attraction in the Gardens. There was safety for them all in the pond. And visitors saw to it that they never went hungry!

The Botanic Gardens were well wooded. We had our favourite trees – chestnuts, hawthorns, and crab-apple trees – favourite, indeed, because each of these yielded up their harvest to us boys year after year. How often in the springtime I went through the Gardens, searching the trees and bushes for birds' nests. What pleasure it was to discover a new nest – all by one's self!

Many spots in the Gardens come back to my memory as I write these lines: the many flowerbeds with their exquisite floral designs; the huge glass conservatories where tall palms and other oriental plants grew in a steamy, hot atmosphere. In one of these conservatories some alert students from the university recently spotted a few plants of cannabis growing. They quietly proceeded to make use of their knowledge, until a recent court case put an end to it all.

Our interests as children in these conservatories were the huge bunches of green bananas actually growing on trees, the broad leaves of the water-lilies afloat on the indoor pool, the luxuriant tangles of jungle ferns spreading along the walls – and through it all, the hot, hot oppressive and steamy atmosphere which at last drove us outside to stand breathing deeply in the clear cool open air.

I suppose the prettiest part of the Gardens were the two long 'rose walks'. There in summer months one moved through a world of red, yellow, pink, white, cream, and pale lemon roses, freely displaying their glorious colours and filling the air with their perfume.

On a lawn near the rose walks in the summer months various bands from the city came to play. The night's programme of music would be affixed to a noticeboard for all to read. We all had our favourite pieces, no doubt, but I think the one most popular with us boys was the well-known march, "Colonel Bogey", which afterwards was used as the theme song of the famous film, *The Bridge Over the River Kwai*. The band of the old Royal Irish Constabulary played it magnificently. It was interesting and pleasing to observe how inspiring this stirring, delightful march was to all the people – and particularly to all the children.

On those band nights in the Botanic Gardens we youngsters ran about, played our games, or listened to the music. Nights of childhood filled with undiluted joy and fun!

What a fine variety of games we had in those distant days. We had no TV sets, no noisy transistors, no record players, no albums of pop stars' songs; but in their stead we had plenty of games, which brought us all the amusement and excitement we needed.

Our games cost us not one penny – it had to be that way, for as boys, my companions and I ranked not among the affluent. Our games were free and laden with innocent fun. Played as they were in the open air, they were healthy and wholesome. How we enjoyed them! We had 'ball in the caps', 'Relievo', button games, 'dab-at-the-hole', follow-my-leader, leapfrog, 'Limpy', hare and hounds, and that age-old favourite, hide-and-seek (in this last game, one gang had to find all the members of another gang).

As each month came round, messages – from the angels, surely – called forth the appropriate games. Thus in due season we emerged with our hoops, spinning tops, ball and bat for rounders (which Americans still proudly refuse to acknowledge is the embryonic form of baseball), or conkers (we called this game "cheesers"). In summer, it was marbles. We had some rare contests in our marble games. There were three holes to play, up and down, with two or three pairs of boys playing against one another. Excitement, tension, arguments, urgings of spectators, rebukes for mistakes, near misses, good shots, the dreadful pain of being knocked far away from a lovely position of advantage – all this, and then the intoxicating joy of winning the game!

One of our summer games was cricket of course. This we played with equipment much below Test Match standards. Our wickets and bails often existed only in paint on a gable wall. I need not say that disputes arose as to when a batsman had been bowled out! Anything faintly resembling a cricket bat was used by the batsman. The ball, particularly when we played on the streets, was a soft rubber one – which indeed broke windows but never human bones!

For the greater part of the year our game was soccer. If we had no ball, we promptly made one from a handkerchief or an old piece of woollen stocking, which we stuffed iron-hard with paper. Unfortunately such soccer games wore away the toes of our boots. This was a serious drawback. Our parents rightly complained, for boots were expensive and money was scarce. They reasoned with us; we listened and agreed. They forbade us to play and we promised obedience – then went out and collapsed in face of the first temptation. Despite threats of dire punishment, despite sound, reasoned arguments, we would fall at the first opportunity.

I can explain, but not justify, our disobedience. Perhaps in extenuation of our guilt I might say that the temptation to play was excessively strong, nay, vehement, and indeed overwhelming. There was the open ground ready for the match! There were the coats and caps placed in heaps, at a suitable distance apart, to mark our goalposts! Our two leading players picked their teams. If you, a member of the gang, were picked to play (and we all were so picked, but in order of merit), how could you resist?

(Here a Reader intervenes in my narrative to say, "You could shun the danger! Avoid the occasion!" St Augustine says that in the face of great temptation, the only safe rule is to run away from it. I answer, "Thank you!" St Augustine gave that advice when he was in middle age and did not know our circumstances! I shall ignore his advice – the man never played soccer with our gang!)

You were selected! That was enough. The delicious feeling of boyish zest and energy for a game wiped all thoughts of promises given and impending parental retribution out of your mind.

And so you stepped forward like a man, played the game, enjoyed every minute of it, and then went home slowly and thoughtfully to face possible inspection of toe-caps and the subsequent penalties incurred. The boots we wore became silent, impartial witnesses against us.

Football on the street once landed me in the Police courts. A group of us were chatting when a beautifully coloured, bouncy ball came over near us – it belonged to a little boy on the other side of the street. Some of our gang played about with this ball, tipping it over to one another. I stood idly watching them. John Tennis, a policeman, coming out of his house on duty, saw us! He stopped play, took all our names – and in due time we were summoned to appear before the magistrate. We were all fined one shilling each, with one shilling and sixpence costs. That two-and-sixpence fine is doubtless recorded against my name in Belfast Police records. Nobody will ever bother to take notice of our appearance in these records – anyway, the whole episode was absurd. Another sensible officer would have warned us and gone on to his duty without making a fuss about it. I was fined for something that I did not do. One point I must add: at home my parents did not beat me or scold me over my 'crime'. I think they knew I was speaking the truth, when I insisted I had not been kicking the highly coloured, bouncy ball.

In autumn and winter we had one simple game which was good fun. We called it 'first-and-last'. I have always thought we ourselves had invented it – but now I learn that ours was but a slight variation of similar games of ancient vintage. We played it in this way: standing before a well-lit shop window, we slowly inspected the words printed on the goods displayed there. One boy selected the first and last letter of some word thus shown in the window. Announcing these two letters to us all, he challenged us to find this particular word in the window. If after some time we still had not discovered the missing word, we would demand that he should "give a glimpse" – which meant he had to come to the window and glance at least once in the direction of the word. Most times his "glimpse" was so swift, universal, all-embracing, comprehensive and fugitive, that it gave us no help whatever. The game went on until we admitted defeat or one of us gained the victory. The victor then chose another word, again announcing its first and last letters, and challenging us to find it. It was all very good fun: it was interesting, it engrossed us for a while, and it cost us nothing.

On Sundays we played no games. Nearly all our companions were Presbyterians, who kept the Sabbath very strictly. So games were out! Therefore on Sundays we often went for a walk in the country beyond the suburbs of the city. Generally on our walks we had a purpose – seeking birds' nests, or gathering primroses, blackberries or chestnuts. From our games and walks we learned much: these sharpened our wits and taught us some of the elements of initiative and teamwork. As we roamed the countryside, we came to know the names of all the common trees in the woods; we were able to identify the various birds and their eggs; we could name most of the wild flowers of field and hedgerow. The countryside was our book: our companions, our teachers.

It is interesting to observe how boyhood's tastes linger on in one's life. Now, after almost sixty years I still love to wander through the fields – looking all about me, standing near streams and rivulets, and gazing at hedges, flowers and trees. The other day in the quiet, secluded garden of the Abbey, I even found myself peering into the hawthorns and holly bushes for the nests of birds.

So far I have been speaking of boys' games. The girls, of course, had their own games. In contrast with our boisterous, rough-and-tumble stuff, their games were a combination of gentle, graceful movement and singing. One of their favourites was "Green Gravel". Here are the words they sang:

> "Green gravel, green gravel, your grass is so green
> The fairest young lady that ever was seen
> We washed her, we dressed her, we rolled her in silk.
> And we wrote down her name with a glass pen and ink
> Dear Annie, dear Annie, your true love is dead
> And she sends you a letter to turn round your head."

In this game, girls linked hands with one another and formed a ring. They then circled around, singing the words to a slow, sad tune. When the last lines were sung, the girl whose name was mentioned turned round and faced the outside of the ring, with her back to the centre. This movement and singing were repeated until all the children were facing the outside of the ring.

I could never understand what this game meant. Now I know! It is, of course, a funeral song or game. The green gravel is apparently the fresh gravel on the grave. The young lady is dead and is laid out for burial in silken cerements. Her name is inscribed in the parish books. The last two lines form a message from the dead girl. Her loved ones must now mourn her death. They do so – they turn away in sorrow.

A very popular game with the girls was skipping. There was a sequence of actions to be carried out: anyone who broke this sequence was "out". Usually the girls beat out a rhythm in their skipping, by chanting a rigmarole of words that suited the timing, eg:

"All in together, girls, this fine weather, girls," or "Who will be my husband? A tinker, a tailor, a soldier, a sailor, a rich man, a poor man, a beggar man, a thief."

If you recite those last two lines in a slow monotone, you get the skipping time perfectly for that game.

Hopscotch was also very popular with girls. It is a game which is perhaps popular among children everywhere – for I saw a form of it played by Filipino children in the Central Visayas of the Philippines.

Other games played by the girls in those days included: 'Queenie, Queenie' (a guessing game), 'schoolteacher-and-class', 'shopkeeper and customers', 'tea for visitors' and swinging. For this last game a tree was the ideal. We had plenty of very suitable trees in the Botanic Gardens, but unfortunately the park rangers did not allow swinging. The next best thing available was any street lamppost. A rope fixed round the lamppost at its cross-section was sufficient. That lamppost became a maypole, around which the children kept swinging and twisting and turning.

With such a repertoire of games to hand, Belfast children were rarely at a loss in amusing themselves. If the day was fine they spent most of their leisure hours in the open air. Only when the day was rainy or stormy did they touch boredom. Belfast, like most cities, became quite depressing on a wet day. How often we children stood at a window looking out at the rain – hoping it would stop, so that we could go out to play. The rainy scene was familiar to us: often a persistent, light rain would keep falling all morning, and sometimes well into the afternoon. Tiny rivers of rainwater flowed everywhere. Shining rain pools on the road erupted quickly, spasmodically, as heavier rain splashed down. Wet papers glued themselves to the pavement. People hurried past with umbrellas bent against the angled lines of rain. Crowded electric trams came clanging heavily along the street. And still the rain kept falling, falling, and still we stood at the windows gazing at the sky and hoping to see a sunlit break in the clouds.

A rainy or stormy day hit us worst of all when we had no school: it meant that we were cooped up in the house all day long. Ennui took hold of us and made the day endless.

Normally we played our games and spent our free moments on the banks of the Lagan or in the streets near our homes. If we had a good spell of freedom, we went to the Botanic Gardens. Once in a while we would go farther afield to the Ormeau Park. It was much more extensive than the Botanic Gardens. It held attractions of its own. For example, at the upper entrance on the Ormeau Road side of the park there was a neat, well-kept bowling green. How often, as children, we stood watching the shining bowls rolling so smoothly and silently along the closely-cropped grass – like so many billiard balls on the green cloth of a billiard table. Most of the players – at least to our young eyes – were elderly men, so that the set-up was a distinct reversal of the roles described in Goldsmith's "Deserted Village", with the old contending while the young surveyed!

The Ormeau Park had also many playing fields where our local football teams exhibited their energetic enthusiasm and moderate skill in Saturday afternoon matches. Nearby was the wide pond where our 'land sailors' launched their model yachts and tested them in races. All these games and hobbies were interesting and diverting for us. We had plenty to see, plenty to discuss.

Encircling the playing fields and the pond were two concentric racing tracks, where trotting ponies were trained and cycle-races held. On one of these tracks, which was about a mile in length, I watched with wonder, as the soldiers of artillery regiments of World War I trained their horses to pull the guns. How strong and well-groomed and fresh those teams of horses were when arriving in the Park! After a series of efforts with the heavy, cumbersome gun carriages around those tracks, they stood glistening with sweat and trembling with exhaustion.

One day I wandered off the usual paths to explore the Ormeau Park with a boy's curious eyes. In one remote and desolate corner I saw bits of coal and cinders lying about. I took note of the spot and the next day I came back to it with a small sack. In next to no time I had the sack filled with sizable pieces of coal and cinders. What I brought home in my journeys from that corner of the park helped to keep the kitchen fire going at home.

In another part of this park I was able to gather twigs and small, broken bits of timber: these also were very welcome at home. My collecting efforts gave Mother some help. I was only about ten years old at the time. I could not earn money in a job, as school had to get priority over jobs and wage-earning. In the small ways open to me I did a little to help Mother. Any trouble involved in my efforts was repaid when I saw how pleased she was with the bits and pieces I had found. What hard, anxious days she went through in the years of the war!

Recently I spotted a plentiful supply of cinders spread across the rose beds in the Abbey garden. Instantly my mind went back to those days in the Ormeau Park. Once again I had lit upon some "black gold". As I stood gazing down at the cinders, there crept over me a certain sadness for the bleak impoverishment Mother had endured.

As a boy I took delight in bringing 'things' home to Mother. I can clearly recall my blackberrying expeditions. On a Saturday morning in autumn, Mother would give me some slices of bread for my lunch, and off I would start, carrying a fair-sized can, for the Giant's Ring. This is a pre-Christian burial ground out in the countryside, about four miles or more from my childhood home. It consists of a large circular mound or rampart enclosing a flat green field, in the centre of which stands a dolmen. Other boys had shown me how to find it: you had to go up Malone Road to Shaw's Bridge, cross the bridge, turn to the right and walk about a mile, then turn to the right again and follow that lane to the Ring.

In autumn the Ring was surrounded with blackberry bushes laden with ripe, juicy berries. On my visits there I had the entire place to myself. There were no rivals, no competitors – the harvest was all mine. How I enjoyed those days! The open-air whetted my appetite. The lunch I brought with me always proved insufficient for my needs. As its accompanying beverage I had the clear bubbling water of a nearby well. Dessert, in the form of innumerable blackberries, became the main dish. I ate and I worked. Yet somehow I filled the can with fine ripe fruit. Late in the afternoon I arrived home, hungry, weary – but happy. Mother was highly pleased. She was able to fill a small shelf in the scullery with pots of blackberry jam.

### The Chapel Fields

In all these memories, which I here record, there is one outstanding event that meant a great deal to us. I now wish to speak about it.

When I was a boy, there was a vacant ground on both sides of Alfred Street, as you approached St Malachy's Church from the Ormeau Avenue end. These pieces of ground were known to us as "the Chapel Fields". They were drab, black-cindered spaces where we played football with rival teams.

Every December, a few weeks before Christmas, a circus and funfair came to transform these melancholy grounds into a bright, colourful fairyland.

How did this circus arrive? I went down to see – I had read of circuses arriving in other towns, and I was full of excitement. There would be a procession. It would be heralded by a meagre but enthusiastic brass band. Then would come the cavalcade of high-spirited horses and prancing piebald ponies, all calmly controlled by circus riders in gorgeous red and blue costumes. Then would come the clowns in their ridiculous clothes, smiling and bowing and doffing their hats to everyone. There would be wild animals, of course, prowling about in strongly-barred cages. We would probably see monkeys hopping about on the red and yellow painted wagons.

Alas! This circus arrived without procession or display. One day the Chapel Fields were be bare and desolate; the next day circus wagons, caravans, and circus equipment would fill the area.

One event I do remember was the speedy setting-up of the 'Big Top'. On arriving at the Chapel Fields the circus hands jumped to their various jobs. The big tent had to be got ready at once for that night's performance. The workmen darted here and there, like surface flies on a pond, running from one spot to another as the need arose. There was much pulling of ropes, smoothing out of the canvas, hammering of tent-pegs and shouting of orders.

The same night that the big tent went up, the sideshows were ready, and the circus and fun-fair were open. "All Welcome! Free Admission to the grounds!" Oh, thrice welcome these words to young men like myself who then lived in a Micawber-like state of financial embarrassment!

In the first of the two fields were two sets of swing-boats, six in each set. The smaller size was for children; the larger for the grown-ups. These swing-boats were very popular. For a few pence you could, with a friend, swing away until 'the man' decided you had received enough value for your money. He then braked the boat by raising a long beam beneath it.

As a small boy I used to stand and stare in alarm at the dangerous antics of some youths in these swing-boats. By the aid of hand ropes hanging from the upper cross-beam, the swingers could gradually increase the height of their swing until it seemed the boats must come right over the crossbar. Each boat had seats, but your dare-devils ignored these: they preferred to stand, pulling strongly at the ropes and exerting the full pressure of their weight by bending their knees at the right moment, so climbing higher in the air. The entire wooden and iron structure of the swings creaked, groaned and trembled, as five or six of the boats swung to and fro, up and up, up and up, with then a slight pause, and a mad, sweeping rush downwards to ascend again to the heights. There was more than a trace of exhibitionism in some of the very wild "swingers" – for the thronging crowd would with excited shouts often keep urging them to go higher!

Other attractions in the larger field gradually drew the crowds away from the swing-boats. There, in the circus tent and upon the payment of sixpence, one could behold "The Wild Man from Borneo" (probably someone with a name like Bert Brown, hailing from Manchester), "The Bearded Woman", "The Amazing Alvanez Acrobats", "The Freak Sheep" (it had five legs), "Joe and Charlie – the famous European clowns", and, of course, "The Sensational Performance of Baron Meier with his World-Renowned Wild Animals from Africa's Wildest Jungles". To a boy this was intoxicating stuff – and all for sixpence!

This was the heart of the circus. Without the big tent and its performers, there would have been no circus – we all sensed that. And yet there was one other attraction which almost eclipsed these: the merry-go-round, or, as we called them then, "the hobbyhorses".

The great circular platform of the merry-go-round stood in the centre of the field. It kept life surging through the entire scene. This great circular structure with its high steps, and rows and rows of fierce grinning steeds went round and around for hours, till the crowds thinned out and people started to go home. These hobbyhorses, as we called them, were fascinating to the eyes of a child. Up and down they went, in crude imitation of the galloping horse: up and down in monotonous regularity, round and around – they seemed to form a mechanical cavalry guard for the gilded steam organ in the centre.

That calliope worked hard. Its strong, strident music could be heard distinctly a half a mile away. It was a huge, ornamental affair. Several carved mechanical figures of women stood on what I must call its façade. I used to stand watching one of these ladies as she mechanically struck a small tambourine in true puppet manner. At length I concluded that she did not really strike the tambourine: she merely pretended to do so. She was there for appearances' sake only. Had she struck the tambourine, her tiny musical effort would have gone unheard in the murderous noise around her. She dwelt apart from the noise – quite detached from the surrounding hubbub, like a clock in a busy city centre. Hour after hour she maintained her counterfeit playing on the tambourine and stared fixedly into the distance with sightless eyes.

Part of the clamour in the grounds was caused by the holders of the sideshows shouting the attractions of their stalls: "Come and buy! Come and buy!"; "Try your luck! Hoopla! Hoopla!"; "If you don't speculate, you cannot accumulate!"

Of these side-stall attractions, "hoopla" was one of the most popular. Delicately perched on tall, narrow blocks placed irregularly on a wide circular table were many glittering prizes – watches, small clocks, rings, necklaces and money. For your sixpence, you received three or four small wooden rings. Then, standing behind the barriers, you tried to throw a ring over the prize you coveted. If you ringed it – it was yours. It all seemed childishly simple till you tried it. I cannot recall any person winning a worthwhile prize. Several cheap pieces of jewellery stood on blocks near the throwers of the rings, but the worthwhile prizes were farthest away and most difficult to ring. The three or four wooden rings you had were small. Each prize rested not on one block but on two – one being slanted to balance on the other. It needed but a gentle knock to make both blocks topple. Unless your ring settled down gently and easily around the prize, like a snowflake, you knocked prize and blocks down. I never had much fun at this sideshow. I thought the odds of winning stood too heavily in favour of the stall-keeper. Still, I liked to see the frowning concentration of determined competitors, who sought in vain to win a particular prize.

More satisfaction for one's money could be found at the shooting galleries. Here, for your sixpence, you were allowed six shots with strong, solid air rifles at a fixed target or at ping-pong balls dancing on tiny fountains. In those years during and after the 1914–18 war, there were many service and ex-servicemen among the crowds at the Chapel Fields. Occasionally, by virtue of his accurate marksmanship, one of these men would gather around him an applauding group of spectators. It was an ordeal for any amateur, unpractised in the arts of war, to take up one of the rifles after these accurate gun exhibitions. The crowd melted away: the contrast in skill levels was too painful.

No skill, however, was needed at the roulette table! All you required there was a stack of money and tons of good fortune. Afire with the gambling instinct, men, women, boys and girls pushed and shoved and crowded around all sides of the long table. Bets dotted the various numbers and colours. For those who lived on lesser financial means the favourite bet was either red or black. As the alert croupier called out, "No more bets", he spun the wheel and sent the white ball racing round it. Silently the gamblers watched the shining ball spinning and bouncing along the numbers and colours, until it finally settled in the winning compartment of the wheel. Those who had won reached eagerly for their winnings. Usually they stayed long enough to lose all their gains. In the end, with doleful countenances, the losers would turn slowly away from the table. Yet for each gambler who left, two or three more were ready to take his place.

All I have been trying to describe was fun and excitement for a boy. It was fun to be one of the crowd and to see all that was happening. Even though you stood around with empty pockets, you could enjoy watching others trying their luck and spending their money at the sideshows.

Today, after sixty years, I can recall most vividly the good-humoured throng of people laughing and chattering as they slowly sauntered along; the hoarse, glaring, flaring blaze of the hanging naphtha lamps; the old, catchy tunes of the impersonal calliope; the encouraging, appealing, raucous cries of the sideshow men; the queue of giggling girls outside the small fortune-telling tent of Madame Rita (yellow headscarf, black hair, huge earrings, sallow complexion – a gypsy type akin to those gypsy girls on the right bank of the Seine in Paris, who stand on the street accosting all passers-by and offering to tell their fortunes); the shouts and whistling of boys calling their chums; the tall policeman standing quietly to the side and calmly surveying the swirling human tide around him.

The Chapel Fields exist no longer! Factories and workshops have taken over the area. The fairyland of my childhood has gone forever!

In those days particular events in my life came with the seasons. Winter brought us the circus and funfair. Spring offered us bird-nesting opportunities and haphazard country walks in search of wild flowers. Another event is also associated in my mind with the arrival of spring. Each year around this time, Mother always prepared a tonic for us children. She called it "the mixture". Father, in true Victorian manner, referred to it as "the electuary". We called it "the lecture"! Authorities will tell you the word "electuary" is derived from the Greek word meaning, "to lick up", but I assure you we did not lick up this particular potion!

In an effort to make it attractive to our taste buds, Mother solemnly assured us it was "full of golden syrup and treacle"! I have no doubt that there were measures of both in it – but their presence was almost nullified by the other distasteful ingredients it contained.

On a certain spring morning Mother would instruct us to call at a greengrocer's shop in Cromac Street on our way home from school. There, we were to buy bog bane and other herbs. We needed no further information – Mother was preparing "the mixture". She never allowed us to see her mixing it: that was all done when we were at school. The complete recipe was known only to herself, and she kept the secret. With no greater care did the monks of La Grande Chartreuse safeguard the secrets of their famous liqueur.

When "the mixture" was ready, we were lined up for it each morning. We had no option: we had to swallow a dessert-spoonful. Mother compounded it and kept it in a chocolate-coloured, earthenware crock on a high shelf – out of our reach – in the scullery. That crock held more than one would judge from its size. It took us weeks and weeks to finish its unforgettable contents.

Is this springtime electuary or tonic or medicine a widespread and prevalent custom in Ireland today? One of our priests, a native Irish speaker from the Aran Islands, off the Galway coast, always took a tonic or mixture or medicine at the beginning of spring – or, as he used to put it, "at the budding of the leaf". Is it just a fetish? In a recent book an Irish doctor gives examples of Irish taboos and fetishes: for example, cold air must not touch the skin of a perspiring infant, an infected tooth must not be removed until the swelling has gone down, etc. He insists that the most popular and most beloved of all the Irish fetishes is "the tonic".

I am inclined to think that my grandmother Mageean believed in "the tonic", and prepared one for her children. From her, then, Mother learned about "the mixture" and made it up it for us. She always assured us that it purified our blood and saved us from boils and pimples. True, we never suffered from these maladies, but I often wonder was our good health due to "the mixture" or not rather to the healthy, open-air life we led. Reasonings and convictions on our side did not matter: Mother's views, and not our feelings, decided our fate. To us children, spring brought bright days, the song of birds, fresh green leaves – and "the mixture".

There are other memories of mine which I associate with spring – such as our entertainers! In spring in the streets around my home, we frequently had entertainments of a kind. We could never predict their coming. They always arrived unexpectedly. They were always a surprise – and a free entertainment at that.

Sometimes it might be a man with a barrel organ. Of a sudden the afternoon quietness of the district would be shattered by a loud, lively dance tune or a stirring march. The sounds could penetrate streets and doors for they issued from the strong steel lungs of the barrel organ. All at once, doors were opened and children poured into the street. Others came running from where they had been at play. Laughing and chattering, they gathered round the organ to enjoy every note of the strident music. We would watch the man turning the organ handle: we wondered how that little handle could produce such startling music. To us it was a kind of magic. And all the while, the man would keep turning the handle, changing hands when one hand became tired. Relentlessly the music was hammered out, devoid of any trace of feeling or interpretation. But oh, how it thrilled us! And how we loved our very own Pied Piper!

Perched on a horizontal stick by the side of the organ, a green-and-yellow feathered parrot would sit, eyeing us with a stony, unblinking stare. For one penny the man would lift the parrot and let him pick your card of fortune from a box nearby.

Apart from these moments when he dealt with fortune-seeking clients, the man at the organ had his eyes on his companion and partner, who would now be going from house to house in silent quest of money as a token of appreciation. I guessed that eight pence or a shilling was as much as they would receive for each performance.

The one great drawback in this welcome appearance of the man with the barrel organ was the brevity of his performance. We children could have stood around him listening and watching for an hour. Yet, here he was, after five or ten minutes, moving off to other areas. In those days we ordinary folk had little music in our lives. Some homes boasted of a piano or tinny gramophone, but there were no radios, no televisions, no transistors, no popular dance bands. We sang a few songs at school. On Sundays we sang hymns at Mass and heard the church organ playing. Occasionally a band of the Salvation Army played for us in the streets, and some of the city bands played in the public parks. That was all. The early departure of the man with the barrel organ depressed us. Whilst he was with us, we were enchanted. His lively music turned our grey streets into a gay and happy playground. Alas, the principal performer was not a fully dedicated public benefactor. As soon as the judicious collection of money was finished, the performance on the organ was ended. One man took a firm hold of the shafts of the organ cart, the other inserted himself into a belt looped over his shoulder. A strong pull now – for the organ was quite heavy – and off they both went, dragging their temple of music to a new bunch of worshippers.

We would stand silent in the street and watch them depart. There was nothing we could do about it. Some older children followed them for a distance. Had there been another performance in a nearly street, we would have willingly trooped after their rickety, creaky cart, as once the children of Hamelin flocked after their own Pied Piper. Our initial dismay, the keen, speechless dismay of children, soon passed. Five minutes later we were deep in our games and the barrel organ was forgotten.

On another day we might have had a visit from "the man who sharpens knives". He had a movable workshop. It was an ingenious contraption, with hand shafts and a main central wheel. On this central wheel he pushed his workshop along, as on a wheelbarrow. When he halted and made a few adjustments to the apparatus, he had a work bench, standing four square on the solid earth, and complete with grindstone. The main central wheel was now off the ground. He now affixed a belt to it and to the grindstone. Very efficiently, a foot pedal now turned the wheel and grindstone.

The man himself was a frail, wrinkled, bespectacled little person. His street cry was meant to be, "Any knives sharpened cheaply!" But what reached our ears was, "Any knives sharp sheep!" He kept calling this out in a high-pitched, quavering voice until some customer appeared with a knife or scissors, which needed his attention.

He was a reticent man. He never spoke a word to us children as we gathered around him. He devoted all his attention to the matter in hand – the sharpening of a knife. His foot moved up and down on the pedal; the light-brown grindstone spun round swiftly; the blade of the knife, pressed expertly against the stone, hissed and hissed and hissed; and a fountain of glittering sparks would rise up into the air like miniature fireworks. The job must not be hurried. He worked with patient care. Again and again he pressed the blade against the stone; again and again he lifted it up, peered at it closely, and tested its edge with the ball of his thumb. Down it would go again, the sparks would fly and scatter, and the knife on the stone hissed and hissed as he whetted the blade to his liking.

He was a conscientious worker: no knife left his hands until he was quite satisfied with its new, keen edge. His charge for sharpening a knife was only a few pence. He won his livelihood by genuine work. I wonder how many articles he had to sharpen to earn, say, ten shillings or a pound.

Another honest toiler was our local cobbler. I include him also as one of our childhood entertainers – not because he was amusing, but because a visit to his den was so interesting. We visited him only when we had boots or shoes to be mended. We would find him in his little dim room, crouched over the shoe he was repairing. Close beside him was a long, wooden tray divided into sections. These held what he needed: small nails, metal protectors, rubber heels, sinister-looking knives, punches, waxen cord and stumps of blacking.

A tiny, blue jet of gas nearby melted the hard blacking when he used it on boot or shoe. Propped against the wall of the room were a number of clean brown sheets of new leather. The room was all leather: it smelt of leather: it was filled with leather. Bits and pieces, cut into queer shapes, lay on the floor, like parts of a larger jigsaw puzzle scattered at random. Boots and shoes, repaired or to be repaired, lay here and there. Surrounded by the leather havoc he had caused, the cobbler pursued his tasks.

When we brought him footwear for mending he allowed us to stand watching him at his work. It was fascinating to see how ruthlessly he cut and ripped off an old sole, how speedily he carved the new piece of leather to the shoe's size, and then how deftly he nailed or sewed the new sole to the shoe on the shining iron last before him. He never hesitated. There was a briskness and certainty about his every action. With his long experience he could tell in a few seconds what treatment had to be meted out to any footwear brought to him.

He had one habit which really astonished me. One day I saw him putting a handful of small nails into his mouth. I was horrified – for a moment I thought he was going to swallow them. Then, to my relief, I saw him picking them one by one from his lips and hammering them with swift accuracy into the leather. You could see that every part of him worked – his brain, hands, eyes, mouth, lips, arms, trunk, and even his foot, for he kept that shoe he was repairing firm and steady on the iron last by a looped strap across its instep which he pressed down at its lower section by his foot.

He too, like my man of the knives and scissors, was a man of few words. And what he did say was gruffly said. This was his manner: it was not, I am sure, due to any unkindness. We bore in mind the fact that his mouth was full of nails. None of us wanted to see him swallowing any of these: we did not expect words from him.

Perhaps conversation did not come easily to him. He had no companion workers: almost his entire day was spent alone. Day after day he was to be found in that semi-dark room, seated on the long, low bench, surrounded by the instruments of his trade, with only the bright little gas flame to keep him company. Whenever in later years I came upon the proverb about the cobbler sticking to his last, I thought of this steadfast cobbler I knew in my childhood.

As I grew older, I discovered new entertainments. Some of them were farther away from my home. I came to know of them gradually. From some of the boys at school, I learned for example of the Customs House entertainments.

One Sunday afternoon I went down to the Customs House steps to see and hear the fun. I can best describe this spot by saying that on Sunday afternoons it became a Hyde Park Corner for preachers, propagandists, quacks, oddities, charlatans, and promoters of causes silly or lost.

When I arrived at the wide square of the Customs House I saw small crowds of people here and there listening to speakers. The first crowd I came to was increasing every minute. I slowly wormed my way through the people to see what was going on. In the open space stood a tall black man. He was gazing around the crowd and speaking in a loud, solemn voice:

> "Ladies and Gentlemen, I repeat it! Please give me your attention! My name is Valentine Hannibal! I come from British Guyana. Kindly gather round me! This bag you see on the ground beside me contains a wild animal rarely seen by the eyes of men. Come, gather round me, please!"

He was a fine build of a man. His voice was clear and strong. He had a small Gladstone bag on the ground beside him. A white handkerchief was tied to its leather handle. After a few more beguiling words about this mysterious wild animal, he slipped away from the subject by saying it would be too dangerous to risk its escaping from the bag! But he had another equally wonderful thing to show his audience – this was the amazing medicine he had discovered and compounded from the herbs and plants of the jungle whence this wild animal had come. He assured his listeners that this medicine would cure ever so many ailments and diseases. Some of the crowd snorted their annoyance at this denouement and walked away. But most of the people remained to listen to this fluent medicine man. He was a good speaker – one worth listening to. Anyway, what did it matter? It was free entertainment!

On those Sabbath days the Customs House steps and Square were full of eloquent gentlemen. The preachers sweated out their most urgent messages to the callous and indifferent. The salesmen had a more subtle approach – they showed they were expert psychologists who had graduated from the school of life. They stood in the midst of their wares, utterly confident and self-assured. They knew how to wheedle money out of their audiences. In turn they were friendly, communicative, persuasive, commending, mildly warning, and then winning customers with a gentle smile. The Square was an open-air market for their wares – not groceries, not household goods –

but quack medicines, second-hand books, herbs and herbal cures, knick-knacks, and cheap, flashy jewellery.

The steps of the Customs House were numerous and spacious. They provided many amateurs with a pulpit for their strange discourses. Each speaker was on his own – he had no seated semi-circle of supporting speakers behind him, waiting to take up where he left off. No, he was a lone campaigner! He held forth regularly on his own section of the steps. If people wanted to hear him, they knew where to find him. His subject might be "Repent and be Saved", or "The Evils of Drink", or "Taxation: a Curse to the Nation", or "Communism" or "Socialism". Some of the speakers were popular, not because of their message or eloquence but for the entertainment they unintentionally offered. The humourists in the crowd would often ask the perspiring orator very embarrassing, awkward, or utterly irrelevant questions that would raise a laugh: "Where are you going for your holidays?"; "What about an under-sea tunnel to America?"; "Could a man marry his widow's sister?" All these and similar queries, put to a speaker who perhaps had been laboriously trying to unravel the knotted obscurities of astrology, were amusing to the crowd and very unhelpful to the discussion.

Sometimes the speaker won a victory by neatly turning the question on the questioner. It was all very good-humoured.

"Can you tell me how old the devil is?" shouted one joker.

"Sir!" replied the preacher, "Keep your family's secrets to yourself!"

Some speakers had no audience: yet they persevered valiantly, shouting their messages into the empty air. You could stop and listen, and then move on. It was generally a wise plan to go to the speaker who had a crowd round him: if he held the crowd, he must be worth hearing. Some speakers were natural if untutored orators; some would never become good speakers. All of them were in deadly earnest. But earnestness, like enthusiasm or patriotism, is not enough.

In all my visits on Sunday afternoons to the Customs House area, I was alone. In my own company I was quite contented. I could stop, move on, change my route or plans without having to suit a companion. My procedure was decided by what interested me. My eyes and ears furnished me with all the company I needed.

On some Sunday mornings after Mass, I used to wander alone down to the harbour and dockyards along the southern bank of the Lagan. Nobody stopped me: any watchmen about saw I was alone and merely out sightseeing: they left me in peace to wander here and there. The names and flags on the ships carried me far away to distant lands. As a boy I took it for granted that I would never visit any of these faraway places. These ships, I thought, would doubtless be my only contact with these strange countries. Foreign sailors on the deck, washing clothes, reading papers, fixing gear, or smoking strong, pungent mixtures of tobacco, helped me to form my own pictures of their native lands. What magic there is for a boy in a harbour of ships! The hours flew by! In the end, the knives of hunger drove me home. I remember I used to feel weak with hunger as I wearily plodded homewards up the Ormeau Road.

New sights and experiences were also made known to me by my companions at school. They told me about "the slaughter house" – now more politely called "the abattoir". Boys were not allowed there, but my friends told me to bend down low and run beneath the window of the gatekeeper's office: he would not be able to see us, and the rest would be easy. With the gang I did what I was told and ran up to the sheds where animals were being killed. The cows and bullocks were moaning in a fearful manner. My chums said the animals smelt the blood in the sheds and by instinct knew what was ahead of them. As those were not the days of humane killing, the killing of the animal was done in most crude fashion. A rope was put through a ring in its nose and also through a ring in the wall near the floor. A man pulled tightly on this rope and thus brought the animal's head down low. The "killer" wielded a long-handled, steel hammer. With all his strength he swung the hammer down on the forehead of the beast, just above its eyes. This seemed to stun and even knock the animal senseless. The man struck it a second similar blow. The beast fell to the ground. He kept striking it until it was dead.

The sight of all this has never left my mind, even though my one visit to those sheds of death took place over sixty years ago.

The school companions, who led me to unusual sights and places by word or example, were children strongly moulded by their circumstances. Born in that busy district of the Belfast Markets, they saw plenty of life and stir around their homes. They matured at an early age. While still young they were alert to all opportunities of earning money: for example, by helping to drive cattle to the ships or the market, watching horses while their owners or drivers had a meal or a drink, or helping older boys in their jobs at the market stalls.

As a rule these boys were intelligent: some were as sharp as needles. A number of those in my school class could have done very well at college and university. Unfortunately they belonged to families who could not afford to pay the necessary fees. Some of their parents were counting the days till their boy was fourteen years of age, able to leave school, and earn money at any job available. A few boys from our primary school went to St Malachy's College. They did not stay there very long. Their families' need of money compelled them to leave the college and take a job. They were clever boys. Shortage of money kept them back from a degree in Law or Medicine or Engineering. I have always thought it a pity that no fund or trust then existed to help such lads through university. Some system of repayment, once they qualified and were earning money in their professions, could have been devised.

One particular boy with whom in later years I used to walk to College every morning was very intelligent. He had a great desire to become a lawyer. For lack of financial backing however, he was not able to go on to the university. He left the college and took a job in a publishing firm. He was capable of much more than office routines. His wife once told me he used to come home, have a meal, and sit down and read law books. With his keen brain, he could have become one of the city's best lawyers. I meet him once in a while. Our friendship is unbroken. His conversation is always lively and thoughtful. Sometimes I feel sad when talking to him. I never reveal my thoughts on the matter, but when listening to him, I keep thinking of what might have been.

## St Malachy's College

In 1918 I sat the entrance examination for St Malachy's College. I passed the examination and was accepted as a day pupil. Quite frankly, I doubt whether I was up to the required standard. I have often thought that the then President, Fr PJ O'Neill accepted me, not on my own merits, but because of my family's associations with the College. I had not gained by attending the primary school in which my father was Principal Teacher. The teachers did not thrash me, when I richly deserved a thrashing. I stayed in Father's class when I should have been in another. I think now I "got away with murder". I should have been sent to another school where I would have received strictly impartial treatment. The result of my antics was this: I read a lot – more than most boys of my age – but I was weak in many subjects I should have known well.

Be all that as it may! Fr O'Neill accepted me as a day boy in the College. I have ever since been mindful of his kindness. I have tried to repay him by my prayers. Rarely have I gone into the cemetery at home – Milltown Cemetery – without going to his grave to pray for him. I feel quite sure he is in Heaven.

Still I ask him to take my prayers and my visits to his grave as tokens of my grateful remembrance.

As a student, under him, I must regretfully confess I shed no lustre on the College. My academic achievements were nil. The record had better be forgotten. My lack of success was due to my neglect of study. Two points I must mention here. Firstly, the common opinion among the boys was that study was silly, and that anyone who did study was foolish. They mocked and jeered at boys who were true students: there was an attitude of hostility and resentment towards those boys who devoted themselves to their books.

This influenced me very strongly. I should not have allowed it to affect me. I was eleven or twelve years of age, impressionable, fond of games, not really interested in my text books – and I idled. I did the minimum amount of studying. I never made myself get down to it. This is the first point.

The second is this – I think I did not know how to study. In my last year at the College, I studied fairly well and felt I had a good grip of my work; but up to that time, my work was desultory and held little interest for me. Something of my primary school attitudes had continued.

I got much different treatment from my College teachers, however: they thrashed me when I deserved it, and sometimes when I did not deserve it. In this respect the French master took a particular interest in me. Each night as part of our homework, we had to learn a number of French verbs and nouns.

In class this master would call a boy to the blackboard, give him a piece of chalk, and say to him, "Write down the French for this sentence: 'I was writing the letter when the postman knocked at the door'!" (This was a trap for the unwary boy!) If the boy wrote the sentence in correct French, he would get another to text to translate. "Write down the French for: 'I have gone to visit my brother'."

In this sentence lies another trap. If a boy wrote the obvious, "J'ai allé …" he got no further! Behind his back stood the tall master who would now ominously begin to chant the French verbs which are conjugated with the verb être: "Aller, to go; venir, to come", and so on. All the while he was reaching for his cane and getting a firm grip on it. He finished his chant and then told the unfortunate lad to hold out his hand. Then with all his might, he would give him three or six of the best – or the worst!

How often I stood at that wretched blackboard before that silent class of boys and that grim master! How often I really did know what was to be written on the board – but how often the whole set-up knocked it out of my head. The master never uttered a word of encouragement. He never gave you the slightest hint or help. You went out to the board and you sank completely or swam back to your desk safely. He was over six feet tall. He towered over us as youngsters. We were indeed small fry. At the time when he was almost daily thrashing me, I was eleven years of age.

Thanks to him and to his drastic methods though, I acquired a very sound knowledge of French. To him I have always felt very indebted. All my life long, French has been of immense value to me, as a student, a priest, a missionary, and particularly as an army chaplain. How handicapped I would have been without it! Without those thrashings, I might not have had more than a smattering of the language.

While I say all this, I look back with horror to my days in that teacher's class. I have been told his thrashing methods of teaching would be quite unacceptable today.

In his book, *A Portrait of the Artist as a Young Man*, James Joyce describes a boy being thrashed in class. He uses a simile which I think is very apt, when the master strikes the boy on the hand: "A hot burning, stinging, tingling blow, like the loud crack of a broken stick, made his trembling hand crumple together like a leaf in a fire." That was my hand!

In St Malachy's College I received good teaching in mathematics. My teacher was Reverend Dr Hendley. He was competent, clear and just. He had no 'pets' in his classes. All boys got impartial treatment from him. If you showed you had done your best, he encouraged you in a bluff sort of way with a smile and a kindly word. I have always been grateful to him. When he became Parish Priest in St Paul's parish, I used to visit him. In many ways I let him see that I remembered all he did for us and that I was very indebted to him. He was an inspiration to us all! A teacher who was very brilliant and had clarity of expression! More than that, he was first and foremost a priest – priestly in his manner and his outlook. I often wonder how many of his students were inspired to become priests by his example.

Except when it rained, I walked from my home in Agincourt Avenue to the College each day. The distance was two or three miles. Classes began at 9.00 am and went on all morning without a break until 12.30 pm. We then had a break for a half-hour, during which time I ate the bread and butter lunch which Mother had made up for me. If I needed a drink, the fountain in the college grounds supplied me with free draughts of clear, cold water. Classes were resumed at 1.00 pm and finished at 3.00 pm. As soon as classes ended, I gathered up my books and faced the walk home.

On arriving home, I had dinner and then went out to play. Homework was done after tea. Those who had homework to do occupied the table until 9.30 or 10.00 pm. At times it was very difficult to concentrate on our lessons and themes, because talk was carried on around us. The truth is that I often found the conversation of parents or visitors much more interesting than my books!

A comfortable, quiet room would have been ideal for our homework. We could not have that in our home. The living room where we worked was warm. All the other rooms in the house, for most of the school year, were icy cold – no child could be put in there to study. We had not the luxury of central heating. Coal was at a price beyond our means. The one fire we could afford to keep burning was in the living room. And so that was the only place possible for our work.

The summer holidays granted us by the College lasted three months. During these holidays I used to take a job, usually that of messenger boy in some of the shops or businesses in the city. The ten shillings I earned each week was a valuable help to Mother in running the home.

## The Troubles (See Appendix 6)

One summer evening in 1920 as I was coming home from my work, I saw a crowd gathered at the Cromac Street end of Ormeau Avenue. I was seated in the top section of a tram, going up Bedford Street. Some people on the tram said that rioting had broken out between Catholics and Protestants. This was the beginning of a series of incidents that changed the whole course of our family life. These riots continued for two years in different parts of Northern Ireland. Nearly three hundred people were killed in that period. Most of them died in the streets of Belfast.

The tram in which I was travelling brought me home safely. Mother was standing at the garden gate, anxiously looking down Agincourt Avenue as she awaited my arrival home. Groups of people were at the street corners, excitedly discussing what was happening in the city. At home, we were uneasy. Few Catholics lived in our neighbourhood. If a mob came to attack our home, we could do nothing to prevent its destruction. The wildest rumours were abroad – so many people had been shot, so many houses and shops burnt to the ground! We stayed indoors. While feeling against Catholics ran so high, we did not dare venture out.

Unrest simmered for several days in our district. Other parts of the city echoed with the sound of rifles and revolvers. Ambulances and taxis sped swiftly through gun-swept streets to the hospitals, carrying wounded men, women and children. On the Kashmir Road, beside Clonard Monastery, seven people were shot dead in one evening's bitter fighting.

Our district was not disturbed. There was much tension – especially in my home, due to the eviction from their homes of Catholic families in other parts of the city; there was no gunfire, however.

Then one day the disorder came close to us. Some men brandishing revolvers stopped a bread van in front of our house. It was a van belonging to the Catholic bakery firm, Bernard Hughes & Co. Taking the horse out of the shafts, these armed men burned the van in front of our gate. I still vividly recall the black ashes and debris of the van lying on the road. The driver of the van, a Catholic, was allowed to go away with the horse. This incident alarmed us. The trouble was now at our doorstep. Mother saw one of the men who burned the van running away from the scene. He was not from our district, but Mother recognised him as he ran up the entry or alleyway at the back of the houses. He was a Protestant from McClure Street. Mother then realised that danger for us and for our home would probably come, not from our good neighbours, but from thugs living in other areas of the city. McClure Street Protestants evicted a number of Catholic families from their homes. They piled their bits of furniture on the open street and burned the lot. I saw this happening.

My memory is that on one of those days, some Protestant friends gave my Father a warning that he might be shot when passing McClure Street on his way to school. So it was deemed advisable for him to go and live with some friends in Joy Street, a Catholic street near St Malachy's Church. That was one of our problems solved.

As the days passed by, the rioting grew worse in the city. The *Belfast Evening Telegraph* presented the news in frightening headlines, viz, "The Battle of Kashmir Road"; "Six Shot Dead in Belfast Street"; "Bomb Explodes Among Children"; "Two Belfast Publicans Murdered". It was a time of great anxiety for Catholics living in Protestant districts.

One afternoon, Mr Sloan, our Protestant neighbour came to our house and spoke quietly to Mother. "Mrs Cummings, where are your children?" "They're up in the Botanic Gardens," Mother replied.

"Very well, I will send my boy, Arthur, up to the Gardens to bring them down. There is going to be trouble tonight in this district. Keep the children indoors. We will try to see that nothing will happen to you."

Mother thanked him.

Young Artie Sloan came up to us in the Gardens and told us we were to come home at once. We saw by his manner there was something wrong. We returned home at once – Eileen, Annie, Margaret, Mary and I. After our evening meal the four girls (aged eight to fifteen years) were sent to the home of Miss Crosgrove, their music teacher. She, a Protestant, had kindly agreed to give the girls shelter for the night. She lived quite near us. My two older brothers were sent to Catholic friends living in the Falls Road district. I, a boy of thirteen years, was left alone with Mother in our home.

Mother now showed her courage. She did not panic. She knew exactly what she was going to do. First of all, she sent me upstairs to the front attic. There from the dormer window, I was to watch the whole length of Agincourt Avenue, from our house down to where it joined the Ormeau Road. Standing on a chair, I had a clear view of the avenue. Knots of people were standing about, especially at the street corners, talking earnestly and looking down the avenue. They were all Protestants, and they knew trouble was coming.

For some time I kept vigil at the attic window and saw nothing to alarm us. Then I noticed more people were gathered at the end of our avenue and on the Ormeau Road. And now it happened!

A mob turned into the avenue from the Ormeau Road. I watched it surging along, like a black tide, coming nearer and nearer to our home. It came up the avenue two hundred yards to a spirit grocer's shop owned by the Catholic family of McSorley. There the mob halted. The shop windows were soon smashed and the place looted. I ran downstairs to tell Mother. To my astonishment she listened to me quite calmly. She bade me go back to the attic window and keep watching: if the mob came past McSorley's shop, I was to come down at once and tell her.

"If they come up the Avenue to wreck our house, what are we going to do?" I asked her.

"I have everything ready! There are your coat and cap and some things you will take with you. I am ready! The small suitcase is packed with what I need. My hat and coat are on that chair. In that tin by the couch I have plenty of paraffin – I will burn the house! If I have to leave it, they will not get it! It will all go up in flames. You and I will go out by the back and make our way up the alley." Thank Heaven, however, the crowd did not come past McSorley's shop – probably it contained all the drink they were seeking. So that night we were left in peace.

But that was not the end of our anxieties. Day by day, night by night, we were very tense, not knowing what would happen next. A rumour reached us that a crowd from the Sandy Row area and one from McClure Street were to join forces and invade the Catholic homes in our district. Mother and I were at the mercy of every wild rumour. And every rumour alarmed us, for we felt that in the turbulent state of the city, anything could happen.

Then one day, in the midst of all the tension a man came from the Falls Road area and offered us a house there, which a Protestant family was willing to exchange for ours. Mother gladly accepted the offer. Our new home was situated on the Springfield Road, three hundred yards from the Falls Road.

Somewhere and somehow my eldest brother secured a lorry next day. On it we piled our bits of furniture. When it was ready to move off, we noticed that some of the articles were in danger of slipping off. I was the solution to this problem. I was helped up to the top of the pyramid, and it was my business to see that nothing fell off en route to our new home. As the lorry lurched forward, I held on tightly to the leg of a table. I instantly realised that on this trip the true danger was that I, the guardian and overseer, would myself topple off. In this manner I said goodbye to the house where I was born.

The driver of our furniture lorry drove past Sandy Row, a bigoted and aggressive Protestant area. In Victoria Street a dense crowd had assembled: our lorry was forced to stop. Down a side street leading to Sandy Row, I saw some Catholic homes in flames. The mob was enjoying the blazing spectacle. Some Protestant boys in the crowd spotted me perched on top of the lorry and pointed to me, shouting: "There is Cummings! There is Cummings!" I knew of course what was on their mind. Like the ogre in the fairy tale they had 'smelt the blood' of a Roman Catholic and wanted more. They were not interested in me any longer as Dan Cummings, the chum they knew –oh no! At that moment they saw me as another Roman Catholic who needed to be dealt with now.

Fortunately, the delay in the street was not a lengthy one, and after a couple of minutes the lorry was able to move on. Soon we began to edge our way slowly through the crowd, through a carpet of faces showing anger and impatience at our brief interruption of their fiery sport.

Looking back on my childhood, spent in that Protestant district of Belfast over sixty years ago, I recall happy days and sad days. Our games were happy: the games which we played, Protestant and Catholic children together, in the streets or in the Botanic Gardens. When for some reason or other my gang had no games to play, trouble for me was always liable to start. That would be the way, particularly if a Protestant bully or bounder from another area was in the gang. He would soon fasten onto me: my own close friends never bullied or badgered me.

I was a Roman Catholic, a "fenian", a "mickey", a "teague": I was not really one of the crowd. I did not really belong. I was there to be baited. I know that people will find this very hard to believe. You have to be born a Catholic boy in a Protestant district of Belfast to experience and understand the hostility latent in the hearts of some Protestant children against all persons and things Catholic. People in the South of Ireland have no true comprehension of the realities in the Northern section of our country. Many of them do not wish to hear about the Northern Catholics' difficulties – they are not interested; they could not care less.

How often I was surrounded by Protestant boys, who shook their fists in my face and cried out to me: "Curse the Pope! Cummings! Come on! Curse the Pope! Curse him!" We Catholic boys knew well that in the circumstances to curse the Pope was to repudiate and renounce your Catholic faith. Thank God, so far as my memory goes, I never cursed the Pope. I was often punched, pummelled and stoned, as payment for my obstinacy.

As a boy, therefore, I lived under a constant strain with my Protestant companions. I never could foresee when the bullying would begin, nor when the old familiar test might come. But, as I have said, my close friends among the boys would never think of bullying me – the trouble usually came from one of two who lived on the fringe of our area and knew me only slightly. These latter were unpredictable. If in a hostile, aggressive mood, revived and stimulated by Orange parades and anniversaries, they could be quite callous and cruel. (See **Appendix 7**.)

When the orange lilies showed in the gardens of our district and the renowned Orange anniversary day, 12 July, came round, we Catholic children had to remain inside. Feelings at that time of the year ran high against us: it was safer to stay behind closed doors.

How one's early life remains with one! I always think of our childhood's fears in 77 Agincourt Avenue, when I read those words in John 20:19: "Late that Sunday evening, when the disciples were together behind locked doors, for fear of the Jews…"

Dislike and discrimination – these I encountered frequently as a child. One day, playing near a garden by a river, I was seen by an elderly Protestant woman living there.

"Who is that boy?" she asked my companions, pointing to me.

"Cummings!" replied my friends.

"Oh, he is a Roman Catholic! Tell him to run away from here. We are all 'True Blues' here!" At this time I was about nine or ten years of age.

On another occasion I was snubbed in a most hurtful way, simply because I was a Catholic. A mile or two from my home lay an extensive demesne called Belvoir Park. Its hundreds of acres of wild woodland held tremendous attractions for us youngsters. In spring, you could explore the woods for the nests of some rare birds. There were grand trees to be climbed, flowers to be gathered by the armful and, in autumn, chestnuts falling in plenty from the chestnut trees. It was indeed a boy's paradise. To enter Belvoir Park, however, you needed a pass. A friend who had a pass could bring you with him.

One sunny afternoon a Protestant boy, a newcomer to our district, joined our group and produced a number of passes for Belvoir Park. He gave passes to all the boys, but not to me. And he made it quite clear why he was doing this – he abhorred Roman Catholics, and he had discovered I was one. So, on that Saturday afternoon, there were passes for everyone, but not for Cummings, the Roman Catholic! I still see the hatred and contempt for me written all over his round, red face. To grown-ups this might seem very trivial – not so to a boy! All my comrades went off, laughing and chatting, to Belvoir Demesne. I went home, alone and with a very heavy heart.

While I was a member of the Community in Belfast's Clonard Monastery, I had frequent encounters with the Reverend Ian Paisley, the self-appointed Moderator of the Free Presbyterian Church. He often used to raise the question of the persecution of Protestants in Roman Catholic Spain. I reminded him of the Protestant persecution of Catholics in Northern Ireland. I gave him instances from my own childhood.

"You are always talking about that!" he cried out.

"Why should I not talk about it? I did not read about it – I endured it!" My point was that Protestants can be as guilty of intolerance as any Catholic prelate, priest or Pope.

The dark memories of my childhood relate to events which happened a long time ago. They are, however, almost as firm and clear in my mind as events of this morning! Memories vivid and ineffaceable!

Quite recently I went across the city of Belfast to view again the district in which I was born. It was not a dark night: there was a fresh breeze and broken clouds were sweeping across the sky. I walked from Shaftesbury Square up Botanic Avenue to University Street, thence to Carmel Street and the other streets where I played as a child.

To my great surprise, the streets were empty! No children were to be seen. In my boyhood, at that time of night – about 7.30 pm – there would have been plenty of children playing their games in the streets; plenty of noise; plenty of fun. But no. The streets were silent! The children were gone! The area was as empty of youngsters as Hamelin was when the Pied Piper took the town's children away by the alluring magic of his flute. It then struck me that the television screens in people's homes now supplied the magical attraction he had once provided.

The streets I knew and loved so well were empty; they also seemed smaller. My child's judgements of the local distances were radically adjusted when I walked the pavements on that October night recently.

"The Plains" – the fields where we played football – are now covered by factories and houses. The high, broken banks of the River Lagan have been replaced by stone embankments and broad concrete boulevards. Lower down, near the harbour, they have dammed up the river, so that the permanent new water-level of the river now hides the awful stretches of mud we used to see at low tides.

Were my childhood in Agincourt Avenue to be given back to me miraculously, where would I play? With whom would I play? These quiet, empty streets, echoing with my own footfalls, are not the friendly, happy streets I knew long ago. The neighbourhood has so changed! One has to be prepared in life for plenty of changes. The Belfast my Father once knew was altered a lot in his lifetime. So also has it been with the Belfast I once knew. So we are back to the truism that cities, streets, areas are as subject to change as man himself.

I now come to deal with that period of my life which began when we moved house to the Springfield Road, in the Falls Road area. All our neighbours and all my companions were now Catholics. This was indeed a change in my affairs, a change both pleasant and interesting. In mixing with other boys, in conversation with them or at games, I was henceforth free from that hidden, gnawing fear that my Catholic faith would sooner or later be mocked and derided.

In this new Catholic district I soon made friends. A number of the boys who attended St Malachy's College with me lived in the district, and through them I made the acquaintance of others. However, this was but the silver lining to a very dark cloud! My newly found comfort of having so many Catholic friends was marred by the bitter pogrom being carried on by Protestant extremists in the Catholic areas in the city.

Our evenings and nights were often filled with the crashing, cracking sounds of rifle and revolver fire. Kashmir Road, near our new home, lay on the fringe of the Catholic district. In that summer of 1920 very heavy fighting took place there: one evening, six or seven people were shot dead.

Members of the Irish Republican Army took part in defending the Catholic areas: but for their armed help, many Catholic families would have been massacred. These Republican soldiers also waged their own war against the armed forces of the Crown.

A typical incident would be this: two policemen or "Black and Tans" would be strolling along a street or arcade in the city, when a couple of Republican soldiers, dressed in their usual civilian clothes, would step out in front of them and shoot them down. The police or the Black and Tans had no chance of defending themselves: they were suddenly confronted and killed. These are horrible events to describe – dreadful acts were carried out by the two sides in this guerrilla war. Those were days of appalling bitterness and bloodshed. I must speak about them here because they played a part in the life I have lived.

On each occasion when these city shootings took place, reprisals followed that very night. For every policeman shot in the city, a Catholic would be murdered that very night. A curfew had been imposed on the city: no one was allowed on the streets without a permit between the hours of 10.30 pm and 6.00 am. This curfew allowed the Crown forces and their agents to carry out murderous reprisals without any civilian interruptions. It was a terrifying time for Catholic families.

We lived in the midst of it all, yet knew very little of what was happening around us. The daily media told us what was going on publicly in the city, but there was much that did not appear in the newspapers. The IRA executed all informers. Secrecy was vital to their movements. Our people were always on their guard never to know or to say too much. So tight was the secrecy and security screen, that most of the people knew nothing about the IRA men and their activities.

For instance, our next-door neighbours were a quiet, elderly couple who had no children. Years later I learned that on those murder nights, six or seven of the leading IRA members stayed with them. Had the night murderers visited that house, these men would have met them with gunfire and wiped them out. It was just as well that we, the next-door neighbours, did not know our own circumstances.

Meanwhile life went on in the city. People tried to behave in their normal way. Shopping had to be done; children had to be fed, clothed and set off to school. Life had to go on!

In travelling to St Malachy's College, we had to cross the city. This meant passing through several danger zones where Protestant gunmen were active. Sometimes in the mornings the sniping and shooting was so vigorous that we were reluctant to cross certain streets. Sometimes, perhaps with too great haste, we decided it was unwise to attempt to reach school. So we turned back for home. This meant a free day for us!

On one occasion when we had taken a free day in this manner, our new French master, Monsieur Magout, asked us next day why we had been absent from school. We smugly explained that the sniping and shooting in the streets had prevented us from reaching school. Monsieur pooh-poohed this excuse, however. He raised his arms to heaven – he laughed us to scorn. We were not true soldiers! This was disgraceful! Monsieur twisted his moustache. He marched proudly up and down the classroom. He knew what real fighting was – had he not served with the French army at Verdun and Douaumont? Ha! The shelling and the machine guns on the Verdun front – these had been truly *formidable*. He, Jacques Magout, knew what he was talking about: he knew real war. "But here, a few shots in the streets, and you boys, ha! You go home to your mothers. Bah!"

We sat silently at our desks and watched his indignant performance with inward joy. Why? Because we had had our free day, and moreover, the longer he re-visited Verdun and the French army, the less time remained for lessons. We listened, but we were unimpressed. We were young boys and we had no remorse.

At night in curfew hours the police sometimes raided a Catholic street. They searched the houses for particular men or for arms. So often did they use violence in these raids, so often had murder been done at night, that people were thoroughly alarmed when police lorries came to their streets. They adopted an unusual mode of resisting these raids. As soon as the lorries arrived in a street, every upstairs window was flung open and all the people would scream as loudly as possible. The screaming of an entire street full of people created an appalling noise. Neighbouring streets took up the scream, and in no time a vast area was wild with sound and fury. This shook the nerves of any group of men bent on quick, silent violence or murder. The screaming put an end to their aim of carrying out certain operations and then silently slipping away into the darkness. A woman's frightened scream, particularly at dead of night, is a fearful, horrifying sound. When many street-fulls of women are screaming simultaneously, the noise is terrifying. It accomplished its purpose: it unnerved the police.

On the night of 25 September 1920 two policemen were shot dead at Broadway on the Falls Road. Later on that same night there were reprisals. A Catholic hairdresser named Eddie Trodden, who lived on the Falls Road, was killed in his home. About 2.30 am, four men, with blackened faces, carrying rifles, hammered at the door of his shop.

"Who is there?" shouted Eddie from an open window.

"Military, on a raid!" was the reply.

Eddie's son went down to open the door. The raiders rushed in. The boy attacked them with a chair. Throwing the chair at them, he ran upstairs to warn his father. The raiders fired at the child but missed him. They hesitated to follow him up the stairs. Cutting down the clothes-line in the kitchen, they gathered the clothes from it and set them ablaze.

"Come down, Trodden, or we will burn you out!" they shouted.

Finally they captured their man. Bringing him out to the backyard of his house, they riddled him with bullets.

On that same night Sean McFadden was shot dead in his home. He lived about ten doors down from us in the same terrace of houses. About midnight, during the curfew hours, my brothers saw the killers going down the Springfield Road to the house. They were a small group of men wearing trench coats. They crossed over to our side of the street and went along the terrace until they came to McFadden's house. In a minute or two there was a volley of shots. I remember, as a boy of thirteen, lying awake in bed that night. I heard these shots that killed Sean McFadden.

I do not think I realised the strain my parents endured that night – I was too young to appreciate the horror of it all. Our home was a house of fear and tension. My cousins, who lived near the spot where the policemen had been killed, came to stay with us for the night. They were in grave danger in their own home. We youngsters were put to bed: the grown-ups kept vigil all night until dawn. I remember how they walked about silently and spoke in whispers. Standing well back in the sitting-room which fronted the street, they kept watch all night long.

Sean Gaynor, who lived farther up our road, was also put to death that night. Neither he nor Sean McFadden were the men the raiders were really after. The murder gangs abroad in the streets of Belfast that night were seeking the brothers of these two men.

Another sad memory comes back to me from those days of bloodshed. On Saturday, 25 April 1921, in the very heart of Belfast two auxiliaries – part of the British forces – were shot dead. That night, as a reprisal, two brothers named Duffin, who lived in Clonard Gardens, were riddled with bullets in the kitchen of their home.

I can recall the tension on the next morning, a Sunday. Groups stood in the streets discussing the murders. I went to the Duffins' home and was allowed to see the bodies of the two brothers. They were laid out in the front room downstairs. Both were robed in the brown Franciscan habit. This visit was something beyond me. I could not determine my feelings or reactions – the whole affair left me numb. I came away from the house, thinking that we were helpless. It seemed our fates lay not in ourselves, but in the guns of the night-raiders.

That morning all kinds of rumours were heard. So pent-up, so nervy were the Catholics that any alarming rumour was seized upon, twisted, exaggerated, and then sent forth on fresh travels. Those April days of spring sunshine in 1921 were days of black gloom in Belfast.

Isolated events come back to my mind. Tom O'Boyle, a chum of mine, persuaded me to join Fianna na hÉireann – the Republican Boy Scouts. Our Captain was Jimmy McShane. He taught us simple rifle drills, semaphore signalling, and Republican Scout discipline. Our unit was the proud possessor of an old Snider rifle, which had probably been brought back as a souvenir from the Boer War. What care it received from all of us! No weapon in modern warfare received more attention and veneration than that "old Fenian gun". It had only one drawback – it was too heavy for young boys to handle easily. Jimmy McShane played about with it as he pleased: the rest of us watched him and tried to learn his technique. Our drilling took place once a week in a hall in the city.

Republican funerals were the occasion of a display of Irish Republican Army strength in Belfast. I witnessed one of these. In May 1921 a Flying Column of twelve volunteers from the First Battalion of the Belfast IRA was sent to operate around Lappinduff Mountain in County Cavan. Soon after the Column's arrival they were surprised by British forces: no doubt a spy or an informer had done his work well. In the ensuing battle four Republicans escaped, seven were captured, and one was killed.

The dead man's name was Sean McCartney. He hailed from the Falls Road district. His funeral cortege to the Milltown Cemetery in Belfast was one of the largest and most impressive even seen on the Falls Road. I followed it all the way to the cemetery. Police in armoured cars cruised around, but did not interfere with the funeral. The volunteers of the IRA marched behind the coffin in military formation. A Republican Tricolour covered the coffin.

Six of the dead man's comrades carried the coffin. I stood close to the grave that day. The priest who recited the prayers at the graveside gave an oration, lauding the noble virtues of patriotism and sacrifice. Just before the coffin was lowered into the grave, eight men of the IRA suddenly came forward and stood to attention, four facing four, on either side of the coffin. At words of command from an officer, who stood at the head of the grave, they produced revolvers, presented them, and fired three volleys into the air. It was my first time ever to be so near to guns firing. Those who knew this salute would be given were prepared for it – the rest of us, who had no idea of what was going to happen, were stunned by the noise.

By the time we had recovered our wits, the firing party had slipped quietly away into the crowd and disappeared. Any policeman on duty in the vicinity must have been startled by the sound of the firing. When the funeral service was over and we emerged from the cemetery, not a policeman was to be seen anywhere. Perhaps they thought it more prudent to keep out of the way.

At the graveside I noticed that one member of the firing party was a student from one of the senior classes in St Malachy's College. He afterwards qualified in medicine and practiced as a doctor in Belfast. I wonder, does he ever think back to the firing party at Sean McCartney's funeral?

The priest who spoke the oration at the grave was Fr Charles O'Neill, then a curate in one of the city parishes. He was the brother of Fr PJ O'Neill, the President of St Malachy's College. He composed the words of the well-known patriot song, "The Foggy Dew". Members of the Belfast IRA learned the song. When some of these were interned in Ballykinlar Camp, they sang the song at the camp concerts. Republicans from all parts of Ireland learned the song from them – and these men, when released, spread the song through the length and breadth of the country. In this way it became, and still is, one of the most popular patriot songs of Ireland.

Before leaving the subject of Sean McCartney's funeral, I must say a word about his seven comrades, who were made prisoners when he was killed. All seven were imprisoned in Crumlin Road Gaol, Belfast. They were tried and condemned to death. While they lay under sentence of death, Lloyd George made a truce with the Republican leaders. A treaty of peace was signed. At the signing of this treaty, all seven men were released. Years later I met one of these men – Sorley McCann. He told me that but for the signing of the treaty, he and companions would have been executed.

So that was the story in those fearsome days – executions, internment, death sentences, raids, murders, search parties. On the Falls Road, all men and even older boys, were suspected by the Crown forces of being members of the IRA. For many years to come, walking on the Falls, you were liable to be halted and searched by troops at any hour. One night I was stopped at the corner of the Springfield and Falls Roads. The soldier searching me found something hard as metal in my vest pocket.

"Hello!" he exclaimed. "What have we got here?"

He took out the object and put it back at once. It was a crucifix I had won in some examinations in the Redemptorist College, Limerick. He asked me no questions: he merely smiled in a sheepish kind of way and signed to me to move on.

The police knew quite a number of the IRA by sight and by name – such men, in the phrase of the times, had to go 'on the run'. Yet the IRA drilled regularly in the Falls Road area. I know, because I would see them drilling close to an open road. The Fianna section of the IRA actually camped out on the mountain near Divis. More than that, I once saw the entire Third Northern Division of the IRA on parade in a field near the mountain. Looking back on it all, I am quite sure the police authorities and the troops knew all about this activity, but decided to keep out of the way of trouble.

# CHAPTER FOUR
# The Redemptorists

## Clonard Holy Family

WHEN MY FAMILY went to live in the Falls Road area, our new home was near the Redemptorist Church and Monastery at Clonard. On some Sundays, instead of going to our parish church of St Paul's, I went to Clonard. Apart from the missioners who conducted missions in St Malachy's Church, I had never seen religious devotees working out their apostolate. Clonard fascinated me. I observed the priests and brothers in their distinctive religious dress. I saw them at their work – the priests visiting in the district, the brothers quietly and reverently attending to the altars and sanctuary, and their monastic duties. In addition, there was the glory of the church itself, and the fine choir and organ under the guidance of that great organist and choirmaster, Monsieur Arthur De Meulemeester. Above all, I noticed the impressive sermons of the priests and the obviously devout attention of the congregation.

In 1921, when I was fourteen years of age, I joined St James' Section of the Men's Holy Family Confraternity. I attended the weekly meetings faithfully. The priest who was Director of the Confraternity was not a star preacher: many of his listeners sank their heads on their chests and dozed quietly. But there were other factors present to compensate for this drawback. First, there was the inspiration I found in the church, crowded with men of all classes – labourers, barbers, teachers, tram-drivers, doctors, bakers: young and old, all of them faithful to the Confraternity. Secondly, there were the wonderful monthly Communions of all the men, who numbered about two thousand in total. Thirdly, there were the retreats preached to us yearly, and half-yearly, by some of the most effective preachers among the Redemptorist Fathers of the Irish Province. All these factors had a strong influence on me.

Something else happened at the end of 1921, which – trivial though it was – somehow affected me deeply. I had understood that I was to play in a hurling match for my team on a certain Sunday. By chance, on the eve of that day I met one of the other players who told me that another boy had been given my place. This was unfair. It had all been fixed behind my back. Not a word had been said to me. Disappointed and disillusioned, I left the team and the crowd of boys who ran its affairs. The team committee had treated me unjustly. At that time I was very keen on hurling – I suppose this explains why the incident annoyed me so much.

This incident started a serious train of thought in my mind: I saw clearly that people, even my own companions, would readily disappoint me; I saw that the world of men could be to me a source of much sorrow. This train of thought, coupled with the ever-present life and example of the Redemptorist Fathers at Clonard, led me to a decision – I would become a Redemptorist! I would give my life to a Friend who would not disappoint me.

All this occurred over fifty years ago. I have no regrets about that decision – except perhaps that I did not always live up to all the ideals of the Redemptorist Rule. I regret that – but I bless and thank God for the grace He gave me in the opportunity to become a Redemptorist Priest.

## Limerick: The Juniorate

Having made my decision, I lost no time in making it known to Mother. I remember the moment well. She was polishing the brass fire-irons in our sitting-room. She listened to me carefully. Right from the time I told her, she helped me. That very morning we both went up to the Redemptorist Monastery to see the Fr Rector. The Brother who opened the door to us ushered us into one of the reception rooms. It was a very bare room – just a few pictures on the walls, four or five chairs, and a table covered with green baize.

The month was December. The room was chilly. We sat there patiently for about an hour, but no one came to speak to us. At long last the Rector came. Having heard about my studies and being evidently satisfied on that score, he went on to discuss the financial side of the matter. There was apparently only one obstacle to my entry into the Juniorate in Limerick: namely, the £60 pension to be paid by each boy annually. Fr Rector said he would write to the Fr Director of the College in Limerick. For weeks we heard not a word. We then went back to see the Rector. There had been some misunderstanding: this second meeting solved the difficulty. Mother had explained she would try to pay the money by instalments. This was agreed on. So, on 5 January 1922 I left home for the Redemptorist College, Limerick. I had just passed my fifteenth birthday three days earlier.

Mother came with me as far as Dublin. There we were met by my uncle, Fr Mageean, who was then one of the Deans in Maynooth College. Under his guidance we had a pleasant day in the capital. I remember we went to the zoo in Phoenix Park. There I saw animals which had hitherto existed for me only in words and pictures. The various keepers put on special performances with their animals for our interest and amusement. January was a slack time of the year in their work, and I suppose they welcomed the break in their daily routine.

Evening came: the time for me to leave Dublin approached. The pleasant day was at an end. On the platform of Heuston Station (then known as Kingsbridge Station) I said goodbye to Mother and to my uncle, and boarded the train for Limerick at about 5.00 pm. It was now a dark winter evening. Dublin was looking anything but cheerful. As my train moved through the suburbs I looked out at the dismal red-bricked houses and the melancholy waters of the Grand Canal. A deep feeling of loneliness came over me. I felt isolated and a stranger to the world around me.

In the railway coach where I sat, I could hear two or three old parish priests talking in low tones at the far end. There were no other passengers in the coach. The Irish Civil War was at its height. Few people travelled in those sad, grim days. I sat by myself in an open apartment of the coach all the way to Limerick – a very lonely boy. I had never been so far away from home before. I was going into the unknown. I was leaving my kith and kin for a new world.

Fr Director of the College had sent a senior boy to the Limerick railway station to meet me. With my bits of luggage piled on top of a jaunting car, he and I made our way through the streets of Limerick to the College. I was not used to jaunting cars – a two-wheeled carriage for a single horse – so I clung on tightly, especially when we careered round sharp corners.

Thus I entered the Redemptorist Juniorate. The initial novelty of it all passed very quickly, and then came the monotony and the homesickness. Of the latter I feel sure I had a super dose, for I was exceedingly fond of home. Like everything else in life however, the homesickness passed away, and I gradually fell into the way of life in the college. To a limited extent I began to enjoy it all. I liked the handball and football games. In my classwork, I was weak in Latin, but far ahead of the other boys in mathematics. As time went by, I began to improve slightly in my Latin work. I had also to take up the study of Irish, a language about which I knew nothing. In St Malachy's College, you took either French or Irish: you could not take both. I had opted for French. Fr McDonnell helped me in a special way with my Irish lessons. I caught up with the class slowly.

Study in the college was compulsory. This was a new feature in my life. I had never been under this compulsion before, and I assure you it was shock treatment!

Owing to what Dr Hendley had taught me in mathematics in St Malachy's College, I was now able to give more time to my weak subjects. Chiefly due to him – and years later as a priest I made this clear to him with very great gratitude – I passed all my examinations up to and including Senior Honours.

## Dundalk: The Novitiate

In August 1924 I entered the Novitiate in Dundalk: I was seventeen years of age.

It is neither easy nor pleasant to write about one's Novitiate. Novitiate year is not meant to be sweet to human nature: its precise purpose, as I understood it, was to tame wild human nature, to conquer it in accordance with the dictum of St Ignatius, *Vince Te Ipsum* ("Conquer Thyself"). Human nature was "the old man" spoken of in such a derogatory manner by St Paul. This "old man" had to die, and the slow, painful days of the novitiate were intended and shaped to put him down ruthlessly and forever. The instruments of subjugation to be used were self-denial, bitter herbs, cilices (arm bracelets of wire mesh with scores of sharp points), denial of food, hours of prayer, stiff obediences, and a rigorous daily timetable which left few crumbs of ease or comfort for a boy's human side.

And so, we had no games, no visits from friends (parents were allowed one visit per year), no holidays, no newspapers, no storybooks, and no communication with any of the Fathers and Brothers of the Community in which we lived. We never got a day at home. We had innumerable retreat days, during which we never uttered a word to anyone. Our recreations were very often a torture. The priest in charge of us used these periods to find cause for reproaching us collectively (which was bearable) and individually (which was ever so much sorer). Among ourselves, as a last resort, we drew up a rota of our turns to go with our Fr Master (as we were taught to call him). This rota was followed rigorously. When recreation began after meals, the whisper would go round amongst us: "Whose turn is it to go with him?" And there was no choice: whoever was due for his company had to march out to the front of our group and join Fr Master. Then in a leisurely way, suiting Fr Master's speed, we walked for half-an-hour round the garden. Next we went inside the monastery to the Novices' Common Room. There for the remainder of the hour we worked at the making of Rosary beads or the rough, corded whips we used at the bi-weekly discipline.

In the Juniorate we had been more or less steeled to endure the Novitiate's tests and trials. We were told alarming stories of its monotony, its weird, humiliating obediences, and its prolonged inhumanity. In a way all these stories prepared us to take what was coming to us, and yet we suffered when the troubles came. You may know someone is going to strike you – it helps you to get ready to receive the blow; but when the blow falls, it still hurts.

At the beginning of my Novitiate year, we had "common recreation" with the Fathers. This was exceptional, because novices were forbidden to talk to the Fathers. During that particular common recreation, an old Father said to me, "Almighty God will give you your Novitiate!" I am certain he was right. God sent me many trials. The Novice Master and my seven fellow novices proved to be keen instruments in his hands. The two novices who treated me badly took their vows, but afterwards left the Redemptorists. I was not the only one to go through the mill of trial and suffering in the Novitiate: we all had to take our share of tribulations. Looking back across the years to those hard days, it now seems to me that God permitted, but certainly did not will, some of the treatment we received. Those who were in a position to hurt us were as much bound by Christ's command as I was, and am: "Treat others as you wish them to treat you." (Luke 6:31)

A young novice is in great need of kindly help, guidance, and generous understanding. He is still a person with an inalienable right to ordinary common respect and consideration. It is unfair to crush his dignity and self-respect. At times in our Novitiate, we were treated as though we were criminals. Day after day we were pilloried and harassed – first one, and then another. Personal abuse was our daily fare.

Angry personal abuse, in public especially, is no help to a novice – it only hurts and embarrasses him and leaves him bewildered. The vivid awareness of one's mistakes and blunders and failings will sufficiently teach one true humility: nothing else will.

Those in charge of us novices thought they were acting rightly. They were good men, following the traditional methods of training novices. In the words of the popular spiritual writers of their time, they were "schooling the novices in humility and obedience". And they went about their task in a ruthless manner. Unknown to themselves, they were following that erroneous principle, "The end justifies the means"! I hold nothing against them: they thought they were doing their job correctly.

I am sure they gained much merit for their dedication to our training. But it was all wrong! Nothing could justify their treatment of us.

Spiritual writers teach that humiliations will make one humble if one accepts them for Our Lord's sake. Now, how can one accept and agree to what one knows is the wrong behaviour of others? Must one accept what one knows is displeasing to God? Must one not wish only what God wishes?

All of this puzzled me for years. I now see that acceptance of unjust treatment does not mean agreement with it. Our Lord accepted dreadful treatment, but did not say it was fair or just treatment. He said on the cross: "Father, forgive them, for they know not what they do!" Some commentators say He was referring not to the Jews, but to the Roman soldiery around His cross. In either case he excused his executioners without approving of their crime.

I now see that suffering inflicted on us unjustly deepens our love for God when we willingly accept it. Stoic acceptance of pain is the Christian's way of meeting suffering.

I now see that God permits injustices and unfair treatment to happen to us – even at the hands of good, holy men. He does not will them to happen but in the suffering we endure, He offers us a way of helping in the work of Redemption. This is what St Paul teaches in the first chapter of the Epistle to the Colossians:

> "I now rejoice in my sufferings for you, and fill up those things that are wanting of the sufferings of Christ."

The New English Bible translates this passage thus:

> "It is now my happiness to suffer for you. This is my way of helping to complete in my poor human flesh, the full tale of Christ's afflictions still to be endured, for the sake of His body which is the Church."

St Paul may mean that a disciple of Christ has to add his measure of suffering if he is to carry the graces of redemption to the world. Or he may mean that Christ, the Head of the Mystical Body (the Church) has suffered and now wills His mystical members (ie, our own selves) to suffer likewise. In either sense we are meant to accept patiently and with love for Christ the sufferings God permits to happen to us. The Second Vatican Council has said:

> "By suffering for us, the Son of God not only provided us with an example for our imitation but also blazed a trail: and if we follow it, life and death are made holy and take on a new meaning."
>
> (*Gaudium et Spes*, 22)

Are we never to resist injustice? Are we never to fight against what is unfair? The only general answer I have to those questions is that the Holy Spirit of God will show us what is right to do in each set of circumstances.

I have digressed somewhat from the story of my Novitiate days. What I have said may give some meaning to what we endured as novices. Whatever of suffering and insults came our way, we cheerfully and prayerfully accepted, I hope, for the sake of Our Lord and our vocation.

I say again that our Novice Master was a very pious man. I am quite sure he acted in good faith and with the best of intentions. He was merely treating us in accordance with tradition. I am sure he reached a high degree of holiness; but to me, by his temperament and mental equipment he was little help in learning the true way of religious life.

As a result when the time came for me to take my first religious vows, I had some strange ideas of the implications of the vow of chastity. The truth is that I did not know the facts of life. I was appallingly ignorant. Neither the Father Director of the Juniorate nor the Fr Master in the Novitiate had ever given us any information about what they called "the holy virtue". Of course during the years I passed under their care, I got lectures on purity, obedience and poverty – but the lectures on purity or chastity extolled its glories and passed lightly over its problems and difficulties.

The usual text chosen by the priest for a talk on purity was this one: "How beautiful is the chaste generation with glory!" (Wisdom 4:1) However the text in the Douai Version of the Bible is inaccurate. The Revised Version renders the same passage: "Better to be unwedded than to live without virtue." The Jerusalem Bible translates it: "Better to have no children, yet to have virtue."

In the talk there was never a word about what sex meant in the physical sphere in and outside marriage: the entire stress was on the glory of chastity and its privileges. I had taken final vows and had reached my twenty-second year before I got to know the facts of life. Because of my atrocious ignorance, I suffered agonies through my constant dread of sinning some way or other in the matter of purity.

Long years have passed since then: what I have narrated happened over fifty years ago. One's memories live on, however, and are part of the life one lives each day. All I endured in those Novitiate days frequently comes back to me. I trust God forgives my miseries and distresses of the past. I was often worried and depressed, bewildered and unhappy. I do not count for much: I am a very small unit in creation – but perhaps my life in those Novitiate days, and my reactions to what happened to me, may comfort and encourage those who have been similarly afflicted.

A number of us stuck it out in the Novitiate. How did we succeed in doing so? The only explanation for my own case is that God must have assisted us with His graces. We needed divine help, for the life there and all it entailed was far beyond what human nature could stand.

At the end of the Novitiate we made fifteen days' retreat in silence and prayer, in preparation for pronouncing our first religious vows. During that retreat I was tormented by the recurring thought that I had not a true vocation, that I was a hypocrite, that the monastery was no place for me, and that I should go home. I wanted in my heart to live a true Redemptorist life, yet these disturbing thoughts kept me depressed and confused.

I decided to speak to my Novice Master. Timidly, I knocked at his door.

"Ave Maria!" he answered in a rather loud voice. (It is our custom to invite entry into our rooms to anyone who knocks at the door, by saying "Ave Maria".) I opened the door and went into his room.

He stared at me over his spectacles. "Well, child, what do you want?" he said gruffly. (Child! I was eighteen years of age! Young men at my age were getting married! This "child" form of address was part of the Novitiate technique of reducing you to minimal size and training you to be utterly in the hands of the superiors.)

"Father, I have come to tell you that I feel I have no vocation and that I ought to go home!"

"Very well!" he replied briskly. "Go to Fr Bursar and get your train fare and go home!"

"Oh, I don't want to end it all like that! But what am I going to do?"

"Go away, child, you are wasting my time!" came his reply, as he turned back to his desk. So I left the room. I came away from him even more miserable than before.

I wandered around, quite distraught. What was I going to do now? Suddenly I thought of the novices' Confessor. I would speak to the priest who had been my Confessor during the year's Novitiate.

He received me kindly. Having listened to my tale of distress, he assured me I had a vocation. Because of his advice I was able to go forward a few days later to take my vows. On that memorable day of the vows – even though I was convinced I was right to take the vows – in some mysterious way, I felt miserable and depressed. Without feeling any trace of exhilaration or exultation, I knelt that day on the sanctuary of St Joseph's Church, Dundalk, and pronounced my vows. The day was the 8 September 1925. On the next day, with my four companions, I journeyed to the House of Studies at Esker, near Athenry, County Galway. There I would begin my years of study for the priesthood.

## Galway: The House of Studies

Life as a student was in many ways much easier than that of a novice, but it was by no means an easy life. At first I found the abstractions of philosophy quite intangible and baffling. For several weeks I almost despaired of grasping its elements. The older students assured me that mine was a common experience: patience was the only answer. The mind must gradually accustom itself to abstract ideas. I persevered, and daily plodding and frequent revision work brought a slow, faint dawning of light.

The older students gave me encouragement. They had already run the gauntlet of philosophers and knew the difficulties. Very often they would explain tough points. How pleased they were when you showed them they had helped you. Indeed among the students there was a great spirit of helpfulness and consideration: they were obliging. They had their disputes, disagreements, preferences – sometimes even with a sharp edge in these – but they never refused to help where help was needed and could be given.

Our everyday life as students was severe. For my six long years as a student, here was the daily programme:

5.25 am Rise (to the merciless hammering clanging of what had once been a ship's bell)

5.55 am Recital of the Angelus by all in the Oratory

6.00–6.30 am Meditation (this consisted of opening prayers, then the reading aloud by a student reader of a passage from a meditation book. All lights were then switched off and we were left in darkness to meditate and pray.)

6.30 am Holy Mass: we received Holy Communion at the beginning of Mass.

7.00–8.00 am Make your bed; tidy your room; study.

8.00 am Breakfast, followed by recreation in the garden.

8.45 am Study

9.45 am Class

11.00–11.30 am Recreation or free time

12.15 pm Class

1.00 pm Recreation in garden or free time

1.15 pm Particular Examination of Conscience in the Oratory

1.20 pm Dinner

2.00–3.00 pm Recreation

3.00–3.30 pm Siesta if you wished, or free time

3.30–4.00 pm Spiritual reading in one's room

4.00–5.00 pm Study

5.00–6.00 pm Class

6.00–6.30 pm Free time

6.30 pm Visit to Blessed Sacrament: done by all the students

6.35–7.10 pm Study

7.10–7.30 pm Reading of the Bible

7.30–8.00 pm Meditation in the Oratory

8.00–9.30 pm Supper and recreation

9.30 pm Night prayers and free time

10.30 pm Lights out

We thus had a daily programme of three hours and 15 minutes of study and three hours of class. Whether you liked it or not, you had to "scorn delights and live laborious days".

Our mediations in the community Oratory were always made kneeling – only for a sufficient reason, accepted by the Superior, could one sit during them. One's knees became covered with rough, tough skin like that of a lizard, because of the frequent, long periods of kneeling: soon, your knees hurt less and less. At times however it was all very wearying.

A bigger problem was the long interval between our meals: five hours between breakfast and dinner, and seven hours between dinner and supper. It was a long, hard day for growing young men who needed plenty of food and no lengthy spells between meals. Only because we were young, eager, enthusiastic and light-hearted, were we able to pull through. We studied diligently; we played strenuous games; we went for long walks frequently – and oh, how often we felt need of a good square meal!

Later on, some concessions were made: the students got a bowl of soup at 11.00 am and a cup of tea with bread and butter at 6.00 pm. These were granted many years after my student days.

I recall one morning at breakfast during our holidays when all thirty or forty students had bacon and eggs, because we had volunteered to do certain manual work in the garden or the grounds. Only one student decided that, since it was holiday time, and therefore a free morning, he would prefer his free time to the extra fare the volunteer workers received. I remember all this, because I was that student. In a lofty, superior, 'holier-than-thou' manner, I teased and railed some of my friends for selling their liberty for a mess of potage – or its equivalent.

Usually in seminaries the professors give lectures, during which the students listen and take down notes. Often a student is too slow in his writing to cope with a fast-speaking lecturer: as a result he is in doubt frequently about points in the lecture. He must then consult other students. He must revise his notes by comparing theirs with his own. Thank Heaven our system was more sensible – we were given a textbook and told to learn so many pages for each day's class.

Having assembled for class, we recited some prayers and sat down. The professor would open his copy of our textbook and question us in turn on the matter he had told us to study. This done, he would explain any point in the lesson we might not have grasped clearly: we were free to write a point like this in our notebooks. He then went on to explain the next day's lesson.

By this system, I studied Philosophy, Church History, Physiology, Hebrew, Dogmatic Theology, Moral Theology and Scripture during my six years at St Patricks, Athenry, County Galway. In all these subjects we had textbooks: the taking of notes was reduced to a minimum. The system was a sensible one, for the average student is kept busy enough in learning a textbook written by an authority on the subject, without having to write out and decipher unpublished lectures. If a professor thinks his lectures are worthwhile, he should have them printed – without torturing his students with sessions of hurried writing. This is what St Alphonsus thought and said. Most students, I think, would agree with him.

Of course no textbook is entirely free from defects. To remedy this, our professors supplemented our textbooks with useful points from other authors. Wise men agree that a student should master one book thoroughly. When he has a good grip of one standard work, he may consult other authors – but not before that. Young, immature students, who go dipping into various books in the belief that they will thus learn their subject more easily, are usually wasting their time. One must first learn to swim in the shallows before venturing out into deep waters.

I knew some students who would spend time with an author none of us had read. That was all very well, but these same students would frequently slip up in the ordinary daily lesson in class. Most of us followed the system I described above, and we tried to do each day's work well. By dint of constantly revising the sections of our textbooks (which we had been through thoroughly in class), we knew our subjects well for our examinations.

One day Fr McMahon, a fellow student, told me about, and recommended, Bishop Hedley's book, *Lex Levitarum*. I read it and was much taken by the Introduction which the Bishop wrote for the main subject matter of the book – namely the Lex Pastoralis of Pope Gregory VII. From the pages of that book I learned what student industry really means. What valuable help this volume gave me in my student days! Lest I should not be able to lay hands on the book later on, I wrote out all that Bishop Hedley had written in his Introduction. As well as was in my power, I followed the Bishop's advice regarding a student's attitude to seminary rules, fellow-students, reading and study.

Concerning a student's industry, the Bishop lays down four points, as follows: the student must take a serious view of his vocation and position; he must be strongly determined to concentrate on his work ("stringe mentem" is the phrase the Bishop uses to illustrate the idea that the student must draw his mind tightly around his subject matter when studying, as one draws the strings of a bow); thirdly, he must make steady use of the ordinary means of progress (ie, sticking to his text books, learning each day's lesson well, and so on); fourthly, he must avoid distraction – "no intellectual work can be done without a determination to keep to hours, to cut short idleness and indulgence, and to force the powers to a certain extent". It all boils down to one thing – namely, patient, steady work.

I think most of us will agree that patient, steady work is the key to success in almost any human activity. Some days, when you are in good form, it comes easily to study patiently and steadily; on other days, when you feel out-of-sorts and utterly disinclined to open a book, you must make the effort to keep at your work regardless.

On this point I once found an inspiring passage in an article on "Adolescence" by Fr Marique in the *Supplement to the Catholic Encyclopedia*, as follows:

"Most essential (ie in education) is the discipline of genuine hard work requiring close attention, diligence, application, the putting forth of all one's energy, the conscious, strenuous effort of the will, bent on completing the task once undertaken, no matter how difficult it may seem at the time, or how disinclined one may feel to perform it. This has been challenged by the so-called 'school of interest', ie, where the teacher's chief function is to arouse the interest of the pupil – he should study the child's likes and dislikes, so as to secure attention and apprehension; compulsion is to be avoided as much as possible, not only because it weakens the child's activity, but because his right to happiness is sacred and his personality should be respected. This has done much to soften the harshness, often extreme, of the old school; it has broadened the curriculum, and adapted teaching to the child's capacity. However, when all is said in favour of 'interest', the fact remains that there is in the school, and still more in life, much of an uninteresting nature that must be done, and on the other hand, there are many things in themselves alluring that must be avoided. Life for most of us is no path strewn with roses: it is full of difficulties, set-backs, disappointments, hard knocks, and on the whole, more bitter pills to swallow than sugar plums to taste. If the school is to be a preparation for life, the motto of its work should not be interest but **effort**, for the chances are that the child who has been fed on the diet of interest will be found sadly wanting when confronted with the realities of the workaday world."

For me the clear, reasoned thought in this passage has always enforced its truth. I can honestly say that these words of Father Marique have strongly influenced my life since I first read them. In prayer, study, and all my work as a priest, "effort" has been my motto. God's grace helps one, but it does not eliminate the necessity of making efforts. Was it not the learned St Augustine who said, "Si facimus quod possumus, Deus faciet pro nobis quod non possumus" ("If we do what we can, God will do for us what of ourselves we cannot do")?

In one of her letters, St Thérèse of Lisieux puts the same idea forward in slightly different words: "Energy is the most necessary virtue: with energy one can easily arrive at the summit of perfection." Effort, energy – are they not just other words for fortitude in action?

Student days are always a strain and a test: so they were for my companions and myself – yet we were, generally speaking, a happy, light-hearted bunch of young men. So many things happened in those six years, pleasant and unpleasant, that I could not recount them all. Some events, however, stand out in my memory.

Each day's work brought us one step nearer the priesthood. Each annual series of examinations we passed was an important milestone on the road to the altar. Those examinations loom large in my memory. For many years, any vivid, uneasy dreams I had were about examinations in which I found myself confronted with an examination paper loaded with questions I could not answer. These examinations loom large in my memory because they were such fearful ordeals for all of us. They were both oral and written exercises. Each student had to do both. Certainly the oral examinations were as equally a test of our nerves as of our knowledge.

In the "orals", as we called them, about fifteen examiners sat at tables arranged to face and almost surround a desk at which the student "victim" was seated. Two of the examiners dealt with each student. There was a lot of luck in it all: you might get two "nice" examiners, or you might have two difficult ones. Each examiner had seven minutes in which to question the student. So from where he sat with the particular textbook open before him, he fired questions at the student. I often wondered what would happen if the positions had been reversed. I wondered how many of them would have fared!

All the members of the Examining Board listened and decided the marks to be given to the student. They generally agreed with the marks assigned by the two priests who had examined the student. The written examinations were a better test of a student's knowledge. Strange to say however, in our tradition and system, the oral examinations were considered the chief test. If a student failed in the oral examination, the examiners would enquire how he had fared in his written paper: the written paper then became the deciding factor.

The relief of having finished – and passed – the examinations was indescribable! It was overwhelming luxury, ease and peace.

One feature of our examinations was unusual. Our superiors had estimated the mental ability of each student. If in the examinations you did not reach the standard they expected from you, you were in trouble. Even though you had passed the examination, you were, nevertheless, in trouble. You had to satisfy the authorities that you had studied diligently during the year – otherwise you received a drubbing, perhaps even a penance. If university students pass their examinations, they do not have to worry. For us, passing the examination was not enough – we had to pass it at the level of our ability.

One other difficulty we had to face as students was this: some of the examiners were not competent in the relevant subjects in which they examined us. The Professors on the Examining Board were nearly all competent and well-qualified, but the others with them, namely the Rectors of all our Irish houses, were not, as a general rule, in their proper element.

I remember one such examiner asking me my first question in a long Church History Course, as follows: "To what Pope did the French write to depose Childeric III?" The answer to that question was in half a line in the very thick volume set for the examination. This examiner deemed that this counted as a question – and the first one at that. It was pointless! On its own it was not a proper question at all for an examination in Church History. We could do nothing about such an occurrence, however. We had to take it and keep silent afterwards.

In Philosophy and Theology all examinations were conducted in Latin. Due to the constant practice in answering questions on the daily lesson entirely in Latin, we became quite fluent in the language. Textbooks written in Latin gave us no trouble. We were thus able to consult German, Dutch and Italian theologians whose works were in Latin.

My own opinion about our examinations is that all oral examinations should have been abolished. The written examinations, I think, are a sufficient test of a student's knowledge and ability.

Usually I studied on my own. If requested, or if both of us felt it would help us, I would work with another student. We asked each other some questions and discussed knotty points. At times discussion cleared up difficulties. My fellow students, in addition to being cheerful and light-hearted, were obliging and kind. Many of them were outstanding in these qualities. Some had temperaments and interests very different from mine. In our way of life, you had to accept this and try to get on well with the others. This is everyone's problem in life, no matter what their chosen path may be – barber or brigadier, painter or prime minister.

Esker, where our college was situated, was beautiful in springtime. The fresh green leaves were a symbol of hope. The increasing brightness of the sunlight was a comfort and reassurance that winter had gone.

I did not relish the dark, damp days of the Galway winter, stretching as is it did from October to April. Winter made even more trying the needlessly long walks imposed on us every Thursday afternoon by the priest who had charge of us. It was his wont to lead us out in crocodile fashion, two by two. He would walk at a fairly quick, steady speed for an hour and ten minutes by his watch – through demesnes, across spongy bogs and through the gaps he found in barbed wire fences.

When only one at a time could get through a gap or a break in a fence, wall, or hedge, there was perforce a delay. We had to wait and take our turn. Some minutes would elapse before the last of the rearguard would be through the gap. Meanwhile his Reverence was stalking away from us at splendid speed over the clear fields. By the time the last student had navigated the gap, our Fr Prefect was a quarter of a mile away, looking over his shoulder, as he went on, on, and on, laughing and striding away in excellent good humour. Those of us who had been delayed were compelled to run to catch up with him. This was the story every Thursday: a gap in a hedge would mean a delay, and then a race to keep up with him.

You might say, "Why did you not let him go ahead on his own?" Because if a student or students did not (in the phrase we used) "keep up" on the walk, it was deemed a fault, and not a trifling one. It was a fault for which you were most likely to be reprimanded. (Thinking back on it now after 50 years, it doesn't make sense!)

After an hour and ten minutes of such cross-country galloping, our leader would pause for a short time – about three or four minutes, then, turning for home, he would repeat his performance with similar speed and tactics. He seemed to enjoy all this. Most of us found it anything but amusing. We usually returned to the college so exhausted we could not study. We would arrive back about 5.45 pm. This was ideal timing for our Fr Prefect, as we called him, for it gave him the quarter of an hour he needed to have a rubdown and a change before tea at 6.00 pm. That was all very well for him: he was a professor and he had the privilege of evening tea at 6.00 pm. We were students, hungry and exhausted no doubt, but we were not allowed to have tea then. Our next meal came two hours later – at 8.00 pm. And so we had to grin and bear it, and kneel in prayer from 7.30 to 8.00 pm.

What changes the years have brought! I lived to see that priest, his robust, vigorous health gone, scarcely able to walk upstairs. And in the end it came to pass that I drove the car which brought him to a psychiatric clinic for treatment. I admired many of his qualities: in class he was even-tempered, consistent, and good-humoured. And I look back with deep gratitude to him for his many kindnesses. He was a man of his time, a product of the system, a faithful echo of the traditions handed down.

I have also lived to see the whole system of treating students change radically. Now they are treated as true brothers – kindly and humanely, not as in our time. We were like the inmates of a detention centre, netted round with rules and regulations innumerable. It is pleasant to know that today's students have not the long intervals between meals which we had to endure.

The wheel has turned full circle! "What was, is not; what is, was not!" as St Augustine would perhaps have put it! As in everyone's life, hard elements were mixed with pleasant in our student existences. I have said above that the coming of spring lifted our hearts and beckoned us hopefully onwards. How magically the spring changed the quiet Galway countryside! Our grounds were fairly well wooded. The chestnut trees were always the first to don their new spring raiment, their soft green leaves (as Jörgensen once put it) drooping like the fingers of a lady's green glove. The full-foliaged beeches, the red-twigged limes, the solid, gnarled oaks with their mosses, the slow rugged elms came in their turn greenly clad, each contributing their own share to the beauty of our world. And through the air, along the valley and by the apple orchard, the swallows came whistling, darting, gliding wheeling, speeding effortlessly. How enjoyable were these sights of spring!

It was pleasant to ramble along the Esker banks and come upon a fresh, pale-lemon cluster of primroses or find a wild rose bush covered in blossoms. All these sights heightened our delight with the new world of spring.

When the heat of the days increased and summer drew near, we went swimming in a little river a mile or two away from the college. The Australian students amongst us were expert swimmers. We tried to imitate them! The only triumph we had over them (indeed a very minor one) lay in our ability, when the cold weather came, to stay in the water much longer than they could. Accustomed to the warmer waters of their beaches at home, they used to turn forty shades of blue after a short dip in the chilly river.

Another memory lingering in my mind is that of the countryside seen from the Eskers (the long, level-topped hills in our grounds) on Christmas Eve. It was the custom of the people to place a lighted candle in the window of their homes, to show Mary and Joseph a warm welcome awaited them within. We students looked out on the dark countryside stretching far and wide below us. The gloom was broken here and there by the twinkling lights in the cottage windows. This was Christmas Eve! Anywhere in this countryside Mary and Joseph would receive a most hearty welcome! Each shining light cried out to them, "Cead Mile Failte!"

As students at times we had to put up with a lot of trouble. There were hard things to bear. It is not easy to forget them. There seemed to be an atmosphere of suspicion, spying and distrust around us. From the Rules of the Redemptorists, we knew we would be constantly weighed up and judged by those in authority over us. There were periodic special meetings of superiors and Professors: the subject matter, the agenda, the programme at these solemn gatherings was "the students" – singly and collectively. About each student every member at these sessions could have his say – and all under the cloak of secrecy! A student criticised or denigrated in any way knew nothing about it. He was in ignorance of it all, and of course got no chance of saying a word in his own defence. I am certain this kind of thing happens often in big business; but in a religious order, it belies much of the talk about charity and brotherly love.

There were times when we came up against austere and crushing authority. You could do nothing to help yourself. There were no courts of appeal! Higher superiors made it a point to always defend, protect, safeguard, and uphold the authority of the local superior. So when the crunch came, you kept your mouth shut and patiently waited till the storm and thunder died away in the distance.

I remember a large number of instances of what I am saying. I will relate just one of them here. I laugh at it all now, but I did not laugh when it happened, because the Professor responsible for what happened humiliated and hurt me very deeply.

Here is what occurred: I had written an essay in a kind of poetic springtime mood. Our essays were handed up to the Professor of English who read and corrected them in his room, and in the next class (without mentioning the student author's name) would comment on them one by one.

At the following week's class the Professor read out my entire essay in a mocking, jeering manner, saying among other things that the writer was foolishly trying to ape Fr Collier's style (Fr Collier was one of our highly imaginative, purple passage preachers). He read each sentence of the essay in a laughing, faltering, stumbling kind of way, and collocating words wrongly – and he made a joke of what I was saying in almost every sentence.

Now I have no doubt the essay was very imperfect, but it was a genuine effort on my part and I had taken much trouble with it. The Professor was quite in error to think I was aping Fr Collier or anyone else. My point is that he had no right or justification whatever in his deliberate effort to make the essay ridiculous. In fact, later in the day one of the cleverest students in the class, who did not join in the universal glee, told me, not knowing I had written it, that he thought the essay quite good. I felt miserable over it all: no one likes to be held up to ridicule. In the class I was very embarrassed, while the mockery and raillery went on around me.

There was nothing I could do about it. He had authority; I had none! He had rights; I was taught I had none! Higher superiors would take his part. I would be reprimanded for my want of humility. The injustice of what he had done would be ignored. So I kept my mouth shut. It had been a rough bit of treatment. I simply waited, knowing that "time and the hour run through the roughest day". There was a sequel to all the foregoing. A few days later I had to go to the room of this Professor over some permission I needed from him. He mentioned my essay.

"That was your essay I read out the other day!"

I agreed. I then told him firmly that I was not trying to ape Fr Collier's style. I said I wrote it in a certain mood. He was rather taken aback by this, for he knew I would not lie to him. He seemed to be at a loss what to say. I did not delay in his room.

When I was leaving, he said: "Anyway, it will do you good to get a knock! You never get any knocks!" This truly startled and shocked me. I left his room, dumbfounded. Here was a priest who could not see the madness of hurting someone for the sake of hurting him. I came away from him, thinking that, while God permits this kind of thing to happen, He certainly does not will it.

In my lifetime I have frequently observed that those who are hard on others get it hard themselves, sooner or later, and even in this world. The priest I have spoken of was severe on many others. Before he died, he went through a difficult time. He had few real friends amongst us. He had made it that way. He died alone – in a monastery in which over a dozen priests were living. He was a very distraught, pathetic case in his last months on earth. I pray for him! May he rest in peace.

My general memory of student days is one of strain and effort and monotonous study. As I have said, some of our teachers – through no fault of theirs – were really not qualified to teach their subjects. What we learned was picked up the hard way – by our own unremitting effort and with occasional help from older, abler students. Clever students made progress: weaker men floundered and staggered along as best they could: for them, life in the studendate was certainly no joke.

Our life was spartan in its austerity. Despite this, as I have already said, we young people enjoyed ourselves in various ways. It is impossible for young people to be utterly crushed: they will find some outlet somehow.

For example, we had exciting games of football and handball. The Rules of the Redemptorists forbade all games – golf, cricket, football! Name it, and it was forbidden. Then because the students obviously needed 'games', it was decided by a General Chapter in the early part of the twentieth century that the Latin word *ludus* – the word used in the Rules' prohibition, meant 'games of chance'. Therefore we were allowed *exercitia corporalia* – 'corporal exercises'. The games we played were permitted in virtue of this modern concession. It all smacks terribly of Phariseeism! It all screams "legalism" to our minds today! At the time we did not mind this however, so long as we could play the games we desired.

One day every month the priest in charge of us made a day's retreat – this meant he spent the day only in spiritual duties and prayer. It also meant that he did not come to our Common Room for our recreation. It was our custom to stage a 'shindy' that night among ourselves. 'Shindy' is not the correct word to describe our impromptu concerts, but it was the traditional word and we kept to it.

At these concerts my cousin, a student like myself, usually acted as compere. He was very light-hearted and merry: no-one enjoyed a joke more that he did. He loved these concerts. Normally he had to contribute an item himself, before he could in fairness ask others to do their bit. His item was always the same one: it never varied, and we all knew what it would be. It was an attempt at a song. The interesting point is that he had not a single musical note in his whole being – not even a semblance of a note!

So, behold him rising from his seat and beaming all round him, as he moved into the centre of the floor to give us his rendering of the old song, "The Three Crows"! It was painful to listen to him, very painful: so remote from music was his effort that it became funny. He knew quite well how dreadful it sounded! He was doing his bit to provide some amusement. We laughed heartily at the appalling noises he made. He stopped frequently to join in the laughter. We encouraged him verbally and by our applause. He persevered to the end – it was all very sporting of him.

Once, when I was helping him to 'sing' a part of the High Mass Chant, I reminded him to keep his eyes on the musical notes on the staff printed above the words.

"Watch the notes!" I exhorted him.

"Those black dots?"

"Yes, watch them as you are singing the words."

"I will do no such thing! They put me off!"

This unmusical compere organised our 'shindys'. Amusement replaced a musical hour! Fun was our purpose. No true singers were invited to entertain us. My own share in the shindy was an impromptu speech on some impossible theme, for example: "The Mayor of a seaside resort welcomes a firm of undertakers to the town in the holiday season" or "An inebriated chairman presides at a Pioneer meeting". It all created silly, innocent fun. How the students laughed and shouted and cheered. We were young and high-spirited. This shindy was one of our few opportunities to relax.

Occasionally at a shindy, I impersonated one of our teachers or one of the superiors – this was a dangerous act from many points of view! It was a performance however which always brought the house down. Later on I discovered that one or other of the students reported my displays back to the subjects of my impersonations. These were not amused. So I gave up the use of my 'gift', because it could hurt the feelings of my victims.

Another diversion we occasionally enjoyed was a visit to our part of the countryside by one of the most famous of Irish hunting packs, "The Galway Blazers". Finding a fox in Carnakelly Wood, the hounds often headed their quarry over our fields. It was fine excitement for us to see the fox streaking away and the hounds baying in hot pursuit. The huntsman reckoned our countryside to be difficult terrain, for it was not at all easy for them to keep up with the hounds. There was much wild, rocky country around us, with plenty of crevices, hillocks and hollows. Although the hounds usually pulled down their fox in open country, there were days when they succeeded only in marking him to ground.

Student days. How slowly they dragged along! We thought they would never end. We piled up memories, happy and unhappy! How frequent the spells of monotony and dullness! But the days, months, and years passed by. Our Ordination day came. We were now priests! Year by year, from that college in the West of Ireland we students – now priests – went out to the far corners of the world to spread the message of Christ. Today those of my time still alive are working in the Philippines, India, Australasia, New Zealand, Malaya, Brazil, the Leeward Islands. They are also to be found in Italy, England, the United States and Canada. Many have gone to their rest. Some have left the Redemptorists, but these were comparatively few. The general body have remained faithful to their vocation, their vows, their work in the vineyards of God.

A most interesting point arises here. Life in the Redemptorists in my time has been, until recently, austere and severe. Yet few of our number turned their back on their vocation. Desertion was a rare occurrence. In the last few years however it is not so! The life has been made easier but defection from our ranks has been happening frequently. We lived a hard life long ago – was that precisely the reason why we were able to take what candidates now will not accept? I feel we had a greater esteem for our vocation than young candidates nowadays. We were prepared to go through fire and water to preserve our vocation. Our hard way of life seemed to nourish this attitude in us! The very great rigour of our daily life seemed to steel us in trial and hardship!

When I was working in the Philippines, I often lived with Mill Hill priests. They used to express their amazement at the amount of work our missionaries could do in the Mill Hill parishes. Our energy – long hours in the confessional, strenuous hikes to distant villages and so on – surprised them. I have always explained this capacity for work by the fact that our life at home in the monasteries was rigid and severe to a degree that made the mission work seem easy and even pleasant.

## Ordination: Second Novitiate

All during our years as students, our star of guidance and hope was our future ordination to the priesthood. This meant everything to us. For that supreme day of our Ordination, we suffered and accepted everything. No doubt there were times we grumbled; but we never 'kicked' or rebelled or bore ill-will. Ordination was our horizon, our harbour. Once there, we felt we would be content: troubles would not matter.

On the 28 September 1930 there were five of us for Ordination. It was a happy day, happy for my parents, happy for my brothers and sisters, happy for my friends. We five felt rewarded and at peace.

After our Ordination, we did another year's studies and were then sent to Clonard Monastery, Belfast to do another six months' Novitiate – a "Second Novitiate", we called it. The aim of this Novitiate was primarily to revive our first Novitiate fervour, and secondarily, to prepare our sermons and lectures for our missionary work now due to begin.

There were six or seven of us in this Second Novitiate. Apart from our daily programme of spiritual duties and exercises, our main occupation was sermon writing. One morning each week at 10 o'clock, the priest who had charge of the Novitiate – a veteran missionary, who was given the title of Fr Prefect – advised us on the particular sermon we were to write. He would outline its aim, the plan we were to follow, and what sources we might find helpful in composing it. He would warn us against certain pitfalls and mistakes we might make in dealing with particular points in the sermon.

For the rest of the morning we would sit in our rooms, writing and rearranging our efforts. It was slow, trying work. We had to write about sixteen pages. The sermon had to be fashioned in accordance with a certain traditional schema, with three main divisions, viz, the exordium, the body of the sermon, the peroration. Within this structure, there were some minor sections which we were not allowed to set aside. Each sermon had to contain two or three stories or illustrations relevant to the chief points we wished to drive home. Finding these stories or illustrations was no easy matter. Most of the stories we knew had long since been worn thin through their frequent use by other preachers. Discovering fresh new stories was a problem. So also was the selection of new, apposite texts of Scripture. We were not idle – we lived laborious days. I found it congenial work, however, for it was personal. This was what we had come for! This was priest's work. This was one of our answers to the "Ad quid venisti?" ("Why are you here?") of the monk, St Bernard – a question he repeated to himself while he walked as a novice in the grey cloisters of the Cistercian monastery at Cîteaux. We had come to the monastery and to the priesthood to write sermons and to preach the Gospel of Christ.

When we had composed a 'masterpiece', we had to go by appointment to Fr Prefect's room and read our work aloud to him. He listened and corrected what we had done. He had seemingly no reluctance and no inhibitions about correcting us: when he found fault with our efforts, he had his say, bluntly and emphatically.

I remember writing sixteen pages of a sermon on "Prayer". I went as usual to his room by appointment to read it to him. The time he had set for me was 4.30 pm – a very drowsy, sleepy part of the day. I felt uneasy about the unsuitability of that somnolent hour. However, I had no option – he had decided the time, and I had to go. Perhaps he had some special reason, unknown to me, for fixing this time: perhaps he was going out later, perhaps he would have no other hour available for me. Anyhow I went along to his room at 4.30 pm. He bade me sit down and told me to start reading my sermon. The moment I saw him, I knew this was going to be a useless session, for he was already heavy and sleepy-looking. It was a close, warmish kind of afternoon; he was well on in years; and it was certainly not his hour for mental alertness or concentration. But what could I do?

And so I started to read, and read on steadily, paragraph by paragraph, page by page. After three or four pages of reading, I glanced covertly at him.

He had up till then passed no comment on what I had written. I knew this was not his way: normally his remarks fell in showers. I glanced at his face: his eyes were closed and his chest was rising and falling in slow, gentle, peaceful rhythm as he slept the deep sleep of the sleepy. Meanwhile, I read on. This was both a farce and waste of time but I read on, just to see what would happen.

As I was coming near the peroration of my 'masterpiece', he suddenly woke up. He took about a minute to get his bearings. I finished reading the sermon and looked at him enquiringly. He pursed his lips, looked at the floor, frowned and then stared at the window.

At last he found utterance. "Take it away, Fr Cummings!" he said gruffly. "It sins against all the rules St Alphonsus laid down for our sermons!"

This was a stiff remark from one who had not heard much of what I had written. I felt it was unfair and even untrue, but I could do nothing about it. I went back to my room.

I stood and looked through the sixteen pages which had cost me much effort and trouble. I recalled what I had just now heard: "It sins against all the rules laid down by our Founder, St Alphonsus." I did not agree! I was sure my work was imperfect, but at least the sermon structure was in accordance with St Alphonsus' ideas. However, the Fr Prefect's judgement would have to be followed. What point then would there be in keeping such a production? So, standing over the wastepaper basket – that grave of so many written gems of genius – I slowly and reluctantly tore in shreds my laborious sixteen-page effort.

Knowing my Fr Prefect, I guessed he got rid of me by damning the sermon in general terms! It also occurred to my mind that later in the week he might have second thoughts about my sermon – and possibly come to my room to subtly withdraw the harsh, sleepy indictment of a few days earlier.

And as I had guessed, so it happened! He came into my room a few days later, hands thrust deep in pockets, and went to gaze out of my window.

"Well, Fr Cummings?" he said in friendly manner, "What about a walk this afternoon?"

I agreed at once. All this was an ice-breaker, an overture, I knew. The real purpose of his business was yet to emerge. He came back to the middle of the room, stared at the floor, and then went back to my window to gaze out over the smoking chimneys of Cupar Street nearby. I remained silent. I could not, and certainly had no wish to help him in his mission of peace.

Finally, he turned to me and said, "By the way, what about that sermon of yours on Prayer?"

"I tore it up!" I replied quite flatly. He let out an exclamation and said in an excited, alarmed kind of voice, "Why did you do that?"

"You told me the other day it sinned against all the rules of St Alphonsus! What point would there be in keeping a sermon like that?"

He wriggled and he twisted, he twisted and he wriggled, as he endeavoured to explain away his condemnatory words. He stayed on the hook! I let him talk. I said nothing. He must have known in his heart he had been unfair to me, and that he had fallen down on his job.

I afterwards bore him no resentment. We had a very pleasant walk together that afternoon across the lovely green Castlereagh Hills on the other side of the city. He had served as an army chaplain with the British army in the Balkans during the First World War. As we walked along, he narrated some of his experiences on the River Stroma front, where the allied forces had fought bitter battles against the Bulgarians.

As I have said, I did not nurse any resentment against him in my heart. Life is too short and too precious to waste its fleeting moments in resentment. I think it is best, generally speaking, to overlook the unfairness and inconsiderateness of others. Nevertheless, one should not help the inconsiderate to practice their inconsideration.

If you can bear with another example of this same kind of thing, here it is. While I was still in the Second Novitiate, Fr McGouran, my cousin, who was then Bursar in St Malachy's College, invited me to dinner in the College. This same Fr Prefect, when giving me permission to accept the invitation, said, "Remember, you are not a first novice! Enjoy the evening with your cousin and do not be in too great a hurry to come back to the monastery!"

I took him at his word. I was not back in the monastery until about 8.30 pm – an early hour by present day C.Ss.R. standards, a latish hour by our standards in the days gone by. As I came up the main staircase, I met the Fr Rector of the monastery. He stopped when he saw me coming up towards him.

"Where were you?" he asked sharply, emphasising the word 'you', thus giving an intended edge to the question. I explained what Fr Prefect had told me. This did not satisfy him one bit. He meant to rebuke me and this was not going to put him off. He let me know very clearly that I was in the wrong for staying out till 8.30 pm.

"You should have been back for the 7.30 pm meditation!" he said in a surly kind of way as he dismissed me.

The root of this queer state of affairs was the fact that we second novices had two superiors – our Fr Prefect and the Fr Rector of the monastery. None of us seemed to know which of them could give what permissions. I think the Rector was offended because I had not consulted him in the first instance about my cousin's invitation. It was all very confusing.

As I left the Rector that evening on the stairway and went to my room, I felt quite frustrated. However I soon got over my frustration. I had then learned to take these things as they came. While accepting them and keeping my mouth shut, I knew in my heart however they were not meant to be part of religious life.

On our first Profession Day (the day on which we took vows of poverty, chastity, obedience for three years), we would sing: "Ecce quam bonum et incundum habitare fratres in unum" ("Behold how good and pleasant it is to dwell as brothers in unity"). I say not a word against this text of the Psalmist, but it is necessary to remember that there must be a unity of heart and will among the members of a Community if these words are to be verified. How often in my life in Religion these words have come back to me in most awful mockery! So often have I seen and explained the rows and arguments and squabbles and unfairness that seem to be essential pieces in the jigsaw of life – even religious life in a monastery. The Psalmist's words express an ideal state of affairs, but certainly not the real everyday life of religious.

In our religious lives in the monastery, there are unpleasant things to bear. This happens, as we all know, in every walk of life, from the lowest and humblest road-sweeper to the most well-groomed, opulent business magnate or potentate. We all have to take things as they come. I think the best plan is to keep going forwards and to do whatever good you can by word, deed, or example to as many as possible along the road of life – that is the one wise way of using the few years God grants us here on earth. Brighten someone else's life as you go through the day! It is indeed better to light a candle than to sit cursing the darkness. I have always loved those lines of the Australian poet, Adam Lindsay Gordon, from his poem, "Ye Weary Wayfarer":

"Life is mostly froth and bubble,
Two things stand like stone:
Kindness in another's trouble –
Courage in your own!"

If I have unpleasant memories of those Second Novitiate days, I have also many pleasant ones. For example, it was very enjoyable to offer Mass in our public church at Clonard, because my parents were nearly always present at it. This was some repayment to them for all they had done for me. Mother used to kneel each morning in the benches before the Sacred Heart altar. So, whenever possible, I used to say Mass at that altar. We priests had no choice of altars for Mass. One Father marked us each day for a particular altar. He had the authority, as Prefect of the Church, to do this. We had to obey his arrangements. I always felt pleased when I saw he had marked me for the Sacred Heart altar.

One day, speaking to Mother, I suggested I should give her Holy Communion at that altar. She would not agree: it would be unusual; people would notice it; she would be attracting attention and giving cause for gossip. So that was that!

During the six months of the Second Novitiate, I worked hard at writing sermons. When it came to an end, I had written about twenty sermons and about twelve or fourteen morning instructions. These had all been censored and approved by Fr Prefect. So I now felt fairly well equipped for my future mission work.

When we had finished the Second Novitiate, we awaited our appointments to various fields of work. I was ill in bed with a dose of influenza when a letter came to me from Fr Provincial appointing me to the mission work in the Philippine Islands – sixteen thousand miles away! I did not mind one bit! Looking back now, I feel I did not sufficiently appreciate how sore a sacrifice this remote appointment was for my parents. In those days the length of our assignment to the Philippine Mission was indeterminate: I could be left there for anything up to twenty years! My parents, knowing this fact, possibly thought they would never see me again. This I did not realise at the time – but I was young, and eager to take up my work. The excitement and novelty of it all, after my secluded, repressed life of eight years in our strict monasteries, led me to accept my appointment with a ready cheerfulness bordering on enthusiasm. I little knew what lay before me.

## The Philippines

Four other priests went with me on that long, sixteen thousand mile journey to the Philippine Islands. We left from Belfast on the cross-channel boat to Liverpool. My parents and family came on board with me to see me off. It was far from being a gay occasion for them all. No doubt they remembered my Redemptorist uncle, who had been posted to Australia many years previously. He had gone out there, not expecting to return to his native land. (Before he left Ireland, he had visited my Mother. She was very devoted to him. He told her that perhaps he would never be back in Ireland. At which news she wept. Whereupon the good man bluntly said he would go into one of the other rooms and there read his Breviary until she was done weeping, and then they could continue their farewell chat!)

With many farewells and much handshaking, we said good-bye to Belfast and our native land. I stood on the deck, watching the city lights slowly fade away from our sight.

Next morning we arrived in Liverpool. We went on at once to London. There was no unnecessary stopping: our superiors had arranged our timetable and in wishing us "Godspeed", had done their best to cooperate with Providence in the matter. We had in fact very little say about what we were to see or do en route to our mission in the East. Boats and trams had all been fixed for us. Perhaps it was the best arrangement: for among ourselves, we might not have agreed on any plans of travel.

From London we went to Harwich and there boarded a steamer for Rotterdam. The journey across the dreary, tossing wastes of the North Sea remains in my memory. I then thought how on those grey waters England's Navy, in the Battle of Jutland, had suffered the greatest blow in its history. Many a British sailor had found his last resting place in this sea. These waters had been the combat area of what were once the two most powerful navies in the world.

It was a cold, blustery night. As the steamer beat its way onwards, the wind rose to a gale. Fr Joy and I stood together, sheltering on the lee side of the ship's top deck. A year or two previously, he had been teaching me Scripture and Hebrew. We were on friendly terms, without being friends. Now we stood huddled together on this ship, companions in the new loneliness and gloom arising from our cutting all our human roots at home. The boat was pitching and rolling, so we fortified ourselves against the seasickness with some spirits a wise relation had thoughtfully given me. We were both in need of the stimulant.

Arriving in Rotterdam, we stayed a few days there with our own Redemptorist priests in one of our monasteries. They were kindly, hospitable men. One of them showed us around Rotterdam. The city – with its miles of quays, its bewildering tangle of ships, its slow, heavily-built dockers, its cycle-riding populace (in Rotterdam for the first time I saw a nun riding a bicycle!) and its network of canals – was my first encounter with the great big world outside the British Isles.

In our monastery in the city, I received my first continental shock: I saw all the Dutch Fathers smoking cigars after dinner. In those days this would not have been allowed in the Irish Province of the Redemptorists. Things have changed a lot since then. Now amongst us, the non-smoker is the exception.

In the same monastery the Brother whose duty it was to answer the doorbell had a small room or office beside the main door. To open the front door, he pulled a connecting chain from the hatch where he spoke to his callers. This arrangement saved him the long walk which our Irish Brothers have to do when answering the door in any of our Irish houses. In our Dundalk monastery, for example, the Brother has to walk about thirty or forty yards down a corridor each time he goes to answer the door. In a given day, he might have to answer the door bell twenty or thirty times – each time requiring a walk up and down the corridor. To fulfil the requests or requirements of a particular caller might entail four corridor trips. Thirty or forty yards is not a great distance, but when that distance is walked regularly for about sixteen hours a day, even a sturdy body will grow weary. Our door Brothers had always been men well on in years: their maturity was supposed to give them the reserve and prudence demanded by their work. These older men felt the length of the corridors and the long hours.

I think of a somewhat similar case in army life: a Lee-Enfield rifle is a reasonable weight for a strong young soldier to carry; but, if he has to carry it right through the day, he feels its weight more keenly, no matter how strong he may be. I have never forgotten that admirable arrangement in Rotterdam: it was thoughtful and efficient.

One more point I add here: people who call at a monastery should remember the distance the Brother may have to traverse before reaching the door. Many callers become at once impatient if the door is not opened almost immediately after they ring the doorbell. Of course, children are the worst offenders on this score: they expect to see the door opened almost as soon as they ring the bell. Grown-ups, however, are often equally impatient – and they should know better.

While one of our Dutch Fathers was showing us around the city of Rotterdam, we passed a street vendor who was loudly shouting about his wares. I asked the Dutch Father what the man was saying. Now, we did not speak Dutch and the Father did not speak English, so our medium of communication was Latin. When I asked him in Latin what the man was shouting, he stopped on the street, listened to the man, frowned, shook his head, and turning to me said just one word in Latin, "Nescio" – "I don't know"! Which incident, coupled with my own experience in the streets of Irish towns and cities, led me to think that too many street vendors concentrate on vocal noise rather than on the distinct, articulate communication of the message.

Our few interesting days in Holland soon passed. At night, when our visit was ended, we went down to the docks and boarded our vessel for the East. The ship was one of the Norddeutscher Lloyd Line boats. She was named *Coblenz*: a passenger-cum-cargo vessel of about ten thousand tons, bound for Manila and Japan.

That same night, the ship steamed out of Rotterdam. Fr Jack Ryan and I shared a cabin. We were comfortably placed. We slept soundly during our first night aboard, for we were both tired after all our touring and sightseeing in the city.

When we had finished saying Mass that first morning, we went on deck. It was a grey, misty morning. Visibility was poor and there was not a sight of land – but I knew we were well down the English Channel, somewhere between Sussex and the coast of France. We were passing through waters to which I would return many years later, during the World War II invasion of Normandy.

I walked the deck alone, looking around me at the cold, leaden sea, moving beneath us restlessly, tipped here and there with foam. I noted the colourless sky, the empty sea, the steady hum of the ship's engines, and the many white seagulls gliding along effortlessly, up and down, on unmoving wings, beside us.

The ship was clean and tidy. As the days passed and we got to know its layout, we felt more at home. The food was good. And young as we were, with healthy appetites we put on a sound performance at every meal. To the passengers aboard the amusements provided were diverting. To our small group the deck games particularly were enjoyable to watch. We would have very much liked to take part in them, but never dared to volunteer. Nowadays this seems absurd, but for us, then, it was quite in line with our daily practice of living apart from the world. You must realise that this sea journey was the very first occasion in our lives since entering the priesthood when we were living amongst ordinary people. We were all in our mid-twenties, we were grown-up, in a certain fashion we were educated – and yet we now felt ill at ease. We watched and studied the people around us far more than they studied us.

It was all so strange and novel to us, who had been so long and so carefully segregated, so bound by rules not to mix with people. We were now thrown into this situation, untutored in the common human ways of ordinary adult society.

Needless to say, we kept ourselves to ourselves; needless to say, we were unbelievably slow to speak to anyone or to make friends. We were six weeks on board that ship and at the end of the voyage we did not really know more than a few fellow passengers. You can now understand why we took part in none of the games played by the other passengers. We, who were meant now to work among human beings, were ourselves somewhat less than human.

It was not our fault: we were in no way to be blamed – we were the faithful, standard products of a system.

Our first port of call was Barcelona. There we were met by some of our priests of the Spanish Province. They brought us to their monastery and showed us every kindness during our stay there. My memories of Barcelona are of wide streets, a burning hot sun, the freakish structure of the Church of the Holy Family, and the panorama of the city and deep, deep blue expanses of the Mediterranean lying beneath us, as we stood on the summit of the Tibidabo mountain.

Meals in our monastery there were unusual: at breakfast, for instance, we were offered raw, uncooked bacon. Wine appeared on the table at dinner and "supper". At home, except on Feast Days or a special occasion, we were not given wine at meals.

Some of the Fathers and Brothers who showed us such hospitality in that Barcelona monastery were put to death a few years later by the Spanish Communist army in the Civil War. In that war the monastery in which we had stayed was burned to the ground.

Our next port of call was Genoa. No sooner had our ship tied up there than a swarm of officials and hawkers came aboard. Also came a small tubby little gentleman, a voluble talker in broken English, who with much bowing and gesticulating, declared himself to be the very person to guide us around the sights of Genoa. We reached agreement on his charges and hired him for the entire afternoon.

He brought us on a grand tour. Up and down the hilly streets of Genoa we walked, rode on trams, and sauntered. He brought us to historical houses associated with Christopher Columbus – perhaps he thought we were Americans. He also guided us through the work-shops of some of the city's jewellers. There we watched men and women engaged at filigree work. How delicate and finely wrought were some of the pieces they showed us! In such places all you needed was tons of money – which we did not have. I fear we were very, very unsatisfactory visitors.

Any guidebook can tell you much more about the principal sights of Genoa than I can. My recollections are that the city was irregular and uneven, the trams were noisy and grinding, and the roads and streets all seemed to fall away to the harbour. The famous Campo Santo cemetery, with its unusual array of monuments sculptured in Carrara marble, alone impressed me.

We went by tram to the cemetery. Sitting opposite me, beside his mother, was a young Italian priest. Obviously, like myself, he was but recently ordained. As I took stock of him, engrossed in reading his breviary, I thought, "Here is one who one day may be Pope!" After this momentous consideration, I looked at him again with a new interest. I have often wondered what his career was afterwards. Perhaps, as I write, he is on his way to the Triple Tiara of the Papacy.

From Genoa we sailed to Benghazi on the north coast of Africa. Here we took aboard in steerage about fifty or sixty Mohammedan pilgrims bound for Mecca. We watched them coming out to our ship in small launches. On arrival at our starboard side, these men and women, swathed in voluminous white robes, came clambering perilously from tossing launches onto a platform at the bottom of a ship's ladder. As they reached the deck, they all began some wailing kind of chant. We listened to their cries in astonishment. Some of the German sailors began to imitate them. Suddenly, however, our small martinet of a captain appeared from nowhere and, with one fierce roar, cleared them all from the ship's rail and sent them about their business.

Once aboard, the pilgrims soon settled down. Day by day the menfolk gathered on one of the cargo hatches. There they squatted in a semi-circle around their teacher, listening attentively to his expositions of the Koran and putting questions to him. At their communal prayers the whole group chanted a refrain, as we ourselves do in the responses in the Catholic litanies. What they chanted sounded to my ears like this: "La ilaha illah Allah", which I am told means: "There is no God but God".

At specified times during the day, the men would individually face towards Mecca, kneel down, bow low several times, and recite their prayers. This is all familiar knowledge to us, but what impressed me mightily was this – these Mohammedans had no human reserve whatsoever. Watched and observed by the ship's passengers or crew, solitary or stared at by scores of 'infidels', they were bent on the daily performance of their religious duties, and they would fulfil them. Many of us Catholics and Christians would be very slow and reluctant to act as they did. Yet the Mohammedans' behaviour somehow did not repel or irritate the onlooker. One's reaction was: "I would not do what they are doing, but I admire their courage and sincerity!" I feel that we Catholics are often too timid, too hesitant and shy about the public performance of our religious practices. How many join their hands properly going or coming from Holy Communion? How many never go round the Stations of the Cross, lest others see them so engaged?

From our anchorage, Benghazi (where we had collected our pilgrims) looked a poor, forsaken spot. We could see only a low line of palm trees, a few white houses huddled together, and, along the shore, the biscuit-coloured sands stretching away vaguely to the farthest distance. Later, in World War II, the town became the scene of some very fierce fighting, and the port would become a precious asset to the warring armies.

How time and circumstances change the value and importance of places as well as of men! Look at Saudi Arabia! Not so long ago it was deemed too poor to be snapped up by the big colonising nations – it was thought to contain only sand. None of the great Powers coveted those sands. But now they do! Now those sands have become the Kingdom of Black Gold! The rich oil-wells have made those sandy countries the envy of the world. The Arab rulers live there now in a wealthy splendour rivalling Solomon in all his glory.

Alexandria was our next port of call. We then sailed through the Suez Canal. On our way through the Canal, we passed El Kantara, where the Holy Family crossed from Palestine into Egypt. There I looked around with interest. What a dreary, monotonous scene it was! Miles of sand and endless stretches of arid desert, dotted here and there with scrub and rock. There was nothing to please the eye or win the heart of the beholder.

At Jiddah, the port for Mecca, we bade farewell to our Mohammedan pilgrims. As we approached the port, they gathered along the rail of the ship to gaze at the starting point of the last stage of their journey to the Prophet's shrine.

How does one explain their extraordinary loyalty to Mohammed? How does one account for their continued devotion to this man who died so many centuries ago? I wonder, does their religion attract the young people nowadays in Mohammedan countries? I saw no young folk among the pilgrims on our ship. Has modern life and especially modern communications at last weakened the hold of Mohammedanism on the Eastern nations which have hitherto clung to it tenaciously?

Colombo, Singapore, Manila were our last three ports of call. In these places nothing worth recalling happened to us, except on our one night in Singapore. We had gone into the city to see around us and to get away from the ship for even a little while. On our way back in the tram, the Malayan bus conductor tried to cheat me in the change due to me after paying our fares. I guessed somehow that he was cheating me. I was not well versed in Singapore coinage; but I was not going to allow him to hoodwink me. So I immediately protested and demanded the correct change. He threw his head back, burst out laughing, and gave me what was due. No one in his right mind will accept cheating! On our arrival at Manila, some of our Australian Fathers met us. In a shed at the docks we spent a tedious hour getting all our belongings safely through the Customs. Finally all our luggage had been examined and passed, and with great relief we drove out to our monastery at Baclaran on the shores of Manila Bay.

I was weary, so that first night in the islands I slept well. At dawn I awakened to the bedlam of a multitude of crowing cocks. Every native house around us seemed to have a number of these cocks. They were all screeching their best.

In the cool of the late afternoon of my first day in the islands, Fr Frean and I went for a walk along the shores of Manila Bay. How strange and alien to my eyes was this Eastern environment – the nipa palm huts, the penny-brown, bare-footed Filipinos, the ring-barked palm trees along the sand banks, the bamboo groves so dense and impassable.

Many children were playing here and there on the hardened smooth soil which served as a thoroughfare between the houses. With some astonishment I paused to watch some of them playing a game similar to that of the hopscotch played by children at home. Elsewhere in the Islands I later saw Filipino children playing 'Jacks' with small stones.

Fr Vincent McNabb OP used to say that children are often inspired in what they say and what they do. I have often thought that the children's angels teach them and remind them of the games to play in due season. The Lord's Providence is often most marked in what attracts the least attention, as in this example, viz, the recurring seasons and the recurring corresponding games which children play.

As Fr Frean and I came to an empty piece of ground above the quiet shore, we found a mimosa plant – the first I had ever seen growing. It is not an uncommon plant in the Philippines: I was to see many of them in subsequent months. It is an odd plant! When you touch its leaves, they shrink and fold up like daisies in the evening. The leaves must be hypersensitive. Ever since seeing that first mimosa, I have often likened myself to it. As a child I was highly sensitive. It was a drawback which remained with me for years. I suppose I still am sensitive – but not to the same degree. Years ago all snubs, cutting remarks, insults, blunt rebukes used to make me wince and shrink into myself. Here, I think, is one of the reasons why I am, and always have been, quite happy and contented in my own company.

Apparently in the old days at Oxford in the nineteenth century, one of the Dons met Newman out walking by himself, bowed to him, and said gently, "Never less alone than when alone!" He spoke it in Latin: "Nunquam minus solus quam solus!" How neatly the Latin language expresses it. I think, however, that the English phrasing of it is equally terse and forceful.

All my life long I have been happy with my own mind, thoughts, and interests. In this lies a selfishness: I hope I have not yielded to that vice. Experience and the passing of the years have taught me to think of the troubles of others and to be less mimosa-like in my relations with them. My own sensitivity has led me to have consideration for the feelings of others and never unnecessarily to wound or hurt them.

The mimosa plant Fr Frean and I saw on the shore of Manila Bay has led me into the foregoing digression: I will return to my narrative of my first walk in the Philippines. As Fr Frean and I walked back to the monastery, the sun was setting. Manila Bay was ablaze with colour reflected from the crimson sky. The very houses and trees were bathed in a crimson glow, which grew fainter and fainter as the sun slowly dipped into the China Sea. For the first time I was now witnessing – and regretting – the so swift passing of twilight and sunset in the East. Sunsets in the Philippines are glorious; but as elsewhere, their quick arrival and departure leave one with a feeling of sadness. They are a passing glory one would hold for ever: a happy picture fading before one's eyes, a very dear friend waving farewell.

Little did Fr Frean and I think as we returned from our walk that the shore we had tramped, the quiet bay, and the silent, tree-clad hills on the Guadalcanal arm of the bay, would in less than ten years become a battleground of blood and death. In World War II the Japanese fought Filipinos and Americans over every section of this calm scene, turning it into a maelstrom of death and destruction. The names of Cavite, Guadalcanal, and Manila Bay will figure forever on the pages of the world's history of wars.

I stayed a few days in our house at Baclaran. While there I somehow contracted dengue fever and had to go to hospital for a few weeks. When still convalescent, yet in rather a weakened state, I set sail in the SS *Vizcaya* for the town of Iloilo, the capital of the island of Panay in the Central Philippines.

Soon after my arrival there, I started in earnest to learn the local dialect of the Visayan language. The only grammar book available had been compiled by a Baptist missionary from a neighbouring American college. It gave us some inkling of the structure and style of the language, but it did not resolve many of our difficulties. It then happened that some notes on Visayan grammar, written by Fr John Kawfmann of the Mill Hill Fathers, came our way. These were very helpful. In those, my salad days, I could learn with fair speed. Soon I had a moderate grasp of the language's basic grammar. Two further difficulties yet remained: one was to gather an adequate vocabulary; the other, to distinguish words and phrases when Filipinos spoke to me. Time was needed to overcome these difficulties – it could not be done overnight.

To assist me in my language efforts, I was sent to a town called Janiway, situated about twenty-five miles from Iloilo in the hinterland of Panay Island. There, as a guest of the parish priest, Fr Ciriaco Serrano, I was to acquire a spoken knowledge of the language.

The priest's house in the town was formerly the residence ("convent" in Spanish) of the Spanish Friars who worked on the Islands in the days before the Filipino revolt against Spain at the beginning of the century. Its many rooms were spacious. The ceilings were lofty, the floors of polished broad boards of a Filipino wood akin to mahogany. I had a large room to myself. In one corner was my bed, shrouded in the white gauze of a mosquito net; over near the shell-windowed shutters I kept my wash basin and towels; in the centre of the wide shining floor was a small round table. At this table, morning after morning, I sat studying my notes and my lists of new words.

In the afternoon and evening I used to go out to the town plaza in front of the church and watch the children at play. I used to speak to them – at first, brokenly and haltingly. I asked them the names of various things around me. By dint of saying, "Anano ina?" ("What is it?"), and "Liwat na ina" ("Say that again!"), I got them to teach me new words and phrases. I listened to them at their play. I gathered them around me and won their attention and friendship by some simple sleight-of-hand tricks and also by gifts of religious medals and badges. They were quite unaware they were teaching me. After a session with them, I would retire to my room and write down all I had learned. I must confess that the children were the most efficient instructors: they were patient, articulate, and very good-humoured.

Thus gradually, *peu à peu*, I secured the desired working knowledge of the language. Next, I timidly began to preach short sermons in the language, and hear the people's confessions. The sermons gave me much trouble at first. I would write out the discourse, first in simple English, then in Visaya, and then bring my effort to one of the teachers in the school to correct it for me. Next, I learned it by heart, and thus prepared, I mounted the towering pulpit in the old Spanish church beside us during one of two of the Sunday Masses and did my best to preach my message to the assembled people. I now wonder did they understand much of what I said!

As the days passed by, I began to make friends among the people of the town. I found the townsfolk well-mannered and very friendly. Those with whom I came in contact were invariably kind to me. In my mind's eye they come up before me as I write these lines – I wonder how many of them have survived the Japanese invasion of their country and the years since then. Good friends they were, warm-hearted and sincere – to know them was to love them.

One special friend of mine was an engineer named Polycarp Fabian. He was an excellent Catholic, very intelligent, a man of most upright character. He used to come to the *convento* in the evenings to have a chat with me. I need hardly say that our conversation was in English, which he spoke accurately and fluently. Sometimes in the cool of the evening we would walk together in the town plaza. He helped me quite a lot in my study of the language. I used to consult him about new words which baffled me.

One morning my friend came to ask me to offer a Mass for his brother. Concerning this brother, he told me the following strange story: "When I qualified as an engineer at Manila University, I arranged with my brother that he should do the same course I had done. Out of my own earnings, I would pay his university fees and his expenses. He attended the university, but he did little or no study. He wasted my money. He failed one examination after another. I refused then to go on helping him. I could not afford to do so: I needed the money he was wasting. He left the university and emigrated to the United States of America. All that I now tell you happened a number of years ago. He never wrote a line to me. I lost touch with him completely.

"So that was the situation up to a few weeks ago. Then one night I had a most vivid dream about him. I dreamt I saw him lying on a bed. To my horror the bed was covered in blood. This dream upset me – I felt worried about him. For some days I wondered what I could do to get news about him. I finally decided to contact the American police. I wrote to the police in Los Angeles, giving them all the information I thought might help them in tracing him. That was a couple of months ago. Since then I heard not a word from them – until this morning when I received this letter."

As he said these words, Polycarp handed me a letter to read. It was from the police department in Dallas, Texas. In it the police stated that they had traced his brother. He had been working in that area. They regretted to inform Mr Fabian that on a certain night some time ago his brother's room was entered and, as he lay sleeping, he was murdered. Even now, I well remember the last sentence of this letter: "From evidence available, it is clear that robbery was the motive of the killer."

"So now, Father," said Polycarp to me sadly, "I want you to offer Mass for the repose of his soul!" Apparently God uses dreams when necessary. Thus it was he helped St Joseph on several occasions. So also did he speak to St Peter, Pilate's wife, and many others. Polycarp Fabian, I believe, was informed, in his dream, of his brother's need.

On this subject, a few weeks ago my cousin, Fr Bobby Quinn, wrote the following to me:

"I read the Death Notice of Fr Tom Loughnane while I was preaching a mission in County Roscommon. He had died on 29 April. On the morning of 30 April I had a strange dream, in which I saw Father Tom. His face was thin, long and yellow, with a peculiar white ash like that of turf ashes on one side. His body seemed to be clothed in a sort of dark, smoky vapour. I knew instantly he was dead. I was surprised to hear myself question him: "In the name of Jesus Christ, who are you?"

He looked at me, as if confused. I put the question to him a second time, and then he answered in a low voice, "Tom Loughnane". He replied to my second question, which I had in mind but had not put into words, by saying, "I got a short Purgatory."

On hearing this, I felt delighted and then asked, "Could you give me some helpful advice?" He answered, "Be attentive to work and to Confession!"

Soon after this, I awoke. I looked at the alarm clock and saw it was 5.15 am I was in no way frightened. Thinking over his advice, I realised it was very sane and logical. The part about Confession could apply to the making and also the hearing of confessions..."

My cousin was reluctant to talk to others about his dream. I accept it as a message to us from a priest and confrère, who was a good friend of us both. Between my cousin and myself, we were able to arrange to say Mass for the repose of that good priest's soul.

And now to resume my story of my days in Janiway. There were close on twenty thousand people living in the parish. I was the only white man among them. My presence soon became known. The people would come to me with their business if it happened that Padre Ciriaco, the Parish Priest, was absent.

One day, when Fr Ciriaco was away in Iloilo, I had to go on a sick call. The men who came for me brought with them a kind of *sedia gestatoria*, the ceremonial throne used to carry a Pope from place to place, made from fibres and stout pieces of bamboo. They told me it was the custom to carry the priest shoulder-high on this chair to the house of the sick person. I instantly shrank from this proposal. I said I would have none of it. I told the men quite firmly I would prefer to walk to the house, no matter how distant it might be. So, off we started, all walking together up into the hills. I attended the sick person and walked back alone to the *convento*.

Meanwhile the parish priest had returned. He had been told what had happened and how I had declined the offer of the *sedia gestatoria*. From one of the *convento* windows, he saw me walking back across the plaza. When I mounted the stairs, he was waiting for me. He attacked me verbally for what I had done. I had set aside the long-standing custom of the priest being carried on sick calls. What would happen when I left Janiway? He would have to attend all the sick calls on foot, no matter how far away they were; no matter how difficult the trail in the mountains! Why did I walk? Did the men not offer to carry me? So it went on, until he got tired. I said nothing to incense him: it was an instance of "least said, soonest mended". Later on he calmed down somewhat. Even though he went "off the boil" – like a kettle taken off the fire – he continued to seethe and murmur to himself for the rest of the day. Some days passed by before he showed me any signs of making the peace!

And so the first few months elapsed. I now had a fair grasp of the language and could speak it with reasonable fluency. A letter came for me one morning, telling me to return to the monastery at Iloilo. My days of preparation for the missions were ended. Up till this point in my life, I had been occupied with study! Now I was to begin my life's work. That was some forty years ago now. Only one of the priests with whom I then worked is alive today. The others have all gone into eternity.

Soon after my return from Janiway, I was sent on my first mission. The slow country train brought me to a station a mile from the town where the mission was taking place. I left my bag with my belongings at the station and walked out to the town. The night session of the mission was in progress when I arrived. To my astonishment I saw that the church, large though it was, was filled with people.

When the session was ended, I met the Fathers. They gave me a warm welcome. They explained the work and the circumstances of the mission. Until that very night the attendance had been rather slack. Why then had there been such a sudden improvement in the attendance? Fr Jack Scanlan claimed that Our Blessed Lady had attracted the people – for this was the special night of the mission devoted to Our Lady, the Madonna! "As usual," concluded Fr Scanlan, "she has brought them along to the church!"

Because of certain unmentionable little creatures who waged war on me, I slept very little that night. For the second night, however, one of the Fathers, who was immune to their attacks, was kind enough to swap beds with me. On subsequent missions I learned how to use petrol or paraffin to repel and defeat these bug invaders before the night began. This meant treating the cane interlacing of the bed, the legs of the bed, and the corners and seams of the pillows. Such knowledge gained was of more practical value to me than the paradigms of Hebrew, or other horrors, over which I had spent many grinding hours during my student days!

Thus was I launched on my first missionary task in the Islands. Day by day I heard Confessions, took my turn at preaching, and tried to play my part in any work to be done. The older Fathers were there to advise me and show me the best methods of doing my work. To my many questions, they readily supplied the answers. But, as in other lines of work, there remained much I had still to learn from my own experience.

The mission lasted three weeks. I then went home with the others for a short rest. One week at home (that is, from Monday night until Saturday morning) soon passed, and then we were off again to another mission in a different part of Panay Island. I was happy and contented in my work. I was twenty-five years of age, active, enthusiastic, and eager to do as much good as I could. While that was true, I still found some of the missions very demanding. We gave a mission in Pototan which I will never forget. Nowhere else have I worked so hard as I did there.

Pototan had about three or four thousand inhabitants, with its outlying villages surely trebling that number. Four of us priests were detailed to preach this mission. Each night sermon of the mission lasted about forty minutes. Yet the preaching of the sermons was not the really difficult part of the work. What wore us down was the daily seven hour stints of confessional work – except on Sundays. This confessional work went on for three weeks. It must be remembered that we did all our work in the native language. Frequently we had to instruct a penitent in the rudiments of the Faith. Doing this for penitents for two hours – quietly taking each one and helping him or her to make a happy confession bringing peace – was tiring work. Seven full hours of it in one day was however far more tiring. What do you think our state was when we had to keep this up for three weeks?

I remember one night in particular. We had finished the work of the day. After our evening meal we went out as usual to the town plaza in front of the church, and sat down there for a while before going to bed. I was utterly exhausted. As we were sitting there silently, I turned to Fr Scanlan beside me and said wearily, "Fr Jack, if I do not talk, please do not mind! I am not in a sulky mood – I am just too tired to speak!" He burst out laughing: he understood. I am sure he felt as tired as I did, but he was able to summon up enough energy to laugh – I could not even do that much! Of course he was older and much more experienced than I was – perhaps he was inured to the work. Down through the years, I have hit some rough spots of work, but never was I more exhausted than during that famous Pototan mission.

Now I see our mistake in the way we worked. We should have instructed the penitents in groups as they came along; we should have elicited from them in groups the necessary acts of acceptance in points of religious teaching! Had we done so, I might not have needed to have made that strange apology to Fr Jack Scanlan on the plaza.

I would like to say a word here about our technique of giving mission in the Philippines in those now distant days. We journeyed to the parish concerned by train, bus, or boat. We set out on Saturday morning, with sermons at all the public Masses in the church. In these first sermons we strongly urged the people to come to the mission, pointing out the graces God would give them during it. At the same time, we also announced the mission programme for the week.

Then, on the Monday, we would divide the entire area of the parish into three or four sessions, according to the number of priests giving the mission. With a list of the villages – or *barrios* – in our own section, and a Filipino boy to guide us, each of us started off to visit these *barrios*. A parish in the country parts of the Philippines might have twenty to forty *barrios* in its outlying districts.

When saying Mass or preaching or officiating at baptisms or marriages, we were obliged by our Redemptorist Rule to wear the black habit or gown of the Order, but for this hike to the villages, we were allowed to wear a white habit. With us we brought a thermos flask of coffee or lemonade with some

Spanish red wine and a few sandwiches. The day lay before us: we had seven or eight hours in which to complete our task.

The day's work was strenuous but not unpleasant. On arriving in a village I summoned the people by striking a metal bar or tube hanging from a tree beside the little village chapel. I waited there: I knew the people would know the priest had arrived and wanted to speak to them. They would come at once. As they arrived at the chapel they would greet me, saying, "Buenas dias, Padre! Maayong adlaw Maayo ang imong pagabut!" – "Good day, Father! Your coming to us is good!" This was their way of saying welcome.

As they assembled in the little chapel, they stood around or squatted on the dry, hard-baked ground. They were rather excited – for in their quiet village lives, this visit of a priest was a very interesting event. While they awaited my talk, they watched all that was happening. We had been taught to speak slowly and distinctly to them. We had been warned to use simple, clear words, and to make sure they understood our message and the purpose of our visit. Bearing these points in mind I would explain who we were. I would tell them their Bishop had sent us to help their parish priest (we always referred to him by name). We would give them a mission. And now their parish priest had asked us to visit them and invite them to come to the mission. I then explained the purpose of our mission and what happened during it. So that during the mission we would marry the couples who wished to marry, and we would baptise any child whose parents desired baptism. We therefore invited and urged them all to come and hear our sermons, make their Confessions, and receive Holy Communion. The mission was a time of grace, and God would speak to their hearts and help them. I would then tell them the times of the Masses and the hours for hearing their Confessions, the time of the evening services, and so on.

The people listened attentively. In almost every instance, they gave us a friendly welcome. Our visits to the villages did immense good. They encouraged the people to come to hear our sermons and to follow the advice we gave them on living holy lives.

At the end of the long day's hike, we would arrive back at the priest's house, weary but happy about the work done. We sat down to a meal. Over this repast we would compare notes and relate our experiences of the day's hiking. We found usually that we had managed to contact almost the entire parish: we had made the mission, its work and its benefits known to the people. Those, who had neither seen nor heard us, would be informed by those who had met us along the trails and in the villages.

In the few weeks that followed the fruit of our visits to the villages was gathered in the church. Sometimes the people walked ten or twelve miles to the mission. They would often camp on the town plaza for a few days, attending the Masses and going to Confession and Communion.

We all knew that if the mission was to be a success, this work of visiting the villages had to be done. So therefore, wherever we went to give a mission we "hiked the *barrios*" – ie, travelled on foot through the villages. If this hiking had been done thoroughly, you could count on a huge attendance and a sincere enthusiasm at the mission. The people would come; the church would be filled; the spiritual life of the parish would be deepened and strengthened. The hiking was well worthwhile.

Sometimes though it was very tiring: if one had to hike through hilly or mountainous districts, one felt very weary at the end of the day. I recall one mission in North West Panay in the Antique country, where when hiking the *barrios*, I had to tramp through soft, yielding sand along the foothills of the mountains. I was very tired by the time I came to this sand, and my progress through it was as slow as it was trying. I sank up to my ankles at every step; I did not lift my feet, I dragged them out before moving a pace forward. It was a day of blazing sun: perspiration gummed up my spectacles and made me most uncomfortable. I thought of a passage in the life of St Thérèse of Lisieux. During the saint's last months on earth, when she was exceedingly weak, she was seen trying to walk in the garden. The effort obviously cost her much pain. A sister said to her, "You should sit down and rest, instead of trying to walk about."

"It costs me a lot to do this now," replied the saint, "but I think of some missionary far away on the missions, exhausted in his work for souls. To lessen his sufferings, I offer mine now to God!" I must admit, as I ploughed through that sand, I felt I qualified for this saint's help!

Sometimes our journeys on these hikes were monotonous enough; sometimes you had very varied surroundings as you journeyed onwards. Sooner or later in the missionary work, you met the lot when it came to terrain and conditions – rice fields, coconut groves, bamboo thickets, rivers deep and narrow or wide and shallow, mountain slopes, wooded valleys, hard-baked clay trails, intensely blue skies, thundering downpours and non-stop lightning, long straight roads close to the shore, and the shining, limitless levels of the China Sea or the Pacific Ocean.

On the narrow trails through fields or forests, I usually asked my Filipino guide to walk before me. I had been advised to do this always. The reason was obvious to the Filipino boys: they could much sooner spot a poisonous snake or a treacherous piece of ground than I could. This practice of mine probably saved my life on one particular occasion. One day a Filipino boy and I were hiking along a very narrow trail. It was a day of blazing sunshine and cloudless skies. A snake, small but deadly poisonous, was basking on the smooth, hard clay of the path we were following. The colour and pattern of its skin merged so perfectly with the background as to make it almost undetectable. As we came along, it was lying at the side of the trail, motionless in the sun. I certainly did not spot it, but my guide did. He shouted as he jumped aside. As he thus warned me, he prepared to strike the snake with his cane. He got no chance however, for the reptile twisted swiftly away into the long grass at the side of the path.

We always had a salutary respect for all snakes. Some of them were viciously aggressive. We soon learned not to estimate a snake's menace merely by its size. On one island near Cebu, there are snakes just a foot long, which carry in their bite a poisonous venom causing swift death.

Snakes on the ground and birds in the air, were the usual living things we saw along the lonely trails. The birds were always interesting. I always took special note of their gorgeous plumage. Blue, red, yellow, crimson, they flashed through the trees like winged jewels. The loveliness of their plumage is perhaps nature's compensation to them for their lack of song. In this respect, the sooty blackbirds or the grey thrushes in the trees and hedges at home in Ireland can easily eclipse them with their springtime songs.

Is there not something parallel to this in the lives of human beings? How often is an invalid a talented artist or playwright? How often is a blind person a gifted musician? How often is a man of meagre intelligence an Apollo in appearance, or a Hercules in strength? You can think up other instances of this. It happens so often that there must be a kind of law of compensation which adjusts to some degree the balance of our lives.

So far I have spoken of the snakes and birds in the Philippines. Now a word about the fish. The seas around the Philippines abound in marine life of many kinds. So much so, that fish is properly one of the staple foods of the Filipino people. Every village along the coasts has its fleet of canoes which put out to sea daily with nets and lines.

Those Filipinos who do not live near the coast can procure fish at times in their own rice fields. Certain small fish live in the water in which the rice plants grow. In the dry season of the year, when there is no water in the rice fields, these fish burrow deep down into the soft wet mud beneath, and remain there until the rainy season comes and the fields are flooded again. When you see men and boys fishing in the rice fields, you know that the waters are in the fields again: the dove to the ark of Noah, and the fish to the rice fields of the Philippines – both messages are similar, both messages are important!

Fish made a welcome addition to our diet in the Philippines. Rice, of course, was the main dish at nearly every meal. What bread is to us in the home countries of Europe, rice is to the Filipinos. They cook it beautifully, and in so many different ways. We could also get chicken, eggs, bread, butter, milk and coffee. Sugar plantations were numerous in Panay and Negros, and so sugar was plentiful and cheap. Sometimes on the missions we received presents of food – generally egg dishes, never lacking in sweetness. Tea was available, but most of us preferred coffee. There were no potatoes of the kind we have in Ireland, but we never really missed them, for the native *camotes*, or sweet potatoes, were a good substitute.

When we worked far away in the mountains, the fare was sometimes scanty. In very remote parts our chief difficulty was to get water that was safe to drink. We always impressed on our Filipino boys the necessity of boiling the water. We often wondered if they understood us. I fear they thought it sufficient to heat the water. I blamed bad, unboiled water for the attack of amoebic dysentery which exhausted me.

In later years Fr Scanlan told me he had discovered the word to use in order to get us boiling water. The boys in the kitchen were told to make the water 'bubble' in the pot. They understood then what was needed. This was too late for me, however – the damage was already done.

When we were in our monastery, we would have normal food, as at home in Ireland. Once in a while friends at home sent us provisions. My mother regularly sent me a cake from home. In her own practical way she evolved a technique suitable for the job. From a local confectioner, she obtained a deep round tin. She baked a cake almost the same size as the tin. She then laced it well with whiskey to keep it fresh on its long journey. Having parcelled it up securely, she wrote my address on it and added the words, "Via Siberia". The Post Office sent it as directed. And so the cake would start on its travels – through England, France, Germany, Poland, and Russia in Europe, and then by Trans-Siberian railway through Russia in Asia to Vladivostok, thence to Manila, and finally southwards by steamer to Iloilo.

Having been so well packed, the cake always arrived in fairly good condition. Moreover, it was big enough to enable me to give a substantial share to all the Fathers and Brothers in the Community. I think its long journey and its safe arrival enhanced its taste for us! To celebrate the coming of a cake, Fr Rector granted us a glass of wine. The Community enjoyed the occasion. It was a break in the daily monotony and routine for all of us.

I say monotony and routine – this applied to our life when in our community in the monastery, for there we lived the strict Redemptorist way of life. Missionary work could also be monotonous at times – but not ordinarily so, for there were generally daily occurrences which brightened our days. For example, we would meet many different nationalities, including Japanese, Indians, Burmese, Chinese, Borneans, Germans, Austrians, Belgians and Spaniards. I picked up a fair smattering of Spanish, which came in useful at times when I found myself in the company of Spaniards.

About the same time, I took up the study of German. Frequently we worked in parishes run by German missionaries belonging to the Mill Hill Missionary Society. From listening to them conversing, I learned the common phrases they used each day. One day, while I was giving a mission in Pandan, a young German priest, Fr Fritz Stoeber, said to me, "You ought to take up the study of German. You seem to have naturally a very good accent and pronunciation in the words and phrases you already know!" So, taking his advice I wrote home to ask Mother to send me my sister Anne's German Grammar. It reached me safely. From then onwards when not otherwise engaged on the mission work, I studied my German grammar. I had to teach myself, but I persevered. It was well worthwhile – but at the time I did not realise that I had taken up the study of the language with the vague idea that it might come in useful sometime. I could not then foresee the valuable use I would make of it in writing my booklets for the Catholic Truth Society; nor could I foresee what a godsend it would prove to be in my future days as an army chaplain in Normandy, Belgium and Germany. I have been repaid a hundredfold for the hours, the laborious hours, I spent studying Anne's German Grammar.

And so life, as I have described it, went on from day to day in the Philippines. The missions were hard work, but we all did our best: there were no idle oars! At times one became nervy and crotchety. Sometimes there was friction. The life and the strenuous work were a strain, and sooner or later small things got on one's nerves. When out on mission work, we had none of that personal privacy afforded in the monastery. We all slept in the same room, and we never got away from one another. We saw each other at dawn when we crawled out of our mosquito-netted beds; we met at prayers, at meals, at recreation – and so it was daily, morning, noon, and night for the weeks and months we were out giving missions. Sooner or later the tensions (that word so beloved of moderns) built up, and there was a flashpoint and an eruption. When the pressures (rather than 'tensions') build up in a volcano there sooner or later is an explosion! So it also is on missions and in monasteries!

What happened amongst us also happens among prisoners-of-war in prison camps. Thrown together so much – exactly our condition – they manifest similar irritations and annoyances. Someone's loud whistling, another's tuneless singing, another's snoring, another's tramping about heavily, his banging of doors, his belongings scattered over the floor, his lack of punctuality: all these and a hundred more similar instances can create tensions and pressures. In my communal days in the Philippines, these things could get on your nerves. To the credit of my brethren however, I must say we usually got over our outbreaks quickly. That was so, for we all admitted and accepted that the world and its people, in the words of William Wordsworth, "can be too much with us".

Despite our ups and downs, the missions went on apace. The work wearied us all – particularly the six or seven hours we spent each day hearing confessions. The work, no doubt, played a large part in making us all, at one time or another, irritable and difficult. The sheer fatigue of the work lowered your resiliency and ability to take what came along.

And yet the work was also magnificent, for despite our difficulties and by God's grace, we infused much happiness into innumerable Filipino lives and homes. It was an immense privilege to be granted the opportunity to help in this work. For the mistakes I made, and the annoyance and trouble I sometimes caused my brethren and the good Filipino people, I have profound regrets. I am very sorry about all that. I am also sorry that I was not able to go on working for many years in the Islands.

## Back to Ireland

In the year 1935 my health gave way. First I had an attack of amoebic dysentery, which weakened me a lot. My Rector at the time dosed me with baking soda, which did not improve matters. I lost much blood. Next came an attack of stones in the kidney, which was quite painful. This was followed shortly afterwards by some form of heart trouble. I went to St Paul's hospital in Iloilo. When I was sufficiently recovered I was sent home to Ireland. With two other priests who, having completed a term of seven years in the Islands, were returning home for a rest, I boarded a Blue Funnel steamer for Europe.

I enjoyed that trip home. The sea air, the good food, the restful days, and the pleasant company of the ship's crew, soon improved my health. There were no Catholics among the crew, but we three Catholic priests were accepted by all of them and made to feel at home.

We called at Singapore, Port Swettenham, Colombo, and Port Sudan on the Red Sea coast of the Sudan. At this latter place, someone pointed out to me a spot in the desert where some missionaries were buried. They had been laid to rest in the sands outside the town.

Months and months later, I used to think of them. In quiet hours, alone with my memories, my mind would travel back to those lonely graves. I used to think then of Fr Wanker, a Mill Hill Father whom I knew in the Philippines. He died in Pandan, where he was Parish Priest, and he was buried by the shores of North East Panay. Eventually this train of thought led me to compose a poem, "The Call of the Dead", which has been published by several journals and has found some favour. I have no illusions about its worth as poetry, but at least it is a product of genuine feeling – for I felt what I wrote.

**The Call of the Dead**
Near white foam creeping
                On coral sands
Near green palms waving
                In sun-bleached lands
'Mid dark pines drooping
                In fields of snow,
Where the sand-clouds drift
                Where the blizzards blow,
We sleep!

Our graves are lonely:
                No marble boast
Doth show our sleeping
                On bare, wild coast –
Where winds come sighing
                But voice ne'er sounds
'Neath a wooden cross
                In our narrow mounds,
We sleep!

Who are we?
We are the dead of the vanguard;
　　　　　We roamed the lonely ways
Over the deserts and mountains
　　　　　And by the bleak Arctic bays.
We are the dead who have toiled long
　　　　　And passed through life, unknown;
We are the legion who faced death –
　　　　　Alone with God alone!

Now on our graves at the vanguard
　　　　　A crimson flame's alight –
Faith's burning torch which we kindled
　　　　　In gloom of pagan night.
Come o'er the seas to these strange lands!
　　　　　Kneel in the sand or snow!
Take up the torch in your brave hands –
　　　　　Come! For the flame is low!

The sea journey to Europe helped my health. I was, however, still far from feeling well when we reached Genoa. We disembarked there and went to spend a week in Rome. Fr General was not too happy about my health. He had me examined by an Italian doctor to see whether I ought to rest in Rome for a while or continue my journey homewards. The doctor judged me fit enough to go home at once.

On arriving back in Ireland, I was granted three days in which to see my parents and relatives. Nowadays our returned missionaries are granted several weeks at home. And usually if there is one of our monasteries near their home, they are appointed members of the community there.

I thought three days very short indeed for my stay in Belfast. My parents neither complained nor murmured. They were worried about me, however, because of my poor state of health. After my years of absence abroad, my very short visit to them brought little comfort, and certainly did not lessen their anxiety for me. My uncle, Bishop Mageean, was dismayed at this meagre visit and asked the Rector of Clonard to extend the time allotted to me. He could not accede to the Bishop's wishes: he had to phone the Fr Provincial in Limerick. And as a result of all this I got three extra days!

When my six days were up, I had to leave Belfast. Feeling very low in

Preserved Mass Rock at old Kilclief Church, possibly used by
Fr Richard Curoe (1742-1844) who was the last priest to conduct
mass in the fields during Penal times.

Fr Richard Curoe, 1742–1844. He died at the
patricharical age of 102 and was known far
and wide in County Down as "The Old Priest".
He is buried at Kilclief.

'Old Dendy' – Daniel Mageean,
1810–1894. 'Old Dendy' had a family of
ten – two girls and eight sons.

Fr Charles Mageean, one of the eight sons of 'Old Dendy' who died within the year following his ordination at the age of 24.

Dendy's grandson , Fr Robert Mageean C.Ss.R., brother of Bishop Daniel Mageean. Fr Robert's life was devoted to missionary work. He spent fifteen years in Australia. He was a great literary figure and contributed to many periodicals and journals. Father Mageean's literary work, in keeping with his career, has always been undertaken with a view to promoting the honour of God and the good of souls. He wrote a book about the Redemptorists, their life and their work which was published in Sydney in 1922.

The Mageean Family. Bishop Daniel Mageean (top right), is next to my mother, Susanna. On her right is Fr Robert Mageean C.Ss.R. The sisters, Selina, Ellen and Margaret are seated in front.

Portrait of Reverend Bishop Daniel Mageean, 1882–1962. He was Bishop of Down and Connor 1929–1962.

Three of his siblings including my mother, Susanna, on the right.

Bishop Mageean (standing) with Pope Pius XII.

The Cummings Family.
Back row l-r: Margaret, Eileen, James, Anne.
Front row l-r: Robert, Father, Mary, mother, myself.

St Paul's winning Billiards Team.
Back row l-r: Robert McCormick, Billy McAlea, Jack O'Hanlon and Billy Austin (manager).
Front row l-r: Father, Dick Mulholland, Jimmy Hughes.

Ordination photographs 1930 showing:
Front row l-r: Relatives Rev R Quinn, R Mageean, myself, The Bishop, J Morgan and R McCall.
Other relatives behind are (l-r) mother, Dan Quinn, Mary Cummings, Mrs McCall,
Margaret Cummings, father, Mrs Quinn, Rita Quinn, Mary Morgan, Bob Cummings, Eileen
Cummings, Joe Morgan, Anne Cummings, James Morgan.

Back row l-r: John Morgan, Aunt Selina, Aunt Molly, Annie, myself, Bishop, Rita Quinn,
    father, Fr Morgan, Dr Dan Quinn.
Front row l-r: Fr Quinn, Margaret, Mary, Mary Morgan, Joseph Morgan (uncle).

My brother James (Jimmy) Cummings (seated) with his wife Mary and five sons.

The wedding of my brother Robert (Bob) Cummings to Cissie O'Doherty.
Back row l-r: Unknown, Bob Cummings, unknown.
Front row l-r: Fr Dan Cummings, unknown, Bishop Daniel Mageean, Cissie O'Doherty, Margaret Cummings.

Dicky Magennis with my sister Eileen and their three girls.

My sister Annie entering Poor Clare Colletines in 1932 with mother.

Sr Anne enjoys a chat with a fellow Belfast woman Mary McAleese, President of Ireland.

My sisters Margaret (left) and Mary (right).

Mary (left), myself and Margaret (right).

My sister Margaret with her husband John Rooney and their family in 1960.

John Rooney

My nieces Rosemary (left) and Clare (right). It was Rosemary who asked me to write my story.

Wedding photograph of my sister Mary to John Holland (left) and, above, Mary with their family.

On board ship heading for the 16,000 mile journey to the Philippines in 1932.

With three fellow Irish C.Ss.R. army chaplains in World War II.
l-r: Peter Mulrooney, myself, Joe Tronson and Luke Hartigan.

Portraits as army chaplain before Normandy (above left and right) and with the Irish Guards (centre).

Mother Gonzague (left), the Prioress, with St Thérèse (right) and three of her sisters photographed in 1894. I met Pauline (1861–1951), then Prioress, Marie (1860–1940) and Celine (1869–1959) when I visited Lisieux during the war. When Celine celebrated her golden jubilee in 1946, Pope John, then Nuncio in Paris, went to Lisieux for the occasion.

Statue of St Gerard hand crafted by a Redemptorist Brother while he was prisoner of war in Germany and given to me at the end of the conflict.

My portrait painted by a Concentration Camp survivor, Hans Baumeister, Germany 1946.

Celebrant at the wedding of Marie McGovern and John McCann, 5 August 1974. Marie is the daughter of my dear friend Mrs Malena McGovern.

As priest to immigrants in Birmingham I regularly visited building sites, as here in the Southern Section of Spaghetti Junction – the Gravelly Interchange as it is now known. All but two men are Irish. One has borrowed my hat and given me his own white helmet. Most of the men left their white helmets – which were compulsory – at their jobs on site when coming to their meal-break.

Some of the men in the Northern Section. They were very shy about posing for this picture. They pushed this lad forward. He struggled to get back into the line – hence the scramble.

All of these men are Irish. I am standing at the extreme right.

All set for the early morning duties working around the building sites of Birmingham (1966-77).

health and spirits, I set out for our monastery in Athenry, County Galway. Superiors thought they were acting wisely in making these arrangements in my regard. They picked for me the monastery they deemed best for bringing me back to health. I am certain they did what they thought was best. The short stay in Belfast to see my parents was in complete accord with Redemptorist traditions of that time.

Why do I linger on all this? It is all over and gone! What matters it now, whether I had three days or three months at home. My parents are dead. The sorrows, troubles, and disappointments of the past cannot touch them now. At the time I felt sorry for them. I knew they would have liked to help me back to health. They would have been contented to see me well again, before I was sent hundreds of miles away to Galway. Those were the days when we felt the hard, ruthless edge of Redemptorist tradition.

That tradition looked on our parents as dangerous potential enemies of our vocation. Our Founder, St Alphonsus, lost so many Italian Redemptorists through the influence of their parents and their homes, that he heard forever ringing in his ears the words of the Gospel: "Inimici hominis domestici euis" – "A man's enemies shall be those of his own household". In his booklet, *The True Redemptorist*, he says that a member of the Redemptorist Order must detach himself from and indeed entirely forget his relations:

> "To show a desire to see or speak with relations is considered in the Order to be a great fault. It would be considered a serious and scandalous fault for anyone to go to his home without express permission."

I wonder how this great Saint, who was a man of penetrating intelligence, reconciled all this with God's commandment: "Honour the Father and thy Mother!" To my mind, his teaching is contrary to what God wants of us. Seemingly the Saint never read St Thomas Aquinas' comment on the text, "A man's enemies shall be those of his own household." St Thomas says: "A man's parents are not the enemies of his vocation, except in so far as they unlawfully hinder him from following it!" Had they thought they were hindering me in following my vocation, my parents would have forced me to leave their company at once. As I have already said, St Alphonsus' attitude to parents was prompted by the number of Italians who left the Redemptorist Order in his day through the influence of their parents and their home. What pain, what hurt, what sorrow has been caused to thousands of sincere

Redemptorists – and their devout parents – in the past two hundred years by the rigid, worldwide application of a rule or policy which was apposite only in the hills of Italy in the eighteenth century.

By religious vows, no matter what form they take, we can never destroy the God-given rights of our parents over us. They always retain the right to our honour, our affection, our esteem, our concern, and our help with their needs. To say, as the Redemptorist writer, Fr Boumans lays down in his book of Meditations, that we must not think of them except at prayer; to say we should keep away from them except when they are seriously ill or some urgent necessity is present; to say we must cut ourselves off from them – all this I have never been able to accept in my heart. Nor have I been able to reconcile it with the command of God to honour and love our parents. Forever echoing in my mind have been the words of the Apostles: "We ought to obey God rather than men." (Acts 5:29)

St Alphonsus, in his efforts to preserve his Redemptorist Congregation, pushed things too far. Times, however, have changed, and Redemptorist ideas have changed: our parents are no longer permanent suspects. Now they, and our other relatives also, are rightly regarded as benefactors and friends of the Redemptorist Institute. Now parents can visit their Redemptorist sons and be visited by them regularly. Their true relationship, based on Christ's charity, has been acknowledged and accepted. In my past years in the Redemptorists, it has been far otherwise. Our new Redemptorist Rules now say:

> "The relatives, especially the parents of the confreres, the benefactors of the Institute, as well as its devoted helpers, are closely linked with our religious family. For this reason they have a special claim to consideration and affection, particularly when they are weighed down by stress and difficulties."

These fine words should have been written into the Rules once the Redemptorist Institute spread outside Italy.

In the past some of our members were not allowed to go home on the occasion of the death of a brother or sister. Many years ago one priest was permitted to officiate at the wedding of a brother or sister, but was not allowed to go into the house. So, good fervent man as he was, he held converse with his family while standing in the garden at an open window. Ludicrous, were it not dominantly pathetic! But goodbye to all that. Thank God the truth has prevailed at last!

And now I will leave this unpleasing subject aside and return at once to my story. I was sent to the monastery in County Galway near Athenry, where I spent my student days. To recover my health, I followed one wise plan: on all fine days I stayed out in the spacious monastery garden. I had written a book on the Philippine Islands and now had ample time to read over the manuscript and correct it. Not having a typewriter, I was compelled to write it in longhand. This was a distinct disadvantage to me, because you fared better with our Institute's two censors if your submitted work was in typescript form. Having finished correcting my book, I sent it along to the Provincial Superior for his approval.

As usual he passed it on to two of our priests to censor it. These censors had a wide mandate: not only were they to look for doctrinal or moral errors, but also to say whether or not the manuscript submitted was worth publishing. Moreover, they were unknown to me, and so could pass judgement with that admirable courage and forthrightness that is bestowed by anonymity.

Anyhow, they promptly rejected my work. I have no illusions: probably my effort was very amateurish and crude, and they were quite right to pitch it out. But at the time I felt it had been damned before it was even read!

First, my penmanship betrayed me to the censors. Here was a young man aiming at being a writer! The Provincial, at that time, was not keen on his young men turning out manuscripts. The young priests should concentrate on their mission work: the apostolate of the pen, so warmly encouraged by our Rules, was not for them! Missions, missions, missions were to be the work of the young men – not the trade of writing!

I could be quite wrong in my surmise. Later on, however, I thought I saw good reasons for thinking my interpretation of events was correct. Two or three years later, I was for lengthy periods sitting idle in the Dundalk Community, with no missionary work to occupy me. I wrote a series of articles on the Philippines for the *Irish Ecclesiastical Record*, Maynooth. The International Eucharist Congress was soon to take place in Manila and these articles were meant to interest Irish priests in the story of the Catholic Philippines. I used much of the material written in the manuscript the censors had rejected. This time the two censors passed the articles as I wrote them. The editor welcomed the first four articles and asked for more. I obliged him. On receiving my fifth article, the same Provincial Superior as previously wrote to me a blunt letter, asking me when these articles were going to end. I knew then what was on his mind: he did not want this writing itch to spread among the young priests of the

Irish Redemptorist Province. Mission work was to be their line – nothing else!

Here is now the heart of the matter! Had my mission work or indeed any work at home in the monastery suffered because of my attention to writing, I could have understood and accepted willingly this good priest's obvious resentment at what I was doing. But no work suffered! I was trying to occupy myself and avoid sheer idleness.

In the Philippines when I wrote my booklet, *The Mother of Perpetual Succour*, I had the very same treatment from my Rector there.

Of such stuff is the fabric of religious life made. Others have suffered as well as I. Our own Fr Bridgett, when working hard on his famous life of St Thomas More, spent his morning hours studying in the British Museum – with one eye on the clock! He had to rush home to St Mary's Clapham around noon, so as to be in time for the Particular Examen! It was not easy for him, grown heavy and corpulent, to hasten back to the monastery, all heated and perspiring.

It is now a cause of chagrin to many to see things allowed, which formerly were strictly forbidden or discouraged. There are many of us in religious life who know how trying it is, when one does one's best in a matter allowed by one's Rules, to be blocked by the good men who should encourage us.

Change is inevitable in all human affairs – laws civil, commercial, educational and religious are modified. The Church has changed many of her laws in the past and no doubt will change many more in the future. Religious Orders are also rewriting their Rules – and it is about time they did so.

# CHAPTER FIVE

# Missions in Ireland

MEANWHILE IN OUR monastery at Athenry, I was daily improving my health. Rest, food, and fresh air revived my strength. But it was a slow process, for I had been very low in energy.

Some months later I was appointed to our monastery in Dundalk. No sooner had I arrived there, than the Rector asked me to give a mission – all on my own – in Haggardstown parish near Dundalk. He left me little option in the matter. Informing me he was in "a bit of a hole", and that I alone could extricate him, he clearly showed me he did not want "no" for an answer.

I was reluctant to accept the work, because I had never given a mission in Ireland. Normally, too, a young priest beginning mission work is sent out with a mission veteran who steers him through his first mission experiences. Here was I, confronted with a mission – my first mission in Ireland – all to be done alone! I had at hand plenty of written sermons, but had preached them only in their Visayan translations in the Philippines – never to a live congregation in their original English versions.

I often wondered, had it happened before in the history of the Irish Redemptorists, that one of their young priests gave his first mission all by himself? Only after many years working with senior Fathers is one usually allowed to give a mission by oneself. So I was now faced with a mighty challenge. Haggardstown is one of the chief parishes in the Archdiocese of Armagh – and here I was, a greenhorn in the work, coming to give the unfortunate people a mission by myself. There was no turning back! I felt like David facing Goliath – instead of his sling and his five smooth stones in his shepherd's pouch, I was coming with an attaché case filled with sermons. As I write about it now, I break into laughter at my colossal nerve.

But at the time I had to just go ahead. So I started into the work. I refurbished my bits of sermons and learned them really well. I preached them as well as lay in my power. I tried to help the people who came to me in the confessional. Thank God everything went well and there were no serious hitches.

The two weeks' work was very strenuous; but thank God too, my health stood up to it. At the end both priests and people seemed pleased with the mission. To me it all brought one lasting benefit: henceforth the preaching of any mission would never daunt or dismay me. By dint of that sudden shock treatment, I had in a sense become a veteran!

As the months and years went by I gave many missions in parishes in Armagh, Meath, Louth, Tyrone, Fermanagh, Donegal, Down and Antrim. In point of fact, with one or two exceptions, I gave missions in every diocese in Ireland. Some of them were easy and pleasant; some quite arduous; but none of them ever equalled the work and trying conditions of the missions I gave in the Philippines.

## Teaching

I now pass over three or four years of such mission work, and come to the year 1940. In that year our new House of Studies had been built and was ready to receive our students. In August of that year I received a letter from Fr Provincial, appointing me Professor of Scripture in this new House of Studies in Galway.

This was indeed a surprise appointment. I had worked hard at Scripture when I was a student. I liked Hebrew and had kept up my interest in it. There now was being offered to me an opportunity to improve my knowledge of the language. More importantly, I now had a chance to immerse myself in the Scriptures.

And yet I could not feel at ease about my appointment. My other teacher colleagues had had years of teaching experience, or had but recently completed postgraduate courses in Rome in the subjects they taught. In my new work I, on the other hand, had none of these advantages. I saw that I would have to work very hard – perhaps constant daily toil would compensate in some measure for my disadvantages.

I began to study the Scripture Course for that year. I exerted full pressure on myself and kept it up. Fortunately the students were using the same textbooks I had studied in my student days. I knew my way about them. I foresaw the difficulties the students would meet. I was able to forestall most of the awkward questions the students could put to me. An old cynic might have said that my greatest asset was that I had neither degrees nor training! The students worked well for me. All of them had ability; some were brilliant. Due to their own talent and industry they put on a fine display in the annual examinations. During the year, on several occasions when the going was heavy, I made good use of their brains. In spite of my drawbacks, I enjoyed my work. Some of the students were of the same cast of mind as myself. We became very good friends and have remained so through the years since then. I enjoyed their company.

I enjoyed also the friendship and companionship of the other Fathers who were teaching with me. Many a happy hour we had together. They were men of exceptional ability and learning. Their conversation was an education to a good listener.

Twice a week with one of them, I went for a long walk through the surrounding countryside. On one of those walks I remember how Fr Sean O'Loughlin and I passed through the Menlo district, which was then completely Irish speaking. A man was working in a field beside the road. We greeted him in Gaelic and stopped to watch him working. His face glistened with sweat. He was trying to open up a new field which had never been cultivated before. To our eyes it seemed to be nothing but rock. Here and there, it had some little depth of surface soil, but over most of it a light covering of soil merely concealed layers of grey limestone.

I remember commenting to him in Gaelic on the severity of his task. He answered me in Gaelic, agreeing with me it was very hard work and adding, "I am wondering, Father, is it worth it?" We both came away from him, also wondering if it was worth it – for he was using in that field not a spade, but a pickaxe!

How often it has been said to us Irish: "You people live in the past!"; "You Irish will not let bygones be bygones!"? May I say that the Irish people have long memories of England's rule in Ireland, because they *still suffer* from what the English invaders did to them in the past. The Plantations of English settlers drove our forefathers out of their good green land into the barren rocky regions such as that in which that unfortunate Menlo man toiled. Can the Irish peasant – with sweat glistening on his brow as he toils in rocky field or bog – be blamed or derided for remembering the Plantations and their pillage? What happened in those distant days now explains why the Menlo man needed a pickaxe and not a spade to cultivate his acre.

Two years of my teaching passed by. At the end of that time I had covered the entire course in Scripture. I reckoned that things would be much easier for me henceforth. I had certainly broken the back of the work, and I felt I could face my third year of teaching with a less anxious mind. Little did I realise that my teaching days were now at an end.

# CHAPTER SIX
# World War II

## Army Chaplain

WORLD WAR II began in 1939. From its commencement, Ireland had remained neutral. In 1942 Monsignor Coughlin, the Senior Catholic Chaplain at the War Office in London, appealed to our Fr Provincial for some priests to act as army chaplains. In July of that year Fr Provincial sent a letter to all our monasteries in Ireland, inviting volunteers to come forward for the work.

I well remember the morning his letter was put on the notice board in our Galway city monastery where I was teaching. I was sweeping my room, when Fr Tom Murphy came to me and said very brightly, "Go off and join the army! You are the man for that!"

"Why? What has happened?" I asked him.

"The Provincial has asked for volunteers to act as chaplains in the British army. His letter is on the noticeboard downstairs! You should volunteer! There is a shortage of chaplains."

He grinned at me and went away. I confess that at first I reacted somewhat impatiently, saying to myself, "This is England's war! Why should I get mixed up in it?" In this mood, I went on sweeping and tidying my room. And then slowly I began to rethink the whole matter. I reflected on the good work I might be able to do among the soldiers. I thought of my modest, but fairly serviceable knowledge of French and German – how useful these languages would be in this war! I would have to rough it in the army, but this caused me no disquiet, for I had had plenty of the rough life in the Philippines.

Should I or should I not volunteer? There was a picture of Our Lady of Perpetual Succour hanging in my room. I turned to God's Mother, and asked her to enlighten and guide me. To guide me: that was my prayer! I honestly did not know what to do. I repeated my prayer several times. And then, suddenly, I saw my way clear. I knew what to do. Hesitations and doubts were gone – I would volunteer!

The Provincial was then visiting us in Galway. I decided to go and speak to him at once. I finished tidying my room, brushed my clothes carefully, rectified my unruly hair, and made my way along the corridor to his room. At his door I paused for a moment, and then boldly knocked with two clear distinct knocks. In his usual languid voice he answered from within, "Ave Maria!" I entered. "Well, Fr Cummings, what is it?"

"I have come to volunteer for the army!"

He burst out laughing: "Get out! There is no question of you going as a chaplain!"

"Why? What is there to prevent me?" At this crucial point I outlined quite modestly, but in salesman-like fashion, my qualifications!

"That is all very well," he replied, "but you have overlooked one thing!"

"What is it?"

"Where am I to find someone to take your place as teacher of Scripture?"

This stumped me! I had not thought of this problem. I retired from his room to consider it and find its solution. Back in my room I consulted the list of Fathers in our Irish Province of the Redemptorists, anxiously seeking possible candidates for my job.

Next day I went back to the Provincial. I gave him two or three names of priests who were well qualified to take my place.

The Provincial noted these names and said to me, "Very well, I will consider the matter. If you are appointed to the army, I will inform you during this approaching vacation!"

I then asked him to make my appointment, if and when it should be made, not merely an announcement of my readiness to serve as an army chaplain, but a command given me to so act in virtue of my vow of obedience. He agreed to do this – an arrangement which contented me greatly.

Our students were allowed a month's holiday every summer by the sea. We, their teachers, were allowed to spend that month in some of our other monasteries. During that vacation I received a telegram from Fr Provincial, appointing me to the army, and directing me to report to a certain doctor in Dublin for an army medical check-up.

Three other Fathers had also been so appointed. With them, I reported to the Dublin doctor – an ex-army man. We all passed the medical test. Next we went to our monastery in Belfast, where the Senior Army Chaplain in Northern Ireland, Fr Tom Duggan, interviewed us. He briefed us about our uniform allowance, equipment, duties, and other similar matters. He gave us army travel vouchers, which would bring us to the locations of the Command Chaplains in England. These were to assign us for duty to various units in each Command.

And so by the end of August I was in uniform and was making final preparations for my life and work as an army chaplain.

My parents put no obstacles in my way. They must naturally have been concerned about my future safety – but I had explained to them my reasons for going into the army, and they were too religiously-minded to raise objections. Nevertheless, they must have been anxious about my welfare.

In the first week of September 1942, we four new chaplains crossed over to England and journeyed to London. We stayed in our monastery at Clapham overnight. Next day we separated: each one of us was to report to the Command Chaplains in different areas. I went to Reigate in Surrey, the Headquarters of South-Eastern Command. There I met Fr Basil McCretan. We lunched together and then went out to the garden of the large villa which the army had commandeered.

It was a warm, sunny day. We sat on the grass. Fr McCretan went over a number of important points I had to be aware of in my work as a Chaplain. After about forty minutes chatting and questioning, he told me of my appointment – I was to be attached as chaplain to a brigade in the 53rd Welsh Division. I would report to the local Senior Chaplain in Hythe, Fr Fox, who would introduce me to the officers of the Brigade Headquarters and get me a suitable billet.

Leaving Reigate that same afternoon, I went back to London and thence to Hythe, on the coast of Kent. Fr Fox met me at the railway station and put me up for the night in his billet. He was a very genial and friendly priest. He made me feel at home. His billet was quite near the sea. That night with the steady, hoarse murmuring of the sea in my ears, I fell into a deep sleep.

I was awakened at dawn by the thunderous sound of aeroplanes, humming loudly at no great height above us. I wondered if it was a German raid. Going to the windows, I could see no planes in the morning sky. Since there was no sound of bombing or of gunfire, I concluded that the planes were British. At breakfast Fr Fox told me I had heard the planes of the British Dawn Patrol.

That same morning we started off together for my new field of work. Within a half-hour or so, we reached the Brigade Headquarters of the Welsh Division. To my dismay, the acting adjutant knew nothing about my appointment and did not know where to place me. Finally, after much phoning and discussion, I was sent to a billet of a Royal Army Service Corps section in 'The Friary' – a fine old mansion outside Maidstone. There I was reluctantly accepted. This particular unit normally had no Padre living with them. They put me up under protest: it was made obvious to me that the sooner I was moved elsewhere, the sooner they would be pleased. It was neither an easy nor a pleasant situation.

I was to share a room with three other officers. One of them happened to be on leave, so I had the use of his chair and camp bed – I wondered what would happen when he returned. I settled in as best I could. Within a few days however the atmosphere in the Mess, which had been initially one of rather cold courtesy, changed completely and I was both accepted and established. When the members of the Mess saw I minded my own business and was honestly trying to cope with a new way of life, they helped me in many ways.

In the first few days I was concerned about the arrangements of my Sunday Masses for the soldiers of the different units in my area. I got all this dealt with as soon as possible, because I had to notify the Battalion and Company Headquarters about times and places: they would then inform the Catholic men. Someone must have guided me in all this, for I knew nothing about what was usually done in the area.

And so on that following Sunday, I said my first Mass for the soldiers and preached my first sermon to them. That Mass was offered in a castle a few miles outside Maidstone. It had all you expect to see in a medieval castle – a moat, in which the circular green leaves and pale white flowers of many water lilies floated, a drawbridge, a portcullis, iron-studded doors, icy stone passages, and a banqueting hall, where I offered the Mass. To get me to the castle with my Mass kit, the unit let me have a car. I had no car of my own.

Everything went well. I heard some soldiers' confessions, preached during the Mass, and met some sergeants whom I knew would be helpful friends. On that first Sunday I felt I had made a fairly good start.

But when the day was over and I set myself to think of ways of contacting the Catholic men in my Brigade, I was at a loss to know what to do. The units of the Brigade were scattered over a wide area of the countryside. Without a car at my disposal, I could not hope to keep contact with them. As the days passed by, I saw that my position was impossible. This was an infantry Division: I ought to have been billeted with one of the Battalions and in direct touch with Brigade affairs, whereas I was now out on a limb – attached to a small unit away from the bulk of my men. It was clear to me that, apart from the Sunday Masses, I would not be able to contact the men. I decided to write to the Senior Chaplain at Reigate, Fr McCretan, putting the facts before him and asking his advice and help.

I had done the wise thing in writing to him. He took action at once. Within three or four days, I was transferred to the 126th Infantry Brigade and attached to the Royal West Kent Regiment in Hythe. The popular name of this Regiment in army circles is "The Buffs". With them I was well circumstanced. My chief wish was fulfilled: I was now able to meet the men of the Brigade, for I was billeted with one Battalion, and quite near another – the King's Liverpool Regiment. The third Regiment in the Brigade was positioned a mile or two away, but I now had a car and could reach the men in a matter of minutes.

In the Brigade I had some Catholic officers who advised me about suitable times and places for the Sunday Masses. It was all very encouraging: I now felt I was getting into the real work of an army chaplain. There was good camaraderie in the Mess. Until I got to know the officers, however, I remained rather reticent. I spoke in a friendly way to all who addressed me and thus gradually became accepted. I kept feeling my way in this fashion. I was ever conscious of my very limited knowledge of the army way of life. So I watched, I listened, and I made mental notes. At first it was all rather bewildering and, for me, slightly intimidating. Gradually I got to know the officers of the Mess and felt at ease in their company.

All this may sound very trivial and childish in a way, but you must remember that since boyhood I had lived almost the entire time behind the walls of a most strict monastery. The silence, the strict discipline of mediation and duties in the monastery, the constant asking of permission for anything we wanted – even to get bootlaces, soap or toothpaste, a box of matches – the countless prohibitions against such things as smoking, concerts, films, walks on certain days, holidays or visiting of friends – all this did not prepare me for army life, in which I had to fashion my own work and daily programme.

My life hitherto did not help me now to make decisions on my own: the monastic rules and my superiors had always determined everything for me. Even when away from the monastery, in the Philippines or on missions at home in Ireland, I was always under obedience and played little part in the shaping of my own life and work. We had been taught to have no will of our own, but rather to live and act by the rules and the will of our superiors. In those early days in the army, I felt my blameless immaturity very keenly. You might say I had come into the army life almost depersonalised.

With awe, I stared at young officers of twenty-two or twenty-three, wielding command of hundreds of men. I, aged thirty-five, compared their poise, self-assurance and maturity with my own bewildered reactions to my new way of life. It took me quite some time to achieve what I will term a measure of normality.

Monsignor Ronald Knox used to tell of his visit one day to a convent. To the Sister who opened the door to him, he passed the remark that it was a nice day. The Sister replied, "I'll go now and ask Reverend Mother!" This is an extreme example of the kind of thing from which now I had to move away.

I received much help when I went to a Conference of Catholic Chaplains in Maidstone. There I met a Fr Gilmartin. He was an expert on the work of a Chaplain. After the formal meeting of our group, he and I had a cup of coffee together. He told me how to get through my work, how to arrange my day, how to get lists of the Catholic men in all my units, how to arrange a "Padre's hour", and how to meet the men in the canteens. I put all my questions to him and he gave me the answers. I was very much indebted to him for his helpful advice. I still think of him with gratitude. I felt saddened when I heard a year or two later that he had left the army and started work as a waiter in a London hotel. It seems he had a row with one of the senior chaplains – some heated words had passed between them. The upshot was that Fr Gilmartin left the army and the priesthood. I have often wondered since what happened to him. Perhaps he has returned to his priesthood – I hope so!

I have never forgotten him. He was a timely help to me in those early days of mine in the army. I learned from him the right approach for my work. Henceforward I was able to go to work with complete confidence. I got to know the Catholic rank and file of the Brigade: they became my friends. I knew them rather as Catholic men than as soldiers. They were always ready to help me when possible. I began to feel pleased that I had volunteered for the army: I liked the life, the work, and the men.

The Senior Chaplain, at one of our Chaplain Conferences, asked us not to confine our activities only to the men of our respective Brigades, but to contact and help all the units in our area My area stretched along the south-east coast of England, from Folkestone in the east to Dungeness in the west; inland, it covered about eight miles. To find the other units in this area, I learned how to interpret map references accurately. Seated in my car beside my driver, with the map open on my knees, I was soon able to go directly to any given unit.

Often on these journeys we were held up by air raids or by shelling. One day Fr Gilgunn, the Chaplain in the neighbouring area, was machine-gunned on the open road by a lone German raider aircraft. He died instantly. These daylight raids were reconnaissance missions; yet the German airmen often used their machine guns or light cannon on vehicles or soldiers on the roads.

I have mentioned the hazard of shelling. Facing us on the French coast, about twenty-five miles away, were some of the German coastal defences.

The Germans had taken over all the guns they found in the Maginot Line. They had planted several of these on the cliffs at Cap Gris-Nez. Hence these guns of our French allies were now pointing towards England, frequently pouring shells into Dover, Folkestone and other British towns. A large section of Dover now lay in ruins because of this. Normally the shells were more harassing to the nerves than destructive of lives and property, but at times they killed many. One evening one of the heavy guns fired a single shell at Dover. It burst beside a queue of military personnel – aircraftmen and sailors – and a number of civilians. The street was a shambles.

In the course of the war the British discovered that the Germans seemed to be tied to a schedule of attack, rest, attack, and so on. Thus in many sections of the battlefronts, the British 'old hands' could foretell when the Germans would be active. However the Germans at Cap Gris-Nez followed no pattern – they were unpredictable.

In Hythe they did not wreak the destruction done in Dover. In German eyes, the town was doubtless of minor importance. It was watched, shelled once in a while, and visited fairly often by fast-flying planes. These planes flew very low – they would come in swiftly from the sea, skimming over the housetops. This was a devilish move on the part of the German pilots: they flew so low that our anti-aircraft guns could not be depressed sufficiently to fire at them. Nevertheless the anti-aircraft guns fired and kept firing. Usually the noise was ear-splitting. For its size the Bofors gun created an enormous din.

The experience of being near guns when they are firing is at first nerve-racking – but, as with everything else, one gets used to it. In a shore battery near the Romney Marshes an officer took me down to one of the six-inch gun casemates to watch a firing practice. Out of the way of the gun-crew I stood to one side, watching the drill. The propellant charge, I noticed, was about twice the length of the shell itself.

When the command "Fire!" came over the loudspeaker, the noise was appalling. It seemed to go through every bone and muscle of my body: it crashed its way through me. The feeling was ever so much more than hearing a very loud noise – this noise was too big for my hearing alone: it filled my whole being. I wonder whether others have a similar experience when close to firing guns for the first time.

When I was visiting a certain battery, the crew of one of the guns told me an interesting story. One day previously they had been firing high-explosive shells. Their gun was working perfectly – and then suddenly something went wrong! They had carried out the drill of loading the gun correctly, as they thought, but when they tried to execute the order to fire – the gun would not discharge. They were puzzled. They decided to reverse the drill: the breech of the gun was opened, the charge was withdrawn and examined, as well as the firing mechanism. Looking up the gun barrel, they saw the shell itself lying where they had placed it. All seemed well. So they replaced the charge, closed the breech, and again tried to fire. Once more, nothing happened!

A second time, therefore, they unloaded the gun – but this time, they also withdrew the shell itself. One of them then looked up the barrel of the gun. He shouted in alarm! His comrades also had a look. To their horror they saw, lying far up the barrel, the bakelite safety cap which is screwed on the nose of the shell and removed before the shell is inserted in the barrel. Someone had slipped up in his duty: the cap must have been loosened but not removed. When the shell had been put into the gun, the cap had fallen off and lay in the barrel. Had the gun fired when the men tried to fire it, they would have died: there would have been a barrel burst – dreaded by all gunners – resulting in destruction and death.

While telling me all this, the men were very solemn and serious. They themselves could not understand how they had escaped death. They had only one possible explanation – the prayers sent up daily to Almighty God by their wives and families at home. Not one of these soldiers was a Catholic, but they were glad to get a chance of testifying to someone that they knew God's protective hand had saved them. Here was a signal proof that He was, for us all, Our Father in Heaven.

In my army life I found the rank and file very interesting. My uniform and my priesthood afforded me a certain link, a comradeship with them. I invariably found them – with a few rare exceptions –decent and friendly.

GK Chesterton stoutly maintained that everything is interesting. My experience is that human beings are far more interesting than anything else. In my army life I was confirmed in this view. I enjoyed meeting the different types of men. I liked to hear a man telling me about his ideas, his convictions, his work in the army or on civvy street. Because I was a priest, because I was genuinely interested in them, the men often opened their minds and hearts to me. Catholic or non-Catholics – it did not matter! They told me their plans, their troubles, their problems.

The world's masterpieces in painting and sculpture are to be seen and admired in museums and art galleries. I have seen them in the Vatican, the Louvre, and Prado Museum in Madrid. There are gems of beauty and craftsmanship in jewellery – like the Crown Jewels in the Tower of London. In the East and West, there are panoramas of scenery, glorious sunsets, and lovely snow-capped mountains. Yet, while all these have their own peculiar value and attractiveness, they cannot hold the interest and wonder found in our fellow beings.

Some of the ordinary soldiers were very talented – more so than some of the officers who commanded them. One could always learn from them. I used often to leave a man's company, saying to myself quietly, "There is a gentleman who will go far!"

Some of the men were unusual, in an interesting kind of way. Going through an army camp one day, I met a soldier who informed me he was not a Catholic. He said he had his own way of belief, for he belonged to the Society of Peculiar People. This information intrigued me. At first I thought it was another of those odd groups which are plentiful in America. They have grandiose, highfalutin names and the members don bizarre costumes and hats to parade in the streets. However, I was wrong in my thinking. There and then, this soldier expounded his creed. His is a truly religious group existing principally in Dorset and south-west England.

Relying on the text of James 5:14, a man called Banyan founded the Society in London in 1838. He taught his followers that when sick, they should not consult doctors, but should instead depend on prayer, oil and nursing. In brief, they are faith healers.

I liked to associate with the men. I used to go into their canteens and have a cup of tea with a group of them at a table. We had many discussions – some serious and some nonsensical – but nearly all humorous and light-hearted. It was a tonic to me to be able to set them laughing and joking. In these sessions we all got away from the world of the war and our involvement in it.

We had many football matches. These were of First Division standards. A battalion of the King's Liverpool Regiment was in my Brigade. Nearly all the players of the Liverpool team at the time were in its ranks. In the matches we played, they always put on a grand display of football. These games were usually held on Saturday evenings. All the men looked forward to them. For them, and for me also, "the match next Saturday" brightened the prospect of the weekend.

The Liverpool Regiment men were very friendly and I got on well with them. I used to go to the firing ranges with them in the army trucks. I watched the accurate and the not-so-accurate shooters amongst them firing their rifles or machine guns. The language of the sergeant-instructors was always picturesque, sometimes slightly vulgar, but mostly impressive and convincing. I had better not give any examples of their vigour and humour: these phrases and expressions, which made you laugh in spite of yourself, seem to lose their piquancy when put down on paper! All this time, as I kept moving around among the units of my area, I was becoming better known. When the Catholic men came to Mass on Sundays, they all knew me: I was not a stranger – I was one of them. They accepted me; I had their goodwill. I felt that they would hearken to what I said to them in my Sunday discourses.

If the men were interesting to me, so also was the area in which I worked. Even now after thirty years, I can see the shore and the waves beating on its banked masses of brown shingle. I think again, as I thought then, that Matthew Arnold had this very shoreline in mind, when he wrote in his poem, "Dover Beach":

"Come to the window, sweet is the night air!
Only, from the long line of spray
Where the sea meets the moon-blanched land,
Listen! You hear the grating roar
Of pebbles which the waves draw back, and fling
At their return, up the high strand,
Begin, and cease, and then again begin,
With tremulous cadence slow, and bring
The eternal note of sadness in."

To the west of Hythe lay the Romney Marsh – a place which brought to my mind boyhood stories of a French schooner in a hidden cove, a secret path up the cliff, and a line of rough, ruthless smugglers carrying kegs of French brandy to some house, lonely and remote in the Marsh.

One night in winter, returning from a distant unit, my driver and I took what we deemed to be a shortcut home through the Marsh. The network of roads, combined with the wartime absence of signposts and lights, left us confused, and we lost our way in the darkness. It took us a long time to emerge onto the main coast road. When we finally reached home, we both agreed "No more short cuts through the Marsh at night!"

I have since used that incident in my book, *The Facts About the Catholic Church*, as an illustration of the disastrous ease with which one can lose one's way in the journey of life, unless one has a reliable guide, namely the Church.

## Dover Castle

After some months spent in and around Hythe, the entire Brigade was moved to the Dover area. I was billeted with the King's Liverpool Regiment in Dover Castle. This move meant that I now had to re-plan all my work. I was not worried over this – I knew how to set about it now.

On Sundays I would say three Masses: one in the Castle itself, one for the South Lancashire Regiment and the Buffs in an army gymnasium near the Grand Shaft Barracks, and a third for some artillery and Army Service Corps units in a convent chapel at St Margaret's Bay. As soon as possible I updated my list of units now to be attended to in my new area. Contacting these, I got a nominal roll of all Catholics in the units, and by regular visiting, got to know them.

I was pleased to be stationed in Dover. The town interested me: it had so often figured in books I had read. One outstanding example was Dickens' *A Tale of Two Cities*. He brought Dover also into *David Copperfield*. One day, as I was passing some houses in the centre square of the town, I saw a plaque affixed to the wall of one of them. There were four or five steps leading up to the front door of this Georgian house, and the plaque was on the wall close to these steps. I stopped and read with interest the following words: "On these steps Charles Dickens represented David Copperfield as resting in his search for his aunt, Betsy Trotwood."

I have referred earlier to the damage in Dover caused by German shelling. There was one particular road, Grace Dieu Road, which I judged had suffered most: it was a shambles of wrecked houses. The people in the town told me the German guns were on a fixed line of fire, and that this one road was on that line. The road itself seemed to indicate the truth of this: it was an avenue of ruined houses and heaps of rubble.

The Catholic parish church was situated on this same road, yet somehow it had remained untouched – except for one part of the wall, which had been slightly damaged. The priests of the parish lived in the adjoining house, and carried on their parish work to the best of their ability. This sort of exemption or preservation of churches and holy places happened so often in the war that one ceased to be astonished at it. In my experience, the most striking example was the Carmelite Convent in Lisieux, where St Thérèse of the Child Jesus had been a nun. The houses and shops all around this convent were in ruins, yet the convent was intact.

In Dover at night, when the German batteries on Cap Gris-Nez started a bout of shelling, I used to stand on one of the town's white cliffs and watch for the flash of the German guns as they fired a salvo. From where I was standing, those guns were twenty-three miles away. As soon as I saw the lights flickering in the darkness at Cap Gris-Nez, I started counting the seconds up to the shells' arrival. Usually about fifty-five seconds passed and then came the thundering crash and deafening explosion, as the shells landed somewhere in the town.

As I stood counting the seconds on the cliffs in the utter darkness of the wartime blackout, I confess it was a matter of considerable interest to me to know where those shells were going to land. It somehow adds a horrible new element to all the death and ruin in Dover, to recall as I have stated already, that all these guns and shells used by the Germans on Cap Gris-Nez were French guns and shells which the Germans had captured in that awful fiasco, the Maginot Line.

In Dover I had very good attendances at my Masses by the soldiers on Sundays. I heard confessions before the Masses. Quite a number of the men availed of this opportunity to receive the Sacraments. I always preached at the Masses – not a long sermon, but something lasting about ten minutes. I always selected subjects suited to the men's unwonted circumstances in their army life.

Each week I tried to hold a Padre's Hour with the Catholic men in the different units of my area. After these meetings, I made myself available to any man who wished to see me. To the men at the Sunday Masses I sold dozens of copies of *The Universe* and *The Catholic Herald*. The men passed these papers to their comrades. The Catholic Women's League was very generous to me: at my request, they sent me corded rosaries and Catholic booklets for the men. I distributed all they sent me.

Later on, in France, Belgium, Holland and Germany, many a Catholic soldier went into battle – and many of them to their death – carrying with them their blue-corded rosary. The men were always glad to receive a rosary, a crucifix or a blessed medal. Some observers have seen in this happy eagerness of the soldiers a naïve form of superstition – something like the belief or confidence in lucky mascots or trinkets often manifested by forthright atheists. I see it differently: the Catholic soldiers, and indeed ever so many of the non-Catholic soldiers, took these religious objects and made them their own as a sign, on their part, of their belief and confidence in Almighty God, and as a token or pledge on God's part of His Fatherly help and protection.

If the men were questioned, they would not perhaps have said explicitly what I am saying. Even if highly articulate, they probably could not have clearly analysed their mental attitudes – yet I discerned their true deep thoughts and feelings. A man's eyes, voice, gestures can be a most clear expression of these. I base my conviction on what they expressed through their eyes, their gestures and tone of voice: all of their outward responses to these sacred objects. Some no doubt saw in these objects a kind of lucky charm and nothing more, but these men were the exception.

I also distributed Catholic booklets to the men. One day a bundle of these arrived from the Catholic Women's League. They were devotional pamphlets which some convent school had donated for the soldiers. Before giving them to the men, I glanced through them. Inside one of them, I saw written the name of the girl who had owned the booklet: it was the same name as that of a French general, then Head of the Free French Forces in England, one who would later save France from chaos. The name I read was, "Elizabeth de Gaulle".

During those war days, lack of reading material was a real hardship for many of the soldiers. Hence these booklets which I distributed after my Masses on Sundays were readily accepted by the men. The soldiers stationed near St Margaret's Bay were particularly pleased to get "something to read". They were very isolated; their off-duty hours were often tedious and boring. An interesting booklet made the time pass quickly.

Aware of this isolation, I made sure to give them a Padre's Hour as frequently as possible. The proper name of their location was St Margaret's at Cliffe – a name most apt, for one arrived at it via a road steeply descending from the clifftops to almost sea level. The convent chapel of a French Order of nuns was at my disposal there for Sunday Masses and also for my Padre's Hour. Early in the war the nuns had evacuated to a quieter inland area. Their convent, which had been partly damaged by German bombing and shelling, was a godsend to me in my work.

St Margaret's Bay was in England's front line of the war and so it remained, until the capture of France and Belgium after the Normandy invasion. The cliffs above it, the surrounding countryside, the very shoreline: all were pitted with shell holes. The entire area had been – and was still being – shelled by the Germans again and again: it had also been bombed by their planes in their many lightning raids along the coast.

On the cliffs adjoining the road which descended into the village, lived a family named Stone. In their home, after my Sunday Mass, I used to get a cup of tea. All around the house lay damaged buildings with gaping, chalky shell holes: yet Mr Stone, and his wife and children, had remained in their home ever since the commencement of the war. Whether they wished it or not, they had a grandstand view of the Battle of Britain. They likewise had witnessed a number of the British Navy's sea encounters with German ships in the Channel.

When I reflected on their dangerous situation, I was amazed that they had not long since gone off to some safer area, astonished that they had not gone away as nearly all their neighbours had done. Mr Stone gave me his reason for staying where he was: he and his family had nowhere to go! So he had no option but to stay in what was then popularly known as "Hellfire Corner". What fortitude those parents showed – anxious as they were for their children's safety and the preservation of the house that was their only home and refuge! Scarce a day passed without air-raid warnings, air raids, gunfire and shelling. Yet despite the peril and the mental strain they lived through, these parents remained courageous and cheerful to a remarkable degree.

In days of peace this Kentish coast was a summer holiday area. As I saw it then, in those days of war, the holiday touch had most definitely vanished! The hotels and guesthouses were either ruined by shelling, or boarded up for the duration of the war. The streets were deserted and silent. Roads were blocked by squat concrete pillars. Here and there one came upon a patrol of soldiers. The sea still rose and fell in its tides; the waves still murmured on the sands; the cloudless blue skies of summer were overhead. All was as attractive as ever, but no holidaymakers were there to enjoy it all. The emptiness and silence spelt danger: this was no area now for fun-seekers. If the German guns kept quiet, the roads and streets and promenades were safe enough; but the sea and the sands were permanently closed by dense rolls of barbed wire – and also by one's keen awareness that the entire shore was thickly mined.

Once I was the only visitor in Margate on an August Bank Holiday. I reflected how crammed with people the promenade and adjoining streets would be in peacetime. I saw only one person in the town that day – a policeman walking his beat. Through the exigencies of war, Margate had become a ghost town. It was the same story in Ramsgate, Deal, Folkestone and Dover. These towns – apart from army and navy activity – were empty and silent. Life for those who had to stay in them was dull and monotonous. Normal town life, normal social life had ceased. Soldiers in these areas knew ennui and boredom. Very little happened to break the monotony.

I can recall one incident in our Brigade which caused some stir. Three of the soldiers, about to be court-martialled for some misdemeanours, were put in the guardroom. I recall the alarm, the excitement, and the humour among their comrades when the word went round that all three had escaped. It soon became evident that no one had connived at their exit from the guard-room. Those boys had ingenuity and imagination. They studied their prison surroundings. To their delight they spotted one fact which would help them towards freedom – the hinges of the heavy iron-studded door of their cell were screwed to the inside of the door. Throughout the night the three prisoners, with knives or spoons purloined from their meal trays, worked steadily at these hinges until they had unscrewed them. At a suitable hour in the dead of night, they quietly slid the door aside and made their way to freedom. I cannot recall whether they were found. Usually such men made for London – and if they reached the metropolis, went into hiding. It is a curious fact that such men were somehow able to contact people who would conceal them – and all this in wartime when the country was fighting for its very existence.

## The 43rd Division and Carthusian Monastery

Not long afterwards, I was transferred to a Brigade Headquarters of the 43rd Division. This was located in the Kentish countryside at Betteshanger, seven or eight miles from Dover.

This was a change of billet for me. I was now living with 129 Infantry Brigade Headquarters. My Brigadier was a Catholic. He served my Mass every morning. The Brigade staff were very friendly and helpful. All were very well-educated and most intelligent. What interesting discussions we had!

Our billet was a beautiful mansion dating from Elizabethan times. Given time and opportunity, I felt I might easily have discovered in it a priest's hiding place or a secret room where Mass would have been offered in Penal Times. The walls of the main rooms downstairs were panelled in oak. The floors were of broad oaken boards so old and polished, they were now dark and shining. In those years of war, the extensive grounds and garden had grown wild – but one saw enough in them to appreciate the former lovely grace of this very English home.

Since I had first joined the army, this was perhaps my most pleasant assignment. Summer was with us. Roses grew around the house in profusion. The cloudless skies, the long calm evenings, the quietness of the fields and lanes, the matin song of thrush and blackbird – these helped to make life pleasant for all of us.

My work was satisfactory. I now had transport in the shape of a Norton 500 cc motorcycle. I knew the location of all my units, and I was able to visit them regularly. It still took me some time to become acquainted with the officers and men of the three Regiments that made up the Brigade.

In one of these Regiments the Adjutant was a Catholic. He told me he had been a theological student in one of the English seminaries at the outbreak of the war. He felt he should join the army and do his bit for his country. His Archbishop, Dr Amigo, had assured him that if he carried out his plan he would certainly lose his vocation. And this is exactly what happened!

When this officer and I became well acquainted, he one day admitted to me he no longer desired to become a priest. He had no inclination whatever to resume his theological studies, for he now intended to marry. His future bride was one of his cousins. We remained very good friends. Yet I could not help feeling some regret about his case. He still retained a very Catholic outlook on everything; he had also a certain priestly flair in his manner and work. I often came away from him, reflecting that in the normal way of things he might have been working with me in what would soon be the red vineyard of the Lord – the battlefields of France.

His Battalion and all the other units of the Brigade then moved to a camp in the west of England close to Dorchester. I went with them. As we were to be under canvas, I loaded my motorcycle with my necessary gear and started off for Dorchester.

En route I called at the Carthusian Monastery at Parkminster. The day was Pentecost Sunday. I attended the Community's High Mass. It was interesting to observe the Carthusian form of the Liturgy. The Guest Master who took charge of me during my visit told me that only one Mass was said in the monastery on the more important feasts. This Mass was said by the Abbot. The Guest Master explained that the Carthusian 'idea' was to keep the Community rapt in contemplation – a multiplicity of Masses, it seemed, would distract the monks. I could not then make sense of what the good man said: today, after the lapse of many years, his explanation still baffles me.

Another point about that High Mass comes to my mind: when the Deacon had sung, "Ite missa est!" ("Go in peace! The Mass is ended!"), the entire group of monks present sang the response, "Deo Gratias", and straightway left the Chapel. They took the Deacon at his word! Nowadays it is normal for the people at all our Masses to leave when the priest says the above words.

In 1943, when I called at Parkminster it was not their practice: at High Mass a last Gospel had to be read; at Low Mass there would be, in addition, the recital of the Leonine Prayers. What I witnessed in Parkminster that day showed me now that the current new practice is really a return to the ancient practice of the Church.

The youngish Carthusian Guest Master who was my host at the monastery was very affable and friendly. He was interested in my work and its problems. I asked him about his own way of life – what in it, for example, did he find most trying? Without a moment's hesitation, he told me it was the monotony of the life. The daily routine never varied: it continued till you died. Day after day after day the monastery bell gave the monks commands, summoned them here, summoned them there; they prayed, worked, took their meals, slept the quota of hours fixed by their religious Rules, arose in the dead of night to chant the Divine Office of Psalms in the bleak chapel of the monastery. It was always the same routine, day in and day out, always the same faces and the same voices, always the same corridors and rooms: one's life alone, day after day, month after month, year after year, till death would call. All in all, a life dominated by a solemn dedication to God. An extraordinary life, needing an extraordinary vocation!

Each monk has his own set of rooms. The cloisters are in the form of a square and enclose a garden. On the off-side of the cloister corridor, at regular intervals, the monks have their rooms or cells. These cells are too cold and cheerless and bare to be called 'apartments' – a word which connotes something of comfort and homeliness.

In his cells a monk will have a ground floor workshop, where he may usefully employ himself at some handicraft. Upstairs he has two rooms – a living room and a bedroom. Outside his cells, but accessible only from the lower cell, is his own small garden which he tends himself. Such is his home for life.

Once a week the monks take their principal meal in the Refectory (community dining room). They also assemble in the chapel for Mass or the chanting of the Divine Office. I am told their rules have been eased somewhat, and that they now all go for a walk together through the countryside once a week. Apart from these occasions, each monk lives an isolated life. His meagre meals are brought by a Brother from the kitchen and handed to him through a small hatchway beside the door of his hermitage. To preserve the strict monastic silence, each monk has a number of printed cards, on which are messages he might want to convey to the Brother, eg: "More bread!", "Half a loaf", etc. Using these cards as required makes it unnecessary to hold conversation with the Brother who brings the monk his meals.

The Carthusian boast runs: "Never reformed, because never deformed!" It is a valid bit of boasting: down through almost a thousand years, they have persevered in their stern, strict life of solitude, prayer, penance and work.

I must confess I left that Carthusian Monastery with a certain feeling of relief. As I sped through the lovely open countryside on the motorcycle, I felt a sense of freedom and release after all the isolation and stern seclusion presented to my eyes on every side within those monastic walls. Particular elements in the Carthusian life attracted me, and I admired the men who lived that life – but I felt I could not imitate them. Theirs is a special vocation, an exceptional way of life.

"We do not aim at having great numbers of monks – we prefer to remain few in number!" said the Guest Master. I cannot say what his point was. I do think, however, that the Carthusian monasteries will never have too many applicants.

I went on my way to our new camp, near Dorchester. Our stay there under canvas was quite pleasant. The weather stayed fine. The days passed quickly. As we were located some distance away from the ordinary social amenities of a soldier's life, we had to amuse ourselves as best we could in our free hours. On an evening in the Mess tent, the young officers would conspire to deprive me of the Roman Collar I wore. They would suddenly move in on me from all sides: in a moment, four or five of them would be piling on top of me. However, I would not yield without a fierce struggle. I twisted and turned and rolled and wriggled. I was always conquered, because they were too many for me. However, I held one small advantage over them: although they could finally pin me down, they could not decide what would be the best way to denude me of my collar. Often, while they were at loggerheads over this point, I threw them off me – and the struggle started all over again. Overwhelmed in the end, I had to submit to partial defrocking, and they were all puffing and blowing before the shindig was over. Wrestlers have a mat, a good thick mat on which to wage their combats: we had none, and so in that Mess tent the struggles took place on the bare grass.

I got along very well with those officers of the Wessex Regiment. I often mused over the fact that their predecessors in the regiment had campaigned in Ireland against the Irish Republican Army. They had had some bitter encounters with the Republicans. How utterly impersonal their side of it was – but here I was, an Irish priest, living with them, working with them, yet in no way made to feel a stranger. I was among friends.

In nearly all the units with which I was associated in the army, I experienced the same fellowship and friendliness. I felt at home with them, and many of the officers and men became my good friends.

On my return from camp, I took up life again at the Brigade Headquarters. As usual the Brigadier served my Mass every morning. He derived great benefit from his faith and from the Mass: these had a profound influence on his daily life. I had clear proof of this, on one occasion when I returned from leave. On the morning of my reappearance in the Mess, the Brigade Major greeted me warmly, exclaiming, "Thank God, Padre, you are back with us again!"

"Why?" I asked. "What has happened?"

"The Brigadier has been impossible since you left us!"

"And what have I got to do with that?" I replied.

"Oh, don't you see? That morning Mass of yours keeps him in order!" he rejoined.

What surprised me in this incident was the plain fact that these non-Catholic officers saw a change in the Brigadier when I went on leave, but also knew the change was due to his not being at Mass and Holy Communion in the mornings. The Brigadier was a fine soldier. He had won the Distinguished Service Order decoration for his bravery and leadership at the time of the Dunkirk debacle. He was also an excellent Catholic. What I have said above shows this.

Tragically he met his death during the campaign in Normandy. Returning one day from a routine inspection of his Brigade's positions, he spotted an ammunition supply lorry parked near his temporary Headquarters. Getting out of his car, he went over to the lorry driver and told him to park his vehicle some distance away. While he was speaking to this soldier, a German shell landed close by. The lorry blew up. All those in the vicinity, including the Brigadier, were killed.

I was not attached to that unit at the time. I was told the Brigadier died instantly. It was all very tragic: dying in the prime of life, he left behind a young wife and several children in Somerset.

My work among the soldiers of my Brigade went on as usual. I visited the three Regiments in turn, holding meetings and discussions with the Catholic men. My three Masses on Sundays were so arranged, regarding times and places, as to make attendance easier for them. I became known in the Brigade, and my influence widened. I was happy and contented in my work. Suddenly one morning however, out of the blue, came my appointment to the 32nd Guards Brigade in the Guards Armoured Division, then stationed somewhere in Yorkshire.

With deep regret I left the officers and men of the 43rd Division. My stay with them in Kent had been a pleasant one and I was sorry to leave them. In the army, as in life, one soon learns that nothing lasts.

Having said goodbye to all my friends in the Brigade, I journeyed to York and there reported to Colonel Monsignor Parisotte, the Senior Catholic Chaplain in Northern Command. Having warmly welcomed me, he directed me to my new unit, bidding me join the Irish Guards 3rd Battalion at Malton in Yorkshire.

## The Irish Guards

On reaching Malton, however, I found all the billets empty, except for some sentries and holding personnel. Someone informed me that the entire Battalion was on manoeuvres – a "scheme", it was called in army parlance. Without more ado, I set off to find the Battalion and join it. After some hunting around, I discovered them in South Yorkshire. All were surprised that I should come out to join them in the middle of a scheme – most newcomers would have stayed in the comfortable billets in Malton, and purred with pleasure at escaping the bleak rigours of a wintry scheme on the bare Yorkshire Wolds. My action was neither virtuous nor admirable, however – I joined the Battalion when out on the scheme because I thought that was the normal, proper duty.

Anyway by doing what I did, I gained much. First of all, I received a cordial welcome from both officers and men – more cordial perhaps because I came out to them on the scheme, which I need not have done. Secondly, I became instantly known to the entire Battalion: I dined with all the officers in the Battalion mess tent and I mingled among the Guardsmen in the fields where we pitched camp. The result of this was I had become accepted and established myself as "the new priest" before we returned to Malton.

I was not long with the Battalion before I realised my life was going to be very different henceforward. A few days on that scheme opened my eyes. Even though the minds of the officers and men were much taken up by the war-like operation they had embarked on, they soon showed me by word and demeanour that the Battalion's Catholic Chaplain held a special place in the affairs of the Irish Guards. Every man of them, Catholic and non-Catholic, would look up to him. He was one apart: to him all would turn with their problems and their worries. Quite frankly, I was unprepared for this: I wish I had been told about it. The attention and courtesy shown me left me slightly bewildered. In all my units hitherto, I had been a kind of appendage: an extra of sorts, someone more or less out on a limb. All that would now end. As one Guardsman said to me, "The priest is an important man in the Irish Guards!"

In the Irish Guards a lot of the life and activity of the Battalion circles around the Battalion's priest. He organises concerts, solves domestic problems for the men, smooths out differences and misunderstandings even among the officers, gives lectures, visits men sick in hospital, advises authority of the Battalion's problems, supplies the men with Catholic books and papers, helps those in trouble – visiting them in the guardroom, and discussing their cases with their respective officers. And far away above all else, he says Mass for the men, and in his Sunday sermons and addresses, keeps up the tone and the morale of the Battalion.

In the Irish Guards the mode of addressing and referring to the priest differs from that in all other army units: he is not called "Padre", he is not referred to as "the Padre": he is addressed and referred to as "Father". This has been the custom adhered to since Queen Victoria established the Irish Guards Regiment after the Boer War. All the Guardsmen – Protestants as well as Catholics – called me "Father". Protestant Guardsmen from the Shankill Road or Sandy Row areas in Belfast, as well as Catholic men from Galway or Tipperary, were now my close friends. I had to work for, and be interested in all of them: they, on their side, looked to me as a friend, not a stranger.

I realised that the special place held by the priest among the Irish Guards is due to the heroism and selflessness of the priests who served with them in war and in peace. The names of these priests live on in the traditions of the Battalion: their bravery and their sayings are still remembered. In the Mess, how often stories were told about Fr So-and-So, what he did and what he said when "we" were in Norway or in North Africa. These chaplains were men of unusual calibre, utterly devoted to the welfare of the Guardsmen. Now, in following in their footsteps, I had their example to inspire me. In my heart I knew very well I could never measure up to them: I would however do my best.

As I have already said, I made a lucky and auspicious start. All the Guardsmen were rather pleased with me because, instead of lounging in the comfortable billets in Malton, I had preferred to come out to them on the scheme and share its concomitant discomforts.

My memory of that scheme is now rather jumbled. It seemed to consist of interminable road journeys, prolonged purposeless delays, sleep in awkward, makeshift shelters for the night, and days which brought forth a medley of new faces and new situations.

One event, however, stands out clearly in my memory, namely, our arrival at dawn – after a wretched night on the Yorkshire roads – in a field where we were to bivouac for some hours. Weary though I was, I stood watching the Battalion spreading out into the field, company by company. Then I observed two interesting and unforgettable episodes.

The first was this. I saw the non-commissioned officers going among the guardsmen and giving them the following order: "Every man to be properly dressed for breakfast when it is ready!" Now this phrase "properly dressed" is polite, peremptory and sinister! How many Guardsmen have been "awarded" (thus they daintily describe it in army pronouncements) punishment because they were not properly dressed? What then does this phrase mean? In its strictly complete sense, it means that everything about your appearance as officer or guardsman must be clean and correct – you hair neatly trimmed, your boots gleaming, your belt and equipment polished, and nothing about you slipshod. But that morning on the scheme, the phrase meant, "Every man must shave before breakfast." Seeing that we were away from our billets and bivouacked in a muddy field, no more could be demanded. Nevertheless the command was the limit of the possible and had to be carried out. I watched the Guardsmen on that raw, bleak morning searching the fields and the neighbourhood for water for shaving.

The second episode was as follows. The officers supervised the Guardsmen's breakfast: they sat, each company commander beside the company cooker, seeing to it that every man got a substantial breakfast served out to him, piping hot. The men queued up for their meal, mess tin and mug in their hands. For every one of them, the officer had a cheery greeting. Often there was a quiet enquiry about a man's stamina and his well-being, such as, "How is your ankle faring, Sullivan – able to stick it?" You could see the astonishing effect all this had on the spirits of the men. Only when the last Guardsman had been served breakfast, did the officers go off to attend to their own needs.

These two episodes made a deep impression on me. Hitherto in the army I had never witnessed such deep concern for the men.

Tradition in the Brigade of Guards assists the Guardsmen in two ways principally – by rigid discipline and by the personal interest of officers in every one of them. Regarding discipline, a basic ineluctable law is this – "a

Guardsman must be spotlessly clean and tidy in his person, his uniform, and his equipment". In other words a Guardsman must always be properly dressed by Guards' standards. This means his boots must sparkle, his uniform be brushed and pressed, his kit shining, his face shaved daily, and his hair cut and trimmed every week. In my time with the Battalion, hours were devoted weekly to these tasks. In the Royal Navy it is maintained that a clean ship is a happy ship: in the Guards, it is likewise believed that a clean Guardsman is an efficient soldier. In theory this might be questioned; but it works out effectively in practice. The man who disciplines himself to be always "properly dressed" will certainly discipline himself to carry out his duties. I saw proof of this principle in practice every day of my life with the Guards. Their basic thinking was correct: it worked. It worked on parade; it worked at drill; it worked in training sessions; it worked in war and on the battlefield.

So much for the rigid discipline of the Guards. Now a word about the personal concern of the officers for their men. I knew that the officers had a genuine interest in their men. How often they came to me about the troubles and problems of some one of their men, and showed how anxious they were to help: "Father, if money is needed to fix up that man's domestic troubles, let me know!"; or again: "Father, Guardsman X is in the Guard Room on detention – do please have a chat with him: I think you can help him!"

The officers' genuine interest in their men gave them great influence over them. The Guardsmen saw they were being treated as human beings – and, more than that, as individuals! There was fair play. And while they were kind and considerate to the genuine Guardsman, they were ruthless with anyone who was 'idle'. That simple word, 'idle', in the usage of the Guards, retains its original meaning: it connotes more than being merely unoccupied. A man who is idle is a slacker, a good-for-nothing specimen, one who is a dodger: lazy, shiftless, and little better than dead wood.

Such a Guardsman, unless he quickly reforms, is going to have a very unhappy time in the Guards' Regiments. Such a man yields and breaks, or is broken and then yields. The Brigade of Guards has a staunch tradition of service and courage: it will not allow any individual to lower these standards.

I would also say that undoubtedly this would apply to officers as well as to the rank and file. The officers who are commissioned to the Guards' Regiments have all passed severe tests in discipline and efficiency. They did of course have the service of a batman to see to the polishing and cleanliness of their kit and uniforms, and so it involved less trouble for them to be properly dressed. Yet an officer who is careless in these matters will remain so despite the valiant efforts of any batman. I must say, however, that any Guards officers I knew set an excellent example in terms of personal neatness and efficiency.

When that first scheme ended, we returned to Malton, a small town lying between York and Scarborough. I was assigned a billet near the centre of the town, so that I was easily approached by any of the Guardsmen who had problems and were needing my help or advice. It was a small billet, consisting as it did of the front room on the ground floor of an ordinary dwelling house on one of Malton's main streets.

My official status now was Roman Catholic Chaplain, 32nd Guards' Brigade. I was attached to the 3rd Battalion of the Irish Guards. I had to attend to their spiritual needs and also to the needs of the Welsh Guards in Rillington (about six miles from Malton), and of the Coldstream Guards in Scarborough (about twenty-five miles away). These three Guards' Battalions formed the main body of troops in the Brigade. There were in addition some smaller units: a Field Ambulance Company, a Company of Scots Guards, a Support Group from a county Regiment, and a Brigade Signals Group at Brigade Headquarters. All in all, I had about five or six hundred Catholic men to look after, with nearly three hundred of these being in the Irish Guards' Battalion. On Sundays I would say my first Mass in the parish church at Malton, and my second for the men in the Support Group located in the countryside several miles from Malton. The Welsh Guards always had transport to bring them to the Mass in Malton. The Coldstream Guards in Scarborough were very near the Catholic Church there, so it was pointless for me to travel twenty-five miles to say a third Mass for them, when they had a number of Masses being said next door to them. Hence I did not tend to say a third Mass, except perhaps when the Division was out on a scheme.

I soon framed for myself a structured way of work and life in my new area. I started off with several advantages: I had a car, a batman driver, clear maps and plenty of good roads. Thanks to the cooperation of my various units, I was able to give the men in each large section a regular Padre's Hour.

In my own Mess the officers were very affable and helpful. Life with them was pleasant. The Mess atmosphere was easy and informal; conversation was entertaining, and there was much good humour. The affairs of the Mess were run most efficiently.

The officers, junior and senior, addressed one another by their Christian names. There was only one exception – the Commanding Officer. While he addressed the others by their Christian names, he was himself always addressed as "Sir". In speaking of him, all referred to him as "the Commanding Officer". He always got his proper title in full: he was never referred to as "the CO", as is commonly done in other army units. This Guards' custom subtly strengthened his authority.

The dominant feature of life in the Irish Guards' Mess was the fine courtesy and comradeship displayed by all. That was the tradition – one easily maintained by the officers, for they came from homes in which courtesy and friendliness reigned. A stranger entering their Mess and meeting them for the first time might have a wrong impression: to him, these officers might seem a whit too refined for the ruthless, bloody business of war. Such a judgment would be both hasty and erroneous. Later on, in Normandy's battlefields, I saw with my own eyes how rock-like and steady they were when guns were blazing and men were dying around them. Their gentlemanliness and ease concealed immense reserves of courage and fortitude: the gloves were velvet; the hands themselves were steel.

Observing them in the Mess, on the parade ground, at the firing ranges and in their battle training, I used to repeat to myself Asquith's succinct summing up of Balliol men: "the tranquil consciousness of effortless superiority". That is an exaggerated statement in their regard, but it gets close to what I am trying to convey.

Although I was friendly with all the officers, I was more friendly with a few. Major Connolly McCausland of Drenagh, Limavady, our Second-in-Command, was perhaps my closest friend. He had become a Catholic while in the army. We were drawn together by these two facts: we were both Ulstermen and we were Catholics. We used to have long discussions about religion, politics, the structures in the institutional side of the Church, the morale of the Battalion, the welfare of the men, and so on.

The Guardsmen held him in high esteem. He had proved himself a fine soldier in their eyes at the time of the evacuation of Dunkirk. His courage and leadership then won him the Military Cross. Of all the Battalion officers he was perhaps the most respected and popular. Always cheerful, affable and approachable, he hid from others the acute anxieties which must have occupied his mind. One of his chief worries was undoubtedly his deceased Father's will.

According to the terms of the will, his father, Marcus McCausland had left the entire family estate to Connolly. The will, however, was conditional: if Connolly became a Catholic, he forfeited his inheritance. So far as I can recall, he was not initially aware of this conditional clause. You can imagine his shock on becoming a Catholic at learning from the family solicitor that he had forfeited everything.

Cyril Nicholson QC, a personal friend and neighbour of Connolly, kept urging him to contest the will. He was aware that Connolly was minded to leave the matter alone and to abide by what his father had decided. In the end Connolly agreed to put the will to the test in the courts. When I was going home on leave to Northern Ireland, he entrusted the relevant documents to me to bring to Cyril Nicholson.

Finally the case came before the courts. Connolly rested his case on the indeterminate nature of the will in its conditional clause; for no one on earth could say at what moment of time it became operative. Canon Law was invoked, and experts from Maynooth College were called in to testify on this point. Connolly had been baptised and had no formally heretical views or teachings to rescind. When he decided to accept the Catholic Church and its doctrines, was that not enough to join him to the Church? So it was argued and debated. In the end the judgment passed was this: Connolly was to have the use, but not the ownership, of the estate while he lived, and on his death the entire property would go to his eldest son. It was a suitable decision: the forfeit clause in the will was, of course, an unjust denial of Connolly's right to follow his conscience.

Marcus McCausland probably knew that Connolly had leanings towards the Catholic Church. In the will he did all he could to ensure his son's loyalty to the Protestant faith.

Another good friend of mine in the Battalion was Prince John of Luxembourg. He was known to us as "John Luxembourg". A junior officer, he was unassuming, always ready to play his part in any duty or Battalion activity, and ever pleasant in manner. We used to go on walks together. We were never short of topics for conversation. He knew a number of our Redemptorist priests in Luxembourg. He had been a boarder at Ampleforth College for years. He was a devout Catholic and set a splendid example to the men of the Battalion. An accomplished linguist, he spoke fluent English, French and German. We had no one in the Brigade to equal him in linguistic ability. He carried his dignity, as he did his knowledge, with ease and assurance. He was in no way affected. No one ever saw him putting on an act. To all of us he was just a fellow-officer, carrying his share of the daily tasks and burdens.

I have a vivid memory of seeing him on a cold winter's morning, the countryside white with frost, emerging from his night's rude bivouac in the lee of a bank. His men had slept in the open that night; he did likewise.

When we took part in the Normandy invasion, Prince John was attached to Brigade Headquarters as a Staff Officer and interpreter. This position enabled him to use his knowledge of German and French effectively. I now had less contact with him and would just occasionally meet him on my rounds.

Later on, in the Normandy campaign, I received information that the Division was going into battle in a few hours' time. I first attended the men of the various units in the Brigade, and then went off to find John Luxembourg. I found him seated near his slit trench in an apple orchard. I told him that in view of the fact that we were going into action, I had come to see him.

"Give me a few moments, Father!" he said quietly, "I would like to go to Confession."

I wandered off to see some of the other men at Brigade Headquarters. On my return, John knelt on the grass beside me and made his confession. This readiness to avail of the Sacrament of Penance was a normal feature in his life. He was a Catholic who lived up to his Faith. I have always been pleased that he came safely through the campaigns of France, Belgium and Germany.

These foregoing paragraphs about Prince John, however, have brought me too far ahead in my general narrative. I must resume my account of my fellow officers in the Mess while we were in England.

In our Mess I was one of the older officers (as Chaplain, I held the honorary rank of Captain). I had perhaps a wider experience of some aspects of life and travel than many of them. I had read more – not the clipped, jejune stuff you get in military manuals, but books in the general run of literature. I had also read a lot of philosophy and theology. All my reading and my experiences as a priest stood to me when discussions began in the Mess about current affairs or other matters of interest.

In our Irish Guards' Mess, as in all army Messes, discussions on religion and politics were taboo, but points often came up which touched on these two taboos. I can recall only a few occasions when religion came up as a subject, and on both occasions I was somewhat embarrassed. I will explain what happened.

One Boxing Day the BBC gave a news summary of the Pope's Christmas address. I and a number of other officers were sitting in the anteroom of the Mess, reading papers or listening to the Radio News. On hearing this summary of the Pope's address, one of our junior officers, not a Catholic, stretched out his arms, looked around wearily and in a clear distinct voice exclaimed, "Did anyone ever hear such drivel?" Instantly the atmosphere became electric! All the officers present looked at me. There was a moment's silence. Putting down the paper I was reading, I looked directly at this officer, called him by his Christian name, and in a calm deliberate voice said to him, "That remark in an Irish Guards' Mess is in very bad taste!"

He tried to laugh it off, saying, "You know, Father, I am not one of His Flock!"

I would not let him away with it, however.

"That is not the point! The remark you have just now made is in very bad taste in an Irish Guards' Mess!"

He rose from his chair and left the room. The other officers spoke not a word. They saw and heard all that had happened. I went on reading my paper.

There was an interesting sequel to all this. Three or four mornings later, that particular officer waited to speak to me after breakfast. In most contrite manner, he apologised for what he had said:

"I am terribly sorry, Father. I do not know what made me say it. I hope you will forgive me!"

On another occasion a religious issue came up in the following way. One Sunday I was seated at lunch in the Mess, when four or five other officers joined me. Of this group only one was a Catholic. At the table one of the non-Catholic officers, referring to the non-Catholic service they had been attending that morning in the town said, "That vicar preached a jolly good sermon this morning!"

To my astonishment the Catholic officer replied, "Yes, it was a fine sermon – I enjoyed it!"

Then, looking over at me, he said in a rather mocking kind of tone, "Father, shall I go to Hell because I attended a Protestant service?" He knew very well what he was saying. He knew he was creating an awkward situation for me. All the officers stopped eating and wanted to hear my reply. Now, it must be remembered that in those distant days in 1944 the question he had brought up was, in the circumstances, an awkward one. The ecumenism of Vatican II with its subsequent theological development had not yet arrived, and theologians were then agreed that active participation in a non-Catholic service was a serious matter, involving grave sin. As this officer had attended such a service and presumably taken active part in it, I would have no option but to repeat the common teaching of theologians in reply to his question. But how was I to say bluntly that his action was blameworthy to such a degree?

Fortunately another line of approach came like a flash into my mind. Calling him by his Christian name, and remembering the school he had attended I replied very quickly,

"It is not for me to teach a Downside boy the answer to that question!"

For the remainder of the meal, he was silent. I think he regretted his attempt at smartness. I still believe I gave him a rebuke as well as an answer. He well knew the answer to his own query. I knew he knew it – but whatever imp of mischief, whatever quirk of humour, perversity or cynicism was in him, he threw an embarrassing question at me in company and left me to deal with it as best I could.

I often think of him and pray for him. He lost his life some months later during the fighting in Normandy. While resting in his slit trench beneath a tree in one of the orchards of the Bocage country, a German high-explosive shell burst in the tree above his head. A splinter of that shell ricocheted downwards and pierced him. He died instantly.

Such were the two incidents touching on religion while I was a member of the Irish Guards' Mess. They do not distract from anything I have said about the good manners and bonhomie which prevailed in the Mess.

## The Stolen Car

About six or seven months after my joining the Guards' Armoured Division, the Catholic Chaplain of one of the Brigades in the 15th Scottish Division asked me to preach a spiritual retreat to his men. With the authority and encouragement of the General commanding the Division, he had secured a suitable place in West Yorkshire, not far from Ilkley. While I was engaged in this work, one of the soldier retreatants slipped away, stole my car, and careered in it over the rough roads of the Yorkshire moors. He ended his wild trip by firmly embedding the car in a marsh alongside one of the lonely roads through the moors. Needless to say, the car was a complete wreck.

The local police were very soon on the soldier's trail. They were not long in catching him. I went to visit him in his cell at the local police station. I was very annoyed and indignant. The loss of my car was a serious one: without it, I would be hampered in my work. How was I to carry on my usual duties? How was I to visit distant, scattered units? As I sat with the culprit in the police cell, I pointed all this out to him. He expressed regret for what he had done. He assured me he did not know it was the priest's car.

I left him. There was nothing I could do about it. My car was a write-off! Someone would have to give me a lift back to Malton, and I would have to make a report.

Some days after our return, Hugh Creaney, my batman, was called to account for what happened. He was severely reprimanded for not immobilising the car – as per army instructions – by removing the rotor arm. In the weeks that followed, I felt the loss of my car. Nor did it lessen my annoyance to think that one of our Catholic soldiers, one for whom I had been working, should do me such an immense disservice. It was small comfort indeed to have heard his prison cell assurances that he did not know it was the priest's car!

We all knew the Invasion of Europe was imminent. It was vital that I keep close contact with all my Catholic men: they needed me now more than ever. And here I was – immobilised! Many months passed by before my car was replaced. By that time I was in Normandy, living on the battlefields, close to death and destruction.

The loss of the car was an exceptional incident. At the time, I used to say to myself, "To you, out of all the priests in the army, this had to happen!" Now that the years have passed, I see things differently. It seems to me now that Providence may have used the loss of the car to save my life. Had I the car in Normandy, I would certainly have moved around a great deal: this necessarily would have exposed me to more danger, for I would have been compelled to use roads observed and shelled by the Germans. A moving car raised clouds of dust, which would have attracted the attention of the German gunners. Many soldiers lost their lives because of that tell-tale dust. Not having a car, I had to make my way to units around the battle zone by crossing the fields and taking near cuts, always keeping away from the roads. I was thus in less danger. I had to face a fresh hazard however, in crossing possible mine fields – I could do nothing about that.

Sergeant Douglas, one of our despatch riders, who used to give me a lift on the pillion of his motorcycle to see frontline troops, was later shot dead on his machine by a German sniper. So perhaps not having a car really did leave me better circumstanced.

That is one aspect of the stolen car incident which impresses me now. Another aspect is this: since there was no regular and continuous frontline of either armies in the Normandy battles, it was quite easy to find oneself in enemy-held territory. This was exactly what happened to another priest in my Division. Having lost his way, he drove into a German position.

The Germans quickly surrounded the car, told him and his batman to get out, and then searched the car thoroughly. The priest explained what had happened and produced his Geneva Red Cross document, which showed that he was a priest and a non-combatant. The German officer-in-command spoke excellent English. He listened to the priest's explanation and examined his documents. While he was thus engaged, a German soldier who had been searching the car came forward with a bolt of Sten gun ammunition. He showed it to the officer.

"If you are a non-combatant, how do you explain this ammunition found in your car?" asked the officer.

Now, according to King's Regulations, the priest's driver should have had his Sten machine gun with him: that day however, luckily, he had forgotten to bring it. So when the officer put the question, the batman spoke up with a bland explanation of how he had come upon the ammunition while crossing the battlefield and had picked it up as a souvenir. This explanation seemed to satisfy the Germans – after all, no gun was found in the car. Demanding that both priest and driver give their word of honour not to reveal the German positions, the officer permitted them to turn the car and drive back to their own lines.

If this happened to one priest, it could have also happened to me in my car – perhaps without my being fortunate enough to encounter such a reasonable and magnanimous German officer. Maybe for me, it was a blessing that I had no car in those early, haphazard days in Normandy.

The ways of Providence are not our ways. Providence can use our losses as well as our gains. Setbacks as well as successes can all be fitted into the eternal design. I recall another illustration of what I am trying to say which also impressed me. In a sermon, Dr Weatherhead described what he saw when watching some Persian weavers working at one of their famous carpets. Facing that side of the hanging fabric on which the design would show, the artist directed the work. On the reverse side, the workers inserted the coloured threads. If in error one of the workers put in a wrong stitch or thread, the artist would not raise a row or threaten recriminations; instead he would use his skill and experience to weave and blend the mistake into the pattern. If the artist were a master of his craft, the finished design might be somewhat different, but not less beautiful. From their position on the reverse side, the weavers could see little or no design: from their side, the carpet was but a confused tangle of coloured threads. When the work was completed, however, the artist would call them to his side to see the finished design. They then saw what his skill had contrived from their work and their mistakes!

God can and does use all that happens for the good of those who serve Him. St Paul tells us so: "In everything He (God) cooperates for good with those who love God!" Thus the New English Bible translates Romans 8:28. The Jerusalem Bible puts it even more clearly: "We know that by turning everything to their good, God cooperates with all those who love him." Writing these words now brings all this home to me; but at the time, I confess I was not able to view the disastrous loss of my car in this light.

In describing this car incident, I have digressed at length from my account of my life and work with the Guards' Armoured Division. I will resume that account now.

I have spoken about the officers of my Irish Guards' Battalion. About a dozen of them were Catholics. In the Welsh Guards, I had four Catholic officers – Captains Pereira, Bedingfield, Worrall, and Turnbull. Excellent Catholics, they each cooperated with me in all my work. In the Coldstream Guards, I had not one Catholic among the officers. In both these Battalions all the officers were invariably courteous and helpful to me. Their manners were refined; their conversation pleasant and friendly; their work thoroughly efficient. To know them was one of the assets of army life.

So much for the officers of my Regiments: now a word about the Guardsmen. Most of the Catholic men were Irish. With them I had one special advantage: having given so many missions and retreats in different parts of Ireland, I very often knew a Guardsman's home town or parish. Such knowledge furnished me with unfailing topics of conversation in their company: every soldier likes to talk about his home.

In my visits to the various units of the Brigade, I sought each man's home address. If he had no home address, I got from him the name of his next-of-kin or of some close friend. While taking down the details, I used to say: "It is good for me to have these addresses, in case anything should happen!" I think each man knew quite well what I meant.

Adjutants and Company Commanders were, as a rule, reasonable in granting me facilities for meeting the Catholic men under their command. I generally succeeded in my aim of giving the three bigger groups in the three Battalions a weekly Padre's Hour. I tried to give the men talks which were suitable for their army life and at the same time interesting.

I realised too well that life in the army in England during those pre-Invasion months was a period of stress and temptation. The men were away from all the healthy influences of their home lives, while the war itself and its perils were as yet remote from them. The wayward example of other men was ever present to their eyes, and the decent, upright men found it hard to keep to the straight and narrow path.

One constant source of danger was drink: it was available and it would often lead to trouble. Men who knew when to stop – and then did stop – were able to steer clear of subsequent rows. Others, who took more drink than was good for them, often ended up in the guardroom because of disorderly behaviour. I used to warn them all about the evils and horror of excessive drinking. Most of them listened and did what I advised, but some heard with unheeding ears and then went out to walk their own path of folly. That was the way they wanted it to be, and I could do nothing about it. You cannot stop a determined drinker.

Sunday, I found, was the best day for my real work. I say "real", because during the week I often spent time with the men on domestic problems in which I could render very little help. If a husband and wife are constantly quarrelling and bickering, no outsider, no matter how well-intentioned, can create harmony between them: peace and understanding must come through their own mutual agreement. Then again, if particular men were in trouble in the Battalion, I had to spend time talking to them and to their officers, in an effort to sort things out and restore normality. All this, of course, was quite distinctly in my line of work as Chaplain, and I was always pleased to help men in this way. But as I have said, my true priestly work happened on Sundays, when I was no longer a kind of welfare worker, but a priest, offering Mass in the presence of the men and preaching the word of God to them. It was for this that I had come into the army.

To my Mass in Malton Parish Church came all the Catholic officers and men of the Irish and Welsh Guards. During the Mass I would preach for about ten minutes: I may or may not have succeeded, but my desire was to preach a sermon that would help these khaki rows of Guardsmen sitting before me to prepare themselves spiritually for the coming Invasion of Europe and all that that entailed. In my other Mass, out in the countryside for the men of the Support Group, my purpose was similar.

The one point I kept stressing was the sheer necessity of faith and the vital importance of our living in accordance with it. I realised that all these men gazing up at me would sooner or later be facing the grim and bloody realities of war; a number of them would certainly be killed. It was my duty now to prepare them for what lay ahead. At the Masses I would give the times for

Confessions to be heard in the church during the week, as well as making any necessary or useful announcements.

Every week after Mass I would set out for sale six dozen copies of *Universe* magazine, and an equal number of copies of *The Catholic Herald*, something I made sure to feature in my announcements. Before each Mass, if time allowed, I would hear Confessions; after Mass, I did not rush away but stayed around for a while, in case any of the men wished to speak to me.

As the weeks and months passed by, we all became increasingly conscious of the approaching British invasion of Europe. We knew for certain we were one of the Divisions taking part in it. We also knew that the Army Commanders would expect a great deal from our Guards' Armoured Division. There were certainly rough days ahead of us all! The Germans were as yet far from being defeated. Moreover, in their usual expert manner, they had mounted strong defences against our landing anywhere along the coasts of Holland, Belgium, and France. They would offer stubborn resistance: for them, this invasion of the countries they occupied, would be the beginning of victory or defeat in the long-drawn war.

Envisaging the stern tasks before us, we went ahead steadily with our training for D-Day. We had more schemes, and I recall some very bleak nights on the roads of Yorkshire and Lincolnshire. Then the word went round that we were to practise invasion-landing tactics somewhere on the coast.

## The Duke of Argyll

A few days later we moved to Inverary, at the head of Loch Fyne in Argyllshire. There the Battalion was billeted in the grounds of Inverary Castle, the residence of the chieftain of the Campbell Clan, the Duke of Argyll.

Shortly after our arrival in his demesne, the Commanding Officer of my Battalion asked me to call on the Duke and inform him that, as soon as we had settled in, he with the other officers would call on him. Behold me then, approaching the Castle of Inverary on a spring evening. It stood apart, with no other buildings near it, four square with turrets at each of its corners. Against the evening sun its black stone became ever so dark and sinister. Every part of the building seemed to be cold and cheerless.

As I neared the castle, I thought of David Balfour in Stevenson's *Kidnapped*, approaching his Uncle Ebenezer's house – the "House of Shaws":

"The nearer I got to it, the drearier it appeared... At last the sun went down, and then, right up against the yellow sky, I saw a scroll of smoke go mounting, not much thicker, as it seemed to me, than the smoke of a candle; but still there it was, and meant a fire, and warmth, and cookery, and some living inhabitant that must have lit it; and this comforted my heart."

From no part of the castle could I now see any smoke arising, however. I began to suspect no one was living in it.

I came at last to the front entrance. On the massive, black door was a knocker in the shape of a heavy iron ring. I lifted it with a little effort and knocked hard on the door. For some minutes I stood there, listening for footsteps inside. I waited. Then faintly to my ears came the sound of someone approaching. I heard chains rattling and bolts being drawn. The door was opened slowly and a white-haired retainer or butler peered at me darkly, and said in a gruff voice, "What do you want?"

On hearing my business, he ushered me inside, shutting and locking the iron-studded door behind me. He left me standing there and went off, presumably to see the Duke about my visit. I found myself in a high-vaulted entrance hall: on the walls around me hung many trophies of war and the hunting field. I saw claymores of various sizes, daggers, circular shields embossed with figures and designs, stags' heads and antlers, long tapering swords, thin-bladed rapiers, dirks, blunderbusses, horse pistols, and muskets: there were enough exhibits on those walls to furnish a museum room! As I gazed on them, my mind instantly went back to Glencoe, the Vale of Weeping, and the Clan wars of Scotland; and I wondered what strange and bloody events these silent exhibits had witnessed.

After a couple of minutes my white-haired friend returned and signed to me to follow him. Conducting me silently along some darkish corridors and through some well-appointed rooms, he at last brought me to the Duke's study.

The Duke greeted me with quiet courtesy and offered me a chair. We had an interesting conversation touching on many subjects – the war, the friends he had in my Battalion, the Roman Liturgy, and Roman Missals. I felt quite at ease with him. He was in his sixties, I reckoned, a scholarly type of man, refined in manner and speech. He seemed to be religiously minded. I noticed with particular interest the slender, graceful, ivory statue of our Blessed Lady, which stood on a small shelf or ledge near his chair.

I spent the best part of an hour with him. It was an enjoyable visit. When I rose up to go, he accompanied me to the entrance hall and front door.

He gave me some verbal messages for certain officers in my Battalion. He asked me to convey to the Commanding Officer his welcoming good wishes, saying also that he would be very pleased to receive a visit from the officers and himself at the castle.

Some time later, the officers visited him. When they were leaving him, he invited, through them, the Guardsmen to come and view the castle. A number of men gladly accepted the invitation. On the morning of the day on which we left Inverary, a group of the Guardsmen visited the castle. The Duke himself showed the visitors around. They were shown the Great Hall and Armoury, the State Apartments, the gallery of pictures, the tapestries, and the eighteenth-century furniture. It was all very interesting to the Guardsmen as they followed the Duke from room to room.

Some straggled behind the general body, and for this reason there was a painful sequel to this castle visit. That evening when the Battalion had arrived at the railway station in the mountains, where they were to entrain for Yorkshire, a messenger came up the road on a noisy motorcycle. He said the Duke had sent him to inform the officer in charge that a number of articles had been purloined from the castle that morning. Among other things, it seemed that his Grace could not find his own Tam O'Shanter, his fountain pen, and various other odds and ends. He suggested – as the police do when they have "got their man" – that some of the Guardsmen who visited the castle might be able to help him with his inquiries.

Major McCausland was in charge of the entraining Guardsmen. Because half the men were already aboard the train, and especially since we had to keep to a time schedule, he decided to do nothing in the moment about the missing articles. At Malton next morning, he would deal with the matter when all the men would descend from the train. He was very annoyed over this development! He was also very clear in his own mind what to do about it.

We travelled through the night. When the men got off the train at Malton, they were weary, cold and hungry. The NCOs lined them up on the windswept platform. Major McCausland addressed them all and told them what had happened at Inverary Castle. Then he spoke sternly to the offenders. He would give them all three minutes to shed the missing articles. During that time, the officers would turn their backs on the lines of men. If, at the end of the three minutes, all the missing articles were not on the platform, all the Guardsmen would stay on the platform until they were found. There would be a man-to-man search and full kit inspection – any culprits detected, he declared, would be very sorry they had ever gone near the castle. They could have it whatever way they wanted now: "Shed what you have stolen and nothing more will be said about it, or stand on this platform, without hope of breakfast, until the guilty men are found!"

For this occasion I temporarily demoted myself from the rank of Captain – which was only my honorary rank anyway. I watched with interest to see what was going to happen. For about one long eternity of a minute, nothing happened. Then quite suddenly a shower of articles fell here and there. The offenders made sure to throw them some distance away from themselves. As the officers heard the stuff thudding on the platform, their eyes opened wider and wider: the avalanche was more than they expected – some of them must have been wondering if there was anything left in the castle! The thudding continued as the souvenir hunters disgorged their treasures. My memory is that all the souvenirs were packed up and promptly returned to the Duke with most sincere apologies from the Commanding Officer. So far as I can recall however, the Duke never recovered his Tam O'Shanter!

As youngsters raid orchards for apples and pears and feel no great qualms about it, soldiers have their eyes open for souvenirs in any new field of their activities. I am quite certain not one of the Guardsmen who "lifted a souvenir" in Inverary Castle thought himself a thief for doing so. This ancient army practice in soldier's eyes is akin to a 'immemorial custom' which is such a magnificent loophole in so many awkward laws of the Church.

Any man who has served in the ranks knows what goes on: he can understand what you mean when you speak of "scrounging" or something which is "buckshee" (a corruption of the Arabic "bakhsheesh", meaning a tip, an alms). Things which come in these ways are accepted, and their origins better left unquestioned.

Not long after our return from Inverary, I received an official notice of a Catholic Chaplains' meeting to be held in York. This meant that all we priests in 12th Corps – the Corps preparing for the invasion of France – would assemble in a hotel in York, have a conference together, and following it, a meal and a chat. I looked forward to this conference: it was always a bright event in my life as a chaplain. I enjoyed meeting my fellow chaplains, hearing their experiences and learning the answers to problems I had met in my own work.

## Our Last Meeting

When we gathered in the hotel in York, Monsignor Coughlin, the Senior Catholic Chaplain of the Army, was there to meet us. His presence indicated that this meeting was a special one, for usually the chaplains of the various commands were addressed only by their own Senior Chaplain. We guessed this was our "preparation for Invasion" conference.

It was interesting to gaze round the room and see the other priests who would go with the Divisions selected to invade Europe. We numbered about twenty. There were others with their units in different parts of England. Our Senior Chaplain, Fr Guilly, first of all introduced Monsignor Coughlin.

The Monsignor began his talk in a very light-hearted manner: "Well, my dear Fathers, this is our last meeting in this world!"

At this we all smiled and looked at one another cheerfully!

"Yes," went on Monsignor, "we shall never be together again. As you know, the invasion of Europe is to take place. You are all to take part in it and if you all carry out your duties as priests, some of you are certain to be killed! That is why I say we shall never be together again."

At this we all fell silent.

He went on to speak of his confidence in us, and how he relied on our Faith, our zeal, and our courage. Although he spoke encouragingly, he certainly did not mince matters when he spoke of the ordeals before us. Later on we saw how correctly he foretold the deaths of some of us. Before the Allied invasion armies reached the Rhine, about nine priests of our number had been killed. One of the chaplains with the first waves of invading troops never reached the dry sands of the Normandy shore: he was shot through the head and fell dead in the water.

Before leaving us to go off to another Chaplains' Conference, Monsignor Coughlin gave us his blessing. When he had gone, it was Fr Guilly's turn to address us:

"Fathers, this is our last conference together. You must all have a fair idea of what lies ahead. I have seen the invasion plans. This is going to be a grim affair. If anyone amongst you feels he may not be able to stand up to it, let him speak to me after this meeting. Let him leave it all in my hands: I will have him posted to a home-based unit. But I stress the fact that he must speak to me immediately after this meeting."

He went on to discuss certain details of our work. As he spoke, we all took notes of necessary or useful points. There was then an open discussion. We all offered suggestions, asked questions, and tried to anticipate some of the problems that would confront us once the invasion had begun. The meeting lasted about two hours. At one o'clock we lunched together, and then said goodbye to one another, "till we meet again somewhere in Europe".

After the meeting, not one of those priests asked Fr Guilly to transfer him to a home-based unit. I can speak only within my range of knowledge, but I doubt, however, if anyone among them even began to ponder the question within himself. They were a cool, level-headed, matter-of-fact bunch: they would take things as they came, but they would not entertain the idea of drawing back from the invasion set-up. They were going to see this grim business through.

Priests, as we well know, are very human: they have many faults and failings. At times they receive the criticisms, mild or harsh, of layfolk. It ought to be remembered that they have, for the sake of the Kingdom of God and for souls, deliberately made sacrifices others have not made. For example, to a very great extent they have yielded up their human liberty – not for a period of service, as in an army, navy, or in another job – but for life. They have also freely given up the comfort and stability of a home of their own. Both these sacrifices weigh more heavily on a priest as he grows older. On occasion also they must readily face death, even most violent death, for the sake of their work.

That morning in York, I saw priests at their best. Everything was done in a plain, matter-of-fact way: they had a job to do and they were going ahead with it.

Later on, in Germany, when the invasion was a thing of the past and hostilities had ceased, I often heard non-Catholic officers and men praising the Catholic chaplains they knew. They wrote their praises in books and letters home. And I think I am correct in saying that the facts justify their praises: for of all branches of the army the Catholic Chaplains' branch had in relative terms the highest percentage of casualties in the war.

The day of invasion was drawing nearer and nearer. My Division was assigned to its embarkation area on the South Coast. We were to travel from Malton to Eastbourne. I watched the first contingents moving off. Down Malton's main street they came, marching with that dignified, disciplined step of the Guards, past the shops and cafés they knew so well, past their many friends among the townsfolk who lined the streets to bid them farewell, on to the railway station, where their train awaited them. As they marched along, they made remarks among themselves: some of these raised a muffled laugh; others, a groan.

As the train, in clouds of steam, edged slowly out of the station, many of the men hung from the carriage windows, waving to their friends and gazing back at Malton, the town they had come to know so well. Nearly all of them would never see it again.

In our new surroundings in Eastbourne, the Battalion's training went on apace. We were nearing the final days. All vehicles were 'waterproofed' (ie made viable in the shallows of the invasion shores by affixing to the engines an air-pipe or tubing – something akin to the snorkels used on submarines).

There was tension among officers and men, for all were vividly aware that the supreme test of the Battalion was at hand. Perhaps it was to ease this tension somewhat that a Battalion Sports Day was arranged. I decided to enter for the Officers' hundred yards race!

## The Battalion Sports

We were given a week or ten days to prepare for the Sports Day. I stopped smoking; I went out early in the morning to run on the Common above the sea-cliffs. The Guardsmen started to lay bets about the different events. In what I later decided was a moment of folly, I jokingly advised one of the Guardsmen to put his money on me in the Officers' hundred yards. That was enough: the word sped around the Battalion that I was a certainty for that race. How I regretted my impulsive advice to that unfortunate Guardsman! What on earth made me say what I did? But the damage was done! In consequence, I nearly ran myself to death in my morning practices on the Common.

The fatal day of the race dawned. As if in mockery, the sun beamed from a clear blue sky. As I lined up for the race, I saw with dismay the rows of Guardsmen staring at me with great, smiling confidence. I interpreted all this at once: they all had their money on me! Why, oh why, had I even joked about my prospects?

Two of the non-competing officers, who had racing traditions in their blood, were acting as bookmakers. One of them came over and spoke to me: "Father, if you win this race, I will never forgive you." That remark did not help me one bit!

We lined up. We got set. At the starter's gun, I ran, ran and ran as fast as my legs could carry me. I glanced neither to left or right. I had only one idea in my mind – to reach that tape first! Reach that tape first!

I won the race, much to the chagrin of the bookmakers and much to the delight of the Guardsmen. One of the men said jokingly to me afterwards, "Father, keep up that bit of speed you have got – it might come in useful when we meet the Germans!"

The Sports Day had been held in the spacious grounds of the Duke of Devonshire's estate in Eastbourne. When the last event ended, all officers were invited to the house for refreshments. I did not go: I went back to my billet. I was not in the mood for visiting that house at that particular time. Why? Because a few days earlier a prominent Catholic girl, sister of President John F Kennedy, had married a son of the Duke of Devonshire – Captain Lord Hartington, an officer in the Coldstream Guards in my Brigade. I surmised that both of them might be in the family home on that occasion, and I did not wish to meet the lady. Her marriage was a registry office marriage: one that was not valid in the eyes of the Catholic Church. What she had done was a cause of scandal and offence to Catholics. I did not wish to meet her.

Her husband, known to us in the Brigade as "Billy" Hartington, was killed in Normandy four or five weeks after our landing there, and she was left mourning the loss of the man for whom she had broken the law of the Church. She herself died in an air crash a few years later. Her brother, who had been best man at her wedding, was killed before the end of the war.

During these days in Eastbourne my thoughts were of the Invasion of Europe, which I knew was very close at hand. I did my best to prepare the men for whatever it might bring – wounds, suffering, death. Particularly, I preached to the men about the necessity of contrition and the value of the Act of Perfect Contrition. I had it printed on a small card in a shortened form. I made sure that every Catholic in the Brigade got a copy. I also blessed and distributed rosary beads among the men. I gave them ample opportunity for Confession.

My sister Annie was a Poor Clare Colettine and her order in Belfast sent me a supply of Sacred Heart badges – these also were given to the men. I used to lie awake at night, thinking what more I could do to prepare for the grim days that lay immediately before us.

The men responded in a half-hearted kind of way. Some of them were very conscious of the perils ahead, and made good use of the opportunities I offered to prepare themselves spiritually. All listened, heard and understood my urgent sermons, yet some remained strangely unconcerned. To them the war was still remote: they were not going to worry or trouble themselves until they were up against it. What more could I do? I could not compel or force them.

One day there was a great commotion outside my billet. I went outside to investigate. Three of the soldiers had a firm grip of a fourth, who was squirming and struggling.

"What is going on?" I asked.

"Please, Father," said one of the three 'warders', "this man is going to Confession."

I brought the reluctant penitent into my room and bade the others to leave him with me. I then had a quiet chat and a smoke with my guest. He gradually calmed down and we got on well together. Before he left me, I fixed him up! He went away contented and happy.

His was an exceptional case. His companions' robust apostolate was not a form of zeal infectious or widespread among the men of the Brigade. I had to rely on each man acting for himself. On my side, all I could do was to offer the opportunities for any man who wished to avail of them.

# CHAPTER SEVEN
# Invasion of France: The Red Vineyard

OUR EASTBOURNE DAYS came to an end. One night in the anteroom of the Mess, the Commanding Officer called me aside and gave me a top secret message – we were leaving at 2.00 am the next morning. He was telling me ahead of time, guessing I would require a few hours to get packed up and organised for the move.

And so, with the willing and efficient help of Hugh, my batman, I got my belongings together and had everything ready about 10.00 pm. I then left my billet and went down to see the local parish priest. Apologising for the lateness of the hour of my visit, I asked him to hear my Confession. I knelt at his chair and he heard my Confession. Afterwards we sat down for a chat. I had always found this English priest very friendly and helpful – that night he was particularly so.

"You know," he said smilingly, "without your telling me, I can guess why you have come to see me at this time of night!" He then went on:

"Before we say farewell, I want to offer you some advice. I was a chaplain in the First World War. I have a fairly good idea of what you will be up against. Take my advice: in battle, you must always be where the wounded are. Be with the wounded! I know how you will feel during a battle: you will be like the rest of us – anxious to show the men you are neither scared nor afraid to face the dangers. That should not be your line of action however: your business is to stay alive and help the wounded. Therefore you should not expose yourself unnecessarily to danger! Do not wander about the battlefield! If anything happens to you, what will the wounded do? If the men are left without a priest, even temporarily, it would be a great pity. Moreover, how is a new chaplain, who has come to take your place, going to be accepted and established? No one in the Brigade will know him. He will be greeted with suspicion everywhere. He will meet many obstacles. I take it that everybody in your Brigade knows you, at least by sight. They will *not* know him! Because of all these points, my humble advice to you is: 'Be where the wounded are!'"

I thought his advice was sound. I thanked him and promised to follow it. It was very kind of him to be interested in my work and welfare. Before saying goodbye to him, I knelt in his sitting room for his blessing.

## Normandy

Our Division landed at Port-en-Bessin on the coast of Normandy. With the Guardsmen I left our troops' transport and went aboard a landing craft about a mile or two from the beach. When we reached the shallow water, a ramp was put down. I then went ashore in a Bren Gun Carrier. The sea between the ramp and the shore was about five or six feet deep, becoming shallower as it neared the sands. We lumbered down the ramp and splashed through the water. We got wet, but were not completely soaked.

Dead bodies floated in the sea. Wrecked vehicles and smashed landing craft lay at odd angles here and there along the shore. White tapes indicated the mine-free paths through the sands to the higher ground beyond: we followed these taped paths until we arrived at a road which led directly inland.

This was France at last. The roads were deep in a kind of whitish or chalky dust. The sunlight was strong: it showed up the fresh scars of war on the trees, the walls, and the houses that still remained standing. The clamour of the moving lines of army traffic filled the air: somehow it deepened the silence of the deserted villages through which we passed, just as a match or a cigarette lighter suddenly flaming up at night intensifies the darkness around you.

On that first night we bivouacked in the orchard of a French farm. My slit trench was under a tree – a bad place to dig a trench, because you have to cut through many roots. As I stood there near the apple tree, the darkness was suddenly split open by long white shafts of light from our searchlight batteries. These clean corridors of intense brilliance crossed and re-crossed the velvet sky, seeking enemy aircraft or furnishing direction to our anti-aircraft guns. I heard the sharp *crack, crack, crack* of the Bofors guns and the steady hammering of machine guns. Red tracer bullets climbed high into the darkness in seemingly lazy fashion, pursuing the German planes which were attacking the masses of allied shipping at the beaches. For a little while, all would settle down into silence: then low in the sky, I could see the sudden flash of our heavy guns speaking their "monstrous anger" to the German enemy farther inland.

On a day of cloudless blue sky and warm sunshine, the Battalion moved up, with the rest of the Division, to occupy positions to the north-west of the town of Caen. I marched up with the Guardsmen of one of our Companies. The Platoons, in alternate order, marched close to the hedges on both sides of the road. This was it!

211

The men were rather silent. Now and again a few forced efforts at humour evoked a few forced laughs. Not that the men were in bad mood or low in spirits – but nearly all of them were new to the dark realities of war, and doubtless each was wondering what was in store for him and how he would stand up to it. Now they had no illusions; now they were entering the actual battlefield; now it was either kill or be killed!

We passed through the silent, abandoned hamlets of Mauvieux. In a house there I saw a woman lying on a bed, naked and dead. She was covered with a sheet. There was a long, deep bayonet wound on her body – inflicted, I was told, by a soldier of the German SS. The score of houses in the hamlet were in perfect order, but not one person remained in them. As the tide of war approached the hamlet, the people had fled.

When we arrived at our positions, I instantly realised that the set-up would block my chances of contacting the wounded in my other Battalions. The wounded of the entire Brigade would pass through our field ambulance. Back In England we chaplains had agreed that our best place in battle was with the field ambulance, and that we should normally be found there. In quiet intervals we could go up to the positions held by the three Battalions. I think now that it should have been arranged differently in my case. If one of the other chaplains in the Division had looked after my field ambulance, I could have stayed with the Irish Guards. But what could I do? It was too late now to readjust matters. My orders were clear: I was to stay with the field ambulance and, when feasible, go up to the Battalions in their positions.

I did what we had been told to do. Unfortunately, as it seemed at the time, I had no car, and when I wanted to go up to the lines, I had to scrounge a lift from someone. Sergeant Douglas frequently brought me up with him on his motorcycle. On a flat, open stretch of road, quite visible to the Germans holding Carpiquet aerodrome, he used to roar along on his Norton 500 cc. I clung to him like a leech, for the road was rough and bumpy. On that bit of road we were exposed to sniper and mortar fire. We always got through safely. Later on in the campaign, as I have mentioned, Sergeant Douglas was killed. A kindly, friendly type of Catholic soldier, he hailed from one of the finest parishes in Antrim – Loughgiel. God grant him eternal peace!

Along that same exposed stretch of road I carried out my first burial. One of the Coldstream Guardsmen, an Irish lad from the west of Ireland, was the first fatal casualty among the Catholics of the Brigade. We dug his grave in a low piece of ground beside the road. I wore no white surplice: to have done so would have attracted the attention of the Germans. So, wearing my purple stole, I read all the prayers, and blessed the humble grave and badly wounded body. Around his neck this Irish lad wore the Irish horn rosary beads I had given him in Scarborough. Before we lowered his body into the grave, I wondered if I should take off his rosary and send it to his people at home. But I quickly decided against this: in life and in death, they were his. So I buried him as he had fallen, in his uniform, a humble soldier with the sign of his faith in the rosary beads he wore.

In those days, death stalked abroad in the fields and on the roads around Caen. It made its presence felt in the sickening crash of shells, the ringing, bursting explosion of the mortar bombs, and the quick tattoo of machine guns. Death's presence was felt even in the intervals of silence: it seemed to brood in the quietness. The smell of death was in the air. In out-of-the way places, German soldiers were found dead and badly decomposed. In the fields, the cows were lying dead.

At times the silence was sinister. One day I went into a village nearby. Neat, red-bricked homes lined both sides of its one short street. All seemed to be as in the ordinary days of peace. Blue smoke spiralled slowly from a chimney; white curtains swayed gently in the breeze at open windows; flowers blossomed in the little gardens; red roses garlanded the trellis work around some of the doors; hens went strutting about and pecking in the empty spaces. Inside one of the houses, a fire burned or smouldered on the open hearth; on the wall the clock ticked the hours away; a red lamp glowed before a sacred picture; cups and dishes stood in clean array on the kitchen dresser. Yet there was not one person in the whole village. The people had left everything suddenly and fled. This was now the battlefield! The village was dead! It was being shelled. Death was gripping it in its relentless hands. By nightfall it would be in ruins. Shells fell nearby as I moved about. It was not a spot in which one delayed unnecessarily. I went on my way. When I turned to look back at the place, it was hidden in a cloud of smoke and dust.

That was only one of the Normandy villages that were abandoned. North-west France was in turmoil. Many refugees passed through our positions. Usually the village Curé came, heading a procession of villagers – a pitiful group of women and children, most of them red-eyed from weeping for the loss of their dear ones. My heart went out to these people – simple country folk, whose lives were so torn up and disrupted by this bitter conflict of the nations. I tried always to help and comfort them as best I could. On such occasions, I thanked God I could speak to these distressed people in their own language.

There was grievous distress and suffering on all sides in those invasion days in Normandy. We, in the invading army, had our own share of strain and stress. Day by day more of our men were killed or wounded. We were living in a state of constant tension. You could never escape the realisation, "I may die at any moment!" You were safe nowhere. We used to say in fact that the positions nearest the Germans were the safest!

## The Picnic

One evening, somewhere and somehow, I met my two fellow chaplains in the Division, Fr Tronson and Fr Hartigan. We agreed we ought to take a day off and have an outing together. Each one would contribute his share of food to the commissariat! But where would we go? Now it so happened that in my movements through the area under allied control, I had spotted a quiet place by the bend of a gently flowing river. I have now searched maps of North Western France in an effort to identify this river. All in vain! It must have been one of the tributaries of the River Aure. I told both priests about its peace and quietness, and suggested we should meet there. Neighbouring farm folk would make tea for us. This would be an ideal place where we could have a break from our daily strain. It was the month of July: we could count on the weather remaining fine. I gave my fellow priests the map reference of our rendezvous.

Thank goodness, all worked out as we had planned. It was a sunny day. We had the whole place to ourselves. We sat on the riverbank and chatted. We exchanged any news we had. We discussed our work and our difficulties. We talked about the future. Our meeting together was very helpful and reassuring. We had no inhibitions with one another. Here we were – three priests who together had joined the army for the one purpose of helping the soldiers spiritually. Our shared ideas and aims were a wonderful help to each of us as we tried to solve our common difficulties.

In World War II we priests had problems in our work which would not have arisen in the First World War. In the First World War there was a regular front line, with a particular section assigned to each Battalion in one's Brigade. A chaplain, therefore, knew where to find a particular unit. In the Second World War things were different: we had no regular front line, only strategic points here and there to be held. Units were frequently changing their positions; there was very little stability of place. Our problem was firstly, to find our units, and secondly, to discover for them some suitable place nearby for Mass and the Sacraments. It was one vast moving battlefield, like a cauldron close to boiling point. There was little or no standing still.

Now that we priests were discussing these matters, it became clear that our own efforts and good intentions were not sufficient: we needed favourable circumstances of time and place. No Commanding Officer was going to permit us to assemble a considerable number of his men in areas subject to lightning air raids, or mortar attacks, or shelling. We had to accept that. Our one hope was to wait until a unit came to the back areas for a rest period, and then to approach the senior officers for necessary permissions and arrangements.

As we sat on the river bank, talking and talking, I remember Fr Tronson remarking how cooperative the men and officers now were – more so than they had ever been when we were back in England in pre-Invasion days. The situation had indeed changed considerably since then: they were all now face-to-face with danger and death. What a welcome they now gave the priest when he walked among them! This confirmed what the Royal Air Force used to say about comrades who had to bale out of their aircraft and come down into the sea: "There are no atheists in rubber dinghies!" In England we had been politely accepted and tolerated by so many; here we were welcomed by all. We three agreed about this change!

So we talked and talked as the day wore on. The heat of the sun turned our thoughts to a swim in the river. Without more ado, we put on our bathing togs and plunged in. We laughed and splashed about and raised great spurts of foam with our vigorous kicking. We tried to duck one another. It was enormous fun and most enjoyable.

We forgot about the war. It went on without us. We could hear the guns up near Caen, booming in that sullen, angry way they have. Somewhere closer, a machine gun went into action. In the intensely blue sky above us, some Typhoon planes swept on towards the German lines. We knew their mission – they carried rockets of immense power: I was told a single rocket could blow a tank off the road. When our forward units encountered very strong German positions, they radioed back for Typhoons to come and break the German resistance.

We lay on the grass, watching them go into action. I pitied any Germans who had to face those winged messengers of death and destruction.

Shortly after midday we decided to have our meal. I produced what I had brought; the two others did likewise. What a mixture! Each of us had followed his likes and dislikes in making up his contribution to the Commissariat. And, of course, what suited one did not suit another. We laughed and mocked at each other's tastes in food. It all came out of the "compo rations" which were issued to us in Normandy. The basic essentials, however, were present: bread, butter, sugar, and tea.

Officially appointed, there on the river bank, as French interpreter for our triumvirate, I was sent to the nearby French farmhouse to get milk and a kettle of boiling water for the tea. It was a solid, old-fashioned Normandy farmhouse. About it there was an air of comfortable prosperity. Madame made me very welcome. I explained who we were and what we wanted. It made everything pleasant and easy when she realised we were Catholic priests. She bade me bring the other priests to the house. *Messieurs les Curés* would have their meal at her table! I went back to the riverbank and fetched Fr Tronson and Fr Hartigan. Madame welcomed them in a few charming words of French. She was all smiles and eagerness to help us.

She had already filled a kettle with water for our tea. While we waited for it to boil, we sat down and looked around us. The house was spotlessly clean. Everything in it seemed to date from older times – the straw-woven chairs, the dark mahogany kitchen dresser, the quaint ornaments in china and brass, the religious pictures hanging on the walls.

There were some faded photographs on display. I asked Madame about one of them, which showed a French *poilu* in the uniform of the French army in the First World War. She told me, with a certain sadness, that it was a photo of her father, who had been killed at Verdun. I reflected then that the 1914–18 war involved all the French people. The trenches of that war were indeed dug in the fields of Flanders and Lorraine, but the homes of France fought the war –and here was one home in a remote corner of the country which had suffered because of it.

The outsize kettle on the fire began to boil. Madame prepared to make the tea. We gave her the tea we had brought with us; we also gave her directions about the amount to use – none of us had much confidence in any French or continental methods of tea-making. While the tea was put to one side of the fire to draw, Madame bustled about and soon had the very wide kitchen table covered with a snow-white cloth, and on it, neatly arranged, all we needed for a meal. She now boiled some fresh eggs. She also gave us some of her own home-baked bread. How pleased she was when she saw us sampling it with enthusiasm.

As we three sat at the table enjoying this unexpected hospitality, we watched Madame cooking a goose. It was being roasted in barbecue style. The goose was impaled lengthwise on a steel spit which revolved slowly before the red fire. It worked away without any assistance: a strong spring mechanism, previously wound up by some muscular arm, furnishing the power. In a long pan beneath the goose, the hot, dripping grease was collected. None of us had ever seen one of these contraptions in action. We stood watching the goose turn slowly as the fire made it browner and browner. Madame was amused at our interest in what was as normal as a boiling kettle or a saucepan in the life of a Frenchwoman.

As we took leave of her, we thanked her for her kindness. We did not offer her any payment in cash – we felt she would have been offended by that. But we left with her a package of tea and some chocolate. With these she was perfectly pleased.

On our return to the river we found that some American soldiers had arrived and were getting ready for a swim. They were very high-spirited indeed. At first there was pretended reluctance about going into the water – one was trying to push the other off the bank. Then suddenly there was a rush, and they all jumped into together. We sat and watched them, swimming and splashing about. They were as happy and noisy as a lot of schoolboys on an outing.

One of them would solemnly announce he was going to give a diving exhibition. No matter how good his performance was, the others jeered at him. They teased one another; they ducked one another; they came up quickly behind unsuspecting 'victims' standing on the bank, and gave them a mighty shove into the river. They shouted and roared as they fought and grappled with one another in the water. It was all done in the best of good humour! Some, who had been ducked and in the process had swallowed more river water than they liked, rose to the surface spluttering and coughing, and breathing fearful threats and vengeance on their enemies. For us the entertainment they provided was as good as a water circus!

We knew the American landing forces had suffered heavy losses in the Normandy invasion. Here were some of the men who had taken part in those landings. We had to admire their merriment and light-heartedness. No doubt they had lost many of their comrades. If these swimmers were a true cross-section of the survivors, the American invasion forces were anything but demoralised. Demoralised men do not behave in such a happy and cheerful manner.

When the aquatic troupe of troopers had gone, we talked about American things and persons. We agreed that America's contribution in men, armaments and food had made the invasion of Europe possible. On a much humbler level of affairs, we agreed that these Yankee boys had helped to make our picnic day.

Before leaving the river, we had another swim. Afterwards we packed up our belongings. We then held a final council of war. We planned to keep in contact with one another as much as possible. We discussed our possible future movements, addresses of Redemptorist houses en route across France, altar wine and altar bread supplies, the laundering of our altar linen. (Back in England, the Superioress of a convent in Hastings had bluntly refused to launder some altar cloths and an alb for me. Years later, nuns of that same Order would come to me, when I had charge of Our Lady's Confraternity in Clonard, asking me to help them to get postulants among the female members!)

The day's heat was lessening and the shadows of the slender poplar trees by the riverbank were lengthening across the fields, as we left the scene of our picnic. It had been a great break for the three of us. We felt the better of it. In meeting one another we had gained a new strength to continue our duties.

All through my priestly life I have found a meeting with other priests to be a source of encouragement. Priests help priests. Priests give strength to priests. Priests are completely at ease in priests' company – and generally speaking, only then! And I think that no brotherhood in the world's history can compare with that found among the priests of the Catholic Church.

Standing on the roadside, we bade each other goodbye – a shaking of hands, and a quick word of good wishes. We never met again. Henceforward we were separated. The moving tides of battle swept us far apart. After the war, two of us came back to our monastery to take up our lives where we had left off; the third left the Redemptorist Congregation and went to work in an American diocese.

On my way back to my bivouac up at the Front, the words of Alan Seeger's poem, "I Have a Rendezvous with Death", came into my mind:

"I have a rendezvous with death
At some disputed barricade –
When spring comes back with rustling shade
And apple blossoms fill the air…

…I have a rendezvous with death
At midnight in some flaming town –
When spring trips north again this year;
And I to my pledged word am true,
I shall not fail that rendezvous!"

We were still in the Carpiquet area. The days were days of danger. German snipers lay hidden in the cornfields. They were chosen men: anyone passing within their range of vision was liable to die instantly. Apart from their skill in the use of weapons, they were possessed of an implacable hatred for all enemies of the Fatherland. Very often they resisted all our attempts to make them surrender. They could not be winkled out alive. They died rather than give up their posts. They had ample supplies of food and drink, and these allowed them to stay behind, when the other German units had pulled out and were in retreat.

Low flying aircraft would swoop over our positions, spraying the area with cannon fire. Shelling and mortaring would start up suddenly at any hour of the day or night. Day after day there were casualties. The Guardsmen would have much preferred to attack the Germans, rather than go on enduring this kind of static, passive warfare. But orders were orders: evidently we were meant to hold our positions, and thus contribute to the general strategy of the campaign. The men were impatient to "get cracking", to see action, to advance. The spreading ennui was unhealthy amongst them. They had daily patrols, daily stand-to, frequent reconnaissance trips to make: they were far from being idle. Yet they longed to come to grips with the enemy. It was for that they had trained so strenuously in England; it was for that they had come to France.

We moved to the eastern side of Vire. The 3rd Battalion of the Irish Guards took up positions at Estry. This was true *bocage* country – fields rich in crops, smallish fields, with deep, intersecting narrow lanes and thick, strongly rooted hedges. Tanks found these hedges and sunken lanes almost impassable. In such country, attacking infantry could rely only on artillery and aircraft support.

The Irish Guards were ordered to attack at dawn on 11 August 1944. There would be a preliminary bombardment by our heavy guns, and Typhoons with rockets would soften up the German-held positions. Although the promised air bombardment never happened, the attack went on.

In such country, those in defensive positions had the advantage in an infantry attack. The Irish Guards were shot down as they crossed the open fields! They failed to dislodge the enemy. They were compelled to retreat. Their losses were very serious. One entire company suffered eighty per cent casualties. At least eight or nine officers were killed. It was a black day for the Battalion. Not until the men reached Holland did they experience a like disaster.

The Regimental History of the Irish Guards gives all the facts about the Estry affair.

## The Children's Party

The dead were buried there in Estry valley; the wounded were taken back to our military hospitals. Reinforcements came out from England to fill the gaps in our ranks. The Battalion was stunned and shocked by what had happened.

The Brigade was pulled out of that valley and sent back to rest in a quiet area. There we learned that we were to prepare for a new effort to break through the German Wall, which was blocking the advance of the invading armies.

This time we were bivouacked in open fields near a small French village which had suffered badly at the hands of the German SS troops. Even the humble village church had been partly blown up by the retreating Germans. The villagers had now returned to their homes, rather dazed and bewildered. Until we had invaded their coasts, their homes and their lives had been calm and peaceful. They could not but look on us as one of the main sources of their sorrows. Generally speaking, the French people became excitedly joyful when we liberated their cities and towns; but in these remote country parts, the Germans had behaved correctly and given the people no trouble, and so when we came invading and their homes were damaged, their stock killed and their crops ruined, they could not but look on us as the main cause of their woes.

The Commanding Officer of the Battalion understood all this very clearly. He had a sincere sympathy for the villagers, and the farming families in the area. One day, therefore, he spoke to me in the Mess tent.

"Father, I want you to organise a party for the children of the district."

"Very well, Sir," I replied, "how many children are to come?"

"Oh, I don't know! Let me see! About forty! Go to see Hastings about the food and supplies!"

Lieutenant Hastings was the Quartermaster of the Battalion.

"What age should these children be?" I asked the Commanding Officer.

"Oh, about ten or eleven, younger perhaps, but not older."

Now, by this time, I had received a car. It was going to be very useful in this undertaking. The next day, with my batman driving, and an area map on my knees, I started out to find children for the party. I went through the village from house to house. There were not many children now living there: most had been sent to families in quieter parts. I then went through the countryside. At all the homes I told them I was a Catholic *Curé* and that I would take good care of their children and see to their safe return home. The poor people were very pleased. Monsignor l'Abbé was very kind! How different from the German SS troops who had blown up their church. Of course their children would certainly go to the party given by the kind English soldiers.

My tour that day was a great success. I lay in my slit trench that night and went over in my mind the houses I had visited. I reckoned I had lined up about forty children for the party. I fell asleep contentedly.

Next morning I went to see Robin Hastings about the edibles and the 'menu' for the party. In true military fashion, he insisted on knowing exactly how many rations he had to draw for the children. I told him I had invited about forty youngsters.

"Right, Father, forty it is – forty it will be!" he replied.

I left Robin and went to have a word with those very important men – the army cooks! I gave them a little talk – soft, but true – about these poor French youngsters, their hunger and deprivations: some had never seen an orange, never seen a piece of chocolate, etc. Their own wives and children at home would be so glad to hear of what we were doing. All this melted the cooks' hearts, and they promised to cooperate to make the party a success.

I left the Battalion cooks and went to the Guardsmen in and around their slit trenches by the hedgerows. When I told them what was being planned, they were all very interested.

"What age are the children going to be, Father?"

"Will they have their older sisters with them?"

"Where are we going to hold the party?"

Questions came at me from all directions. However, I spoke to them with subtlety and cunning, ensuring that I made the running of the party and its success as much their affair as mine. I told them quite truthfully I could not stage this function without their help. They were all to come and to bring with them any supplies of sweets or biscuits they could spare for the children. I outlined my programme for the party. The Guardsmen were pleased: they all liked children – they reminded them of home and their own families – and in any case, the party was going to be a break from their daily routine.

Next I went to the Battalion Pipe Band leaders. They promised to dress in their kilted uniforms and play for the children. I contacted the despatch riders: they agreed to put on a show of stunt driving on their motorcycles.

I arranged my programme on paper. I planned foot races for the different age groups of the children. The winners would receive suitable prizes. For that purpose, I stored up my own rations of chocolate and sweets. I knew what we wanted, and there were to be no delays – on such occasions, people and soldiers hate delays. Whatever events we were going to put on would have to happen without delays, and I impressed this on everyone: "We must keep the pot boiling! If we allow no unnecessary intervals, the afternoon will pass very quickly. There must be no lengthy hold-ups in the proceedings!"

On the eve of the day fixed for the party, I made my final preparations. We would have forty youngsters; a programme of events written down and some copies made for my 'stewards'; good confident, reliance on the kindly nature of the Guardsmen to contribute part of their rations of sweets and eatables. The day was sure to be sunny and warm, and there was plenty for the kiddies to see, to do and to enjoy. All was well: this picnic party promised to be a resounding success.

The venue of the entertainment was a large meadow near our bivouac. It was scheduled to start at 3.00 pm. At about 2.30 pm my batman, Hugh Creaney, came running up to me and panted:

"Father, have you seen what is coming up the road?" His eyes were wide-open with a kind of surprise and horror. "You had better come and have a look!"

When I went down with him to view the road leading to the field of the party, I saw children, plenty of them, coming joyfully and briskly along the road. But to my utter dismay, I also saw that nearly all of them were accompanied by a troop of parents, grandparents, and other 'children' well beyond the age of fourteen! I had not foreseen this turn of events. A crisis had arisen before we had even started! In these new circumstances another miracle of the multiplication of the food was needed! The afternoon promised to be very interesting.

The quartermaster came over to me, red in the face, wagging a warning finger in the air: "Father, you said forty children, right! I have rations for forty! Not one more! Not one more!"

"Robin, that is quite alright!" I assured him. "I promised a party for the forty children – and not for any hangers-on. We will see to the children!" He went away to his kitchens and Mess stewards, only slightly mollified.

Yes, a very, very interesting afternoon lay before me! However, there was nothing for it now: we had passed the point of no return. Therefore I went down to the gate leading into our fields, and, welcoming the children and their friends, I guided them to the place in the meadow selected for our party.

On my way up with them through the fields, I observed with increasing dismay that nearly all the grown-ups accompanying the children carried empty satchels or bags. Apparently they had judged that this occasion would give them an excellent opportunity of replenishing their empty larders at home.

I faced the afternoon with some apprehension. Either I committed suicide on the spot, deserted my post (would it be in face of the enemy and would I be executed if caught?), or I stood my ground. I elected to stand my ground. I would feed the forty – the rest could fend for themselves. After all, I reflected smugly, the others had come uninvited. So I tried to reassure myself anyway, but I still felt uneasy!

My fears, thank God, proved groundless. The party was a great success. The officers and men rallied round in most generous fashion. Everyone helped to make the occasion a pleasant one for the children – and even for their friends.

First came the pipes and drums of the Battalion Band, playing rousing marches. The French villagers, and especially the children, stood in open-eyed wonder as they gazed on the saffron-kilted Guardsmen. They had never seen men dressed in skirts.

"Tiens! Mon Dieu, voyez-vous les jupes?" To them the Band was a most startling sight!

Next came the performance of the despatch riders. They thrilled the youngsters with their daredevil tricks on their motorcycles. They circled around, wove in and out, re-formed, divided, circled, re-formed again, going through a bewildering set of movements. They climaxed their display by driving up in rip-roaring fashion through blazing screens of fire. The children were mesmerised by it all. They loved every minute of it.

Then the Pipers, standing in a circle, played some lovely Irish melodies. By this time, the entire Battalion was assembled and enjoying the fun. They loved it too: it was great fun for them.

Next came the party proper. At this point, much to my relief, the Guardsmen themselves took over. It had to be that way: it was too much work for me alone. So I supervised and helped where I was needed. The Guardsmen ranged the children in one great circle. They gave their mess tins to the youngsters. No child was forgotten. And now the cooks surpassed themselves. What an array of good things they had prepared for our young guests! Distribution was both speedy and efficient. The party was an enormous success.

But what about the unexpected guests? I cannot explain this mystery – but all of them got plenty to eat and drink. The children were indeed given priority, but somehow that did not lessen or diminish the sources of supplies for the grown-ups. I must record quite frankly that the grown-up sisters of the children seemed to do best of all. On this point, let us agree that explanations are unnecessary.

After the meal the children sat around, while a ground platform was placed on the grass. On this platform some of the Guardsmen gave an exhibition of Irish dancing, the pipers playing the music for them. Quite honestly, I confess I did not know there was such a wealth of talent hidden in the ranks of the Irish Guards.

The Guardsmen themselves were in great, good humour. They mixed with the people. Barriers of language seemed to cause no difficulty – signs and exclamations and bits of 'English French' worked wonders. When the dancing was finished, the men played with the youngsters, just as they would do with their own children at home – lifting them up into the air, teasing them with sweets, showing them conjuring tricks.

Next we held the foot races. These were well organised. We had official starters, handicappers and judges. All was done in proper Guards style. Everyone was interested. In each race the parents had their favourite; the Guardsmen had theirs; the children had theirs. There were shouts and cries of encouragement in French, smooth polite English, broad County Antrim tones and Cork and Kerry lilting accents. There was applause for the winners. And when the prizes (chocolates and sweets) were awarded, the Germans could surely have heard the cheering and hand-clapping. To these French kiddies deprived of chocolate by the war, our gifts were a dream luxury.

In the middle of all these events, I saw with some surprise that the local *Curé* had arrived. He was a simple type of man, kindly in manner, unassuming and humble. The officers received him very graciously and conducted him to their Mess tent, where I am certain they treated him royally. He was in good hands.

We organised some games with the children – the Guardsmen quickly teaching them what each competitor had to do. There were more prizes for these. There was then a general distribution of various items – food, sweets, souvenirs, etc – which the men wanted to give to the children. And finally, the Band played another set of marches and Irish songs.

Evening was drawing in when the Commanding Officer assembled all our guests and made a little speech, which I translated for our French guests. And so I informed them all how pleased we were to have them with us that day. We hoped they had enjoyed the party. War days were sad days: we offered the people our sympathy for all they had suffered. Now the dawn of freedom for all of France was at hand. France was a great nation; we were proud to be the liberators of the French people.

When I had done, Monsignor *Le Curé* replied on behalf of his people. In clear, simple French he offered the kind English soldiers thanks of all for the hospitality they had that day received. As an old soldier himself, he saluted the brave English soldiers, the liberators of France. France would rise again, thanks to her glorious allies. He spoke with great sincerity. At the end he led his people in the singing of "La Marseillaise". We all joined in the singing. Any lack of musical finesse in the rendering of this war-song of France was compensated for by our general enthusiasm and goodwill.

There were hand-shakings with all our guests – the French dearly love this hand-shaking routine. Then the function was at an end. The children were tired. With their parents, they slowly wended their way from our meadow. I went with them as far as the road. On the way through the fields I noticed with amusement, that the satchels and bags carried by the grown-ups were no longer empty. I did not enquire how this had happened. There is a time for silence.

The proceedings were at an end, but all was not over. I looked back to the spot where we had held the party. Behold! The Guardsmen were now dancing with the big sisters of the children. That the grass of the meadow was not suitable for dancing was a minor detail. The pipes played their waltzes and the couples danced away merrily in the fading light.

And that was the Children's Party. The Guardsmen enjoyed it just as much as the kiddies. The sight of the children awakened their memories of home. Their kindly hearts opened to the youngsters and they treated them as their own.

Our next move was to an area on the Bayeux–Caen road, not far from the village of Bretteville l'Orgueilleuse. The entire Division was bivouacked on a wide area on both sides of the road. The land was owned by people living in a nearby farm. The fields were soon pitted with slit trenches – it made me think of the numerous holes in a nutmeg grater. Because of shelling, the men were always ordered to dig slit trenches: no one was allowed to sleep on the surface of the field. When I saw the Guardsmen digging, digging everywhere, and throwing up piles of soil and stones, I wondered how any farmer could ever cultivate the land again.

At the farmhouse there were chickens and eggs, butter and milk, vegetables and Camembert cheese available – but not for long: the men were soon knocking at the door and, despite a Divisional order, bartering for these desirable commodities with their own treasures of chocolate, cigarettes, tobacco and soap.

As I was passing along one evening I saw a Guardsman trying to exchange several bars of soap for a goose which a French woman was carrying. She could not speak English: he could not speak French: negotiations had reached deadlock. The woman replied to my "Bonsoir, Madame!" by asking me to help her. She wanted to know the price of soap in England. Shrewd French peasant, she was not going to be the loser in this bit of bargaining. I had to confess that I did not know the exact price of soap in England, but I told her it was very scarce there, and that I thought the soldier was making her a fair offer. She paused, looked at the soap, looked at me thoughtfully – and handed over the goose for the bars of soap.

On our arrival in the area, I visited the family living in the adjoining farm. On learning I was an Irish priest – Catholic, not Anglican – she and all her family gave me a cordial welcome. They were very devout people of the old Normandy stock which has given so many great saints to the Church.

Madame had lost her husband early in the war. Her sister lived with her. She, with Madame's only son, were running the farm. Some local older men helped as farmhands. Madame's sister was a very spiritual woman. She showed me her little library of religious books. To my surprise I saw many of the works of Dom Columba Marmion on her shelves. Noticing my interest, she assured me his books were her favourite spiritual reading. How many girls working on farms at home in Ireland read the Abbot's works? More now perhaps than then! I came away from that farmhouse, thinking within myself: "Perhaps this is one of the reasons why France has given the world so many great saints!"

## Bayeux Cathedral

While we were at rest at Bretteville l'Orgueilleuse, I went into Bayeux to see the Bishop. Here again, my bit of French came in useful! With the Bishop it was to be either French or Latin. We got along all right in French. He was a kindly man, in his late fifties, bespectacled, grey-haired, scholarly-looking. On learning I was Irish, he asked me for names and addresses of Irish Bishops to whom he could apply for the loan of some priests. Many of his parishes had no priests at all. I gave him some names and addresses – I never knew whether he succeeded in obtaining any priests for his diocese.

Before I left, I asked his permission to have a Sunday Mass for the Division in the Cathedral there in Bayeux. He readily granted what I asked. I went off, very pleased at this success. I hastened to contact the other priests in the Division. At once they made the necessary arrangements. A notice therefore appeared on all military orders, from Divisional Headquarters down to Company level, giving details about this Divisional Mass. There was novelty about such a notice as this, hence everyone was interested in attending a Mass in Bayeux Cathedral. I did not know it at the time, but that my initiative to hold this Cathedral Mass had aroused the envy of the non-Catholic chaplains. Many years later I learned that they had made an effort – through General Montgomery – to take over all French Catholic Churches for their services. This move was strongly resisted by our Senior Chaplains. In the end the plan was dropped.

When the Sunday in question arrived, there was no hitch. The Guardsmen, Catholic and non-Catholic, packed the vast Cathedral. I said the Mass. What a pity that it had to be said in Latin! For the hundreds of non-Catholic men present, it had no meaning – it was just a jumble of sound.

One of the other priests preached. In the circumstances I thought his subject was ill-advised. Here were so many men who were doubtless going to die on the battlefields of Europe. They needed a simple, urgent reminder of God, of the importance of belief in Him, trust in Him, loyalty to one's country, of justice and hatred of wrong-doing. And what did they get? An emotional, devotional sermon on Our Blessed Lady! To most of those men a sermon on Our Lady was too much. Their necessary background knowledge being deficient, the subject was quite meaningless. We understood the importance of Mother of God and her place in the economy of salvation: so many of those soldiers however had no idea of her mission. That sermon remains one of my regrets.

Quite frankly, I felt afterwards that I should have preached the sermon and let the other priest say the Mass. Not that I fancy myself as a preacher, but I am quite certain that I would have spoken to those men in a language and about matters they understood. This feeling of mine was confirmed by what one of my officers said to me later that day: "You should have preached the sermon yourself!"

The deed was done, however: I had to abide by our arrangements.

There were bright elements and dark elements in what we had planned. One bright element was this: a Guardsman in my own Brigade – a Protestant from Ligoniel who was a church organist at home in Belfast – played the great organ of the Cathedral during the Mass. This helped to make the occasion memorable.

The dark elements were twofold – as well as the sermon, there were the many collections taken up during the service. While I was engaged in saying the Mass, the French sacristan of the Cathedral and his assistants, unknown to me, made three or four different collections. No one would have raised any objection to one collection: but to have three or four at one service was outrageous. What was done caused much annoyance and irritation. After the second collection the men had no more change to offer: they were quite embarrassed when the collection bags were shoved in front of them a third or fourth time. When I heard what had happened, I was ashamed: it looked as if the Cathedral people were merely cashing in on the presence of so many visitors. Whatever collection customs exist among French Catholics could have been temporarily set aside on that Sunday.

Looking back, I feel pleased however that we were able to hold that service for the Division. It was the first time for about 800 years that an English service (in so far as it was English) had been held in Bayeux Cathedral.

It is one of the great Cathedrals of France. There you will see the Lady Chapel erected by Bishop Cauchon in atonement for his nefarious part in the burning to death of Joan of Arc. Across the street from the Cathedral, in what is now the town library, the Bishops of Bayeux had their residence. I visited the house and there saw the rooms in which St Thérèse of Lisieux met the Bishop and asked his permission to enter Carmel at the age of fifteen years. The few French people to whom I spoke, when visiting the library building, had never heard of the saint's visit there. This surprised me. I was very interested in seeing the place. Hitherto I had pictured it in my mind: henceforth a true picture replaced my imaginative one.

It was the aim of the Commanding Officers of the Division to provide some sports and entertainment for the men while they were at rest. We had a few concerts and singsongs. The men were able to visit the local towns that we had liberated. Some were able, by those devious methods alert members can discover in army procedures, to go on sightseeing tours.

We played a football match with a Bayeux team. The Guardsmen and many of the local people came to watch the match. A great number of Bayeux's youngsters cheered their side with ardent enthusiasm. It was a sunny afternoon. The pitch where the match was played was dry and powdery. All our players were out of practice. We were beaten, but not disgraced. Our team put up a reasonably good show. It was enjoyable for everyone. I particularly enjoyed listening to the chatter of the French people around me. It is one thing to be able to follow what a Frenchman is saying to you in direct conversation: it is another to be able to understand what French people are saying when chatting among themselves. I decided that anyone who can follow their mutual conversation really knows French. I was keenly interested in the children's talk and mannerisms: I thought that St Thérèse of Lisieux must have spoken and behaved as these children did.

## The General Absolution

Our rest days came to an end. We had received reinforcements; companies had been brought up to strength; equipment and arms had been checked, and deficiencies made good. We were now ready for our next move.

One morning I was informed we were to leave at nightfall for a dawn attack in the area north-east of Caen. I guessed that this was going to be a large-scale battle, so I made up my mind to give General Absolution and Holy Communion to all the Catholic men in my Brigade. As the number of Catholic men ran into some hundreds, I realised that the small pyx I carried would not be large enough to hold all the Communion particles I needed. So I procured a new half-size biscuit tin. This I polished up and lined with clean white paper. I filled it with particles – of which, thank God, I had plenty – and at Mass that day I consecrated the lot.

The Commanding Officer of the 3rd Battalion Irish Guards had said he would address the entire Battalion that evening in one of the nearby meadows. I brought my up car to the spot. I let down the tailboard and turned the rear part into a little altar with cloths and flowers and candles. I was ready when the men assembled.

I told the Commanding Officer I wanted to speak to the Catholic men when he had finished his address. He agreed, of course, and told me to get the Regimental Sergeant Major to hold them for me when he had done.

The Battalion almost filled the meadow adjoining the Bayeux–Caen road. I stood to the side while the Commanding Officer, in line with General Montgomery's policy of letting his troops know his plans and what he expected of them, told his Guardsmen the battle plan. The men listened quietly to what he said. They heard him say it was a full-scale attack: if successful, it meant a break-through in the German positions. They heard the part they were to play in the battle. When the Commanding Officer had finished speaking, the RSM in his loud parade voice instructed all the Catholic Guardsmen to remain where they were: all others were to go off to their duties.

The scene comes clearly to my mind as I write these lines. The quiet summer evening, the meadow deep in grass, the long line of tall poplars to our left, the surrounding fields crammed with guns, equipment and transport, the tiny group of French children watching it all and understanding not a word. The Guardsmen were standing before me in wide semi-circles, row on row. I spoke to them very simply and briefly. I told them it was too much to expect all to come through this battle unscathed. The men must therefore turn to God, placing themselves in his hands – the hands of our Father in Heaven. We had to now renew our faith, love and loyalty to God. We had to repent of any sins we had committed and seek God's pardon. As I had so often done for them in England, I briefly explained the meaning of General Absolution. I said I would now give them this Absolution and Holy Communion.

I asked them to kneel down where they were in the meadow. I asked them to repeat silently in their hearts the short Act of Perfect Contrition, which I would now say slowly aloud. I recited the formula I had taught them in England. I said it very distinctly so that all could hear me. I then gave them a small prayer penance to say and then imparted General Absolution: "Ego vos absolvo ab omnibus censuris et peccatis in nomine Patris et Filii et Spiritus Sancti, Amen."

When this was all done, all the men received Holy Communion. As soon as they had received the Sacred Host, the men in each of the semi-circle lines stood up and moved to the side of the field. This enabled me to reach the next row of men. And so it went on. It was like a man reaping ripe corn with a scythe. This was a harvest, not of corn, but of souls.

When all had received Holy Communion, I spoke a few words to them, telling them to do their duty, to help one another, and to face whatever lay before them with brave hearts and trust in God.

All was over now. Many of the men came to me to say goodbye until we would meet again, once this attack was carried through. All were very grateful to me for what I had done for them. Some gave me new addresses of relatives. One man said light-heartedly, "Now, Father, we are ready for the Germans!"

They did not delay or hang about. They had to get back to their duties. A lot had to be done in a few hours. So, with many a handshake, many a cheery word, they left me standing near my little altar at the car. Some of them I never saw again.

I too did not delay: I had further duties to carry out also. I moved off to the Coldstream Guards and the Welsh Guards, and did for the Catholic men in these units all I had just now done for the Irish Guards.

A faint summer darkness had set in by the time I returned to my bivouac – a slit trench in the corner of a field near Battalion HQ. I was tired, but I felt contented. I had done what I could. The rest was in God's Hands.

Late that night we began our move. Steel-meshed tracks had been laid down secretly across the fields. On those tracks, without touching any of the map roads, the whole Division moved to a new position on the western bank of the River Orne. This was a new manoeuvre in war at the time – the moving of an entire armoured Division across country at night by a road which did not exist – according to the maps.

## Pegasus Bridge: Colombelles

At dawn, standing by the roadside, I watched the Allied bombing planes attacking the German positions beyond the Orne. It was a thousand-bomber raid. The planes came in unbroken succession, like a black chain stretching to the shores of England and beyond. The sky hummed and throbbed: the noise of their engines, coupled with the fury of their bombing, made conversation difficult. I stood silently on the road with my batman and a group of ambulance drivers. I thought of the unfortunate German soldiers trying to maintain their positions under such devastating explosions. And yet they fought back: their anti-aircraft batteries blazed into the sky – and with effect: I saw some of the allied planes falter in the air, suddenly bursting into red and yellow flames, and falling like dry, burning leaves in the fields beyond the river.

Later that day I learned that the Allied planes were using a new type of bomb that morning – a high fragmentation bomb which splintered into tiny pieces on impact, without penetrating the ground or losing its destructive power in the soil. This bomb shattered the nerves and the morale of many of the German soldiers. In the afternoon of that same day we took scores of German prisoners. I asked them about the dawn bombing attack. One of them said instantly, "Es war schrecklich" ("It was frightful"). Many of them still showed the effects of that bombing, trembling with shock and nerves. They must have seen for themselves that the German Air Force could do nothing to stop the Allied air attack. When I raised this question with them, they replied ruefully: "We always get the same answer – our German planes are on the Russian Front!"

Towards midday we crossed the Orne at Benouville. The bridge there had been captured on D-Day by men of the 6th Airborne Division. They gave it a new name: "Pegasus Bridge" – Pegasus being the winged figure on the flash of their Division. Lying around the bridge were the broken and wrecked gliders which had brought the airborne men to the area on D-Day morning. The fighting there had been bitter: the Germans knew full well the importance of the bridge and defended it to the last. Without the use of that bridge, our armoured attack that day would have been impossible.

When our tanks and infantry had crossed the bridge, we thought we had the Germans on the run. How mistaken we were! They fought stubbornly all day long. In one particular village however – I think it was Caumont – they quietly allowed our armour to pass through. As they foresaw, the tanks radioed back the news that the village was clear of the enemy. The unsuspecting infantry came jauntily along the village street – to be suddenly greeted by the withering fire of German machine guns carefully sited in the houses.

We felt that day that the attack had failed. We were bogged down somewhere in the vicinity of Caumont. We got no farther. General Montgomery, however, as always asserted that the attack had achieved its purpose – it had drawn off the German armour from the American sector of the Front in the south west. If he was correct in this, it certainly was a tactical victory, for the US armies broke through the South West sector, and pouring into France, forced the German armies to withdraw. But certainly so far as we could see, no territorial advantage had been gained by our attack.

I am in no way competent to judge these high-scale tactics of war. At the time we were aware only of what was happening in our own area: newspapers from home were our only source of information about other sectors. This is understandable: of what use is it to the common soldier to be kept in touch with what is happening to other units, forty or fifty miles away? He is concerned with what is happening around him!

When our attack had come to a halt, the Brigade Field Ambulance, with which I always kept close contact, established itself in the open fields of Colombelles, beyond the town of Caen. These fields sloped up to a crossroads where the local Catholic parish church stood. Although this church had been badly damaged by shellfire, we were able to clear it up a bit and use it as an Advanced Dressing Station. The main altar became an operating table. The surviving statues around the walls looked down on wounded and bandaged men lying on stretchers. There were always some walking wounded sitting in the pews, awaiting their turn to be attended by the doctors and surgeons.

Lying on the floor of the church was a plaster statue of St Thérèse of Lisieux. With the help of a couple of medical orderlies, I brought this statue outside the church and placed it upright against the wall. There was sporadic shelling going on: the Germans had realised the high church tower was a very useful observation post, and probably wanted to see it down. However, we displayed the Red Cross on the remnant of the roof: we hoped the enemy would observe the Geneva Convention and leave our Dressing Station alone. To make doubly sure, I asked St Thérèse to watch over us and keep us safe.

Lower down in the fields close by a hedge was my slit trench. From where I was bivouacked, I could see the church and thus watch for any ambulances bringing in more wounded. Not far from my trench our artillery had sited a heavy gun, which kept shelling German emplacements, bridges, and key roads far inland. That one gun must have caused the enemy a great deal of trouble, for they kept probing and searching for it. Every day planes came over our fields, hedge-hopping and on the look-out for that gun.

All this helps to explain what happened about a week after we had laagered there. It was a day of hot sun and cloudless sky. Apart from shelling, our sector seemed very quiet. I sat down on the edge of my trench to write a few lines to my mother. I was writing the letter, when I heard the sound of a car up at the crossroads. Looking in that direction, I saw one of our ambulances drawing into the yard before the church.

Some wounded men? I could not be sure! Should I finish my letter – or should I go up at once? And then there flashed into my mind the words of the parish priest on my last night in Eastbourne: "Always try to be where the wounded are!" That decided it! Laying aside my unfinished letter, I put on my steel helmet, and walked up the field to the church. In the pockets of my battledress I always carried the Blessed Sacrament and the Holy Oils. So I was quite prepared to deal with any new wounded. On reaching the church, I found that the ambulance had brought in three or four stretcher cases: one of them a Scots Guardsman – one of my own men. (A Company of Scots Guards had been attached to our Battalion). Having attended him I waited in the church, giving a helping hand wherever necessary.

Meanwhile the shelling had suddenly become intense. None of us felt too comfortable. We were an obvious target to any German gunners who had poor ideas about the Red Cross sign. They may have suspected the church tower would be used as an observation post for our artillery.

The shelling had gone on for five or ten minutes when more stretcher cases were brought in. I instantly observed with dismay that they were all completely covered with blankets – they were dead! I went over and examined each man to find out whether any were Catholics. The bodies were still quite warm – but the men were dead. They had evidently been killed just a few minutes previously. I turned to the stretcher-bearers and asked them where they had found these men. They told me the men had been killed by a shell which landed by the hedge where my slit trench lay.

"You should see your car, Sir!" said one of them to me.

"Why?"

"That last lot of shells landed near your trench!"

I waited until the shelling died down somewhat. Going back to my trench, I found that the hedge near my car was stripped white and smashed down, my equipment above ground destroyed, and my car riddled with shrapnel. Surveying the wreckage, I saw clearly that, had I remained to finish my letter, instead of going up to the wounded in the church, I would have been one of the dead lying on the stretchers.

Those were indeed harassing days of strain and unease. We knew little enough of what was going on around us, and nothing at all about the general situation of the Allied armies. Shelling continued. A low-flying German plane, ignoring the Red Cross signs, sprayed our laager with cannon shells and killed some of our medical personnel. Wounded men came into the Clearing Station daily. The heavy gun, close to which I was still camped, kept firing at irregular intervals during the day. The Germans never succeeded in silencing it.

In the middle of it all, my confrere and fellow-chaplain in the Division, Fr Tronson, came over to see me. We talked of our experiences since we had last met by the river near Bayeux. On this day now, our circumstances were far different. We both agreed that if we came safely through those trying days of shelling and air-raids at Colombelles, we would never again complain or murmur about hard times. That was a promise I should like to have kept; unfortunately I have grumbled and groused my way since then, and no doubt will continue to do so in my future troubles.

Our main concern in those grim days was for the wounded. When the ambulances brought them along, we were too busy attending them to be aware of much else. I used to scan the pallid faces of newly-arrived wounded to see were any of my close friends among them. In effect it did not matter whether there were or not – for all, even the German prisoners – were treated with care and gentleness. I used to try to assist the surgeons in a small way with German wounded, translating their questions into German for the prisoners. The answers which I translated in turn helped the surgeons in their work – and also saved a lot of time. Wounds are the dark side of war – wounds and death and sorrow and destruction; the bright side is the fine sympathy and kindness of soldiers and surgeons for the wounded of all ranks.

In most modern armies medical help for the wounded is now at a high level of efficiency. How very different it was in the old days – even up to the nineteenth century. General Mercer, in his journal about the Waterloo Campaign, describes how he spent the night of the day on which Waterloo was fought, ie, Sunday 18 June 1815: he slept on the footboard of a gun limber on the battlefield. It was not a sound sleep, it was rather a series of short dozes. He recounts in his journal:

> "From one of these dozes I awoke about midnight, chilled and cramped to death from the awkward, doubled-up position imposed upon me by my short and narrow bed. So I got up to look around and contemplated a battlefield by the pale moonlight. The night was serene and pretty clear: a few light clouds, occasionally passing across the moon's disc and throwing objects into transient obscurity, added considerably to the solemnity of the scene ... Here and there some poor wretch, sitting up among the countless dead, busied himself in endeavours to staunch the flowing stream with which his life was fast ebbing away. Many whom I saw so employed that night were, when morning dawned, lying stiff and tranquil as those who had departed earlier. From time to time a figure would half-raise itself from the ground, and then, with a despairing groan, fall back again. Others, slowly and painfully rising, stronger or having less deadly hurt, would stagger away with uncertain steps across the field in search of succour. Many of them I followed with my gaze until lost in the obscurity of distance; but many, alas, after staggering a few paces, would sink again on the ground, probably to rise no more. It was heart-rending..."

Comment on this passage from a General's journal is unnecessary. We have moved a long way from those days. In happy and blessed contrast is the excellent and detailed organisation of the British (and other) Army Medical Services. Thanks to what is now army medical routine, wounds which in those distant days so often meant death, are now in most cases but temporary disablements. Not only are the wounded taken care of during war, they are also cared for after the war if their wounds have disabled them. The dead are also a serious concern of the army: they are reverently buried and, where possible, with due ceremony. Moreover, every dead soldier's grave must be precisely noted on a special form with accurate map references. We chaplains had to be very careful about this regulation when we buried dead soldiers. We had to make sure the forms were filled in properly, before we submitted them to the Military Graves Authority.

When war is over, such forms enable the Graves Authority to collect the dead from scattered graves for re-interment in a military cemetery.

Later on in our campaign I spoke to some American soldiers in a Brussels cemetery, who were trying to identify the dead. I was interested to know how they set about this very difficult task. The Sergeant-in-charge explained that they had all the medical and dental records of their soldiers 'missing' in that area. These records helped a lot – particularly the dental records. In blunt language, no two mouths are quite similar – a man's teeth will identify him. This Sergeant said that thus far, they had been very successful in tracing their 'unknown soldiers'.

This has been a rather long digression about the wounded and the dead. I must now take up once more my story of the Normandy campaign.

General Montgomery knew the facts about our attack across the Orne. He insisted that we had drawn off the main bulk of German armour from the American front farther west. His statement is perhaps proved correct by the subsequent events: the Americans broke through on their sector. Up to that time the Allied armies had made little or no headway – now their tanks smashed through the German positions, fanned out into the countryside beyond, and went racing across France. The German armies were forced to retreat. Thousands of them were trapped in the Falaise country; the rest fled back across France, Belgium and Holland, to Germany and its border frontier, the Rhine.

Our area now became suddenly quiet. Before going off in pursuit of the Germans once more, our Division took a few days to re-form and re-group. During those quiet days I paid a visit to some of the local priests. A number of these had remained in their parishes, despite the maelstrom of war which was swirling around them.

Again, on these occasions my knowledge of French was a great blessing! By this time I had no difficulties in conversing with the people. In this, as in everything else, one improves with practice. I already had a good basic knowledge of French grammar, a fair vocabulary and accent – practice improved me on these points. As a schoolboy, I was so often thrashed for "messing" my French lessons. I used to think the French master paid undue attention to my progress in the language. I now see that it was perhaps Providence that whispered in his ear, "Ask that boy Cummings in the second last bench!" I little knew then how useful French would be to me all my life long – but particularly in Europe during those days of war! The thrashings paid good dividends!

## The Abbé Ân

One of the French parish priests invited me to dinner. When I arrived, I found he had invited another guest – Abbé Ân, the Catholic chaplain of the Carmelite Convent of Caen. This priest's amazing cure from illness when he was a student was one of the two miracles put forward for the beatification of St Thérèse of Lisieux. At dinner that day he told us the story of his cure.

At the time he was a student in the Seminary of Bayeux. He fell into tuberculosis. No remedies stayed the rapid course of the then fatal disease: he came to the brink of death. He sank so low, the seminary authorities expected him to die at any moment. He began a Novena to Sister Teresa of the Child Jesus, as she was then called. For four days he showed no improvement. On the fifth day of the Novena, however, he had a kind of dream in which the saint appeared to him and told him he was cured. He awoke to discover that he now felt well. He arose forthwith from his dying bed and went down to the students' dining room. His appearing amongst the students was like Lazarus' emergence from the tomb. They were speechless. He told them what had happened; he assured them he was cured. To prove the truth of what he said, he sat down to table with them and ate a hearty dinner. Word of his cure quickly went round the Seminary. Professors came along to have a look at him. Servants left their work in the kitchens to see the student whom they had expected to bury that very week. They could not believe the reports that he was cured: they came to see for themselves. Yes, there he was, eating a hearty meal – his first proper meal for months.

This reminds you of the Jews who could not believe the report that Jesus had raised Lazarus from the dead:

"A great multitude, therefore, of the Jews knew that he was there: and they came, not for Jesus' sake only, but that they might see Lazarus, whom he had raised from the dead." (John 12:9)

It was both interesting and helpful to meet this priest and hear his story. He was a very affable and pleasant type of man. He seemed to be in excellent health: he had a good colour and, as I can testify, a good appetite. After so many years – for his cure had taken place in the early years of the twentieth century – the gift of health, donated him by Heaven at the intercession of the saintly nun of Lisieux, remained with him. To meet him, to hear his simple and humble account of his cure, deepened ones awareness of Almighty God.

At the time I met him, the *Abbé* was acting as Chaplain to the Carmelite Convent in Caen. Knowing that this convent had been founded by the Lisieux Carmelites, I was very interested in it. Seeing my interest, he invited me to visit the convent.

I went to it the following day. When I arrived, I found the nuns busily engaged in clearing debris and cleaning bricks. In the recent shelling their convent had been damaged: they were intent on repairing the damage as quickly as possible. So, without formal reception or the usual grill procedure, I met the Caen Carmelites in the open air. They seemed to be very shy and reserved. Monsieur *l'Abbé* did most of the talking for them. One request they did make of me: that if I happened to pass through Lisieux, would I be so kind as to inform the Carmelites there that all the sisters in Caen were very well, and that only slight damage had been done to the convent itself. This I promised to do. They knew the Lisieux sisters would be concerned about them: as I have said, they were founded by the Lisieux Carmel and some of them had been novices there. And now the news links between the two convents had been badly interrupted by the Allies' Normandy invasion.

Before leaving the Caen area, I called at the Caen Visitation Convent. Léonie, the sister of St Thérèse of Lisieux, had been a nun there. Both the Chaplain and Superioress of the convent were very kind to me. The latter allowed me to hold in my hands the crucifix belonging to the saint. I revered it and blessed myself with it. That was a wonderful experience for me. Since boyhood I have prayed to this Saint. I felt I had some affinity with her – for the very slender reason that we both have the same birthday, 2 January. This somehow made me feel that she might even take an interest in me.

Soon afterwards our Division left the Caen sector and started its advance across France. While we were en route to the Seine, in the wake of the retreating German army, I decided to make a slight detour and visit Lisieux. I had first to make certain of three points: I had to find out what route the Division would follow in its pursuit of the fleeing Germans; secondly, I had to plan my journey to Lisieux on the army maps in my possession; thirdly, I had to take all the supplies I might need.

## To Lisieux

Having attended to these matters with Hugh, my batman and driver, I started off. Our progress was slow. Many roads were blocked; some bridges were down; we had to make detours; we were sometimes halted by Military Police. Fortunately we did not come up against German units or groups – a likely enough hazard, I learned afterwards, but one which had entirely escaped my reckoning at the time. And so, after much journeying and close peering at the map on my knees, we came to Lisieux.

The town had been partly destroyed by bombing and shelling. Few people were about the streets. Someone told us how to get to Les Buissonets – the childhood home of St Thérèse. An extern Carmelite sister there showed me around the house and the garden. Every room in the house awakened my memories of what I had read in the saint's account of her childhood. What I had so often pictured in my mind was now a reality around me.

Religious souvenirs were on sale. I bought a pair of rosary beads. I take special care of these beads: I look on them as a kind of relic of St Thérèse. I have them beside me as I write these lines.

The extern sister at Les Buissonets directed me to the convent. On our way there, we stopped to pay a visit to the church of St Peter, where the saint had always attended Mass, and where she made her first Confession. Thence we went to the convent. Another of the extern sisters received us there. All the houses and shops around the convent had been reduced to rubble by the bombing and shelling. The sister told us that apart from very slight damage to the corner of one wing of the building, the convent had escaped unscathed.

During the worst part of the fighting around the town, the Carmelite community, in which three sisters of St Thérèse were still living, had left the convent and taken refuge in the crypt of the new basilica outside the town; now they were back in the convent. I explained to this extern sister who I was, and that I brought a message from the Carmelites at Caen. She immediately said I must speak to Mother Prioress, as this good news would please her very much.

Before the sister left us to inform Mother Prioress, I asked her if the sisters were in need of anything. Her eyes brightened at the question. She told me they had practically nothing in the convent: there was little food, nothing for the sick and infirm, and no light in the entire building – their cells were in darkness. I remedied this situation as best I could. Hugh and I gave her all we could spare – almost everything we had. We were not worried: going through the countryside, we knew we could get new supplies somewhere along the road. The sister was very grateful for this unexpected help. We both assisted her in carrying into the convent all the spare commodities we had brought with us. When she returned, she informed me that Mother Prioress wished to speak to me.

I was ushered into the reception room. From behind the screened grille, Mother Prioress – Pauline Martin, sister of St Thérèse – spoke to me in French, thanking me for our gifts. With her were two of her sisters, Marie and Céline. They promised to pray for Hugh and myself and for the men of my Brigade. She gave me three pictures of her sister, the saint. Each little picture was signed by Marie, Céline and herself. I told them about my visit to the Carmelites at Caen, the damage done to the convent and the message the sisters asked me to convey to Lisieux.

The visit was a short one. Now that our mission was accomplished, we were anxious to be on our way. We left the convent, contented that we had done something for those who had helped to give a great saint to the world.

## Through Flanders Fields

And so without further delay, we headed across France. We crossed the Seine at Vernon. There I had the good fortune to meet some of my former comrades in the 43rd Division. They were able to tell me the whereabouts of my own Division. We pressed on and soon caught up with my Brigade.

Speed was the order of the day. The Guards' Armoured Division moved rapidly across Northern France. The retreating Germans offered no resistance. The French Resistance fighters – or the *Maquis*, as they were called – dealt with any pockets of the enemy which put up a fight. Occasionally as we came into towns and villages, we were held up by cheering crowds who thronged the roads and streets. After so many years of repressive German occupation, the people were now delirious with joy at being freed. Garlands of flowers, baskets of fruit, much handshaking, and for the very cooperative Guardsmen, embraces and kisses, were additions to the order of the day. To the men, these compulsory halts and welcoming tributes were most acceptable.

As we moved along the roads, we passed little groups of German soldiers, huddled in misery by the roadside. Some were wounded; all were weary and dispirited. They were now prisoners of war, but no one bothered about them – there was no delay for them; no guards were assigned to them. We kept moving on and on. For them, but not for us, the war was ended. For them indeed, in the words of Shakespeare's Cleopatra, "withered was the garland of war".

On our arrival at Amiens, I went to the Cathedral. It was dim, cool and quiet, after the turmoil of the advance and the greeting, cheering crowds. On the steps of the High or Main Altar, I knelt and placed a bunch of flowers someone had thrust at me as we came along. I meant these flowers to be an offering from my batman Hugh Creaney and myself to Our Lord in the Blessed Sacrament. I asked Jesus to watch over us and help us. I know now, but did not then, what lay before us.

Leaving Amiens, we took the road to Albert. When passing through that countryside, I looked around me with great interest: these fields were once the scene of some of the bloodiest battles of the First World War. Out of Amiens, by this very road along which we were driving, thousands of men had marched to their deaths in the battles of the Somme.

On a low hill by the side of the road, as it went down into Albert, I stood to watch what was happening ahead of us. The Germans were still in the town. We were now close on their heels. Near us was a French farm cart which they had been using. Its shafts were on the ground: there was a fire smouldering, some food, sugar lying in a torn blue paper bag, bits of equipment – and a Spandau machine gun with its barrel partly crushed. All these items indicated a very hurried departure by the Germans. It now seemed they were going to make a stand in Albert. From the small hill I was standing on, I watched the road entrance to the town. While I was there, an officer came over to me and advised me to stand down, as I was in real danger of being killed by snipers. However, there was no fighting. Following the usual strategy of those days, the Division by-passed Albert and left the Germans manning their barricades and fingering their weapons impatiently in the town.

Along the road taken by the Division, my batman Hugh and I stopped to look at a military cemetery. At the entrance was a large notice in German, which said: "Here lie 44,000 German soldiers who died in this sector during the World War 1914–18". The cemetery's enclosed area was a low forest of small black crosses, one on each grave, in most orderly array, row on row, line by line – 44,000 small black crosses, equalling the number of the soldiers buried there. As we stood gazing at this melancholy sight, I thought how impressively the ordered array of these soldiers at rest in death contrasted with the chaos and turmoil of the war in which they died. Hugh turned to me and said, "Father, isn't it terrible to see such loss of human life? And here we are – back at it again!"

It is a truism that war is an indictment of man's folly. The problem is that every new generation will not accept this: every generation repeats the folly. Folly brings its own punishments. We are witnesses of what Germany is now paying for the madness of the two World Wars which they have precipitated since 1900.

## To Brussels

We were now on the road to Douai, through the countryside north of Bapaume. The bare, dark-earthed fields through which we passed, were once coveted prizes won by the suffering and death of so many thousands of soldiers. These stretches of barren land, now still and quiet, were once muddy Gehennas of death, and blood, and destruction. In these fields of Flanders, we are told, England lost the flower of her youth in the war of 1914–18. I looked around me as we went forward, my mind filled with sad thoughts, my eyes seeing only a desolate and gloomy countryside.

At length we came to the streets of Douai. There was nothing bright and cheerful about the town: it seemed to share in the general gloom of the area. We stopped there for the night. From Douai we advanced to Brussels, a distance close on a hundred miles. This advance was made in one day. I was told afterwards it was a record – the furthest advance in a day of any Division in the annals of British military history.

Instead of entering Brussels directly from Douai, the Division branched off from the Douai–Brussels road several miles from the capital, and entered the city's suburbs at Ouderghem. This was "the oblique approach", so dear to the hearts of many military commanders.

We arrived at Ouderghem in the small hours of the morning. Our Battalion, with the other units of the Division, stood to until dawn. As the morning dawned and the city awakened, I saw the local people moving here and there in normal manner, so I decided to find some place where I could say Mass. Since we might be given orders at any moment to move quickly, I knew that my Mass would have to be said in some place near at hand. If only I could find some neighbouring convent or chapel!

A passing Belgian woman informed me that the Marist Brothers had a college and chapel a couple of hundred metres farther along the boulevard.

I told Hugh where I was going. He would wait to guard my car. If we were suddenly ordered to move, he was to come and collect me.

On my way to the chapel, I came to one of our machine-gun posts. I stopped to have a word with the men. I told them where I was going. From where they were positioned, they could see the entrance door of the chapel.

I walked on. Both sides of the boulevard were here well-wooded. I crossed the road and entered the chapel by the main door. I genuflected as usual to the Blessed Sacrament, and then knelt in one of the benches. I was no sooner on my knees than a machine gun started rapid firing outside. I waited for a moment. The firing ceased. I got up and went out into the boulevard.

Guessing it was our own machine gun which had fired, I waved to the men at the post. They waved back. My eyes now turned to the roadside near me. Lying on his side, blood pouring from his body, was a German soldier. Kneeling beside him on the road, I opened his tunic and took out his *Soldat-Buch* – his Pay Book – with all his particulars. There I saw his religion was "Gottglaubich" – "a believer in God". Not waiting to ponder the matter, I there and then absolved and anointed him conditionally. Clinically he was dead, but theologians, reasoning that the soul in such cases does not leave the body at once, allow conditional administration of the Sacraments.

The Guardsmen in the machine-gun post told me what had happened. As soon as I had entered the chapel, this man had come out of the trees on the opposite side of the boulevard. With rifle at the ready, he had approached the chapel door. The corporal in charge of the machine-gun post called to him to halt. He did not halt – instead he tried to make for the chapel or the woods.

"I called on him to halt! He tried to run for it: I gave him three bursts from this Bren gun!" explained the corporal. His aim was accurate: the German's body was riddled with bullets.

The people of Brussels gave us a tumultuous welcome. Cheering crowds filled the streets, as we moved in to selected strategic points. It was a slow process: the people presented us with flowers and fruit; the girls embraced and kissed the willing Guardsmen; the young men climbed on board the tanks, the Bren Carriers, the transport. And all the while the people cheered and cheered – not in bursts or spells, but as one prolonged, thundering sound.

As soon as I could do so, I went to our Redemptorist church and monastery in the city, named St Joseph. There I met one of my confrere chaplains of my Division. We were both standing in the entrance hall of the monastery, when an old Belgian lady came to greet us. Now this confrere was one accustomed to the former ways in the spiritual world, and ever a model of propriety and decorum. I can still see the startled look in his eyes as this kind old dear threw her arms round him and kissed him. Instantly his gentlemanly manners reacted suitably and he played his part with his wonted courtesy.

The Belgian Redemptorists gave us a warm welcome. Their happiness at being freed from the oppressive presence of the German army of occupation was evident. They had endured, with their people, four years of tension and fear. Now they were all smiling and light-hearted. They could not give us the welcoming hospitality they wished, but they did their best. They brought us to the Community Refectory and there gave us large mugs of hot malt. I drank the lot. It was their wartime substitute for coffee. I thought it was quite good – not like the dandelion tea I was later offered elsewhere, which sickened me horribly.

Although we had reached St Joseph's in or near the centre of Brussels, the Germans were not far away. Small pockets of their troops still held out in certain suburban districts. The Irish Guards had one Company holding a post on the north eastern side of the city. I went on a visit to the men there. As we drove through the city, I observed to Hugh that the streets seemed to be deserted. With that some shots rang out!

"Now you know why there is nobody about!" said Hugh, as he accelerated. We had run near a German-held position. And either their inaccurate shooting or our swift acceleration saved us from being cut to pieces by a German Spandau.

During those first days in Brussels I saw one of our trucks bringing in one of these pockets of die-hard Germans. On seeing the German uniformed figures, a crowd of Belgians quickly gathered round the truck. They began to taunt and jeer the Germans. A man in the crowd went up to one of the prisoners, a German non-commissioned officer, and with the back of his hand slapped him hard on the face. To me at the time, it seemed to be an act of the most profound contempt. I seemed to be seeing all the hatred and contempt of the entire Belgian people for their German invaders, summed up and manifested in that one slap on the face.

The fighting spirit of a number of our soldiers died in Brussels. The kindly people, the liberated homes so readily open to them, the free supplies of wine and liqueurs, the quickly-organised black market in army stores, the ease and pleasure of the city's life, coming so suddenly after the hardships and tough fighting in Normandy – all this induced in some of the men a reluctance to face further dangers in battle. And so, when we moved out of Brussels to begin the advance to Holland, scores of soldiers deserted. Newly-made friends hid them. There was nothing much the various units could do about it. The war had to be continued. Lists of deserters were soon in the hands of the Military Police: they would tackle this new problem in their own way. The army's advance had to go on.

Of that advance through Belgium to Holland, only a tangled skein of memories remains with me: our steady progress for an hour or two; halts – some for meals, some forced on us by German resistance; German prisoners standing in forlorn groups behind crude, barbed wire fencing; some of our tanks lying askew by the roadside – perhaps with the message chalked up on them: "Brewed up! Do not touch!" – which meant that the tank had been hit by a shell, had gone on fire, and probably contained dead bodies.

The German armies were by no means finished. They did not let the allies have things all their own way. Here and there, at strategic points, they stubbornly resisted all our efforts to break through. They were highly skilled in the art of choosing defensive positions: at times, thanks to this skill, a mere handful of them were able to hold up the Division's advance for hours.

On one occasion, I remember, a group of five or six Germans, well-armed and with ample supplies of food, picked a position halfway up one of the sloping slag heaps outside a coal mine, and dug themselves in. These men held up our Division for at least two hours. Their emplacement was hard to find and harder to hit. From where they were, they could sweep the main road of our advance with murderous fire. It took our guns some time to winkle them out. When the few survivors of this small but troublesome garrison were brought in as prisoners, I asked one of them why they had attempted such a hopeless task as fighting a Division. One of them replied in a matter-of-fact kind of way: "Ein Befehl ist ein Befehl!" ("An order is an order!") They were true soldiers of the German military tradition: what was commanded had to be done, whether the soldiers deemed it wise or otherwise. All of us respected these brave men – but to us, their stance somehow resembled the mad actions of the Light Brigade at Balaclava.

There is no doubt but the average German soldier thought that an order, no matter what it was, must be carried out. Soldiers of the highest ranks in the German army seemed to accept and insist on this principle. At Nuremberg, during the trials of the Nazi war criminals, many of them quoted this principle to justify the monstrous crimes perpetrated in the Occupied countries and the concentration camps.

## CHAPTER EIGHT
# Into Holland

### The Road to Arnhem

WE MOVED ON through Belgium into Holland. One day we stood on the roadside, watching planes towing gliders. We knew something big was on – but that was all. Later we learned it was the 6th Airborne Division attack at Arnhem. Had the attack succeeded, it would have changed the whole course of the war. It failed, as we know – a failure which was particularly bitter after all our previous triumphs.

Our Division was ordered to push on and relieve the 6th Airborne Division, which the Germans had surrounded. And so, without delay, we crossed the River Maas by the bridge at Grave, and next, the lower Rhine by Nijmegen Bridge.

We got as far as Oss on the Nijmegen–Arnhem road. There we were held up and got no farther. It was not tank country – and when not able to employ and deploy its tanks, our armoured Division was practically useless. Picture a high road with embankments running directly to Arnhem! Down the embankments on both sides of the road, stretching far and wide, lie low, flat fields intersected by canals and drains! That was the area where we were unable to advance to the rescue of the men in the airborne Division.

### Hospital in Brussels

By this time the autumn weather in Holland was worsening. There was a good deal of rain. The countryside was often hidden in white, wet mists which drifted in from the sea. I was out and about in all this, and soon I began to feel the effects of the cold, damp atmosphere. A heavy chill brought on a severe attack of bronchitis, which unfortunately led to asthma. For some time I fought it, in the hope that it would clear up. In the end, it beat me: I had to go back to Brussels to a military hospital.

Although the hospital treatment soon halted the asthma, I was too weak and exhausted to go back to the Brigade. It was arranged that I should go by plane to England. I was made ready and comfortable on a stretcher. I lay in a hospital corridor, awaiting transport to the airfield. While I lay there, our Senior Army Chaplain, Monsignor Stapleton, came to say goodbye and to wish me a speedy return to health. I assured him I would soon be back to normal. Another week in the hospital would put me on my feet. I suggested that, rather than sending me back to England, he should instead assign me to the hospital here, and send its chaplain to replace me in the Brigade. He instantly agreed. So I was taken off the stretcher and put back to bed. My prophecy proved to be correct. A couple of days later I was up and around – well again, but weak. However, I rapidly recovered my strength and energy. Not long afterwards I had taken up my new duties.

What were these duties? I had to attend to the spiritual needs of the Catholic patients and staff of this British military hospital. My flock, therefore, consisted of wounded men, doctors, nurses, and medical orderlies. At first I found the work strange. I had to get to know the staff of the hospital and the layout of the wards. I had to evolve some plan for my daily duties. I had to learn slowly, bit by bit, how to cope with the many tasks demanded of me.

Gradually I got to know the hospital and the staff. I was by then on friendly terms with all, and accepted and established as part of the team. I had a lot to learn, however. I began to feel out the best way of going about my work – for example, how to find out in advance of the arrival of a new batch of wounded; how to discover new arrivals during the night; the best times for visiting the wards; how to visit a ward; how to find Catholic patients, and so on. The work was interesting and varied – more so than I had expected! I have always thought that real variety and interest in life is found in one's personal experiences in meeting different people: people are always more interesting than scenery and sights. Apart from the loss of personal liberty, part of the punishment of prison surely consists in the awful monotony of living with and seeing the same people, day after day after day.

I had not so many Catholics among the staff. As for the patients, if the wounded intake came from a fairly Catholic regiment, I would have perhaps thirty to fifty. The number was variable.

Nearly all the Belgian people who came to help in the hospital were Catholics. It always struck me however that few of them were enthusiastically Catholic. I may be very much in the wrong about this – it is quite possible that they were deeply loyal to both Catholic Faith and Church, but in a manner less demonstrative than we Irish manifest. How friendly and kind they were, though! They daily brought in presents of flowers, fruit and books for the wounded. They did much to brighten the lives of men wounded grievously and slowly sinking into death.

The hospital was one of the main hospitals for the Allied armies. Hospital trains and ambulance convoys came into Brussels from all sectors of the areas where there was fighting. Many of these brought us scores of wounded men. I met many nationalities among them.

On one occasion while doing my rounds, I came to the bed of a Canadian. On hearing my accent, he asked me did I come from Ireland. At my affirmative reply, he bade me sit by his bed while he told me the following story...

He was a journalist working for one of the Canadian papers and attached to the Canadian Division. During the "Phoney War" period (those first few years of the war), nothing much was happening in England or elsewhere. Therefore his editor back in Canada sent him word to go over to Dublin and there find out the views of the man in the street about Irish neutrality. Very pleased at having such a sanctioned opportunity of visiting Ireland, he crossed by boat from Holyhead to Dublin. On the boat he fell into conversation with an Irish civilian. They had a few drinks together in the ship's bar. He explained to this Irishman the purpose of his visit to Dublin.

"Why not start with me?" asked the Irishman. "I am Dublin-born, I am a 'man in the street' – why not start with me?"

"Right!" answered the Canadian, taking out his shorthand notebook. "What are your views about Ireland's neutrality in this present war?"

At this point in his story, the Canadian turned in his bed to look at me fixedly. "Padre," he said, "that boy was really eloquent. He launched forth on the crimes and iniquities of England. He really wanted England to get a good hammering. She deserved it, because of all she had done against Ireland in the past. His language was most vivid and picturesque. He damned England! So I said to him, 'I take it then, that you would like to see Germany winning this war?'"

"Oh no!" that Irishman had replied. "I want England to get a good rocking! But I would not like to see Mr Hitler winning the war!"

"What are you doing about it? You really want England to win: good! But what are you doing to help England? You are just like the rest of them in Ireland – you are sitting on the fence, watching others do the dirty work!"

The Irishman did not reply. Instead, he began to fumble in his pockets. Producing some papers, he handed them over to the Canadian for his inspection. The papers showed that he was a pilot in one of the Hurricane squadrons of the Royal Air Force. He was now going home to Dublin to enjoy a well-earned leave.

The Canadian journalist laughed heartily as he finished his story. He evidently enjoyed that boat episode. He thought it was one of his best stories, and he heard it before he even set foot in any of the streets in Ireland!

## My Sister Eileen's Death

As I was going through the wards one day, I received a message that the Commanding Officer wished to see me in his office. I went along at once. Bidding me take a seat, he told me there was some news from home – news that was not at all pleasant. He asked me about my family at home. He then quietly broke the news to me: Eileen, my eldest sister, had died, rather suddenly.

He kindly offered me seventy-two hours' leave to go home to Belfast for the funeral. He advised however me not to go: the time he could allow me was very short, and the journey would be long and wearisome. I weighed up all the circumstances and decided not to go home.

When he heard my decision, he told me to take the day off. He said I should go away somewhere for the day – an outing would help me to get over the shock of the news. I accepted this advice. I made enquiries in the city and discovered that a bus was going to Bruges that very morning. This suited my purpose, and so I went to Bruges.

It was the wrong decision. I arrived in the town and wandered through its curious, old-world streets. I visited the Beguinage. I stood on the old bridge spanning the canal, and pondered the mediaeval beauty around me. I went to the town square. There, while I was standing before the Market House, the sweet mellow chimes rang out from the belfry. As I listened to them, I suddenly remembered that Eileen and her husband, Dick, had come to Bruges for their honeymoon. This recollection saddened me, and made my visit to Bruges more a sorrowful pilgrimage than a helpful distraction.

My sister and I had always been very close to each other. As children we went to Mass together on Sundays. Most days too, I went with her a good part of the road to our respective schools. She advised me about difficulties and problems in the home. She was intelligent and wise. From her I learned so much. I do not think we had any real secrets we kept from one another. Her marvellous plans for the future, painted for me in vivid colours as we walked to Mass or to school, became to me as a boy almost present realities.

Eileen was attractive, popular among her friends, and always a good sport. She loved fun, and parties, dances, holidays, and she wrung the last drop of enjoyment from all of these. She was very good to Mother. After her marriage, she frequently shopped in the city centre: her normal practice was to buy some article of food or wearing apparel for Mother.

She died from heart disease in 1945. I have never forgotten her. Many times I have offered Mass for the repose of her soul. I pray for her eternal peace every day of my life. The words of the Preface of the Requiem Mass assuaged the sorrow I felt at her passing: "Vita mutatur, non tollitur!" ("Life is but changed, not taken away!") And how often do these words of Cardinal Newman's hymn, "Lead, Kindly Light" come into my mind:

"So long Thy power hath blest me, sure it still
Will lead me on,
O'er moor and fen, o'er crag and torrent, till
The night is gone;
And with the morn those Angel faces smile,
Which I have loved long since and lost awhile."

In God's Mercy, I look forward to the eternal meeting with my parents – and with Eileen.

Our Lord has himself felt the sorrow that plunges through our hearts when death strikes a dear one. At the grave of his friend Lazarus he was "deeply moved", and he wept. He has encouraged us in our grief: "Blessed are they that mourn, for they shall be comforted!" I have always thought that sorrow over a death of someone near and dear, when accepted for Jesus' sake, sanctifies and ennobles the soul, as does sorrow and repentance for sin.

In those days in Brussels, death was a frequent visitor, daily stalking the hospital wards and beckoning to many of our wounded. One day, I forestalled him. News came to me one morning that a Catholic soldier had come into the hospital during the night. He had been badly wounded during a battle near the German frontier. There had been some slip-up regarding the entry of his particulars at the reception office. So I had to go through the wards and rooms, looking for him. In my search I entered a small ward of four or five beds, only one of which was occupied by a wounded man. I asked him his name and his religion. He told me he was a member of a Protestant denomination.

"Has your Padre come to see you?" I asked him.

"No, Sir!" he answered in a low, weak voice.

"I will let him know you are here and he will come to see you," I said, as I turned to go out of the ward.

"Don't go away, Sir!" said the soldier.

I shut the door and came back to his bed.

"What has happened to you?" I asked him.

"Both my legs are gone, Sir!" he replied. He looked terribly ill. His face was ashen. The sweat of death was on his forehead.

"Look here, son," I said to him, gently and regretfully. "You do not belong to my Church. There is not very much I can do for you in the circumstances."

"You could help me to pray, Sir!"

So I sat beside his bed and prayed with him. Prayer and all the necessary Sacraments for the dying were meant by God for men like him. And so whatever spiritual help and comfort I could give that dying man, I gave with all my heart. When I left him, he was contented and at peace. He died some hours later. How good of God to give me a chance to help him! I had gone into the wrong ward and found the one man in the hospital who needed me most.

Not many days later another incident occurred: an incident of a very dissimilar complexion, however. One morning as I was coming from the chapel of the Hospital of St Paul, where I had said Mass, I met three American soldiers. They were standing in the entrance hall of our hospital. As they looked rather lost, I asked them could I help them.

"Yeah!" drawled one of them. "We wanna box a guy!"

It took me, as it is taking you, some time to work that one out! A few questions to them elicited their story and their needs. One of their number had been killed in a parachute jump: his parachute had failed to open. His comrades had gathered only some pieces of his broken, dead body, and not having a coffin available in the moment, had deputed these three men to come to the hospital for one.

I brought them down to the morgue, where we had plenty of coffins stacked along the walls. They selected one and brought it to their truck. As they were about to leave, one of them turned to me and said, "say, Chaplain, where can we get some eats?" I brought them back into the hospital, got them a hot meal, and sent them away happy.

About this time the Germans introduced their famous reprisal weapon, the V-1 (or 'Doodlebug'). Many of these fell on London and the south eastern counties. Many also fell on Antwerp and Brussels. These flying bombs, pilotless and carrying a powerful warhead, came over the city by night and by day. In daylight you could not only hear their staccato-sounding engine as they neared the buildings and streets of Brussels, but also see their flight direction, and you could if necessary take some evasive action. Not so during the night. You had to go to bed to get some sleep: you could not keep staring into the far, dark reaches of the sky during the night hours. It was a trying experience, to lie in bed at night, listening to their approach, not knowing where they were going to fall. Neither was it pleasant to be awakened out of a deep sleep by the sound of their fall and an explosion quite close at hand.

The V-1 was indeed a terrorising weapon. It achieved little or no direct military effect: it merely destroyed dwelling houses and wiped out families – families of ordinary, plain folk who were in no way responsible for the declaration or carrying on of the war. I suppose the Germans would have said the same about the Allied bombing attacks on Berlin, Dresden, Hamburg, and other German cities. The British retort would probably have been: "The Germans started it all by bombing London – let them take now what is coming to them!"

In the two great conflicts of the twentieth century, the people of Belgium and France have suffered, as Britain has suffered. Unless history in our times is going to change the pattern, these nations will continue to suffer the ravages and disruption of war every twenty or thirty years. With good reason has Belgium, for example, been called "the cockpit of Europe".

The weeks and months passed by. The Allied armies finally began their advance: they crossed the Rhine and moved on into Germany.

The time came for us to leave Brussels. I said goodbye to all my friends in the city. I liked the people there: they were friendly and helpful. Many of those I had come to know were very cultured. It was for me an interesting experience to listen to their conversation *en famille*. Their talk was on a high level – thoughtful and well-informed. Only occasionally would I take part in a discussion, however. I preferred to listen to the ideas, counter-ideas, views and appraisals put forward by those present. It seemed to me that the womenfolk were every bit as keen-minded and shrewd as the men: they could set aside domestic problems and turn to discussions on world and social affairs with complete ease and most sensible judgment. I had now to leave them all. Not much warning of our move had been given, so my farewell meetings with my Brussels friends were short and to-the-point.

# CHAPTER NINE

# Into Germany

## Between the Ems and Weser

EN ROUTE TO Germany, what scenes of destruction we passed through! Many Belgian and French towns had suffered extensively, but all that was small when compared to the destruction of the towns in north east Germany. Towns like Kleve, Goch, Geldern and Wesel were total ruins. You can get used to everything, they say, but in the beginning of our advance into Germany, it was startling to see the widespread and utter devastation of what had not long since been prosperous towns. As we advanced, we came to realise that masses of rubble on both sides of the road meant that another town had been wiped out.

We met few German civilians: nearly all had fled before the advancing tide of war. Those we did meet walked slowly past us, with eyes on the ground and very dejected appearance. No wonder! No wonder, for this defeat and desolation was the final outcome for them of Hitler's promises and boasting and the Nazi dream.

Fraternisation with the German people was forbidden, but from the start this law was broken. The Allied soldiers were kind; the average British Tommy loves youngsters. And so in Germany the newly arrived 'enemy' made friends with all, but especially with the children. It seemed to me that the German children reminded the men of their own little ones at home. It was too much to ask them to snub a child or to refuse to help women and elderly folk.

Having crossed into Germany, our route lay through the rich, fertile land which lies between the two rivers, the Ems and the Weser. This is quite a wide area which, until the early years of the twentieth century, had been looked on as merely moorland. Only when the Dutch began to cultivate their side of it, did the Germans themselves bring in their ploughs and start to turn the moor into fertile land. There are great stretches as yet untouched, but many clear-sighted Germans insist that this moor is the land of the future.

Of the future – certainly not of the present! In winter the scene is uninspiring: all one sees is a flat, spreading area of country, broken here and there by dark, lonely groves and forests of fir and pine trees. In summer however, the countryside becomes somewhat attractive: fields here and there are rich in crops; birches gleam along the footpaths and moorland tracks; heather unfolds an immense violet carpet, checked only here and there by black banks of peat.

Our destination was the town of Bassum, which lies about fifteen miles south of Bremen. A few miles outside the town there was a German military hospital. The German medical and nursing staff had moved out with their patients. When we arrived, the Canadians were in charge. Once they were transferred elsewhere, we took charge.

Soon our medical staff had everything organised. We began to receive the wounded. These were dealt with at once, and when fit for the journey, they were sent down to a base hospital in Belgium, or to a transit camp en route to England. In a short time we stopped taking in any large number of our wounded soldiers, because we were crowded with male patients who had been prisoners in the German concentration camps.

## The German Concentration Camps

There were many of these camps in Germany. Belsen, perhaps, was the most notorious. It consisted of three separate camps. No 1 Camp held about 27,000 men of different nationalities. When the Allied troops took over, the prisoners there were extremely weak and underfed. They were, generally speaking, able to be up and about: they could look after themselves. Yet, although there was neither disease not epidemic in that camp, twenty to thirty died every day – obviously from starvation. The buildings which housed those prisoners were overcrowded: a hut which was intended to take one hundred and fifty men was made to hold five or six hundred.

No 2 Camp was the 'Horror Camp'. It was a wired-off area of about 1400 yards long and 700 yards wide. A large section was occupied by German army units and buildings. Into the remaining area, in seventy-nine huts (thirty eight of which were for men), about 50,000 human beings were crowded. Thirty per cent of these were Catholics.

Typhus had broken out in No. 3 Camp. When the first units of the British army entered this camp, seven to ten thousand prisoners lay dead in the huts or in the compound. The remainder were either dying or in grave danger of death. In truth, No 3 Camp was a Gehenna of suffering and death.

No wonder that on 12 April 1945, the Chief-of-Staff of the First German Parachute Army contacted the staff of the British 8th Corps, to ask the British Forces to take over the camp at Belsen. A dreadful situation had arisen there – typhus was raging and matters were out of control.

No wonder the Germans wanted to hand over the trouble to someone else! To the everlasting credit of the British authorities, they agreed to deal with this crisis. The German personnel in the camps left hurriedly, and the British services moved in. For some hundreds of the poor prisoners, they had come too late! When the British compiled statistics, it was revealed that on the first day, in No 3 Camp, 548 people died. Despite the difficulties, however, they were able to rescue about 27,000 in No 1 Camp. Sadly, they had not the same success in No 3 Camp, where Typhus had too strong a hold by the time they arrived.

Hundreds of these prisoners from Belsen and other concentration camps were transferred to our hospital. We had no proper buildings for the large numbers arriving, so they were accommodated in large marquees. Since the weather was quite warm, this was no hardship to the patients.

They were of all European nationalities – Poles, Dutchmen, Belgians, Frenchmen, and so on. Every one of them was suffering from "manition" – or, in plain speech, "insufficient food". Added to this, many of them had TB, and very many had Typhus. They were nearly all young men. Few were over forty; most were in their twenties.

Our British Army doctors and nurses did all they could for them. Some could not be brought back to normal health: their state of health was too low. The deaths each day were numerous, especially at the beginning of our work with them. Many died, because our help came too late.

How did we overcome the language problems of working with so many different nationalities? The answer is simple: they had all been so long in the concentration camps that they had picked up a good knowledge of German. It was the one language they all understood. This fact did not solve our linguistic difficulties, but it simplified things.

My knowledge of German now came in very useful. I was able to act as interpreter for the doctors and nurses when they were working with the patients. Moreover, we had to employ German girls for the work in the wards. When a Sister wanted to instruct these young women in their duties, I would stand by and translate her instructions into German. I was much in demand, thank God! It was wonderful to feel I was lending a really helpful hand.

Two or three times a day, having dusted my body with anti-lice powder – as the doctors had ordered – I donned a long white coat and went round the wards to hear the patients' confessions and to anoint the dying. Those who could swallow food received Holy Viaticum.

For the burial of the dead, we had no coffins. We wrapped them up in army blankets. In a field across the road from our hospital, we had German civilians digging graves, hour by hour, day by day. Into the newly-dug, shallow graves, we lowered the poor, wasted bodies of these young men. In a war not of their own making, they had been torn from their homes and destroyed by cruelty, suffering and disease. Far from their homelands, they now lay buried among strangers.

There was one mania from which these sick patients all suffered – a mania for food. Even when dying and quite unable to eat any food, they still clung to the plate of food given them. It was pathetic to see a dying man trying to nibble at bread or meat or potatoes – for he would insist on getting what the others were getting.

Religion brought them some comfort in their last hours. The Catholic patients availed of all the spiritual help I could give them. Soon I had clear evidence that the Russian patients wanted me to help them also. As I have said earlier, the Poor Clare Colettine Sisters would send me packages of Sacred Heart Badges. With few exceptions, the Russians were most anxious to have one of these badges. When I handed a badge to one of them as he lay in bed, he instantly pinned it on the shirt of his pyjamas. I remember one day entering a ward and finding every patient – Russian or Polish or French or Belgian – wearing a Sacred Heart Badge and displaying it proudly.

In my spiritual administrations to the patients, I made no distinction between Catholics and Orthodox Catholics. These dying men wanted to go to God: they were not interested in doctrinal difficulties. They wanted me to help them, so I attended them. When they died, I buried them with prayer.

The earnest Catholic faith of the Poles did not surprise me, for Poland, like Ireland, has a long history of fidelity to the Faith. But I was very surprised at the faith of the Russians. I should have thought that atheistic Communism had destroyed the Christian faith in Russia. Apparently not, from what I saw in that hospital in Bassum. Perhaps at some future date, when the Russian people shall have recovered the normal freedoms of life, the story of their underground efforts to preserve their Christian heritage will amaze the world.

I have in my possession – somewhere! – a photo of a shrine of Our Lady and the Saints painted by a Russian artist in a prison camp, and erected there by his comrades. It was a work of art. It was also a sign of the faith of those Russian prisoners.

One other Russian memory: while searching for a grave in Bassum cemetery, I came upon a Russian mother with her daughter, weeping and praying at her son's grave. They mourned this boy, then dead a year, and prayed for the eternal repose of his soul. I spoke to them, in German of course, and consoled them through their belief and trust in God.

Russia, converted as a nation to the Faith, may well one day convert Europe, now losing the Faith.

## David's Story

Among the patients we received into the hospital was a little Jewish boy of thirteen or fourteen years. His name was David. He was very worn after his spell in one of the concentration camps. Fortunately his youth, along with good food and proper treatment soon restored his health. I met him as I was walking through the hospital grounds. He was wearing those horrible striped clothes which the prisoners had to wear in the concentration camps. The suit he wore was much too big for him: it made him look very strange. I took pity on him, because he was so young, and I helped him in many ways. One day I asked David how he had come to be in a concentration camp. He told me his sad story…

When he was only eight or nine years of age, the Germans had invaded his native village in Poland. He and his family, being Jewish, were taken away. He never saw his father again, although he had heard a rumour that a Jewish organisation had contrived his escape to South America. With his mother and his baby sister, David was brought to a concentration camp. Because of some trouble that broke out in the camp, the infamous SS troops arrived. David saw them killing his mother and baby sister. Somehow he escaped the slaughter – perhaps they thought he could be useful. He was a sturdy youngster, so some time later the Germans sent him to work in the coalmines.

He worked there for several months. The mines were lit by electric lamps of very high power. David explained that the glare of these lights was very severe on his eyes. I had already noticed how thickly-grown his eyelashes were – abnormally so. On hearing about these strong lights, I wondered if this was nature's response to a young boy's problem of this kind. David assured me that the lights made his eyelashes grow so thickly.

After some months he succeeded in escaping from the mines. Having no home, no friends and no money, he wandered through Germany from place to place, living on alms and the small sums he earned by doing jobs for farmers.

In the end the Gestapo caught up with him. They soon had him back in one of the concentration camps. They also made sure he would no longer be nameless: they gave him a number as his name – it was tattooed on his upper arm. He pulled up his shirtsleeve and showed me the light blue figures marked clearly on his skin.

Why had they done this to a Jewish child? I am quite sure the Gestapo would say: "An order is an order!"

Some months later they had him on the list for execution. With others, David heard his name called out and his number as well. He was to report, with the other condemned prisoners, at the Camp Commandant's office at once. Everybody knew what this meant. The boy bade farewell to the few friends he had come to know in the camp.

He and his companions were now taken in army trucks to the place of execution, some miles from the camp. They were all lined up, with their backs to a long, deep trench. They faced a machine gun. At a word of command, a German soldier opened up on them with this machine gun. In true German style, he did this methodically, firing from right to left. One by one, the prisoners fell backwards into the trench – some were dying, some were killed instantly. David saw the way in which the killing was being done: he decided to anticipate the bullets. As the machine gun came pointing in his direction, he flung himself backwards into the trench where the others lay. There he remained, feigning death, until night fell. In the darkness he then crept out of the trench and crawled slowly and quietly to the nearby forest. Once in the shelter of the trees, he hurried away.

He lived in hiding for some weeks, stealing food from the fields, from houses, from anywhere he could find it. He then had the good fortune to come upon a Polish slave-worker on a farm. This man was from one of the many slave camps the Nazis had set up to compensate for the absence of their own manpower, who were engaged in the war effort. He gave David food, and brought him some clothes. Thus equipped, David started off on his wanderings once more. Again, he was captured; again, he was put into a concentration camp in North Germany. By this time the German armies and the whole German nation were on the brink of utter chaos. No attempts were made to trace David's records: he remained in that camp until he was liberated by the British Forces as they advanced into Germany.

David, as I have said, was about thirteen years of age when I met him. He was the youngest patient we received from the concentration camps. Most of the prisoners were in their twenties. Some were middle-aged, but not many of these had survived their ordeal.

All who had survived had horrible stories to relate. A Polish doctor amongst them told me quite candidly that in his hut, they never reported the death of a comrade at once. They delayed on purpose. In their starving condition, they opened the dead body at night and devoured the heart and the liver. They were starving, mad with hunger! From all I heard, confirmed by all I have read, I think the German concentration camps have no parallel in the horrors and atrocities of the whole of human history.

We all did our best to help these afflicted men back to normal life. It took time and patience. Thanks to my modest knowledge of German, I was able to speak to all of them. How often I thanked God that I had acquired a good working knowledge of the language! Little did I think in those distant days in the Philippines, when I wrote home for the German Grammar my sister Annie had used at school, little did I think that German would prove so useful to me.

When the prisoner patients were well enough, I would sit beside their beds and chat with them. This helped them to realise they were now among friends. In sunny days we brought the convalescent patients out to the lawns. There, in groups, we could together discuss the progress of the war, the likely situation when peace would be declared, and the chances of their being repatriated in the near future.

Some, of course, were too ill to be moved from the wards. I had been for some days keeping an eye on one man, who I knew was near to death. One day I found his bed empty.

"Has this man died?" I asked his neighbour.

"No! He got up and went outside!" replied the man in the adjoining bed.

I hurried outside and found my patient lying on his back on the grass. The sun was very bright and warm. His eyes were closed.

"Why did you come out here?" I asked him.

"I am not going to live! But the sun is shining, and I came out to see the sunlight. I have been shut away from it for so long!"

There was nothing I could say in reply. I sat with him on the grass for a while. We did not speak much: he was too weak to hold a conversation.

He died the next day. His poor, wasted body was wrapped in a blanket and buried in the cemetery across the road.

In addition to my work in the hospital, I had to look after the Catholic soldiers in my area. I said three Masses for them: one in Bassum, one in Sulingen and the third in Diepholz. The church in Bassum where I said Mass was a pre-Reformation church. It was now in the hands of the German Lutherans, who had taken it over at the Reformation. The mosaics and murals on one of the inner walls, however, bore silent witness to the church's Catholic origins, for they showed images and portraits of Our Lady.

For fifteen minutes before every Mass, I heard Confessions. During the Mass I always preached a short sermon. At that time we chaplains were allowed to have a cup of tea between the Masses. This concession, which now seems minor, was then an important one, and we gladly made use of it. The tea made things easier – one thing it did, was to save us from headaches which usually accompanied a long morning fast. Even so, my Sunday mornings were a tiring experience. In each place I had to unpack my Mass kit, get a makeshift altar ready, hear Confessions, say the Mass and preach a sermon, interview any of the men who wished to see me, pack up again, travel twenty or thirty miles to my next Mass location, and repeat the whole procedure there. All this occupied the entire morning. I did not get back to the hospital until one or two o'clock. All that would be done, without anything to eat or drink except the cup of tea!

On these journeys I was alone. I drove an old German army car, a DKW, which I had been given by my Senior Chaplain. The countryside of North Germany is in many parts lonely and desolate. Often along the deserted roads, I met Germans or wandering Russian slave-workers. These men were all on the lookout for what they could lay their hands on. I felt I needed some method of defending myself, should they attack me and try to seize the car and my Mass kit.

Fortunately at this time, I was instructing an officer of the Royal Air Force in the Faith. I consulted him about my problem. He promised to solve it. A few days later he came to me with the perfect answer – a German Luger automatic pistol. (It had nine chambers.) There was one snag remaining – I had no ammunition. I went among my friends, quietly enquiring where I could get some to fit this Luger. Inside three days I was in possession of two hundred rounds of the right calibre. Henceforward I knew I could take care of the car and kit – and also defend myself against all assailants. I worried no more when out driving alone: the sight of the shining loaded weapon on the seat beside me gave me all the confidence I needed. This was all very well – but deep within me, I kept fervently hoping I would never have to use the gun.

So my work went on. I helped local German priests to get travel passes in their parishes and surrounding districts. I procured a large quantity of black cloth for a Community of Nuns who were in need of it to mend clothes and Habits. In lots of ways, I was privileged to be able to assist those in need.

At the very first, the law of non-fraternisation kept the German folk and ourselves apart, but as I have said, this law was imperfectly observed. Little by little it broke down, until we all treated one another in an ordinary human manner. Whereas in the beginning, some Germans would look away from us as we passed by, never giving us any greeting, speaking only when spoken to, and thus seemingly ignoring us, now they would be friendly. Perhaps they were at first afraid of us; perhaps they had heard what the Russians had done in other parts, and feared we would act likewise towards them.

When I was out visiting troops, I would pass neat cottages along the roads. I used to stop the car and get out to look at the flowers in the gardens. Sometimes a garden would be a mass of the loveliest roses – a vivid, rainbow pattern of colour. The people in the cottage would at times come out to cut some of them and offer them to me. When they discovered I spoke German, they soon became very friendly. If the family was Catholic, I was instantly accepted and made to feel at home.

Moreover, the Mess Officer used to ask me to go to some of the local farmers to buy eggs, butter, and poultry. Our army rations were sufficient but monotonous fare: the extras we purchased in the neighbourhood caused hardship to no-one. In fact, the farmers were pleased to be able to sell some of their surplus produce.

And so I came to know Herr Meyer and his family. He lived a short distance away, in a farmhouse by the roadside. With the help of his wife and his two daughters, he cultivated a small farm. Herr Meyer was strongly built – however, his strength was of little use to him now, because he had become almost totally blind. He gave a hand in the farm work whenever possible, but most of the time he could only advise about the work, and let his wife and daughters get on with it.

His wife was a splendid type of German housewife: thrifty, industrious, competent and methodical in her work. How spotless her home was! How calm and self-assured she was in meeting the daily problems of the farm! Her husband's blindness did not seem to upset her life: she never referred to it, and day by day all went on as usual in the home.

Herr Meyer was a very interesting person. Some years previously, before blindness had struck him, he had regularly exhibited his farm produce and livestock at one of the local agricultural shows. On one occasion he won first prize for a sow he exhibited. He had been given a choice between two prizes – a money prize or a watercolour painting. He chose the painting – and his choice had been the right one. The picture hung in his sitting room, and I had been attracted to it at once when I first entered the room. It was the work of some local artist in Bremen. Its title was "Kastanienbaum im Frühling"

("A Chestnut Tree in Springtime"). It showed a half-timbered farmhouse of the local countryside, with walls of a dull red, and a roof of bright red tiles. Beside the house stood the chestnut tree, deep in leaf and blossom – like a huge green chandelier holding aloft hundreds of white candles. A fascinating picture, with such a lovely harmony of colour! And what a pleasing subject – one of spring's own glories!

How gratified Herr Meyer was when he heard me admiring and praising his picture. I congratulated him on his taste and judgment. I have often wondered since then how many of our farmers at home would have preferred a painting to a money prize at a show! From Herr Meyer, I learned of the Russian slave camp some miles away. He and his family were afraid of these Russians. At night they roamed through the countryside, robbing and pillaging! Herr Meyer asked me to come and stay with him. I would be near the hospital and my work would not suffer. I felt, however, that I ought not to separate myself from the Mess. My departure from my billet would certainly create gossip and misunderstanding. So I declined his offer – regretfully, I must say, for I understood his problem. I assured him I would keep in close touch with him. If any marauders were to come to his house by day or night, he was to get a message off to me in the hospital at once.

During their advance into Russia, the Germans had taken thousands of Russian peasants as prisoners. These they brought to Germany to work on farms and in factories. From central camps, they were sent out to neighbouring works and farms. Now they were free – their German guards having fled before the march of the Allied armies. These Russians now looked around and began to lift whatever they wanted or fancied from the German people.

I decided to visit the Russian camp. Since my car was being repaired at the time, I went over to the place on my bicycle. At the camp a group of Russians gathered round me. Having lived in Germany for some years, they all spoke fluent German.

Standing there on the road, surrounded by Russians who were staring at me curiously, I began our dialogue. I introduced myself: I told them who and what I was, and where I was working. They asked me what army I belonged to: was I a Frenchman? I said I was in the British Army and that I came from Ireland. I regret to record that they had never heard of Ireland, for they shook their heads and looked blankly at one another. Observing their obvious ignorance about my native country, I informed them, with true but different meaning, that I came from England. Ah yes, now they knew! England, they knew. They questioned me about life in England: had we nice houses like the

Germans; what were a man's wages in German Marks for a week's work; how much did my bicycle cost; was it hard to get a bicycle if you had the money to buy one?

Clearly they had never learned much about life in England. Nor had they ever met a British soldier. Everything about me was strange to them – my uniform, my bicycle, my accent, my mannerisms. I was their first encounter with Britain. At least I furnished them, I am sure, with some interesting topics of discussion in the miserable camp in which they had been living for years. To me they were quite civil and friendly. I felt sorry for them – whole families uprooted from their Russian homeland, transported a thousand miles away and made to work as slaves.

I have said earlier that bands of these slave-workers went on the rampage through the countryside. They had worked hard under the eyes of their German masters, but once the Allied armies had driven the Germans back, these workers downed tools and set about avenging themselves on the German masters. Local German families, like the Meyers, were terrified of them. One frightened German lady said to me, "Die Russen sind nichts als Tiere!" ("The Russians are nothing but animals!")

Their marauding did not continue for long. As soon as the Germans had surrendered, the Russian government sent convoys of trucks to all the slave-camps and repatriated their countrymen at once. The Germans on their farms cheered those convoys – in their hearts at least – as they went roaring back to Mother Russia.

I must confess, we had little sympathy for the German people as a body, for they themselves had forced the Russians to come to the Fatherland. They had brought the trouble on themselves. After Hitler acceded to power, he continued to receive 99 per cent of the vote from the German people.

Whenever I talked to Germans about the horrors and atrocities Hitler had inflicted on the world, they usually had a twofold answer. First, that they had been deceived; secondly, that they were afraid of the Nazi party.

One day, seated in a German farmhouse where I had bought some eggs, I discussed the whole question of German war-guilt with the people of the house and some neighbours.

"What do you think of Hitler now?" I asked one woman, who seemed to have clear-minded ideas about what had happened.

She answered quickly, "Er hat uns gelogen!" ("He deceived us!") Then, to my astonishment, she burst into tears. She was but one of millions in Germany who now fully realised that Hitler had cheated and betrayed them.

In palliation of the war-guilt of the German people, it must be said that ever so many of them had been terrorised by the ruthless tactics of the Gestapo and Nazi party officials. I learned about all this from the parish priest of Twistringen. This was a small country town south of Bassum. I passed through it very often, and had come to know the priests there. I got them passes from the military authorities which allowed them to travel in their area during curfew hours. The parish priest, Pastor Friedricks, was a spare, spectacled, scholarly type of man, middle-aged, with greying hair. We became quite friendly. We could sit down together and discuss our problems. In the circumstances, you can readily understand we were never short of topics.

On one occasion, over a cup of 'malt' coffee, I asked him about the concentration camps. On hearing the words "concentration camps", he instantly looked round to see was the door of the room open. It was an instinctive reaction, and I could read all it said – the "camps" were clearly too dangerous a topic for discussion, unless all the doors were closed and no-one was listening.

In a lowered voice he told me he knew about them. He said there was nothing the ordinary folk could do about them. Interference of any kind meant instant imprisonment in the camps and probably death. Guards patrolled the perimeter area of each camp. They were well-armed and were permitted to shoot on sight. To help them in their work, they were accompanied by vicious patrol dogs. Anyone, therefore, who went near the camps was asking for death.

Moreover, any prisoner released from the camps was warned to keep his mouth shut about everything he had seen and heard there. Any violation of this order meant that you were brought back to the camp and never released – except by death. So the camps were never talked about or discussed openly. No public opinion could be formed against them. Ex-prisoners refused to open their mouths about the horrors they had witnessed and endured. And thus it went on, until near the end of the war, when the truth about Belsen and other camps was revealed to a shocked world.

It would seem that in the Germany of Hitler, one had to be a member of the Nazi Party to be able to live a normal life. Those who refused to join the Party were hounded and harassed beyond belief. Pastor Friedricks knew all this and explained it carefully and regretfully. He made it clear that some had taken a stand against Hitler and all he represented. His own personal hero amongst these protestors was the Catholic Bishop of his own diocese of

Münster. At this point, as he told me these things, he looked at me steadily and proudly pronounced the Bishop's name: "Sein Eminenz, Kardinal Clemens August Graf Von Galen!" How proud the German Catholics were of that dauntless man! He loved Germany as much as Hitler claimed to love it – but he was not going to throw aside the laws of God to further Germany's interests.

The Cardinal's birthplace, Dinklage, which lay at no great distance from Twistringen, was one spot I would have liked to visit. The Von Galen family, ever steadfast in their Catholic Faith, had lived there for over three hundred years. They were a well-to-do family: their home was said to be the oldest and finest moated castle of the Oldenburger *Münsterland*.

In addition to Pastor Friedricks, I also became acquainted with the parish priest of the neighbouring town of Goldenstedt. He was a man of warm heart, pleasant to meet, and most friendly. He always gave me a hearty welcome. In his quiet country parish I made many friends – especially among the children. Most acceptable to them was my unfailing supply of sweets and chocolate. In those army days, I smoked cigarettes: for me, the cigarettes eclipsed the sweets. I thus had an unused weekly ration of chocolate and sweets for the children of Goldenstedt.

Whenever my car appeared on the stony, uneven streets of the quiet little village, a cry went up from the children: "The English Pastor is here!" The word soon spread and a crowd of children gathered around my car. The youngsters looked with wonder at a small bar of chocolate: most of them had never seen chocolate before – the Allied blockade of Germany had seen to that. To meet the demands of the children, I also used to ask my army friends who never drew their sweet rations to allow me to have them. Needless to say, as the sweet supply increased, my visits to Goldenstedt became more and more popular!

## Rheine

From the local priests in my area I learned that the Redemptorists of our German Province had a house at Rheine in Westphalia. I decided to pay a visit to this house. I studied my maps and planned a route. Rheine, I discovered, was roughly a hundred miles away. I was lucky to be able to get another chaplain to take my place in my absence.

So, one fine morning I took the car, serviced it, and started off for Rheine. The roads, even the main roads, were in disrepair: there were no road-workers to look after them. All the manpower of Germany was devoted to the war-effort. When I came to the Wildeshausen–Cloppenburg road, I saw an unbroken stream of German refugees from Eastern Germany fleeing before the advancing Russian armies. Now I saw Germans suffering the hardships and sorrows they themselves had inflicted on the people of other countries. There they were, shuffling wearily along the road – women and children, occasionally an old man – an endless procession, struggling painfully to get away from it all. Gone now were the arrogant days of uniforms and waving banners, the tumultuous cheering on of Hitler, the thundering cries of "Heil! Heil! Sieg Heil!"; there was no more chanting of the Horst-Wessel-Lied! Now on this broken road these Germans sought only shelter, food, peace and security. In the circumstances I temporarily took it upon myself to waive army regulations, and gave a lift to one of these refugees.

I reached Rheine in the evening. The German Redemptorist monastery there had been destroyed in an Allied air-raid. Our priests therefore had had to find temporary accommodation in a private dwelling house. They were few in number: all the younger priests and brothers were serving in the German armed forces. The few priests remaining in Rheine welcomed me in a kindly way. I sat down with them to a frugal meal, and I soon felt quite at home with them. We chatted about the war, army life, the Redemptorists, Ireland's neutrality, the air-raids, the refugees. As we sat at the table discussing these topics, there was a faint knocking at the front door. One of the Fathers went out to see who was there. We could hear him give a cry of astonishment and then putting an excited series of questions to the visitor. He came back to where we were seated, bringing with him a bedraggled-looking figure. The stranger stood in the doorway, shading his eyes against the light and looking at us silently. Then suddenly someone recognised him and cried out his name: it was one of our own German Redemptorist Brothers who had been away a long time, serving with the German army on the Russian Front. He sat down in our midst. How weary, how dusty and travel-stained he was!

After a meal, he revived somewhat. He had a lot to tell us. He had news of some of the other German Redemptorists who had served with him on the Eastern Front. Slowly, bit by bit, he described how they had died. He tried to give us a picture of the horrors of the German campaign in Russia: the endless, dreary wastelands across which German supplies had to pass; the loneliness of the countryside with its devastation and absence of houses; the dark, impenetrable forests where the merciless Russian partisan bands lay in ambush for German stragglers; and above all else, the appalling cold and snow-blizzards of the Russian winter. It was indeed a horrifying tale: a tale of men who had found death a sweet release; a tale of living soldiers who, though they had escaped Russian bullets and shells, were nevertheless broken by the horrors they had endured.

The Fathers put me up for the night. For a while I lay awake, thinking of all the Brother had told us about his life on the Russian Front. His return that night reminded me of the return of St Isaac Jogues to France after his mission work among the Huron tribe of Indians in North America in the seventeenth century. In order to evangelise this most strange tribe, he went to live among them. He learned their language and their customs.

In a prolonged drought, the Indians suffered many hardships. Their medicine men convinced them that Fr Jogues – "Black Robe" – was the cause of all their misfortunes. The Indian braves accepted their testimony and punished "Black Robe" by making him run the gauntlet. Surviving this fearful ordeal, the priest was further punished: one of the braves chopped off some of his fingers. Later he escaped to the coast and there was able to board a schooner for France.

On a winter's morning at dawn, Fr Jogues landed on a lonely part of the coast of Brittany. Wading ashore from the boat, he stumbled across the fields, and knocked at a farmhouse door. On opening the door, the Breton farmer brusquely demanded of him who he was and why he came at that hour. Fr Jogues said not a word; he merely lifted his maimed hands and showed them to the farmer. The man recognised him at once – all of France had heard of Fr Jogues' work and sufferings – and he exclaimed in joyful amazement, "Fr Jogues! Fr Jogues!"

As I lay awake in bed that night in Rheine, I thought of these incidents. Like Fr Jogues, this poor Redemptorist Brother had been changed and marked by his sufferings in Russia. Like him, although unknown and unrecognised for a moment, he was quickly welcomed heartily for his links with those of us seated at that table, and for what he had endured.

On my return from Rheine I found a new field of work awaiting me. It was work more directly in line with what I had been doing on the mission field at home. The Senior Army Chaplain, who had opened a Retreat House for British soldiers in Germany, asked me to take charge of it and conduct the retreats. Each group of thirty or forty soldiers would go there and spend two or three days attending to their personal spiritual needs. They would hear spiritual talks, and be given plenty of time to reflect on their lives and to receive the Sacraments. I, the priest-in-charge, in addition to giving the talks, would be available for Confessions, consultation and advice. I thought it an excellent project. I admired that efficient enterprise and the strong army influence of the Senior Chaplain who had established the work. My memory of it is that he called his scheme a "Leadership Course"! It is amazing what you can achieve if you have got the right name for your proposal!

A large villa on the shores of Steinhuder Meer, near Hanover, had been selected as the Retreat House. Army sappers and engineers had installed a water system and made the place ready for the first group of retreatants. The army authorities had provided adequate kitchen equipment, beds, linen, tables, chairs, and food. All in all, it was a job well done.

Steinhuder Meer, where the house was situated, is a lake about five miles long and three miles wide. It is not a deep lake: its greatest depth is only about ten feet. In peace times I am sure the whole area is a popular resort among the Germans. The surrounding shores are well wooded. The adjoining countryside consists of sandy heaths and moorland. In winter I feel sure the area is bleak and depressing. However we arrived there at the beginning of summer, when everything was looking at its best.

An army girl from the Auxiliary Territorial Service supervised the staff of Polish women refugees who helped me to run the house. These girls spoke some German, so I was able to instruct them in their duties. They were all devout Catholics. The presence of a priest in the house seemed to make them contented in their new line of work. They were able to attend Mass in the little Retreat Chapel. I saw to it that they had some free time, and that their meals and their accommodation were satisfactory.

Once we were started with the work of the retreats, my routine was clear. I did all my usual Sunday Masses in Bassum, Sulingen, and Diepholz. On Monday mornings I drove the sixty miles from Bassum to Steinhuder Meer. The retreats for the men began on Tuesdays and continued to Friday or Saturday. The talks I gave there were based on my own knowledge of the problems of soldiers in wartime. I tried to be realistic and helpful. It was really good work while it lasted. Week by week, I kept up my routine in a steady and constant fashion.

To my very great regret, I fell ill with a bad bout of bronchitis and asthma. Despite all my efforts to get well, the illness continued. Perhaps I had been beaten by the constant work and the damp, chilly winds, which in the late autumn blew steadily from the North Sea.

In the end I was flown back to England and brought to a military hospital near Preston. After several weeks there, I was transported to a military hospital at Musgrave Park, in Belfast. In due time I recovered my health. Meanwhile another chaplain was sent out to Germany to take my place. I was then assigned to take over his work in County Down.

My two main centres were Ballykinlar Camp and Waringfield Military Hospital. I stayed at Ballykinlar. The camp was near Tyrella, where I had spent my holidays as a boy. Sometimes, in those distant days, my companions and I had visited the military camp: there were shops there where one could buy goods. I one day went into the camp alone. On the firing ranges, rifle and machine-gun practice was in progress. I was thrilled to be near such an impressive and deadly noise. I moved about with timidity and awe. Now, things were different. Now I belonged; now I was a member of the garrison, a sharer in the life of the camp. And although I was a newcomer, I was no stranger there, for I knew every inch of the camp and every building within its perimeter.

In this camp I had a chapel of my own. In the chapels in British Army camps the Church of England officiates – if I may use the expression – all other denominations are allowed the use of the chapel as a courtesy. But here in Ballykinlar, the chapel was Catholic and for the use of Catholics only.

It had been erected by the Sinn Féin internees in the camp in 1920–21. The priest who was then appointed to attend to the spiritual needs of the internees had none of the requisites for saying Mass. He needed sacred vessels, linen altar cloths, vestments, and other articles. My mother's close friend, Letitia McLarnon, had organised some help for the priest, and was able to provide a lot of the essentials. Mother had worked with Letitia to get things ready.

One morning, while saying Mass in the camp Chapel I suddenly remembered about these events of 1920–21. It was then I realised that these altar cloths and other appurtenances around me had come from my own friends and family. In providing for that priest's needs, they were providing, though they little knew it, for mine in the future!

## Demobilisation

At long last the war had come to an end. Month by month, the wartime army was being gradually demobilised. My turn for demobilisation came in 1946. I was instructed to report to the York Demobilisation Centre. There, I received a full new outfit – shirts, clerical suit, shoes, socks, etc. I still have the shoes now, twenty-five years later. I have not worn them except in summer; I am wearing them as I write these lines. Apart from my memories, they are a visible reminder of my army days.

Thus I left the army. A cheerful sergeant wished me the best of luck, and with a warm handshake offered to give me a first-class ticket to London. I declined the offer with thanks. I asked him to give me a ticket for Ireland: I had had enough journeying in the army.

I went back to Ireland very gladly. I had no regrets about leaving army life: I had had enough of it. I was thankful to God that I had survived the war.

I went to our monastery at Clonard. I was glad to get back to the peace and tranquillity of religious life.

One abiding pleasure was mine: I had been one of the Catholic Chaplains who had served the Catholic men in the war. Compared to what other chaplains had suffered and accomplished, my efforts and achievements had been small. But I was one of those chaplains – that thought, even still, affords me much pleasure. As a body, they were hard-working and selfless in their devotion to duty. Many of them were admirable for their sheer heroism.

After the war Monsignor Coughlin, the chief Catholic Chaplain in the Army, wrote of his chaplains:

"From all sources, ecclesiastical, military, and lay, I heard nothing but the highest praise of our chaplains. Certainly they are held in the highest esteem by all with whom they have come in contact. Were I to be asked for proof or evidence of their self-sacrifice and heroism, zeal and devotion to duty, it would suffice to mention that fifteen of them have made the supreme sacrifice; twenty-eight have been wounded; twenty-seven became prisoners of war rather than abandon their men; twenty-seven were awarded decorations, and fifty-six mentioned in despatches; and they instructed and received into the Church over five thousand converts. These are records of which we are justly proud."

# CHAPTER TEN

# Back to Clonard

### Our Lady's Confraternity

Returning home, I was granted some weeks' rest and then assigned to the Redemptorist Community in Clonard Monastery, Belfast. My work was now the ordinary work done in a city Catholic church – sermons: hearing Confessions, giving Masses and leading evening devotional services. Frequently during the year I was sent to other parishes, schools and convents, to preach retreats and missions. This special kind of work required the preparation of new sermons and lectures.

I worked at these until another bout of bronchitis and asthma laid me low. However once more, I got over that attack. My health steadily improved and my strength returned. It is good to experience illness, if one has to visit sick people and help and comfort them. The healthy, robust types who are never ill, know how to spell "headache" but know nothing else about it, find it hard to understand what a sore thing weakness, pain and depression, can be.

When I had recovered my health, the Superior asked me to take charge of the Confraternity of Our Lady. This was reputedly the largest of its kind in the world: its membership totalled 7000. It was divided into three divisions, each division of around 2000 members holding a meeting on one Sunday afternoon in the month.

A meeting lasted one hour. The programme consisted of the five decade Rosary; announcements and the sermon; Benediction of the Blessed Sacrament. The sick and the dead were prayed for, and afterwards members could interview or consult the Fr Director in the Confraternity Room.

It was a new type of work for me. I tried hard to make it a success. I had one rule, which I adhered to strictly: I would not begin my sermon until all those members who were standing had obtained a seat. The members were allocated to sections, each section being named after a saint. Many of the sections could not be allotted enough seats for their members. I made sure that all who could not get a seat in their own section would find a place in one of the other sections. I always bore in mind the fact that, for most of the women present, Sunday was a busy day. They had children to prepare for Mass; they had meals to cook and dishes to wash. When these mothers came to their Confraternity meeting at 4.00 pm, they were weary enough, without having to stand for an hour in the church. At least that was one problem I solved: everyone got a seat.

The women themselves loved the Confraternity and were very loyal to it. In addition to the religious benefits of a meeting, they had other perquisites which were very acceptable: they met all their friends, they had a good chat after the meeting with people they otherwise would not meet, and they had – for their husbands – an invincibly good reason for getting 'out', and away from the four walls of home. His arguments were all useless: she had to get to her Confraternity meeting! The phrase the women would use was this: "It is my Confraternity Sunday". When these words were uttered in a home, a husband knew he was beaten! His arrangements with "the boys" would have to be cancelled, for "she" would have to go to her Confraternity meeting – and he would have to mind the house and the children.

If a member fell ill or was in hospital for treatment or an operation, her name was handed in to me, and it was my duty to visit her. This meant frequent journeys to homes and hospitals in all parts of the city. The journey was easy, if the home or hospital lay near a bus route; but often they did not. In those days we Redemptorists were not allowed by Superiors of our Irish Province to have a car for our work with Confraternities, and so my only means of transport then was a bicycle. How useful my machine was on these sick visits! In pleasant weather it gave me many an enjoyable outing across the city. When the weather was bad, it was not so pleasant. In heavy rain I got a thorough soaking. In cold weather I was numb from the cold. In icy weather I was in danger because of skidding on icy patches. I remember how, on hilly Clonard Street one freezing morning, my bicycle skidded from under me at Odessa Street corner, and I came down with a horrible thump on the concrete road. I was shaken, but undamaged!

How times have changed for us Irish Redemptorists! Now, every priest in charge of a Confraternity has a car for his work. For the six long years I was Director of Our Lady's Confraternity in Clonard, I had neither car nor assistant – now the Director has both. Far from bemoaning my lot, I rather rejoice at the sensible change that has happened. The car is expedite, comfortable, and makes one independent of weather conditions. This is true. However, the bicycle had its own advantages: you met more people in the streets; it was healthy exercise; and in the car-thronged city, you had no parking problems. The constant use of a bicycle ensures that you never become lazy! How many of our present-day ailments are due to the lazy use of the car. In the words of St Peter: "Whatever influence gets the better of a man, becomes his master." (2 Peter 2:19)

## The Mission to Non-Catholics

When he entered my room one autumn morning in 1948, the Rector of Clonard had a question for me: "What about a mission for Protestants?"

"I see so many difficulties about it, I will mention none of them – but let us have a go at it!" I replied.

That was in 1948. The situation then was not at all ecumenical. The atmosphere in such matters has changed completely since then. I now realise I was slow in accepting the idea of such a work, and too doubtful about any good coming from it. My attitude was doubtless the product of my Belfast background: ever since my childhood, I had known nothing in Belfast but antagonism and bitterness on both sides of the two main religious groups: Catholics and Protestants.

"Very well!" said the Rector, Fr Reynolds. "Go to see Fr Sean O'Loughlin! Get together and work out some plan for the six Sunday nights in the coming Advent."

I went to Fr Sean's room and broke the news gently to him. He bore up well! We sat down together and discussed this formidable project. I insisted – and he agreed – that right from the start, our approach to our Separated Brethren would not go along the path of controversy: we would explain Catholic doctrine, and let the truth speak for itself to the hearts and minds of our listeners. At Fr Sean's table we planned our programme of sermons and our procedure for the first mission ever given to non-Catholics in a Catholic Church in Ireland.

You may well ask what prompted Fr Reynolds to hold such a mission, in the tense religious atmosphere of Belfast. Strange as it will seem, it was Protestants themselves who were the occasion of it. Some days previously three Protestant young men had come to Clonard Monastery, hoping to interview any one of the priests. Fr Gerard Reynolds, the Rector, received them. While clearing out some premises on the very Protestant Shankill Road, where he intended to start his own business, one of these young men came upon a short history of the Catholic Church by Rev JF O'Doherty, Professor of Church History in Maynooth College. With increasing interest, this young man read the book a couple of times. There were matters in it which he did not understand – so he had now come to Clonard Monastery, which was the nearest Catholic Church, to get some explanations.

And what about the two friends who came with him? It seems he had coaxed them to accompany him as a kind of moral support. He had never done anything like this before. He had never in his life spoken to a Catholic priest! He did not know how he would be received. His two friends had come along to add their courage to his own.

To their amazement, Fr Reynolds had received them in a kindly manner. To their further astonishment, he said he would arrange a course of Sermons explaining the Catholic Faith to them and their friends. He invited them to come. He would insert notices about these sermons in the daily press. He would first have to ask Dr Mageean, our Catholic Bishop of the Diocese, to give his permission for all these proposals.

The Bishop was consulted and gave the enterprise his approval – but he was doubtful whether many Protestants would attend the mission. The mission was given on the Sunday nights of Advent 1948, in Clonard Church at 8.30 pm. I have written a full account of this mission in the pages of the *Irish Ecclesiastical Record* for the months in 1949. There you will read how surprised we all were, when we saw our church crowded with Protestants on the first Sunday night. Many no doubt had come through mere curiosity – and many of these never came again. On the other hand, some who came were deeply impressed and returned on the subsequent Sunday nights. By the end of that Advent, we knew that the Clonard Mission for non-Catholics was something to be established.

Our words reached not only those who came to the sermons but also, thanks to the published reports in the *Irish News*, hundreds of Protestants throughout Ulster. Other similar missions followed in the Lent and Advent of subsequent years. In an effort to help those Protestants who wanted to hear more about the Catholic Faith, we started Monday talks for them in Clonard Hall. As a result of all this work, many conversions took place. When last I made enquiries, I discovered that, from 1948 to 1968, the average number of converts per year received into the Church by our priests in Clonard was about one hundred.

The Reverend Ian Paisley was deeply interested in all this work we were doing in Clonard. So far as I know, he attended the missions right from the start. During one of my first sermons to our Protestant friends, I spoke about the real presence of Christ Our Lord in the Eucharist. While I was speaking, some listener in the congregation tut-tutted his abhorrence of what I said – it was like the frightened tut-tut-tut of a blackbird alarmed at the sight of a prowling cat or a hovering hawk. I have often wondered if the Rev Ian Paisley was the tut-tut-tutter that night. It is in the compass of his style!

During one of the mission nights I had my first personal encounter with him. I used to take a group of our Protestant visitors on a little explanatory tour of our church. One night he accompanied us. When we reached St Gerard's altar, he tackled me aggressively on the subject of relics. Neither of us would give ground. I defended the Catholic tradition and practice; he scorned it.

About this time, he heard of our Monday talks. So he sent up to these talks two of his 'bright' disciples – a Miss Elsie Taylor and her friend Victor. Firstly, they watched to see who was coming to the Talks, and, secondly, they noted what we said. They then went to Ian Paisley and gave him a full report.

He made good use of all they told him. He first of all published a pamphlet against Fr Moran and myself: Fr Moran was then helping in the work. This pamphlet was a kind of broadsheet, reminiscent of the political lampoons of the eighteenth century, sold for a penny in The Strand or Cheapside. As well as this, he preached every week on Clonard's erroneous teachings about the Saviour and Redemption.

In or around 1950, Ian Paisley founded the "Free Presbyterian Church of Ulster". The group attached to the Ravenhill Evangelical Mission Church on the Ravenhill Road joined him: this Mission Church became Ravenhill Free Presbyterian Church, with the Reverend Ian becoming its Minister. In 1953 he began his sermons against our work. His advertisements in the *Belfast Telegraph* had such headings as this: "Clonard's Priests Challenged!"

His next move was to send me an invitation to a public debate on Catholic and Protestant doctrine. Knowing his antagonism, his desire for publicity, his eagerness to denigrate so much of what we hold sacred, I declined. This was one occasion when the old cliché, "no useful purpose would be served", was true and appropriate. Moreover, those were days when Belfast blood pressures mounted high when religious matters were debated. I guessed also that Dr Mageean had enough problems to cope with and was not going to start more by sanctioning such debates.

For years the Reverend Ian kept preaching about Clonard's errors, issuing challenge after challenge, and holding rallies in the Ulster Hall in Belfast. It is true to say that Clonard's ecumenical work of those years was the ladder up which he climbed to the platform of notoriety. His hostile sermons led Northern Ireland Protestants to look on him as a "true blue", a man after their own hearts, a spokesman who would not betray their cause. And that is exactly how Protestants look on him to this day.

I used to read his diatribes against all things Catholic in the fiery pages of his paper, the *Ulster Protestant*. He now publishes it under the name of the *Protestant Telegraph*. One day, I met him and congratulated him.

"Congratulations!" I said brightly.

"What for?" he growled back.

"On being a Pope! You have founded a Church and you are its supreme ruler!"

"That is ridiculous!" he answered, in an annoyed kind of way.

"It is not ridiculous!" I replied. "You are the Head of your Church!"

This line of talk did not please him, so he went on to something else.

Another day when I was coming from the City Hospital, where I had been visiting some sick people, I met him on the Lisburn Road. He stopped and stared at me. He then tackled me about my being in need of true conversion to the Lord Jesus Christ. Only in that way, he emphatically pointed out to me, would I find true joy and peace.

This was not done quietly, by earnest words alone! Oh no! Standing there on the street, with people passing us, he began to raise his voice, and wave his hands and arms in the air. He ranted at me, as only he can rant, quoting his familiar, worn texts from Scripture. I told him to stop haranguing me. I told him he was only attracting attention in a public street, and that he was quite mistaken about my state.

"My dear sir," I said, "I am perfectly happy the way I am."

"Ha!" he snorted. "What you are suffering from, Brother, is false joy!"

No matter what I said, he was going to win. How could you reasonably debate any subject with a person like that? I was meant to accept his word, but he would not accept mine. In the end he discarded that tremulous, urgent, preaching voice he had put on for my benefit and returned to his normal voice. It was an anti-climax!

He was holding a small bag of sweets in his hand: he had obviously been sampling its contents as I came along. He now looked at the sweets and then at me.

"I don't know whether I'll give you a sweet or not! But anyway, here you are!" Saying this, he held out the open sweet bag to me. I laughed at this remark – and then proceeded to reduce the number of his sweets.

In the bad old days of the West, the Indians used to smoke the "pipe of peace" with their enemies. In the manner aforesaid, I, standing on the Lisburn Road in Belfast, chewed the sweet of peace with Ian Paisley. I have always interpreted his sharing of the sweets as his first genuinely ecumenical gesture.

I have always admired him however for his defence of the Divinity of Our Lord. He publicly burned the books of Principal Davey because, he said, they attacked the Divinity of Christ. The books were piled on waste ground in High Street and sent up in a blaze. That was an act both forthright and courageous: he carried through his convictions. I admired him for that. I thought him sincere but fanatical. But now, as I write, in the light of all he has done since those days, he has become politically ambitious.

I said a moment ago that the Reverend Paisley sent up two of his disciples to our Monday night talks, and that one of these was Elsie Taylor. When I got to know her well, I discovered what a fine Christian girl she was. When I first met her, she was about eighteen years of age. She worked in a factory. She was a pale, anaemic-looking girl, and she spoke with a rather noticeable stammer.

At our talks, she would stand up to raise an objection to some point we had made. From her handbag she would produce her treasured notebook, in which she had written her key passages in Scripture. Standing up before the mixed crowd of Catholics and Protestants, she would read what she saw as the refutation of our statements from her Scripture texts.

I liked her for her courage. She stood up before a crowd of Catholics, atheists and Jews, and asserted her sincere beliefs. When I proceeded to make distinctions and qualifications of her texts, she felt so frustrated she exclaimed to a friend, "That man, Fr Cummings, would prove black is white!"

Gradually, however, I got to know her. With amazement I came to know her penances and her practices of prayer. I am quite certain that Elsie Taylor, this factory girl with meagre education, lived in close union with God. My friendship with her has remained firm and constant down the years and I hope it will remain so. Usually the first letter I receive at Christmas is from Elsie. She is now happily married and lives in Lambeg. I have not met her for years, but I never forget her. She is, of course, still a Protestant, and most probably will die one – but I am quite sure she is very close to God and very dear to Our Blessed Lord.

She has separated from Ian Paisley's Church: his ways did not please her. Moreover, there was one particular point of doctrine on which they differed. I think I am responsible for drawing attention to this difference.

One Sunday Ian Paisley phoned me in Clonard, asking if I would come to a public debate with him. In the course of reading one of his pamphlets, I had discovered that he did not believe in the necessity of Baptism for salvation.

So I tackled him on this important question. Relying on Acts 10:44–8, he was teaching that Baptism was not necessary for salvation. At first, he evaded the issue. "Oh, they can be baptised any way they want!" he said to me.

"I am not asking you that," I replied. "I want to know whether you teach that Baptism is necessary to enter the Kingdom of God."

"No, it is not necessary! Read Acts 10!"

That much was now clear. On a Monday night at our talks, I spoke to Elsie.

"Elsie, do you believe Baptism is necessary for salvation?" I asked her.

"Yes, I do!" answered Elsie.

"Well, Ian Paisley does not believe that!"

"That is what *you* say!"

"Alright, Elsie, don't take my word for it! Ask Ian yourself!"

So the following Monday night, I made sure to have a word with Elsie again:

"Elsie, did you mention that matter to Ian?"

"I did," she replied.

"And what did he say?"

"He asked me, did the Reverend Cummings ask me about that!"

"And am I right in what I told you?"

"Yes, what you said is true: he teaches that Baptism is not necessary. And I don't agree with him."

So she parted from his Church and began to teach Sunday School children in a church near her home on the Lisburn Road. Elsie Taylor – a pious, sincere follower of Christ.

At our Monday night talks in Clonard Hall, we usually had an audience of twenty to thirty people. One night I noticed a newcomer. At our tea interval I spoke to him. He was a Protestant, who worked in the shipyards. He was a regular attendee after that. I became quite friendly with him. One night he opened his mind to me, saying: "All I want is the truth! I am looking for the truth about God and salvation. I have gone from one religion to another, and still I am not happy. I know there must be one true religion. I am still trying to find it."

John lived in Essex Street, a very 'Protestant' street near Agincourt Avenue, where I was born. In due time we instructed him personally in the Faith and received him into the Church. He became a most fervent Catholic. A few years after his reception into the Church, he died. But how did he come to attend our talks on the Catholic Faith in the first place? What led him to the Catholic Church? One day, I asked him these questions. Without hesitation, he told me the whole story…

For years he had been unhappy in his religious beliefs. He went from one religion to another, and in none of them did he find the peace and contentment he sought. It happened one morning that on his way through the city, he passed an old junk shop. As he passed by, he saw at the back of the display of jumble a picture of the Virgin Mary. He walked on some distance, and then turned in his steps and went back to the shop. He went in and bought the picture for half-a-crown.

At home John set about cleaning the picture. He made a good job of it. He wanted to put it on the wall of his living room – but his wife, an ardent, image-loathing Protestant, protested strongly: on no account would a Roman Catholic image be hanging on the wall of her living room!

So John hung the picture in his bedroom. At night, before getting into bed, he used to turn to the picture and beg the Virgin Mary to help him to find the true religion. So his life went on, month after month, year to year.

One day at his work in the shipyards, he mentioned his quest for the true religion to a fellow-workman who happened to be a Catholic. This friend advised him to go up to our talks at Clonard. He took this man's advice – and when he came to Clonard Hall, I met him.

As I have said above, John was duly instructed in the Catholic Faith and was received into the one true fold of Christ. All his prayers were answered. He died a few years later: earnestly devoted to God, Our Lady, and the Church. He died a holy death, a death that was but the echo of his life. All his prayers to God's Mother were answered.

Those were wonderful days in Clonard. The apostolate for non-Catholics was going well. Later on, apathy from some within our own ranks retarded the work. Many – though not all – of our priests from Southern Ireland did not set the same value on the work as we Northerners did. Some did not really feel at home in the North and had little time for Ulster's interests and people.

Their attitude was but the general attitude of the entire Southern section of our divided country. The bitter, unpalatable truth is that fifty years ago, in 1922, the southern Government threw us to the wolves, and has stood silently aside in the years since then, while the Unionist and Orange wolf-packs harried us. We Catholic Irish in Ulster had no illusions: in Southern eyes, we were part of the "Black North" and did not really belong.

The Dáil records attest that in December 1922, Liam Cosgrove, Ernest Blythe and Kevin O'Higgins – a Southern Government trio of plenipotentiaries – went to London and in return for some financial concessions granted by their hosts, the British Government, they in effect sold the Northern Six Counties of Ireland to the Ulster Unionists. This can be verified if you look up Dáil records for that month and year. It was on that occasion that Liam Cosgrove on his return to Dublin solemnly declared in the Dáil: "It is a damn good bargain!" For those words he will be remembered in Irish history.

It was all made public in the daily papers, and it is clear that Dubliners and people of the South in general shed no tears for us Ulster folk. While we Catholics were being subtly and cunningly repressed, and deprived of the common rights and opportunities of ordinary citizens in Northern Ireland, the Southern Government were more concerned about affairs in countries thousands of miles away. In United Nations Sessions, their spokesmen made speeches about international affairs, and, for example, their army helped out in the internal troubles of Nigeria and Cyprus – but Northern Ireland was left alone. We in the North have always known they are not really interested in us: whatever their present attitude may be, we know they did nothing to alleviate our persecution during the past fifty years. Their 1922 agreement with London is the most faithfully kept treaty in the history of modern Europe: apathy on their part seems to be the main reason for their fidelity.

Even when we made efforts to rid ourselves of the unfair burdens and the rank injustices, and the papers reported trouble and street fighting in the North, the common Southern comment would be something along the lines of: "Ah, sure up there, you don't know where you are! One side is just as bad as the other!"

In these matters Dr Mageean knew what he was talking about. In print, in a special brochure or issue of the *Capuchin Annual*, he said what I have said.

It is commonly said that Seán Lemass, head of Éire's Government from 1959 to 1966, thought we Ulster Catholics were indeed a blameworthy, unfriendly crowd, and that what we needed was a super dose of 'neighbourliness'. We got it – some say, thanks to him – and Belfast people can bear testimony to the experiment's failure.

In accordance with the Southern mode of thought as I have outlined it, some of the Rectors in Clonard gave the apostolate for non-Catholics less than their full support. One tried to end our correspondence course; another said the apostolate was not our work. How could any movement flourish, when those in charge had no interest in it! Financially the work was not in the least lucrative. Had it been otherwise – and this is a hard thing to say – the support given it might perhaps have been otherwise too.

In these last three or four years, with the initiatives of the Civil Rights Movement and the activities of the IRA, the work has been more or less stalled. Please God, when a just peace comes, that the apostolate will be resumed on even a bigger scale and carried on successfully.

What I have said is the truth, and I know it. I pay tribute however to the Clonard Rectors from Éire, who did foster the work: Fr Gerard Reynolds, Fr Crotty, and others. These men were splendid – but not all thought and acted as they did.

## The Correspondence Course

I must now say something about the correspondence course, which I mentioned a moment ago.

Between 1950 and 1955, our Apostolate for Non-Catholics went ahead steadily. The Diocesan Priests in Belfast decided to form a group of priests to promote the work in the Diocese. This led to the formation of the Diocesan Board of Down and Connor for convert work. At first these priests concentrated on creating a pool of qualified instructors for converts. They selected a volunteer group of Catholic men and women for this purpose. To these volunteers they gave special lectures on Catholic Doctrine and on the proper method of instructing converts. Within a period of months, a fair number of qualified instructors were available.

A further step in the work of spreading the Faith was taken when the Board decided to start a correspondence course for interested enquirers –a decision inspired by the course run in the USA by the Knights of Columbus. The priests on the Diocesan Board in Belfast asked me to write the new course. I received no guidelines, no plan, no terms of reference. I had clear knowledge of the Board's aims and purpose in starting the course – but that was all!

I knew writing the course was not going to be an easy task, but I agreed to do it because the work of the apostolate in which we were engaged was so terribly important. I counted it a privilege to be able to contribute something to its success. I hoped and prayed I would do this job properly. If ever in my priestly life I needed God's guiding hand, I needed it now!

In facing my task, I decided I would follow the principle we had adopted in the work of the mission for non-Catholics: that there would be no controversial approach; that I would explain clearly and simply the case for the Catholic Church. I would say what we believed in, and I would give the reasons for our beliefs. What we had to communicate through the course was the truth, and the truth would have to make its own appeal to the minds and hearts of those who followed the course.

And with that basic principle to guide my writing, I planned a course consisting of twenty-one Letters. I chose the 'letter' approach, because it allowed me to write in a friendly, chatty, simple style. Each Letter ran to about seven or eight pages in crown octavo, and would thus be the subject of a separate pamphlet.

I worked very hard at the writing of these Letters. I was not exempted from my ordinary work in the church, the house or the Confraternity of Our Lady, other than that for one full week, I was not marked to hear Confessions. This was a help and I got a lot done in that week. Every day I was seated at my table by 8.30 am I wrote steadily all morning; at times I consulted books in our library, studied the best way to explain difficult points, re-wrote some passages, corrected and clarified others. Finally, when I was quite satisfied with the end product, I would type out the whole Letter.

During the writing process, I kept reminding myself that these Letters were intended for ordinary folk – not theologians – and that therefore, accuracy granted, the simpler and clearer I was, the better!

I kept up the effort. Generally I succeeded in writing almost two Letters per week. In those days I was able to do it: I do not think I could repeat the same effort now. In a little over three months, I had the work completed.

I had now to submit what I had written to two Redemptorist censors who had been appointed by the Father Provincial. One of these approved all the Letters. The other found no error in my work, but thought I should have brought more doctrine into some sections. I stood my ground, however! I was writing an introduction to the Catholic Church, not a full treatise on its doctrines. I did not want to cram too much doctrine into any of the Letters – I did not wish to overload them. I had to keep the material light, interesting, and informative – but it did not have to be complete in all branches of Catholic teaching! I knew that, if I succeeded in winning the hearts and minds of the readers of the course, the Penny Catechism would supply thereafter the points of doctrine I had failed to mention: they could get it all in the Catechism! Let me first interest them and lead them to the Catechism.

Monsignor James Hendley, Parish Priest of St Paul's Church and my old teacher in St Malachy's College, was the Diocesan censor appointed to examine my work and approve it. I used to bring him two or three Letters at a time. He found little to contest.

In class as a boy, I must have exasperated him very often. It now seemed I was again a boy and he again my teacher. How pleased I was therefore when, at the end of the censorship work, he said to me, "You have done a good job!"

I find it hard to explain all this: it seemed to me that I had now by hard work – belatedly indeed – offered him atonement for my boyhood negligence. The atonement was graciously accepted and acknowledged: it was a kind of "come home, all is forgiven!" moment. I came away from Monsignor, thinking that, although my effort was a long time coming, it was better late than never!

Once all the censors had completed their side of the work, I quickly had everything ready for the printer. I remember distinctly how, on my way down to the printers, I stopped beside the kiosk which then stood in the centre of Castle Junction. This kiosk was an office of the Belfast City Tramways: in my mind, it was always the hub or centre of the city. I stopped there for a moment or two and, with all the earnestness and faith that was in me, I offered my poor bit of typescript to God, asking him to bless it and make it spiritually helpful to my city and its people.

Two thousand copies of each letter were printed. Thank God I had no worries about paying the printer's bill: the Diocesan Board of priests financed the scheme. Cardinal D'Alton and the Northern Bishops sent me donations for the work. My friends also helped in many ways: Joseph Kavanagh of Smithfield gave me £25 for stamps, while James Elliot, of the Dress hiring firm, brought me 20,000 envelopes.

I advertised the course only in the Protestant newspapers of Northern Ireland. I varied the words of the advertisements from time to time; the usual one ran as follows:

*Free*
*By Post – Confidential*
"The Teaching of the Catholic Church"
Write to:    The Director,
              Correspondence Course,
              4 Waterville Street,
              Belfast.

Since I knew how awkward it might be for Protestant enquirers in small villages to be posting a letter – which the Post Office people could identify – to Clonard Monastery, I put my address down as 4 Waterville Street, which is in fact the Waterville Street door of Clonard.

Each applicant received a letter every two weeks. On printed cards I marked down each applicant's progress in the course.

The first appearance of the advertisements brought sixty applicants. Week by week the numbers kept increasing, until soon we had about three hundred envelopes to address each week. Jack Wright and Dick Magennis came to Clonard to help me in this tedious work. We worked together for two or three hours to finish the despatch. How grateful I am to them! Jack has since died; I am sure he now prays for the work in the presence of God.

And so the glorious work went on, week by week, month by month. When our participants finished the course, we gave them instructions as to what to do if they wished to learn more about the Catholic Church, or wished to become a Catholic. If they lived far away, we would give them names of people near their homes whom they could approach and consult. If they were in Belfast, we invited them to come to Clonard and meet us.

Among those who applied for the course was a Protestant married woman living in a very Protestant district outside Belfast. She had seen our advertisements in the local paper and without consulting her husband, had sent off for the course. She read very carefully each Letter as it arrived. All was working out nicely: nobody knew her secret interest in the Catholic Church; the postman brought each letter to her when the children were at school and her husband was at work. When she had reached the end of the course, she was convinced that the Catholic Church was the one true Church of Christ. She knew she would have to become a Catholic.

But how was she to go about this? Finally she wrote a letter to Clonard, explaining that she could not go to the monastery without letting her husband know. He would want to know everything. He might raise an awful row over what she had done. She suggested she could meet a priest in nearby Lisburn, if some quiet place could be found where she would not be known.

She met our Fr Hugh Arthurs in a room above a certain shop in Lisburn. After much arrangement and planning, she was more fully instructed and then received into the Church. Before being received, she told the whole story to her husband. Being a rather staunch Protestant, he was at first shocked by the news. He listened carefully to all she said; he weighed it up. She told him she was worried not only about his potentially annoyed reaction to her decision, but also about the attitude her Protestant neighbours would adopt towards her once they found out. Having heard her side of the story, her husband said, "I certainly do not view the Roman Catholic Church in the same light as you do – but you are my wife and, if you want to join that

Church, go ahead! Do what you think is right! As for our neighbours, leave them to me! I'll see they will not interfere with you or annoy you."

And so this good woman became a Catholic. She was most fervent. At first it was thought more prudent for her to skip the Sunday Mass attendance. However, she do not want to stay away from Mass and so went regularly into Lisburn to attend it. Later on she came to Clonard with one of her children, a boy of about twelve years of age, who wanted to be a Catholic like his mother!

As the series of twenty-one Letters of the correspondence course became more widely known, many priests and nuns wrote to me asking for it: they said it would assist them in instructing future converts. At first I concurred and sent them copies as requested, but so many subsequently applied for the course that I decided to publish it in book form and sell it cheaply.

When published, it bore the title, *Nothing to Fear* – a phrase I took from a speech made by Sir Edward Carson in the Ulster House of Commons when the Partition of Ireland was established. His point was this: now that the Unionists had control of Northern Ireland, their Roman Catholic countrymen should be made to see that under Unionist Rule, they had nothing to fear. We should have nothing to fear from our new rulers: there would be no injustice, no discrimination, no victimisation, no repression or hatred because of our religious beliefs.

I was therefore saying to my readers: "Here is my code of religious belief! I have nothing to fear."

At the time Fr Hugh Arthurs liked this title also. However I came to realise it was more suited for a thriller or a mystery story than for a book of its kind. Moreover, the title did not indicate the book's contents, and I have always preferred a title of a book which gives me some idea of what I will find between the covers. So, once the first edition of 2500 copies was sold out, I changed the title for second edition to: *The Facts about the Catholic Church*. One of the 'expert' readers of the Catholic Truth Society changed this title in a subsequent edition to: *Facts about the Catholic Church*. I was not consulted, and I was not a bit pleased. No acute knowledge of the English language is needed to discern the two very distinct meanings in these titles. However, there is nothing I can do about it at present. The book is already on the booksellers' shelves.

Up till now, sales of the book have been good, with over 12,000 copies being bought. I hope that the present edition, which I have revised in accordance with the Decrees of Vatican II, will also sell well.

During these years, while the Clonard work for non-Catholics continued,

I was privileged to lead a number of day retreats for non-Catholics. Usually these took place at a convent or college. On average, about twenty or thirty non-Catholics would attend. The day's programme was arranged to suit our visitors. There were three talks, then an hour was given over to answering queries put by the participants themselves, and finally, the Benediction of the Blessed Sacrament. All ended about five o'clock. Our guests received dinner and tea.

The members of the Legion of Mary organised these retreats. They prepared the meals, and at intervals in the programme during the day, they chatted with our guests. Very often these friendly chats helped people towards the Church.

It is not generally known among our Irish Catholics that the true ecumenical apostolate and Christian dialogue, envisaged and encouraged by Vatican Council II, was already for years being faithfully carried on, not only in the Clonard Mission, but also in these one-day retreats organised by the Legion of Mary in Cork, Dublin and Belfast. I led the retreats in these three cities. At them, we never glossed over or whittled away any Catholic doctrine. Pointing out our beliefs held in common with Protestants, we went on to show where we parted from their company. We admitted our faults and failings, past and present. Thus we added force to the truths we maintained. The sincere, candid exposition of our Catholic beliefs is not merely the most effective approach to non-Catholics, but also the only way of winning their true conversion.

While living in Agincourt Avenue in the years of my childhood and boyhood, I was confronted on every side by people professing a variety of creeds. In my own young mind, I roped them all together – they were all Protestants! Although some boys, and indeed some grown-ups, were at times bitter towards me because I was a Catholic, the majority were good friends and neighbours. By and large they were a religious people. In those days, ever so many of our neighbours attended church faithfully on Sunday. As I grew older, I came to realize that they can excel us cradle-Catholics in their love and service of God. What a wonderful asset they are to their church.

The amazing number of advertisements and notices of church services published in the *Belfast Telegraph* on Saturday nights – church services to be held the following day, Sunday – prove that the Belfast Protestant people are still religiously-minded. It has always been so. Even in my boyhood I was in no wise surprised to see good crowds of people attending the numerous Protestant churches in the city. They went to one church; we went to another.

I hope that one day all Ireland will be Catholic: our small country will then begin a second era of missionary work across the earth. The days of Columcille, Aidan, Columbanus, Killian and the host of other great Irish missionaries will return, and the Faith and the Church will again be brought by Irish missionaries to remote and distant lands.

On one occasion, while I was engrossed in the work for non-Catholics, I had to consult some of the writings of St Patrick. I there came on a passage which intrigued me. In one of his visions, the saint saw a tiny flame beginning to glow in the North Eastern part of Ireland – a brightening flame following darkness, a flame growing in size and intensity, until it enveloped the land and spread to other countries. Was this a vision of one event, namely, his own apostolate – or a vision also of a second event, namely the work for non-Catholics that in days to come was to get under way in Belfast? Had we kindled a flame – the tiny flame seen by Patrick in prophetic vision 1500 years ago? Time alone can give the answer.

# CHAPTER ELEVEN
# **Dundalk**

## Prefect of the Church

IN THE MIDST of my work in Belfast, I was appointed Superior of the Redemptorist Retreat House, Limerick. This meant I had to leave my position in Our Lady's Confraternity. This did not cost me any pain: I had been Director there for six years, and expected to be changed to other work at any time. But leaving the work of the correspondence course and the apostolate for non-Catholics gave me cause to regret leaving Belfast. However, in this as in so many other appointments and assignments I had received from Superiors, I had no option whatsoever. Therefore I packed my belongings and set off for Limerick.

My three difficult years in Limerick were followed by my appointment to Dundalk. There I concentrated on the work of missions, retreats, and the normal work of our church there, St Joseph's.

I was appointed Prefect of the Church – this is the title for the priest who has the job of running the church, ie, arranging the Masses, the ceremonies, and any other function taking place in it. In all our churches, we are forever changing and adding to our programme. To retain all the necessary points in his mind, the Prefect needs a good memory. He has equally a need for patience.

On the wall of the lower corridor of our monasteries, a large board is generally affixed. It is a specially constructed board, showing the names of the altars and of the members of the Community; in addition, the whole board is a regular pattern of marking pegs, bearing the times of the Masses and other special functions and duties. With this board, a Prefect can indicate to all the members of the Community what duty each one has to perform the following day. He reorders this board every evening. So often it will happen, when he has everything arranged and assigned, that someone will come along to say he must be exempted from his duty. This can upset all the arrangements the Prefect has made. Often he must undo all he has fixed up and start over again. Genuine excuses were always accepted – but the persons concerned should have warned the Prefect in better time. How often a Prefect has just cause for exasperation!

A sense of humour is most valuable to a Prefect. It really was amusing at times to hear the excuses put forward by some! Sometimes it was difficult not to burst out laughing.

The right idea is to give – and demand from – each person his fair share of work. The basic principles of Community life apply here as elsewhere: "Have some consideration for others"; "Treat them as you would like them to treat you".

I took a special interest in the altar servers. These were about twenty or thirty boys, their ages ranging from seven to fourteen. I always kept in mind the fact that these boys offered their services voluntarily: we had no special claim over them. It was our duty to treat them with kindness and consideration. One ought not to expect the mature behaviour of adults from a crowd of children such as they were.

Frequently I entertained them with stories about the Philippines, or the war in France and Germany. On saints' days, I would tell them something about the life of the saint. I talked to them about their schoolwork and their games. I obtained the Superior's permission for them to play football in one of our fields. This, alas, had to be discontinued, because the Bursar saw them playing there and said it would ruin the grazing for the few cows we kept!

Every year on a day in summer, I took the boys by bus to the sea at Gormanston Strand. The bathing there was very safe. The sanded beach served as a pitch for their games of football and their sports. We brought with us all the food and soft drinks we needed for the day.

The success of the day depended on the weather. Provided it did not rain, the boys enjoyed every minute of their outing. They swam; they practised for the sports to be held in the afternoon; they visited the local shop and bought what they fancied. We could always be sure, no matter what they ate beforehand, that they would put up a good performance at dinner. What we gave them for their meal was eagerly welcomed and praised. Sea air puts a sharp edge on a boy's appetite. We had ham and chicken sandwiches, lemonade, orange squash, cake, fruit, and sweets. To a boy on the sands beside the sea, a veritable banquet!

The sand banks above the strand furnished any summer visitors to the beach that day with a grandstand view of our sports. No records were broken – but the enthusiasm and noise made that fact go unnoticed. The relay races provided great excitement, but the pièce de resistance was the football match.

We had the choirboys also with us that day. Now in our church, as in every church throughout the world, there is no love lost between choirboys and altar boys. The football match of the summer outing was their great contest of the year. From time immemorial, they had been deadly rivals. Now was the trial of strength. I was always pleased when the match ended in a draw. Peace descended sooner after the match, and there were fewer arguments than beforehand.

Some of the boys were potentially good athletes; some obviously would never ever make the grade. However, hope springs eternal in the human breast – and the hopeless hopefully made efforts to succeed. One lad tried the high jump, and failed again and again to go over the bar. One or two of the boys near me said he would never jump the height set: "He has drunk about five bottles of lemonade, Father, he cannot jump with all that inside him!" Although the lad failed to jump successfully, he got more applause and noisy encouragement than any other competitor.

Every Christmas week the boys were invited into the monastery and treated to a party and cinema show. Romantic or psychological films bored these young gentlemen: they wanted films about the Wild West, or murder, or clowns in comedy. They thirsted for blood: the more shooting and bloodshed and murder and explosions in a film, the better.

When opportunity arose, I would tactfully gave the boys advice and counsel. This mostly dealt with attention to their lessons and homework, the folly of starting to smoke cigarettes, the use of bad language – particularly, the irreverent use of the Holy Name – and the importance of prayer, morning and night.

Their sacristy room was close to our church tribune, where the Fathers and Brothers said their prayers. Therefore we had to impose a rule of silence on the boys in that room. This was a very difficult rule to enforce. It proved rather much for youngsters such as ours. One day I had a brainwave: "I will get a set of chess and a board and teach them the game: that will occupy them and keep them quiet!" So I gathered them all together one night and in twenty minutes, I explained the basics on a chessboard: the names, the initial positions and the moves of the different pieces. The boys were very quick to pick up the rudiments of the game. I then played a few games with them, to show how it was done.

Chess fever caught on! Within a few days, they had bought up all the chess sets in the Dundalk shops. They were then playing the game at home with their chums. Some of them became very expert: in fact, two or three were very difficult to beat. On one occasion I received a most humiliating drubbing from these masters. If they had remained modest and quiet about their victory, I would not have minded, but they went around, whooping loudly and telling everybody they had beaten me!

During the Christmas holidays I organised a Chess Tournament for them. There was a Junior as well as a Senior section. "Valuable prizes" (boxes of sweets!) were promised to the winners. This tournament stirred up great rivalry and excitement. All games in the contest had to be played in their own sacristy room. Matches between two of our 'experts' made the other boys stand still, silent and open-eyed. The contestants would not tolerate noise, because this would spoil their concentration! When I saw their interest and eagerness, I felt well rewarded for the little trouble it had cost me to teach them the game.

## Locked in a Cathedral

I frequently left the monastery to give missions or retreats to parishes or special groups. To describe that work in detail would be dull and uninteresting, so I will here speak only of a few incidents which were rather unusual.

On one occasion I was sent to give the annual retreat to the priests of the Diocese of Ossory. This retreat was held in St Kieran's College, Kilkenny. One half of the priests came for the first week, the other half for the second week. When I had finished the first week of the retreat, I was free from Saturday morning until Monday night. The Bishop, Dr Collier, advised me to pay a visit during this time to the Protestant Cathedral in the town.

"It really belongs to us. They took it off us at the Reformation. It was built with Catholic money. Go and see it! It is well worth a visit," he said to me.

Accepting his suggestion, I left the college about five o'clock that Saturday evening and went down the town to see the Cathedral. When I arrived, the Protestant caretaker was working in the grounds. He courteously unlocked the wicket of the main door and allowed me to go alone into the Cathedral. Inside, it was rather dark and chilly. Before examining any details, I walked here and there to form my own general impression of the building.

The caretaker brought in some American tourists – one of whom came over to speak to me. The caretaker was looking in our direction. I thought I was holding up the visitors' tour of the church, so I ended the conversation as nicely as I could and moved away to the end of the transept.

I must have spent about half an hour going round the various monuments and ancient tombs of famous personages of the past. In the gloom, I tried to read their inscriptions written in Latin or quaint archaic English. I was much taken by the impressive solemnity of the building, its noble design and very fine windows. As I slowly moved around, I reflected on the faith of the Catholic people of Kilkenny, embodied in the stones, sculptures, and carvings which formed this magnificent temple of God. I thought also of Cromwell – he who had massacred Catholics in this very building, and then crowned his infamous work by stabbing his horses within its sacred walls.

Time was passing for me, however, and in the fading light, the Cathedral was becoming darker. I felt I had done well enough: I had seen as much as I wanted to see. Moreover, I was but lightly clad and felt the increasing chill of the vast stone building. So I had my last walk around, and then made for the wicket to leave.

To my dismay, it was firmly locked! So also was the main door itself. Then I immediately thought there must be other exit doors still open. I searched for them and found them, but they too were locked. I then tried to enter the sacristy. In vain – for the door leading to it was locked. I thought then of the windows: surely I could open one of these and get out? There were numerous windows, but none of them were helpful. They were narrow – as long and narrow as a plank of wood – they were made of small, leaded panes of stained or clear glass, and every one of them began at least ten feet from the ground. I was not going to escape that way.

I thought then of ringing the Cathedral bell. However, I soon discovered that the belfry was separate from the main building: to reach it, I would need to cross some open ground. Now I felt I really was in a fix: I was securely locked in the Cathedral for the night! Where was the blessed caretaker? Why had he locked the doors on me? He must have thought that when I ended my chat with his American tourist, I had gone out from the Cathedral. But why, oh why, did he not first glance around before locking me up for the night!

Perhaps he was still working nearby in the grounds. So I went, in hope, and knocked and hammered on the main door. It was stoutly timbered and iron-studded: as I went on, hurting my fists and my feet with my beating on it, I knew the noise I made would carry no distance.

I now decided to rest for a while. I went to the seats and sat down to consider the situation. Here I was, alone, and well and truly locked in. No one would come near the Cathedral until the time approached for the Sunday Service – that could mean I would not be released until perhaps eleven o'clock or noon the next day. How was I going to spend the long night hours? In my light summer attire, I could now feel the chill getting into me. Like the character in *The Mikado*, I kept repeating to myself, half-aloud, "Here's a right how-do-you-do! Here's a right how-do-you-do!"

Any Sherlock Holmes-like powers I possessed now had to be awakened and put to work. I would have to do something – something drastic if necessary, for I was determined not to spend the night in that Cathedral. At this point I knelt and asked the good Lord to get me out of this predicament.

Then, rising to my feet, I made another reconnaissance of my prison. And now a most careful survey showed me that I had, like a hare on the coursing field, only one line of escape – the main door. I stood examining it. Then suddenly I noticed that its sliding vertical bolts, above and below, might be freed from their sockets. If I succeeded in doing this, I might then be able to pull open the two wings of the huge door.

The releasing of the bolts required some hefty pulling and straining. The top bolt was rather high for me, and it gave me a lot of trouble. Apparently it was loose in its socket, and a thick wedge of wood had been driven in, to keep it firmly in its place. I kept trying to pull the bolt down; I could reach it with only a few of my fingers. My face was damp with perspiration, and my spectacles became misted up.

I sat down again to recover my breath, to wipe my spectacles, and to offer a prayer that this monster of a door would yield to my seemingly puny efforts. After a few minutes' rest, I went back to the door in a kind of desperation and renewed my struggle. I felt the bolt loosening. The block or wedge fell on me, but the bolt was now freed!

Now to pull the two wings of the door inwards and apart. I somehow got a good grip of both wings and started slowly pulling them towards me, then releasing them, pulling a bit farther each time. So it went on, until with one last big effort, I pulled both sides apart. As the sides swung open, I saw once more the grey, gravelled paths, and the long light of the setting sun on the green lawns.

Thankfully, I came out into the open air, closed the door behind me and walked down the path to the entrance gate at the road. On my way down I saw my friend the caretaker, some distance away, tending a grave. He was obviously too far away to have heard my knocking and hammering on the door. At the crunching sound of my footsteps on the gravel of the path, he swiftly looked up and saw me. In a flash he took in the situation! He realised he had locked me in the Cathedral!

"Oh, sir, were you locked in?" he exclaimed anxiously. "I am terribly sorry, sir! I hope you don't think I did that on purpose?"

"I would like to think not!" I replied with some indignation. "You should have had a look around before you locked it. I was lucky enough to find my way out; other people in the same fix would have been locked in that cold building all night."

Before I said any more, I walked away, leaving him muttering apologies.

And that was my first visit to Kilkenny Cathedral. Now whenever anyone tells me he hails from Kilkenny, I instantly think of that memorable Saturday evening and my enforced stay within the Cathedral's dark and chilly walls.

What I have narrated happened years before ecumenical meetings and services were in vogue. And when I reflect on my experience of that evening, the thought has occurred to me that the leaves must have fallen many times since a Catholic last prayed in that Cathedral as I had done.

## The Swearing Stone

Not long afterwards I was assigned to preach a mission in the little village of Longwood in County Meath. Longwood is a typical Irish country village, with its one wide street, its decent church, its clean shops, and its warm-hearted, friendly people.

On the morning of the second Sunday of the mission, when our work was done, the kindly parish priest asked me to accompany him on a short drive in his car.

"It is a grand morning, thank God!" he exclaimed. "Come out with me for a run in the car! I'll bring you to see the swearing stone!"

"A swearing stone! What is that?" I asked him.

"Wait till we get there! I'll explain everything to you" he replied.

We drove about two or three miles through the lovely countryside of Royal Meath. We came to a demesne entrance and followed a winding, tree-lined avenue for about a quarter of a mile. Rhododendrons grew in thick clumps here and there – pleasant sights, with their colourful blossoms of purple and red.

We parked the car on a grassy space beside the road and set off walking. We had gone but a little distance, when we came to a woodland glade.

What a sight of magical beauty opened now before our eyes! It was a bright, sunny day with a gentle breeze blowing. The trees around us – beech, elm and chestnut – arched broadly over our heads, forming a wide dome like a huge, green umbrella. Looking up to this green dome, you could see darker areas where the foliage was dense, and soft green patches where the sunlight played through the leaves. Here and there, single shafts of brilliant sunshine shot through the trees and fell in pools of tremulous light on the brown path before us.

The priest made his way forward. In silent wonder I followed him. We came to a river, which was about as wide as an average street in any of our cities.

"This is the Blackwater, a tributary of the Boyne river," he explained.

I replied that it had been suitably named. It flowed on silently and steadily, pouring along like black oil. Its surface was like an ebony floor, long and smooth and dark. As I gazed at it, I saw a ripple – upstream, a short distance away: a widening ripple that became a ring on the surface.

"Wait for a moment!" said the priest. "There is a trout cruising around there. He is circling slowly as he watches for flies."

In a moment the fish broke the water, sucked in a fly, and sank back into the river.

On the bank where we stood, some trees reached out over the river. Their shade was broken by a single brilliant beam of sunshine piercing through the foliage. My eyes followed that light down through the water, down to where I could see stones and pebbles lying on the golden sand of the riverbed.

The glade and the river formed a fascinatingly beautiful scene. All was silent around us, except for the occasional trilling song of a thrush or the clear, sweet fluting of a blackbird. In the distance there was the low, hoarse sound of falling water at a weir: it was like unobtrusive background cello music in perfect harmony with the beauty of this faery glade.

"What a wonderful spot this is!" I exclaimed to my priest-guide. "It is like one of those places you read about in a book without ever a hope of seeing it."

"Yes," he replied, "it is quiet and peaceful. I often come here to read my Breviary – which reminds me that I have some Office to read. You should stay around and see everything, while I go and finish my prayers."

And so I had ten or fifteen minutes more to stand or move along the riverbank, and relish the loveliness of the scene around me. Thinking it quite probable that I would never see the like of this spot again, I looked carefully and deliberately around me, in an effort to imprint indelibly on my mind all I saw. I thought of Wordsworth's daffodils which, to use the poet's words, "flashed upon that inward eye which is the bliss of solitude". I desired so strongly to retain this mental picture all my days.

While thus engrossed in my 'imprinting', the time passed quickly. All too soon the priest's voice reached my ears: "I am afraid we will have to move on. We must go to see this famous swearing stone about which I was telling you."

As we walked along, he told me how in reading the history of the parish he had discovered that there had once been a monastery here, with an adjoining graveyard. He had enlisted the help of some volunteers in the parish to tidy the graves and set up a small shrine in the partially restored ruins of the monastery. In clearing the graveyard, he had come across a strange stone thrown down in a tangle of grass and bushes. In shape it somewhat resembled the headstone of a grave, and yet it was too narrow to be one. He had a curious feeling that there was something sacred about it. So he had it cleaned up and erected on a slight elevation in the graveyard. While he was speaking, we were threading our way through the graveyard.

"There it is!" he said suddenly, pointing to the stone.

It was of a rough brownish kind of sandstone, standing about five feet high and barely two feet wide. It bore no inscriptions, no Ogham writing, no marks or signs whatever. Near the top, however, right through the stone, were two oval holes. Each of these was about six inches long and four inches wide.

"This is a Swearing Stone!" said the priest. He then went on to tell me how in very ancient times, an Irish boy, on reaching maturity, was initiated into full membership of his clan by a solemn ceremony. In the presence of the assembled clansmen and their chieftain, the boy would have knelt before this stone, put his hands through these holes, grasped the hands of his chieftain, and promised life-long fealty. Similarly at this same stone, and through these same holes, bridegroom and bride would have joined hands and pledged mutual trust and fidelity.

This stone had clearly a symbolic meaning for the members of the clan. In its steadfastness and permanence, it signified and visibly symbolised the qualities of the promises made before it.

In all of us as we go through life, there is a demand to see external signs of the invisible happenings in which we are concerned. The flag of a nation; the badge of an organisation; the use of the sword in the conferring of a knighthood; a decoration for valour; a uniform; a ring at a wedding: these are all visible signs or symbols of unseen loyalties and qualities. Our Lord used visible signs for invisible effects – the water in Baptism; the bread and wine in the Eucharist. The Church likewise uses visible signs in administering the Sacraments – for example, the holy oils in Confirmation and Extreme Unction. All these procedures satisfy and fulfil the human need to see visible signs for invisible happenings; visible symbols for spiritual effects and unseen realities.

My thoughts ran along these lines as I stood looking at this Swearing Stone. Coming away from it again, I asked the parish priest how he came to know it was a Swearing Stone. He said he had invited a Professor of Archaeology to come and examine it. This expert assured him it was indeed a Swearing Stone, and that only about six similar stones had been so far discovered in Western Europe.

## The Spaniard's Chapel

The story about the Swearing Stone brings to my mind another different kind of monument or souvenir of the past: the Spaniard's Chapel in West Donegal. It can still be seen close to the road that runs from Ardara to Kilcar. I must here tell its story.

During the mission I was giving in Ardara, the parish priest, Fr Boyce, invited me to come with him on a journey to Glencolmcille. As we drew near to Kilcar, we passed a long stone building, now fallen into ruins, by the roadside.

"Have a good look at this ruin!" said Fr Boyce as we approached to it. "It is called 'Supéal an Spainneac' – 'the Spaniard's Chapel'".

As he slowed down the car, I had a long hard look at the building. The gables and side walls were still intact, but the structure was roofless and obviously a long time derelict.

"Why is it called The Spaniard's Chapel?" I asked.

"I would prefer you to hear its story from the parish priest of Kilcar," replied Fr Boyce. "It lies in his parish: he knows the full history."

We drove on and came to the house of Kilcar's parish priest, Fr Carr. We found him cutting the grass on the lawn outside his house. In reply to our apologies for calling when he was so busy, he assured us it was a welcome interruption of his perspiring efforts to deal with the grass. As we stood with him on the lawn, he began to point out – for my benefit – the various landmarks in the attractive scenery around us. On the landward side there stretched out before us a panorama of fields in varied shades of green and brown, broken up by the grey of the rock walls or fences. Out towards the West we could look down on the sea, far below the cliffs, touched with foam here and there, and spreading out vaguely into the dim distance.

After a short time Fr Carr brought us to his house. There Fr Boyce asked him to tell me the story of The Spaniard's Chapel. Here follows the story of his namesake…

Over two hundred years ago, in 1756, a boy named James Carr, who lived in this district, set out to study for the priesthood in the Irish College at Salamanca in Spain. After his Ordination, he returned to Ireland and was duly appointed Parish Priest here in his native parish of Kilcar.

On a stormy winter's night one of his parishioners came to ask him to attend to his father, who was dangerously ill. The sick man lived near the sea cliffs some miles away.

Fr James Carr was soon dressed and ready. By that time his servant had the priest's horse saddled and waiting. Fr Carr decided to take a short cut along the top of the cliffs to get to the sick man's house. The storm was now at its height. The strong, high winds slowed the priest's progress. He could hear the furious seas pounding and thundering on the rocks at the base of the cliffs. He was not the least bit worried about the track he was following: since boyhood he had known every inch of these cliff paths. Moreover, he rode a safe, sturdy horse. Despite the gale winds and the driving rain, he made slow but steady progress.

All of a sudden Fr Carr's horse stopped on the cliff path. In spite of the priest's coaxing and urging, the animal would go no farther. The priest dismounted. This was most unusual. He felt there was something wrong. His horse had never behaved like this before! As he stood there, wondering whether he should leave the horse at once and continue his journey by himself, he thought he heard someone crying out, as if in pain. He heard the sounds again – a piteous cry, down below him on the rocks at the foot of the cliff. Tethering his horse to a bush, he scrambled down the cliff and stood there listening. Guided by the sound of the moaning, he found a sailor lying on the rocks, injured and half-drowned. The priest lifted him up gently, and carried him off the rocks to a dry, sheltered part of the cliff.

Though barely conscious, the poor sailor was able to speak a few words. As Fr Carr bent down to hear what he was saying, he discovered with surprise that the man was speaking Spanish. Now using his fluent knowledge of Spanish, acquired in his student days in Salamanca, the priest was able to give some comfort to the dying man and administer the Last Sacraments to him before he expired.

A moment or two before he breathed his last, the sailor told the priest he had always prayed to Our Lady to obtain him the grace of a good death. He now realised these prayers had gained him his desire. He said he now wanted to do something for Our Lady in return. He told the priest he had some money in the belt he was wearing: would he take this money and use it to build a small chapel in Our Lady's honour? The priest promised to do as he wished.

When he saw that the man was dead, Fr Carr climbed up the cliff again, and recovered and mounted his horse. This time the animal went forward willingly. The priest reached the sick parishioner's house, and was in time to attend him also before he died.

The Spanish sailor was buried in the local graveyard. With the gold found in his belt, the priest built the little chapel in honour of God's Mother. In those Penal Days the Catholic people of the area attended Mass there. Times have changed. Many of the people there emigrated to England and America. When Catholic Emancipation was granted in 1829, Catholics were allowed to build proper churches. The Spaniard's Chapel was no longer used: the new parish church sufficed for the needs of the people. The Chapel is now a ruin.

"As you came along the road, you saw what it is like," said Fr Carr to me as he finished his story. "It is now a hopeless ruin – but once upon a time it was a blessing sent from Heaven to the people of Kilcar!"

CHAPTER TWELVE

# England Again

## Emigrant Chaplain

IN 1966 I WAS a member of the Redemptorist Community in Dundalk. My health, although not one hundred per cent, was reasonably good. I had occasional bouts of bronchitis and asthma – but never did they so incapacitate me, as to prevent me carrying out any tasks or work I was asked to do. Our church in Dundalk, St Joseph's, is popular but it is not a busy church. Dundalk is well supplied with Catholic churches, with three belonging to Dundalk parish and three in the hands of religious orders – the Dominicans, Marists and Redemptorists.

The work involved in our church could easily have been carried on by five or six priests. In the Community, however, there were about sixteen priests. A few of these were invalids or very advanced in years: they could not be counted as active workers. However, the remainder were able for work and keen to get work. Generally, about five or six priests were always available at home to keep the church work going; the remainder would be engaged in the external work of giving missions or retreats.

Unfortunately, in later years, applications from priests or religious superiors for missions or retreats were not numerous enough to keep us occupied for the greater part of the year. As a result, there was sufficient work for all of us for only about three months of the year. During the other nine months, when little or no external work was available, I, along with the other active priests, found myself unemployed in that long period.

I saw the years of my life slipping away from me, one by one. I was not idle: I studied theology; I wrote several articles and booklets; I did my bit in the church work; I was "Priests' Confessor", and heard many priests' Confessions. But no really substantial external work was offered to me – except on a few rare occasions. I had prepared all the sermons, lectures and discourses needed for any work that might turn up, but no work came.

Now, on Tuesdays and Thursdays we were allowed to go for a walk. I used to go off tramping through the countryside. As the others in the Community were not keen on walks, I was usually out alone. I used to say my Rosary and other prayers as I trudged along the lovely country roads and lanes around

Dundalk, Blackrock and Faughart. As I went along, I used to reflect on my life and my work. I could see that there would be no increase in the work available for me in Dundalk. I was not in a contemplative Order! We were supposed to be active workers. I asked myself, "What can I do about this situation? Where can I find work to do?"

It had come to my notice that the Oakland Province of the Redemptorists in California was short of priests. One day on my walk, the thought sprang to my mind: "Why should I not volunteer to go there?"

So I wrote a careful letter to our Irish Provincial Superior in Dublin, asking permission to go to Oakland for three or four years. From all I have said just now, you can guess what reasons I gave him for making my request. I consulted no one about all this; I made up my own mind. No one else knew what I was planning. I am always chary about revealing, even to a very close friend, anything I really want to keep secret. It has been my experience that often people to whom you entrust a secret will remember the secret but forget that it is a secret! Hence it can happen that they will then repeat what you have told them as if it were a matter of common knowledge or an idle bit of gossip.

Having sent off my letter, I eagerly awaited a reply from the Provincial in Dublin. Day after day passed, however, and no reply came. I began to wonder what way my application had been received. It looked as if my request was going to be turned down.

Then it happened. One night I was called to the phone: it was Father Provincial speaking. He said he had received my letter and noted my request. He then went on to say this: "The Archbishop of Dublin has asked me to give him a priest for emigrant work in England. Would you consider this work? Would you accept it?"

Without a moment's hesitation I said: "Yes, certainly!"

And so, in late August of that year 1966, I arrived in Birmingham. I was to live in our own monastery – Erdington Abbey. I would be a guest of the Community. From the Abbey, I was to carry out my work for Irish immigrants.

I have never regretted my chosen exile. I have so often thanked God for allowing me this amazing opportunity of helping souls.

Birmingham was then England's second largest city. It had a population of about 1,500,000 people. I had been in the city on two previous occasions, when I was preaching the annual series of retreat lectures to the Sisters of St Paul at Selly Park. These brief visits, however, had not made me familiar with even the main streets of the city. Consequently, on that August morning in 1966, when I got off the train at New Street Station in Birmingham, I had no idea of the way to Erdington Abbey. A taxi-driver knew all the answers, however, and, having judiciously loaded my luggage into his car, he soon had me moving through the busy streets on the road to Erdington Abbey.

The Archbishop of Birmingham had appointed Fr Maguire of St Catherine's Church to be the guide and mentor of our group – for I was only one of about a dozen – of newly arrived immigrant missionaries.

On a pre-arranged day, I went to see the Archbishop. There I met my fellow chaplains in this immigrant work. Most of them were assigned to work in city parishes which were predominantly Irish. My circumstances were different from theirs, however, for I was to live in Erdington Abbey and work from there through the different parishes in north-east Birmingham. I was not to be attached to any parish as an assistant priest: I had a kind of 'roving' commission, whereby I was to cover a wide area seeking Irish boys and girls who were constantly moving about from lodgings to lodgings: those who had never been contacted by any priest, and were most liable to lapse from the Faith or its practice. The subjects for my work, therefore, were to be these 'drifters' or 'floaters' in the north-eastern parishes of the city.

In that year, 1966, according to the Census, there were no fewer than 800,000 Irish immigrants in Britain. Most of these were to be found in London, Birmingham, Manchester and Liverpool. It was an accepted estimate that in Birmingham alone, there were at least 100,000 such people. How many of these now lived in my area in north-eastern Birmingham, and how was I to set about contacting the drifters and floaters amongst them? No one could tell me the answers!

One of our priests in the Abbey gave me a large map of the city. I sellotaped it to the wall of my room and surveyed it with interest. The extent of the city, and the sheer size of the north eastern area, which was now under my remit, made me whistle!

Where was I to begin? For the first few weeks I went out every morning to look around me and to find out the lie of the districts and streets. I persevered day after day. I had no car; I tramped the streets, hopping and stopping here and there, like a homing pigeon which has lost its way or is breaking its journey. On my way home to the Abbey, I often had to ask the way. The whole scene was new to me, and yet I needed to know it like the palm of my hand. Progress was rather slow. My first step forward was the purchase of a street guide. Equipped with this book, I soon found I could make my way anywhere in Birmingham.

My next step was to contact some Irish workers. I made some notes at the time, which show my tentative efforts to get started at the work I had come to do:

"Saturday, 17 September 1966
Talked to John Maguire, Cavan County, labourer at the railway reconstruction job at New Street Station. Married to a Catholic from Belfast. He says:
1. The Irish lads come and go on this job.
2. Stafford Road is an area to which many Irish boys go. In the evenings they frequent the pubs there.
3. A number of them don't want to work: some of these hang around the subway and the pubs at the Bull Ring.
4. On this building site on Saturday the men work until 4.00 pm.
5. Many Irish are just drifters.
6. His ganger, Paddy Fitzroy, Dublin, married to a Catholic girl, has not been in Ireland for sixteen years. His family are quite Catholic, the children going to Catholic schools. Had a good chat with him. Very decent man."

All this was breaking the ground for me. I was feeling my way and planning future operations.

On Sunday, 18 September, I went to the Dance at the Abbey Irish Club. There I met my first real 'case':

"J.C. from Dublin wants to talk to me. Is married to a non-Catholic, 2 children (baptised). He still goes to Mass. Has been put out of his home by his wife (he lives with his wife's people), because of his drinking sessions. Now he is thoroughly repentant, but she has had enough of him – she won't resume married life with him. He asked me to speak to her.

Monday, 19 September
Went to her address. He came out to speak to me. He said, "she is inside, but she doesn't want to see you". I brought him out with me for a short walk. I advised him:

1. Get a flat or some place of your own – invite her to join you there and bring the children with her.
2. Show her there are, and will be, no more night drinking sessions.
3. Get to Mass: keep up your religion. (He tells me his mother writes to him often, always reminding him about going to Mass, etc)

I encouraged him. He told me he had bad fits of depression. He showed me his wrists, which he had cut in an effort to commit suicide – 18 stitches in one, 6 stitches in the other. He badly needed any encouragement I gave him. I gave him my name and address so that he can contact me.

Came home in bus to Erdington. An Irish conductor, Madden by name: we had a chat. A lot of Irish working on buses. Depot is in Millar Street. I must go there some time soon."

These meetings gave me an idea of what lay before me. I was making some progress. I cannot recall who it was that advised me to go and see Fr Denis Ryan, a Limerick-born priest who had charge of St Mary and St John's Parish, Gravelly Hill. I visited Fr Ryan. We had a long discussion, in which we planned a campaign of visiting every house in his parish. My meeting with him led to the real beginning of my work. In his parish I started to visit every house in a wide area of about fifty streets.

Day by day, I went out to these streets. I took them one at a time. I went from house to house, knocking at every door and inquiring about Catholics living there – particularly Irish Catholics. I carried a small notebook, in which I noted down names and helpful data for a future visit. I was always anxious to know about attendance at Mass on Sundays and the Catholic education of the children. I found out the best time for visiting a house. Anything that would enable me to help them was noted down in a highly complicated code in my notebook.

Week by week, I carried on with this work. On Monday mornings I sat down with Fr Ryan and gave him a verbal as well as my written report of all I had learned in the previous week's work. I frequently brought him news of recent arrivals in the parish. If any tough, problem cases arose, we discussed the most effective manner of dealing with them. When I needed his help or advice, I sought it.

Thus for about three years I tramped the streets of Gravelly Hill Parish, knocking at doors, making inquiries, stopping Irish people in the streets and trying to get to know them. How is it that you can recognise an Irish face? I can! I make mistakes now and then, but an apology is the remedy for that. Usually I am right. I have clues of course: for one thing, an Irish person takes a second or even a third look at you when you are a priest. They recognise you – and they show it! And being alert for this sign, you can spot and interpret it at once. I sometimes came upon an elderly person, an Irish immigrant now become an invalid, to whom a chat about Ireland was ever so welcome. Usually I encountered the following problems: marriages broken or disintegrating; children not baptised or attending non-Catholic schools; alcoholics; young men and women seeking accommodation; Catholics who had stopped attending Mass. I am not saying that these problems were frequent or widespread: I never generalise about such matters here in England: I merely say these problems occur and I met them.

While I was engaged at this work, I met Irish folk who said they often visited the Abbey Irish Club. This was a club started in our Redemptorist Abbey Hall about six or seven years previously. It was frequented mostly by Irish boys and girls. There was a bar attached to the club. The dance hall had a fine maple-wood floor, polished like furniture. I visited it one night and went round among the people. I felt out of place.

A man from Dublin, the worse for drink, challenged me:

"You should not be here! All right around the church! This is no place for you!"

I replied, "Why not? If it is all right for you to be here, it is all right for me!"

He then shamelessly declared his malevolent aims in coming to the club. I will not record them here. He was the type of immigrant who gets a bad name for others from Ireland. His manner and speech were drunkenly aggressive, but he knew quite well what he was saying.

Some weeks later Fr Rector of the Abbey Community asked me to take over the running of the club. I agreed: I saw in his offer an opportunity to do something for the Community, who were both putting me up and putting up with me as a guest! I also saw in the job a chance of contacting more Irish immigrants – particularly unmarried boys and girls, who were drifting about from place to place, and perhaps never contacting a priest. This was the very work I had come to do. I therefore accepted the Rector's offer. Alas! Unknown to myself, I was entering into and stirring up a hornet's nest…

After several weeks of close observation of the club's mode of operation, I was uneasy and dissatisfied. I explained everything to the Rector. He and I agreed a new start should be made. We replaced the committee with an entirely new group of men. To this new team, I pointed out what past mistakes we were henceforth going to avoid. I was determined to profit from the lessons I had learned under the previous committee.

I will soon be entering my fifth year with the club. Since I took it over, I have run it as efficiently and smoothly as possible. For me, this has been a responsibility carrying with it much worry and strain. In the running of a club, there sooner or later arises dissension among the members. Sometimes the committee itself is divided on a policy, an incident, or a proposal. Sometimes one or more of the ordinary members, having taken too much drink, start a rumpus in the lounge bar or on the dance floor. When 'incidents' happen in a club, they seem to happen suddenly, like lightning. In a moment there can be a flare-up which, if not speedily quenched, becomes a conflagration.

The troublemakers will not take any directions or admonitions from a committee member. Normally I have to be summoned to the scene. In fact I have to deal personally with almost every crisis. Realising this full well from the start, I knew it meant my constant and vigilant attendance every night the club is open. So from 8.30 pm until about 12.30 am, I stay in the club.

This is the dark side of the club's life. There is a very bright side to it all also. I make many contacts. I move among the members and become friendly with them all. They often speak to me about some problem in their work or in their homes. I am able to advise the boys and girls about their difficulties. I feel I am the only priest friend many of them have here in Birmingham. That pleases me: I am their friend – they know they can turn to me when they need me.

I must confess, it demanded a real effort on my part to mix with a crowd in a bar or in a dance hall. I had to face a new element in human life: I had to go for the first time among boys and girls, men and women, who were dancing and drinking. I, who had never done this before; I, who for over forty years had been obliged by Redemptorist Rules not to speak to outsiders. At first, within myself, I was utterly embarrassed. And so I smiled grimly and faced it all, feeling utterly self-conscious, as I tried to be pleasant to people in circumstances which understandably repelled me.

Now, after years in the club, it is altogether different with me. I am quite at home among the members, quite at ease moving through the crowded dance floor or sitting with a group of Irish boys or girls who are having a drink.

My club experience has shown me that the presence of a priest is necessary for the true success of a Catholic Irish club here in England. The priest will need a committee of eight or nine reliable members. To them he can assign the various lines of work required. However, he cannot leave everything to them. He must not allow that to happen – if he does, they will gradually take over full control of the club. This easily leads to deterioration of the club's ideals and purposes. It will then happen that when this priest wishes to take action, his hands will be tied. If a Catholic club is to remain what its name indicates, the priest must strive to retain control of its affairs. He must ever be unobtrusively vigilant and watchful. But it is all well worthwhile.

Years ago – like so many other priests – I concerned myself only with the spiritual side of people's lives. My ideas have changed completely. Now I see that the social side of life is also necessary for people's lives, and that the priest, so far as he can, must interest himself in promoting social activities among his people. He should aim at having an adequate social centre for his people. Where there is no such centre in a parish, the local pubs will take its place. When this happens, the priest's sphere of influence is very much lessened.

In harmony with the ideas current in many Religious Institutes in bygone years, we Redemptorists never interested ourselves in active social work. In this way we interpreted the text, "Render to Caesar the things that are Caesar's, and to God the things that are God's." However, Our Lord's words in the "Our Father", "Give us this day our daily bread", refer to the needs of ordinary, everyday life and not merely to "the loaf". We knew all that; but we forgot that, "although man does not live by bread alone", he still lives "by bread".

We preached social justice. We concerned ourselves with condemning the evils we saw in social activities. Outside of this, we did nothing active to promote good social works. Had I the power and opportunity, I would build an adequate social centre near all our monasteries. It would engage in social initiatives of all kinds – amusements, dances, concerts, education classes, housing needs, saving, co-operative work and domestic economy.

When I read through the Decrees of Vatican II, I find passages which encourage and oblige us to act in this manner:

> "Let everyone consider it his sacred obligation to count social necessities among the primary duties of modern man and to pay heed to them."

(*The Church Today*, No 30)

"In our times a special obligation binds us to make ourselves the neighbours of absolutely every person, and to actively helping him when he comes across our path, whether he be an old person abandoned by all, a foreign labourer unjustly looked down upon, a refugee, a child born of an unlawful union and wrongly suffering for a sin he did not commit, or a hungry person who disturbs our conscience by recalling the voice of the Lord: "As long as you did it for one of these, the least of my brethren, you did it for me." (Matthew 25:40)"

*(Ibid.* No 27)*

"Priests cannot be of service to men if they remain strangers to the life and conditions of men."

(Priests, No 3)

Therefore a priest must, to some degree, be involved in the ordinary, everyday life and conditions of the people. He must not go too far in this, however. A proper balance between such human involvement and his spiritual apostolate must be reached. This is not as easy as it seems – but we priests must be clear-sighted about our primary work as ministers of Christ. We must keep first things first: the worship of God, the service of God and the spiritual welfare of men are our primary duties. As Bishop Young says, in the Preface to the *Decree on Priests*:

"Under the pressure of the activities in which his ministry increasingly involves the priest of today, he must not be torn by the dichotomy of work and spirituality."

In one sense that is quite true. In another sense, it needs qualification: for the priest's involvement in human affairs, we must remember, is not a mere sociological requirement, but flows from the very heart of his divine mission as "another Christ". Work for others and our own service of God are the same activity; and if we work in union with Christ by prayer, we are drawing ourselves as well as others nearer to God.

## Visiting Building Sites

I must now speak of another line of work which I took up. I stumbled upon it. Here is what happened.

One day I was walking down Fentham Road and stopped for a moment to watch the workmen engaged in the construction of Erdington Grammar School. Suddenly I realised that most of the men were Irish. I walked on thoughtfully. Why not visit these men? These were the very people I was trying to contact.

I pondered over the matter for a day or two and then made up my mind: I would visit them regularly. I then had to plan how to proceed. Firstly, I would get permission to visit the site from the firm of contractors. It would not be while the men were working, for with the high scaffolding and the heavy machines and cranes, it would be dangerous to divert their attention from what they were doing – no, I would visit them in their canteen hut at lunchtimes, 1.00 – 1.30 pm. Secondly, I would go on a fixed day every week. Thirdly, I would pay short visits at first, gradually lengthening the time as I became accepted. Fourthly, I would aim to gain the friendship and trust of the men. Having achieved that, I could then influence them.

I secured the contractors' permission and, one Tuesday at lunchtime, went along to the men's canteen. I must not exaggerate – but you will believe me when I say it took any bit of courage I had, to flounder through the muddy building site and knock at the canteen door.

My approach was clumsy; I know now how to first approach a site. But I was full of goodwill, and I am sure that men saw I was trying to be friendly. That is true – but at first, they did not know what to make of me. I was not looking for money for some good cause; I was not selling ballot tickets, or chasing after some delinquent; I was not inquisitive about their private lives. I can well imagine one of the Irish lads in that canteen, speaking about me to one of his friends along these lines: "We have an Irish priest who comes into the job to see us every Tuesday. A friendly bloke! He usually leaves us the midday edition of the *Evening Mail*. Any news there is – he has it! From his accent I would say he is from the North of Ireland. He told us his name – I forget it – and I think he said he was from Erdington Abbey, up the road. He never misses a Tuesday. Now we know his knock on the door."

I will not give all the details, but soon I started to visit other big building sites where I saw Irish lads working. Before long I was visiting five sites a week, each time meeting up to forty or fifty men a day in their canteens. Invariably, as I got to know the men, they would ask me: "Would you like a cup of tea, Father?" That was it! I was accepted!

Since I started this work, I have visited the following building sites each week until the work was completed:

1. The Midland Electricity Board offices, George Road
2. Erdington Grammar School
3. The River Tame and Salford Park site
4. Taylor's reconstruction site, High Street
5. The Swan Shopping Complex, Sutton New Road
6. The Gravelly Hill Multi-level Interchange – popularly known as "Spaghetti Junction"
7. The Lancaster Place section of the Aston Express Way
8. The Dartmouth Street section of this Express Way
9. The Honeywell block of offices, Orphanage Road
10. The Birmingham General Hospital Extension

When Cardinal Conway – whom I have known since his earliest days in the priesthood – came to Birmingham, he accompanied me to two of these sites. I knew beforehand that he intended to come along, and I warned the men on the sites to be prepared:

"The Cardinal is coming to see you!" They thought I was joking – they could not see any Cardinal coming to visit them – among the grey mud, the trenches and holes, the heaps of sand and bricks, the bulldozers, cranes, the mortar, mixers, and the narrow slippery planks, which were the only paths through the noisy chaos.

He came. I gathered the men. On each site, the Cardinal chatted with them for about twenty minutes. He conversed with them about their hours of work, their digs, the contact they had with their people at home.

"You earn good money," he said to one man. "Are you able to save any of it? What happens to it?"

"We would all like to know the answer to that one, Father," replied the man laughingly. "It seems to slip away and vanish!"

All the men addressed the Cardinal as "Father" – which after all is a much more important and meaningful title than "Your Eminence"!

By far the biggest site on my current visiting list is the Gravelly Hill Interchange on the M6 motorway: a £12 million scheme. More than 4000 men will have worked on this site before the scheme is completed. By then, most of them will have met me. I have visited the site from the first week it was opened, going twice a week to two canteens at different sections on the site. I go round the tables standing or sitting here and there, chatting with the men and getting to know them better and better. And there is always tea – in a mug lent by one of the lads! Usually it is strong tea, well loaded with sugar. And though at times I have disliked the very thought of drinking so much tea, I have emptied the mug!

I have been asked by confreres if I get results; if the men respond. My answer is this: I judge by the atmosphere my visits create. After three or four visits, you can sense the change! You can see a welcome in the men's eyes when you walk into the canteen. You can see this welcome too, in the way they make room for you at a table, or in the way they turn to you to settle some point under discussion. And if you are welcome in their midst, it means your influence as a priest is there.

These Irish lads know very well I am coming to see them not merely because I myself am Irish, but because they are Irish Catholics and I am an Irish priest. They are not slow to see that I am concerned about them and eager to help them in any way I can. Although I make no distinctions among the men – I sit down with black men, Welshmen, Scots and Englishmen – my main interest is, of course, in the Irish lads.

I stay around when the lunch half-hour is ended, so that men can speak to me privately for a moment if they wish to do so. A change of digs; a catechism or booklet to instruct a child for first Holy Communion; a Mass to be said for a deceased parent; guidance on proper procedure in arranging to be married: these are some of the points they bring up to me.

What I have done is this: I have gone to the men. I have not put up a Gospel Tent in a field, or opened the door of a church and then invited all and sundry to come in. No, I am there amongst them; they have me if they want me. And whether they do or not, my friendly, regular contact with them influences them even subconsciously.

In another few months the Gravelly Hill Scheme will be finished. Meanwhile, I am planning to continue my street apostolate, on an even wider scale. I talk to any Irish person – man, woman or child – I meet on the street. There are a number of elderly Irish people with whom I keep in regular contact. I sit on the public benches with them and discuss all kinds of subjects, from health to social benefits, to home, to Communism, to religion: everything that interests them.

In addition I plan to undertake house-to-house visits in Cecil Road and Minstead Road, because these streets have many lodging houses where Irish boys and girls are living in rooms. Fr Ryan the parish priest backs me up in this plan.

As I see it, all this work is in line with what Christ our Lord did. He walked here and there, speaking to the people along the roads, in the fields, along the seashore. He dined with tax-gatherers and sinners. He made himself known to them, he won their friendship and was able to advise and teach them how to live the life of a true Christian. That is what I aim for! Here in the jungle of Birmingham's streets to meet people, to establish with them a personal relationship and to try to help them through life's problems and to get nearer to God.

It might be a man I meet in the street, or on a bus. It might be a couple of men, repairing a gas or water main in the road. It might be a bus conductor, or an Irish lad in an ice-cream van. All these are the focus of my work. I normally do not scold or preach formally to any of them. No, that is not my way! I gain their friendship first, and then we talk over things together.

## Visiting Birmingham Hotels

Monsignor Leonard, Vicar General of Birmingham Archdiocese, sent for me one day early in January 1973. He asked me to take on the work of attending to the spiritual needs of Irish folk working in the hotels of the city. The priest who had been doing this work was returning to Ireland. Monsignor advised me to consult him, and I did so. This priest had some notes on the work, written by his predecessor. These were presented to me and gave me some help. The priest also advised me against taking on the work at all, because it was so difficult. I had said I would undertake it, however, and I was not intending to go back on my word.

It took some nerve to face management and staff in the high-class hotels of Birmingham. It was all new work to me. Moreover, mentally, my Redemptorist background had conditioned me against, rather than for, hotel visitation.

By this time, I am well-entrenched: I know the staff, the management and the layout of each hotel; I have no difficulty in going through every department. And I agree with the Vicar General that this work is worthwhile and very necessary. In the Decree, "Christus Dominus", issued by Vatican II, we read (Section 18):

> "Special concern should be shown for those among the faithful, who, on account of their way or their condition of life, cannot sufficiently make use of the common and ordinary pastoral services of parish priests, or are quite cut off from them. Among this group are very many migrants, exiles and refugees, seamen, aeroplane personnel, gypsies, and others of this kind."

A large section of the workers in the hotels are immigrants. Some are from Ireland; some from continental countries. It is not easy at times for such people, who live in hotels, to keep up the practice of their faith. I am Chaplain to fourteen hotels in the city – these are the larger ones. In the suburbs of the city, there are up to fifty small hotels. I have concentrated on those situated in the city centre or near it. One of the principal hotels in Birmingham has the following notice in each bedroom:

> "Chaplain-on-call: A clergyman is available at any time to our guests who have a spiritual need. He has both experience and training in counselling, and is acquainted with clergymen of other faiths and with sources of help when referral [sic] is needed. Our chaplain-on-call is —. [Here is given the chaplain's name and phone number]."

My efforts have been focused, not on the guests, but on the staff. When I began the work, I secured a formal letter of appointment from the Archbishop's house. This was intended to establish my credentials, if need be, for any hotel manager who might ask for them. As things turned out, I had to produce this letter on only a few occasions.

First of all, I drew up a list of all the hotels in the city. I then consulted a map and found out their locations. Next I tramped the streets to assess my field of operations, and to discover any short routes from one hotel to the other. I then selected one of the hotels and wrote to or phoned the manager, telling him who I was and asking for an interview. I said I had an important matter to discuss with him, and would explain it in a personal interview. I tried to avoid any further explanations. By meeting the manager face-to-face, I judged I stood a better chance of gaining his approval and cooperation. A manager harassed by some vexatious problems in his hotel, as often happens, might easily give a phone caller a quick brush-off. I wanted to minimise that risk.

In some hotels the manager himself came down to see me; others sent one of their assistant managers. In these interviews, I explained that the purpose of my proposed work would be to pay occasional visits to the hotel to help the staff. There would be no question of my interfering in the work of the staff or the internal affairs of the hotel. In all the hotels – with one exception – I secured the full permission of the management to begin my work. The one exception was a hotel owned and staffed by Jehovah's Witnesses: they soon made it clear they did not want me near the place.

Having secured the hotel manager's permission, I asked him, or one of his assistants, to introduce me to some of the key personnel. In a modern hotel, these will include: Manager; Assistant Managers – the number varies according to the size of the hotel; Restaurant Manager; Head Chef; Security Guards; Head Receptionist; Head Porter; Housekeeper; Housekeeper's assistants – again the number varies according to the size of the hotel. I usually asked the manager to introduce me to the head receptionist, the head porter, and the housekeeper. Through these, I knew I could meet all the others.

In any hotel, the housekeeper is an important person. She controls a department which is perhaps the largest in the hotel. It is advisable to explain your work to her, and it is essential to gain her goodwill and cooperation. My experience is that she can help the chaplain in ever so many ways, viz, informing him of new recruits to or departures from the staff, or letting him know who is in need of help and advice. From the beginning I made it clear to every housekeeper that I would neither hinder nor delay the staff in their work – because I knew she would think that this might happen.

I always asked her about Irish boys and girls working in the hotel. I asked her to let me meet some of them at once – if she told me what floor they worked on, I went alone and met them. I told them who I was, and what my work would be. I asked them to tell the other Catholics that I hoped to meet them all very soon.

In my first visits to any hotel, I tried to take note of the layout of the building, eg, the various floors on which were situated the laundry, linen room, restaurant, bar, kitchen and staff canteen. Some managers or housekeepers wanted me to meet their staff at tea break in the canteen. As a fixed rule, I never agreed to this. If a boy or girl has a personal problem, they are certainly not going to air it in the canteen in front of all the others. But I had to go along with it in the beginning; I never made an issue of it. I knew that I would sooner or later be able to speak to each one alone at their work.

On my visits I always carry a loose-leaf notebook into which I enter names and useful items of information. I dislike taking notes in front of staff, so I usually make these notes when alone on my way from one department to another. In making a note about an Irish boy or girl, I usually add the name of their hometown or parish in Ireland. Why? Because from my work on the missions in Ireland, I know most parts of the country fairly well, and so by such a note, I have always at hand a topic acceptable to any immigrant: I become for them a link with home. I use a loose-leaf notebook because hotel staff are frequently changing, and I have to keep my notebook up-to-date. There is no other solution to this problem. It pays me to take the necessary notes. A glance at my notebook will refresh my memory before I go to the various departments; I can foresee what problems lie ahead.

Little by little I learned my work. Progress was slow at first. I discovered that it is useless to visit a hotel on Saturdays, Sundays, and Mondays, because so many of the staff are not available. I found out the best times for visiting each of the hotels: in some, it was from 10.00 am to 12 noon; in others, it is from 2.00 pm to 3.30 pm. I worked out a method for my visits. By grouping the hotels according to their proximity to one another, I can visit two or three in a morning. If I leave the Abbey at 9.45 am, I can have finished my visits by 12.30 pm.

In each hotel, I greet the reception staff and any hall porters who may be around on my arrival. I then take the lift to the top floor, see the chambermaids working there, and make my way down from floor to floor. Each girl has a trolley which carries all the supplies needed for fixing up a room – soap, towels, bed linen, etc. Usually this trolley will be near the room in which the girl is working. Also, the sound of a vacuum cleaner, or a master key in a door, are signs a girl is working there. From each girl I find out who is on the same floor with her, and if there are any new Catholic workers. On my way down from floor to floor, I normally meet maintenance men and women cleaners who look after the banquet, or function rooms, and so on. I also visit the kitchen. There I will meet the head chef, his assistants (the commis chefs), and the kitchen porters. I try to have a brief word with each of them. If they happen to be very busy, or if there is a row or a group meeting in progress, I leave them alone. I know I will be back again, when things are calmer, and I can speak to them.

What do I say to the workers in the hotels? I talk about their health, work, or problems. If speaking to a Catholic I will also, when necessary, remind them about Masses in the local church, holy days of obligation, and any Catholic function or dance in which they might be interested. Often the chat and its length varies according to circumstances. In reality, the chat is secondary: the important fact is that you, a priest, are available to them if they need your help.

Having visited the kitchen, I call to see the staff in the restaurant, the canteen, the laundry, and the linen room. Then comes the housekeeper's office: I never omit to call with her. If she is not in the office, I get one of the staff to 'bleep' her on the intercom. If she is very busy, I will go to where she is working. She often shares new problems or helps me to solve them. I am mainly concerned with Catholics, but I speak to all: non-Catholics and people of all denominations are treated in the same way. Some of these need encouragement and advice more than the Catholics do, and they are always very grateful for any solicitude you show them.

What about foreign workers in the hotels? There are Spaniards, Italians, French, Portuguese, and Greek and Turkish Cypriots. The French I have learned at school; the bit of Spanish I spoke in the Philippines; the smattering of German which was so useful to me during the war – all these have come in very useful in my work in the hotels. The foreign newcomers pose the main problem in this regard – those who have been some time in England can speak some English. If I am really stuck, I will get one of the 'veterans' among the foreigners to help me.

I visit the hotels regularly. In the beginning I tried to visit them all once a week. Now that I am established in each, I visit them once a fortnight. There are some smaller hotels, which I visit once a month. I try not to let any hotel go unvisited for a lengthy period. Regular visiting is the key to success in this work. I rarely take a meal in a hotel, but if I do, I will pay for it. I try to avoid playing the role of a guest. On only one occasion have I been thwarted! A manager saw me seated for lunch one day, and said to the waitress, "Father's lunch is on the house!" I demurred; he insisted; I eventually submitted. I do not argue with managers! My protest was genuine – I have a dread of even seeming to sponge. The staffs laugh at my fears! Without consulting me, they will place a cup of coffee or tea before me. It is already made, so I cannot refuse it – but my constant endeavour is to make the staff's hospitality end there.

Sometimes the housekeeper or the head porter will offer me unclaimed articles of clothing left behind by guests, with the request that these be given to the poor. I always accept these, but I always arrange to have them collected by an Irish Sister of Charity who is in touch with needy families here in Birmingham.

The basic principle of hotel work is making contact with the staff. The hotel chaplain is involved in the lives of scores of people – to them, he is not a stranger: he is with them, a friend, a brother.

From my work in the hotels I have learned a lot. I have learned, for example, that hotel staff live in a little world of their own. I suppose this holds good for every group of human beings, who are united in a common task. The running of a hotel means close teamwork, day after day, week after week. The many demands made on the staff cannot be met, unless all parties work together. In this sense, the members come into closer association with one another than do people in factories and offices.

A salient feature or element in their lives can be summed up in one word: uncertainty. Their hours of work are so often irregular and unpredictable. Arrangements are upset; mistakes are made about rooms to be prepared, or meals to be cooked, or supplies to be ordered. Chefs fall sick; supplies do not arrive in time; waitresses are ill with colds or influenza; chambermaids do not report for work – everyday something is sure to go awry. One individual, whose spell of duty is ended, may be asked to stay on and do the jobs someone else should have done. A row ensues and then there is talk that he has been sacked. These upsets occur regularly. When they do happen, the word goes around very quickly. Whatever happens in a hotel is soon known by all the staff!

To the chaplain, this fact turns out to be an asset. If in a visit he does not manage to see some of the staff, those he does meet will tell the others about his visit. They will go over it all, repeating his messages and any bits of news he had. They may repeat some of his remarks, perhaps, and comment on them. And so the talk will go on – among the cooks, the chambermaids, porters, waiters, and waitresses. Hotel staff will of course also discuss their guests, but they tend to do so in a detached impersonal way. But anyone who, like the chaplain, is part of their own little cosmos, is discussed in a distinctly personal manner: he is one of their number.

The staff in a hotel form a big family. This is true, even when strict rules seem designed to keep them apart. Chambermaids, cleaners and others are usually forbidden to enter certain departments, such as the kitchen, the bar, the restaurant. However, they all meet in the staff canteen. At meal times they will have a really good chat, and hear all the news. Birthdays are remembered; presents are bestowed. Arrangements are made to visit any who are ill; "Get Well Soon" cards and flowers are sent to them. Such is the hotel life which guests never see.

The chaplain helps the staff. He can advise about family problems; he can help boys or girls preparing to get married; he can arrange instructions for potential converts; he can inform Catholics from other countries where they can go to Mass, and where they can go to Confession in their own language; he can clear up misunderstandings between members of staff. Most of all, he can influence them by his sincere concern for their welfare. His sympathy, his empathy gradually produce a remarkable effect on all. A point is reached when the staff look forward to the chaplain's visits.

The work of the hotel chaplain demands self-sacrifice and energy. You have to forget yourself and think of the interests of all these workers. But the chaplain, as Vatican II reminds us, is not alone: God works with him and through him. The words of St Paul clarify this so well:

"Let us give thanks to the God and Father of our Lord Jesus Christ, the merciful Father, the God from whom all help comes. He helps us in all our troubles, so that we are able to help those who have all kinds of troubles, using the same help that we ourselves have received from God."

# CHAPTER THIRTEEN
# Epilogue

IT WAS GRATIFYING that Fr Dan was able to continue his chaplaincy work right up to his death on 24 May 1977. V Rev Gabriel Maguire who lived in the room opposite Dan in Erdington Abbey, Birmingham, recalls: "I was there when he got his first heart attack and overruled his wishes and got him into hospital. Sadly the second attack wasn't as kind."

It was Dan's wish to be buried in Milltown cemetery, close to the people he had served for so many years. He was very proud of his Ulster heritage and ancestry, and his ecumenical work in the troubled city, so it is only proper that Belfast remains always his home.

His large funeral took place in Clonard on 28 May 1977 and the Eulogy (following) was given by his cousin, Fr Robert Quinn C.Ss.R. The Redemptorists had established a large burial plot for the Order in Milltown Cemetery and Fr Dan was the first to be there interred.

### Homily on Fr Dan Munchin Cummings, C.Ss.R.

Father Dan Cummings has come home to rest from his labours. He has returned to Clonard, so dear to his heart; and to his native Belfast, which he loved so well.

As I stand here, I look around this beautiful, inspiring church and see so many silent witnesses to the things he prized and valued in life. Clonard Church of the Most Holy Redeemer, situated so near to his parents' home on the Springfield Road, drew him to the Congregation of the Most Holy Redeemer. Within its ranks he found and carried out, for more than fifty years, his vocation as a Redemptorist.

The picture and shrine of Our Mother of Perpetual Succour, here beside me, became his guiding star through life, so much so that he wrote and published two booklets in her honour, in an effort to share his devotion to her with others, that they might join with him in praising this good Mother. He was untiring in his zeal to promote Our Lady's Confraternity when he was its Director.

That altar before which he prayed and where he so often offered up Holy Mass was the wellspring of his devotion to Our Blessed Lord.

Over there is the pulpit from which he often spoke to Our Lady's Confraternity, with such winning simplicity of language and clarity of thought that won the hearts of those who heard him speak.

Fr Dan was a man for all seasons. He endured the tension and heat of work done on the foreign missions, in the Philippines, until he had to retire because of failing health. Nevertheless, he was courageous enough to serve as a military chaplain to the Irish Guards on Normandy's beaches during World War Two.

He returned from that war neither soured nor embittered by the cruelty and brutality of men at war – rather, he was more enthused with the love of Christ to work for the uplift of his fellow man.

That zeal for souls inspired him to initiate the Clonard mission for all Christians, even those not of our persuasion, because of his deep, genuine love for the people of the North; and to his credit, be it said, in doing so, he did not arouse animosities or open old wounds of strife. He was too good a workman for the Lord, to go around dropping bricks!

His love for his people brought him to Birmingham, where during the last eleven years of his life, he helped our emigrants to settle down and work in new surroundings.

When I visited him, last April, during his final illness, I was so impressed by the number of people who wanted to see him in hospital that I asked for an explanation. He told me with absolute candour and simplicity, "If ever I could do a good turn for anybody, I always tried to do it!" In other words, he has expressed his own epitaph.

We can do him a good turn by remembering him in our prayers, Masses and Holy Communions.

His last request, at death, was quite consistent with his life. He wished to be buried in the Redemptorist plot, at Milltown cemetery, so that he could be ever close to the people; he wished to be buried in a public place, where people passing by his grave can bestow on him the benediction of a prayer.

It is right and fitting, at this funeral Mass, that we thank and praise God from whom all blessings flow. We are reminded in this Mass that death for His faithful people means that "life is changed, but not ended". Yes! Life for Fr Dan has changed, and changed for the better.

If we have tears, let them be for ourselves who are left behind, not for the departed. Like Christ, who died on the cross, Father Dan has said, "Father, into Thy hands I commend my spirit".

After the burial of Jesus, the holy women went looking for Jesus in the tomb. They were looking for Him in the wrong place: for He had risen to a new life.

Unlike us, who have not yet completed our earthly pilgrimage, Father Dan is now gazing upon the bounty of the Lord, in the land of the living.

May Our Mother of Perpetual Succour comfort, help and sustain us all. May the soul of Father Dan Cummings rest in peace. Amen.

**Fr Robert M Quinn C.Ss.R.**
**28 May 1977**

# Name Anomalies

## Comings changed to Cummings (Ed.)

I HAVE DISCOVERED that Dan's father, Robert Cummings was in fact born Robert Comings. Robert's father was James Comings and his mother was Mollie McClarnon – not McLarnon as Dan had thought. The name McClarnon has been corrected in the text.

Why and when the spelling of Comings was changed is unknown. Citation is: "Ireland Births and Baptisms, 1620-1881" database, FamilySearch, Robert Comings, 19 Dec 1868; citing Antrim, Ireland, reference v1-1 p356; FHL microfilm 101,180. (https://familysearch.org/pal:/MM9.1.1/FPD7-TG9 : accessed 6 July 2015)

## Nicholas Maginn: Informer

In *As I Roved Out*, Cathal O'Byrne refers to an informer named "Nicholas Mageean", who betrayed his comrades in the United Irishmen.

In *Revolt in the North* (Clonmore and Reynolds, 1960) Charles Dickson speaks of Nicholas Mageean (Magin) as:

> "…a young Catholic farmer, born and bred in the townland of Lessans, two miles from Saintfield on the old road to Belfast, a member of the Provincial Committee, a Colonel in the United Irishmen's army, who reported all to Reverend Clelland, Chaplain and agent to the Earl of Londonderry. Clelland reported all to Price of Saintfield, Price to Castlereagh. Mageean bought a farm at Greenhill near Banbridge for £1500, became a drunkard, went to prison for debt, and died in gaol."

In *A Collection of Documents relating to 1798*, published by Her Majesty's Stationery Office, Belfast, a report of a limited Irishmen's meeting is given in the informer's own handwriting – in this document, he spells his name "Maginn". This is also the spelling James Hope gives in his autobiography. The informer, therefore, was Nicholas Maginn, not Mageean.

# APPENDIX 2
# Mother's Sayings

MAY I HERE quote some of the quaint words and phrases I heard my mother use:

"He will sup sorrow with a spoon of grief."

"A hand's turn" – a job, a work, a task, as in: "He has not done a hand's turn since morning".

"hap" – means to wrap up in bedclothes, eg: "Hap that child!" Or, "Hap that child's back!" It is a Scots word.

"I could not hear my ears!" ie, I could hear nothing. This is said when some noise eclipses all other sounds.

"He was as fidgety and jumpy as a hen on a hot griddle."

"lerked" – meaning wrinkled.

"A month of Sundays" ie, a very long time.

"You should never lift your hand to a woman".

"We had words" – ie, we had a verbal row.

"By no manner of means" – ie, never; not at all.

"You are better wanting that" – ie, better to be without it. This is a Scots phrase.

"Mind me to buy some bread" – ie, remind me to…

"I mind the time…" – ie, I remember…

"It was teeming" ie, raining heavily. This is a very interesting word: it is an old Norse word meaning "to flow copiously".

"I missed my foot" – ie, I stumbled.

"Mocking is catching" – said to one who mimics you. (When I deliberately used some of her own phrases to tease her, Mother used to say to this to me.)

"You are a mouth!" – said to one who tells what should be kept secret.

"It is a newance to see you so early" –ie, a new experience

"Are you thinking long?" – ie, feeling homesickness or sorrow

"I rose and put on me" – ie, I got dressed.

"He is a right lad" – ie, a good, reliable lad.

"It was so dark, I could not see a stime before me" – "stime" is a Scots word, meaning a glimmer of light.

"You are to lie at the stock!" – ie the side of a bed furthest from the wall; the outside of a bed.

"You are a stranger!" said to a friend who has not visited you for some time

"That sweet gave me a stune in one of my teeth!" – a "stune" is a sting of pain.

"I wouldn't give a thraneen for it" – a "thraneen" is a small rush growing in damp ground.

"I am all my lone" – ie, I am alone

"All together, like Brown's cows…"

"She had an eye like a travellin' rat" – ie, she saw everything

"He is not at himself" – ie He is not well

"That finger is beeling" – ie, a suppurating sore

"The apple is bad – look at it – it is bose!" – ie, hollow

"The porridge are very salt today…" Mother always used "porridge" as a plural noun; so also, the word "broth". This is Scots usage.

"He checked me for going there" – ie, he chided me

"A fouter": a useless, awkward kind of person; someone clumsy at ordinary jobs.

"A chuckie" – ie, a hen

"All evening he sat there, clocking at the fire!" A Scots word, meaning "hatching".

"She is over there, fornenst the cottage." – ie, opposite to (another Scots word)

"You are all foundered" ie exhausted with rain and cold.

"It is gey hot today" – "gey" here means "considerably". Again, a Scots expression.

Some of Mother's comparisons included: "As clean as a new pin", "As dry as a bone", "as crooked as a ram's horn" and "as sure as a gun".

And now, that word, "trinket". In his Glossary of Words used in County Down and County Antrim, Patterson gives it this meaning: "a small, artificial watercourse made across a field". He does not derive it for us, but he proves that Mother was right – it is a County Down word and it has the meaning she gave it.

# APPENDIX 3
# The Churn

In his *Glossary of Words Used in County Down and County Antrim* (1880), Wm Hugh Patterson says:

> "Granny: The granny is a small sheaf composed of the last remaining, growing stalks of corn on a farm at harvest. The stalks are plaited together, and are cut down by the reapers, throwing their reaping hooks at it from a distance. It is then carried home in triumph, and the person who has cut it down puts it round the neck of the oldest woman of the farmer's family. It is sometimes hung up against the chimney brace, where it remains till next harvest, when it gives place to a new "granny". It is also called "the churn" and "the hare"."

"Granny" here is surely a corrupted form of the Irish word, "grainne", meaning, "a grain of corn".

I have searched books to discover the derivation of the word "churn" in this context, but all in vain. However, in a Lancashire Glossary here in the Abbey library, I find it mentioned as follows: "'The Churn': the Churn-supper is an evening feast to celebrate the hay harvest" (*A Glossary of the Lancashire Dialect*, John H Nodal and George Milner, 1875). So it must be a 'planter's' word – brought over to Ireland by English planters.

～

Since writing these last few paragraphs above, I have found out more about the word, "churn". The word is very ancient – but in a different form. "Churn" is a corrupted form of the Old English word, "cyrnan", and Middle English, "kerne", meaning "corn". The *Encyclopaedia Britannica*, in its article on "Harvest", has the following entry:

> "Harvest has been a season of rejoicing from the remotest ages. Throughout the world, harvest has always been the occasion for many queer customs, which all have their origin in the animistic belief in the Corn-Spirit or Corn-Mother. This personification of the crops has left its impression upon the harvest customs of modern Europe.

In Northumberland, where the harvest rejoicing takes place at the close of the reaping and not at the in-gathering, as soon as the last sheaf is set on end, the reapers shout that they have got the "kern". An image formed of a wheatsheaf, and dressed in a white frock and coloured ribbons, is hoisted on a pole. This is the "kern-baby", or harvest-queen, and it is carried back in triumph with music and shouting, and set up in a prominent place during the harvest supper. Throughout the world, the semi-worship of the last sheaf is, or has been, the great feature of the harvest home."

The term "kern-baby" was in the course of time shortened to the "kern". Northern Ireland farmers soon transformed this into the "churn".

All the foregoing led me to another interesting point. The painting of a village or farm banquet by Pieter Brueghel is not a wedding banquet, despite the fact that art authorities have asserted that it is a marriage festivity. Against this opinion is the fact that, while the bride is at the central seat of honour at the table, there is no bridegroom to be seen anywhere! This was a puzzle the art authorities could not solve.

The picture itself is in the Kunsthistorisches Museum, Vienna. I wrote to the Director, saying there is no bridegroom in the painting, because it is not a marriage feast. It depicts a harvest festival. If you look at the wall you can see, most prominently displayed, the kern: the girl in the place of honour at the table is the Kern-Mother or Harvest Queen.

# Epitaph: Dr Richard Marner

Dr MARNER IS buried in a cemetery adjoining Massforth Church, Kilkeel. His grave is left of the church. It is a raised tomb with a thick slate slab, bearing the following inscription:

"Hic jacet in sperm resurrectionis beatae Rev Richardus Marner DD, PP, VF. Natus apud Kilmore anno 1834 sacerdos factus est 1857. Post elevationem ad statum sacerdotalem munere praesidis collegii Sti Malachiae apud Belfast per multos annos felici exitu functus est. Vices parochi apud Dunsford sibi commissa est 1876 et diligenter administravit. Ab anno 1885 usque ad obitum paroechiae de Mourne Superiore praefuit. Lelo divini cultus incensus ecclesias complevit et ornavit, scholas erexit animarum saluti maxime studiosus verbum Dei indefesse praedicavit. Obiit 14[th.] March 1906. Requiescat in pace."

(Here lies, in the hope of a blessed resurrection, Rev Richard Marner DD, PP, VF. Born at Kilmore, 1834. Ordained priest 1857. After becoming a priest he was for many years President of St Malachy's College with happy outcome. Being made Parish Priest of Dunsford, he diligently administered it. From the year 1885 till his death he was in charge of the parish of Upper Mourne. On fire with zeal for divine worship, he completed and embellished churches, built schools, and most eager for the salvation of souls, he unwearingly preached the word of God. He died 14[th.] March 1906 [at the age of 72]. May he rest in peace.)

My information is that Dr Marner wrote his own epitaph.

# Dr Mageean's Obituary

Dr Mageean (Fr Daniel Cummings' uncle) died 17 January 1962. This obituary is taken from the *Irish Independent* at the time. It is credited as cited.

### Passing of Dr Mageean
### People mourn loss of great Churchman
(*Irish Independent Reporter*)

The Diocese of Down and Connor is in mourning for Most Rev Dr Mageean, the Bishop who never spared himself in his 32 years' reign over his flock of more than 200,000, often beset as he was by problems and difficulties that would have daunted a more robust man, but always reacting vigorously and sensibly to the task in hand. His Lordship had visited Braid parish in County Antrim on Wednesday and became ill on his return to Belfast. He died on Wednesday night. Dr Mageean was Bishop of Down and Connor since 1929, succeeding Most Rev Dr MacRory.

In March, 1960, he was given the high honour of being made an Assistant to the Pontifical Throne by His Holiness Pope John XXIII.

The period of his Episcopate was one of great trial, but whether it was anti-Catholic riots or the death and destruction wrought by the German air raids in the Catholic parishes of Belfast, the slight, serious-minded man with the sudden flash of humour was there to comfort and succour, and if needs be, speak out fearlessly on behalf of his people.

### Defence of His People
He compelled the respect of even the most bigoted partisans because of his ceaseless fight for the rights of northern Catholics to lead their own lives without interference by the State in realms of education, and latterly, in the controversial sphere of health and medicine.

Unionists predicted that the voluntary Mater Hospital, Belfast, would be forced to close its doors once it was starved of State assistance. Some feared that the prediction would prove only too true, but Dr Mageean never wavered in his determination, and for fifteen years kept the institution going in face of great odds.

### His Great Energy
Priests much younger than Dr Mageean, who was the oldest churchman in the diocese when he died at the age of 89 years, marvelled at his energy. Ten years ago he suffered a heart attack from which it was thought he would never recover, but with characteristic resilience he reappeared, refusing the assistance of an Auxiliary Bishop, and instead of reducing his activities, seemed to have acquired new energy.

Newspapermen who followed his many activities were astounded at the number of engagements at which he appeared all over his diocese, extending from the Mourne Mountains to the shores of North Antrim, opening new Primary and Intermediate schools, new churches, renovated churches, parish halls. Rarely did he refuse an invitation to speak at Catholic gatherings, often numerous, and what he had to say was generally very much to the point.

### Official Tributes
Ministry of Education officials recently paid warm tributes to his work for education in his area and said that his record of school building was unsurpassed anywhere in the country. It is a paradox that this mild, dignified man will be remembered as the fighting Bishop from the North and now that he has gone, the Diocese of Down and Connor has lost a great figure, whose memory is enshrined in stone in the churches and schools he has built and in the new parishes increasing and growing in and around the Northern capital.

### Distinguished Career
Born at Lisowen, near Saintfield, County Down in 1882, Most Rev Dr Mageean was a son of the late Mr Daniel Mageean and the late Mrs Mageean, whose brother, the late Very Rev Dr Marner, was pastor of Kilkeel, and at one time President of St Malachy's College, Belfast. His father was a brother of Rev Charles Mageean who, after his ordination was sent as curate to Duneane, but died at an early age.

Most Rev Dr Mageean attended the national school at Doran's Rock, and from which he went to the parochial school at Saintfield. He entered St Malachy's College at the age of thirteen. After spending some years there, Dr Mageean graduated in the old Royal University, obtaining a BA in Philosophy, and immediately afterwards entered St Patrick's College, Maynooth, to take up his theological studies. Here he quickly distinguished himself, and at the end of his course obtained the Degrees of Bachelor of Divinity and Bachelor of Canon Law. During his period at Maynooth, Most Rev Dr Mannix, Archbishop of Melbourne, was President.

After his ordination in 1906, he entered on a postgraduate course in the Dunboyne Establishment, where he studied under the late Dr Walter McDonald.

### College Professor

For some time after his ordination, Father Mageean was curate of Glenavy, County Antrim, but he was soon recalled to St Malachy's College as Professor of English. While in this position he took an active part in the Irish language movement. He was a keen student in Colaiste Comghaill and soon became a fluent speaker. On several occasions he preached in Irish on St Patrick's Day. He spent most of his summer holidays in the Cloughaneely district of Donegal.

He remained in St Malachy's College until 1919 when he was appointed Dean of Maynooth College. Here his deep sympathy, kindness, and his charming personality won him a large circle of friends. For many years, Dr Mageean was editor of the *Irish Catholic Directory* and of the Ordo. He was also a regular contributor to the *Irish Ecclesiastical Record*.

### Appointed Bishop

Father Mageean was appointed Bishop of Down and Connor in 1929 in succession to Most Rev Dr MacRory on the latter's appointment as Archbishop of Armagh and Primate of All Ireland.

During his reign Most Rev Dr Mageean was an outspoken and fearless champion of the rights of Northern Catholics, on whose behalf he made many forceful and eloquent pronouncements in Pastorals and on public platforms.

He spoke vigorously at all times against the injustices suffered by the Northern minority. Frequently he attacked the Northern Government for its partisanship in the matter of grants for the Catholic voluntary schools.

During the 1935 riots in Belfast, he sent an influential deputation of priests and laymen to Westminster to interview MPs of all parties and to demand a public inquiry into the origin of the attacks on Catholic homes and property in the dock area – a demand which was turned down by the then Prime Minister, Mr Baldwin, on the usual ground that the question of law and order in Belfast was a matter for the Northern Government only.

During the late war the Bishop was forthright in his condemnation of the nocturnal police raids and searches of Nationalist homes in Belfast and interments without trial.

The 1948 Health Act, which enabled the Government to take control of the hospitals, found the Bishop waging a lone battle defending the position of the Mater Hospital, Belfast – the only Catholic voluntary hospital in the Six Counties – which, refusing Government demands, was denied financial aid or even payment for the services it renders to the sick and maimed irrespective of creed.

By his inspiration the hospital has since been enabled to collect sufficient funds to carry on without Government assistance, maintaining its freedom from State control.

Devoted to the cause of Blessed Oliver Plunkett, Dr Mageean personally led a number of pilgrimages from Belfast to Drogheda. He also travelled with Down and Connor pilgrimages to Lourdes on a number of occasions.

### The Obsequies

The remains will be removed at 7 o'clock this evening to St Peter's Pro-Cathedral in the heart of West Belfast, where they will lie in state until the Solemn Requiem Mass at noon on Monday. Cardinal D'Alton will preside.

The funeral will take place to Milltown Cemetery, Belfast. Dr Mageean is the first Bishop to be interred there since Most Rev Dr Tohill, who died in July 1914.

# APPENDIX 6
# The Troubles

THE IRISH HAVE names for their rebellions, viz:

"The Troubles" – the Rebellion of 1641. This name was also given to the fighting in Belfast 1920–22.

"The Hurry" or "The Hurries" or "The Turn Out" – the Rebellion of 1798

And of course, "the Troubles" has been again used in 1968 and thereafter.

# Bullying is the Orange Aim
### (from *The Belfast Telegraph*, c1972)

THE ORANGE ORDER has come under a scathing attack from a former Church of Ireland Bishop of Clogher, Dr Richard Hanson. Writing in *Community Forum*, a Community Relations publication, Dr Hanson describes Orange parades as, "an aggressive and provocative show of Protestant strength and a warning to the Catholic to lie low". "They are correspondingly feared by Catholics. No-one who has heard the frightening sound of an Orange drum with its deliberate undercurrent of intimidation could doubt what it means," he adds.

Dr Hanson, who is now Professor of Theology at Manchester University, says: "One of the moulding forces of the social and political climate in Northern Ireland is Protestantism, and bullying has always been part of the tradition of Ulster Protestantism.

"From about the middle of the last century the Anglicans and Presbyterians have joined forces to bully the Catholics. This, as anybody who cares to use their eyes can discover, is the main purpose of those grotesque and quaint parades and processions in which the various Orange and Black Orders indulge to such a vast extent during the summer in Northern Ireland.

"To the English viewer these occasions may appear merely comic, an antiquated march of boot-faced men in bowler hats and Sunday suits, beneath banners carrying references to utterly obsolete religious disputes."

Dr Hanson criticises Catholic attitudes: "Politically and socially the policy of the Catholics has until recently been one of non-co-operation with Protestants and their extremist fringes have never abandoned the policy of political murder when they thought that it would pay.

"In their schools they have tended to combine very old-fashioned religious teaching redolent of the days before Vatican II, with an unrelenting inculcation of hatred for England and all things English."

And he says the claim of Unionist politicians, that all they want to do is to preserve the British way of life in Ulster, is "nonsense": "Ulster never has had the British way of life and accepts it only reluctantly and under pressure." he says.

# APPENDIX 8

# Some of Fr Dan's War Letters

IN THE SECOND World War seven Redemptorists from the north of Ireland volunteered to serve as military chaplains in the British Army. As well as Fr Dan Cummings were Frs Joe Connolly, Luke Hartigan, Peter Mulrooney, Joe Murphy, Jim Scott and Joe Tronson. Their lifestyle was to include keeping a strict Mass account and to inform the Provincial, Fr Kerr, of every occasion when alcoholic spirits were consumed. They were to keep contact with each other and other Redemptorist communities where possible. They were also to preserve regular spiritual exercises, in keeping with circumstances.

Dan Cummings' great uncle, Dr Richard Marner (1832 1905) was the first President of St Malachy's College and Dan's uncle, Dr Daniel Mageean was Bishop of Down and Connor. Other family members who were Redemptorists include his uncle, Fr Robert Mageean (brother of the Bishop) who was a missionary in Australia, Fr Joe Morgan (India), Fr Robert Quinn, Brother Malachy Morgan and Richard McCall who died as a student in Esker. Dan's letters below provide a flavour of a perhaps forgotten part of the Redemptorist contribution not just in World War II but also in the Great War of 1914-1918.

~

Sunday, 7 August 1944

Dear Father Provincial,

I am waiting to say Mass in an adjacent field and I am going to write to you until the moment comes when I have to shuffle off.

Since we arrived in France, our routine has been: arrival in a section of the line; digging of deep slit-trenches; the Germans observe our arrival and the air becomes noisy with the whine of shells and the explosion of Nebelwerfers; a shout for stretcher-bearers and my speedy crossing of a field or two to the ruined house or barn, where a busy doctor is injecting morphine into a writhing, groaning shape covered with blood that a few minutes earlier was a man. In one place, we had this continually for over a week, and frankly, it was as much as a human being could stand. I used to sleep on the church floor beneath heavy blocks of stone, poised to fall at any moment. Each shell or mortar that fell made me open one eye to watch the stones above my head. I became so fatigued and so indifferent that I used to fall asleep, saying: "If that broken wall falls on me, I won't worry nor will I know what hit me." Wounded came in all during the night and the doctors wakened me if any of them were Catholics. Continuous sleep was impossible.

One Catholic lad had several wounds – all seemingly superficial, but somehow he kept sinking despite plasma transfusions. I gave him the last sacraments. The doctors were puzzled. Then they examined a small wound at the base of the nose, between the eyes. There was an open hole where a fragment had ploughed through his head. I buried him under shell fire in the corner of a wheat field, along one of the dusty roads of Normandy.

The cream of the German army faces us here in the west. I have met and talked to quite a number of the SS, who are the cementing force of the Wehrmacht. They are young – 17, 18, 19 years, long-haired and amoral. We meet their work in the ruins of a house or a church or along deep country lanes. "Les SS sont des sauvages, pas humaines, très mechant, des animaux, vicieux." (The SS are savages, they are not human, they are evil, animals, vicious). These are the French phrases I hear so very often.

One SS man came in wounded. I was standing beside his stretcher, helping the doctor to cut away the blood-stained sleeves of his tunic. I felt something knock against my side. I found a fully-primed grenade in his pocket. It was not there by chance, for he had no other arms or ammunition, nor had he any documents.

I asked another, had he been to Russia – "Jawohl!" he replied. "But this fighting is far worse than anything we had to face in Russia." Another took a cup of tea and exclaimed, "This is the happiest day of my life, I am out of the German army!" "Why can't you stop the war?" I said to a German Catholic lad who was slightly wounded. "Befehle ist Befehle," he answered. ("An order is an order"). That is their outlook – militarily quite sound. They keep sniping, using machine guns until our men are up with them. Then "Kamerad, Kamerad" – I will say no more on this point.

The papers tell more than I can. I have seen Bayeux, Caen,

Bretteville, Balleroy, Caumont, Sept-Vents and Carpiquet. There are many places which are just heaps of rubble, which nauseate one with the smell of unburied dead. This is not a tooth-some kind of letter, but war is an image of Gehenna. God has been very good to me, on several occasions. I have had nice escapes. An ambulance beside my car was riddled with canon shells: an aircraft came skimming over the field at 30 feet, machine gunning all in its path. Had its track been a few yards to the left, I would not now be writing to you. Again, an H.E. landed four yards from my car – peppered that car cover, smashed into fragments my canvas washstand, tore open my mess-tins as if they were paper and, strange to say, the car is still in running order. Fortunately, I happened to be up with casualties and missed the packet. Want of sleep is the greatest burden. Fr Luke (Hartigan) was very good to me. He relieved me a couple of days ago so that I could get a decent sleep. We three keep seeing each other as much as possible. You can't imagine the relief it is to lie on the grass and talk about de Valera and the little items of news about the Province. Even a meeting with other priests has not the same ease and tranquillity.

The guns are starting up again. The noise shatters your ears and upsets your thoughts. At night the guns flicker unceasingly in the sky, just like the electric storms you see along Sumatra, trembling and twitching.

If we are spared to return, we shall all be the better for the experience. Living close to death is an experience which changes your mind irrevocably. No meditation, no purposeful thinking, no continued reflection brings that stark reality of death so closely to mind as does this kind of life we now live. The years will not be long enough for us to thank God for his mercies.

Pardon my writing in pencil. There is no ink. I thank you for all your letters. We know what happens out here – you are left anxious. But God is good – and if we come through safely, we will endeavour to repay him. I must go now. With kindest wishes to Fr Rector, Fr Minister, Fr Mageean and the community.

Your dev. serv. in JMJA
DM Cummings C.Ss.R.

12 August 1944

Dear Father Provincial,

I reported five Masses in my letter of 17 July. I feel sure I reported others said since then but alas, I have omitted to make a note of it. However, since 17 July I have said twenty-one Masses for your intention. If you have received a Mass report since my letter of July 17, you can deduct the number reported already. I am sorry about this slip-up, but this last while has been peculiarly harassing and trying. I also wish to report that I have taken spirits two or three times since my last fortnightly letter. Also on a few occasions I took some Calvados, which I am sure is spirits.

The days merge into one another, slowly and tediously. It seems years since our arrival in France. The various battles we have engaged in lengthened the hours. I now think that when the sun stood still in the heavens, the inspired author perhaps viewed the situation from the standpoint of the vanquished. The Germans are beaten – they checked us with small pockets of men strongly armed and fighting till death, but they are broken. The end is not far off. Fr Luke and Fr J Tronson agree with me.

It has been a great privilege to be allowed to help men to die. Some of those whom I have brought back to their faith have thanked me earnestly. And those who come in with shattered limbs and twisted bodies are already prepared. At times in England I felt on the borders of despair. But here it is another story. The General Communions are fully attended. Fr Luke (Hartigan) took over my work for a few days and I got a rest. I get anxious and upset, lest any wounded slip through my fingers – and so at night, I get the medical orderlies to waken me if a gravely wounded Catholic comes in.

I heard a number of German prisoners' confessions. Some were terribly wounded. They are starved-looking: one ate and drank endlessly: he said he had not eaten for three days. Their transport side must be in chaos. I asked him, did he think Germany was finished? "No!" he replied, emphatically, then he asked eagerly, "Is England finished?" So that is that. Kind wishes to all in Limerick. I hope to write soon to Fr Mageean. How I wish it were all over.

Yours ever in JMJA.
DM Cummings C.Ss.R.

26 December 1944

Dear Father Provincial,

In my letter of 3 December I reported twelve Masses: I now report since then fifteen Masses said for your intentions. I also wish to report that yesterday, Christmas Day, I took spirits once.

Yesterday morning, I started my three Masses at 7.30 am. The last one was a Missa Cantata. It was interesting to hear the old French Carols sung as they have been sung for centuries. Candle shortage means that one candle is lighted on the altar at the beginning of the Canon. For the whole of Mass, two tiny reddish electric bulbs glow on top of the imitation candlesticks. I admired the crib, which is composed of screwable sections and erected in fifteen minutes. Belgians focus attention on the crib and not on the rocks, snow, distant hill-scenes, stars, etc.

Wounded men swathed in bandages came down on trolleys and were placed facing the altar. One young boy who had been blinded by a shell saw nothing, but kept saying his rosary. He said to me afterwards, "You know, Father, it all becomes tremendous when your eyes are closed. If I still had my sight, I would be looking around me." Another soldier, whose head wound had injured the motor nerves controlling his speech, lay still and quiet before the altar. Afterwards when I asked him how he liked the Christmas Mass, he just blinked his eyes once to show me he was pleased.

Wounded came in as usual yesterday. One lad from Leeds was brought in dead. He had been drowned in some canal: his face was the most hideous sight in the world – blood and greyish mud, like something in a nightmare.

I have just received a Belgian Liberation Medal. It is beautifully done with the Lion of Flanders and on the obverse: "Fortissimis Liberatoribus Belgae Grati MDCCXLIV". I must end here. I wish you and all in Mt Saint Alphonsus a very happy New Year.

Yours ever in JMJA.
DM Cummings C.Ss.R.

# Index